Constructing Empire

Constructing Empire

The Japanese in Changchun, 1905–45

Bill Sewell

UBCPress · Vancouver · Toronto

28 27 26 25 24 23 22 21 20   5 4 3 2

Printed in Canada on FSC-certified ancient-forest-free paper (100% post-consumer recycled) that is processed chlorine- and acid-free.

Library and Archives Canada Cataloguing in Publication

Sewell, Bill, 1960-, author
Constructing empire : the Japanese in Changchun, 1905-45 / Bill Sewell.

Includes bibliographical references and index.
Issued in print and electronic formats.
ISBN 978-0-7748-3652-4 (hardcover). – ISBN 978-0-7748-3653-1 (softcover)
ISBN 978-0-7748-3654-8 (PDF) – ISBN 978-0-7748-3655-5 (EPUB)
ISBN 978-0-7748-3656-2 (Kindle)

1. Japanese – China – Changchun (Jilin Sheng) – History – 20th century. 2. Imperialism – Social aspects – China – Changchun (Jilin Sheng) – History – 20th century. 3. Architecture, Japanese – China – Changchun (Jilin Sheng) – History – 20th century. 4. City planning – China – Changchun (Jilin Sheng) – History – 20th century. 5. Economic development – China – Changchun (Jilin Sheng) – History – 20th century. 6. Changchun (Jilin Sheng, China) – Colonization – History – 20th century. 7. Changchun (Jilin Sheng, China) – History – 20th century. I. Title.

DS797.59.C536S49 2019   951'.8804   C2018-904918-9
C2018-904919-7

Canadä

UBC Press gratefully acknowledges the financial support for our publishing program of the Government of Canada (through the Canada Book Fund), the Canada Council for the Arts, and the British Columbia Arts Council.

This book has been published with the help of a grant from the Canadian Federation for the Humanities and Social Sciences, through the Awards to Scholarly Publications Program, using funds provided by the Social Sciences and Humanities Research Council of Canada.

Printed and bound in Canada by Friesens
Set in Museo and Warnock by Artegraphica Design Co. Ltd.
Copy editor: Barbara Tessman
Proofreader: Sarah Wight
Indexer: Cheryl Lemmens
Cartographer: Greg Baker
Cover designer: Setareh Ashrafologhalai

UBC Press
The University of British Columbia
2029 West Mall
Vancouver, BC V6T 1Z2
www.ubcpress.ca

Contents

Illustrations

Tables

Preface

This study examines Japanese empire building in northeastern China and its surrounding discourse in the first half of the twentieth century. Two periods are evident – one in which Japanese created an "informal" empire based on contemporary models and one witnessing efforts to build something novel and ostensibly Pan-Asian yet linked also to fascist regimes. Both were short-lived, but that does not diminish their significance. Japan was the first nation outside Europe and the United States to join the imperialist ranks and later sought to overturn the international order in alliance with Nazi Germany and Fascist Italy. Exemplifying broadly shared ambitions, Japanese activities in Manchuria and statements about them were aspects of wider efforts to join and later revise a world order structured by industrializing imperialism. They also reflected shifting definitions of national identity compatible with Japan's evolving international posture.

Japanese in both eras typically perceived their activities in Manchuria through what might be called a civilizational lens, self-identifying as agents of progress. This presumption endured because of its inherent appeal, because pre-war Japanese tended to perceive themselves as Asia's natural leaders, and because their manner of empire building included studying global practices and pragmatically adapting them. As a result, Japanese often perceived their empire to be in the vanguard of development; this was true even in the 1930s, as the goals of the second era seemingly addressed issues arising in the first. After 1945, many Japanese maintained this perspective because the sense of crisis apparent in the second, briefer era intensified altruistic self-perceptions and because postwar Japanese society did not undergo the kind of self-examination witnessed in postwar Germany. Consequently, postwar perceptions of pre-war efforts reshaping the colonial world often remained positive, contributing to an array of international tensions.[1] Some publications even celebrated Manchurian experiences, showcasing pre-war photographs nostalgically.[2] Though problematic, such idealistic assessments offer avenues of inquiry not unlike others have explored elsewhere. Geoff Eley, for example, suggested that to understand fascism's appeal it is necessary to appreciate why people perceived it favourably.[3] In his study of American diplomacy, William Appleman Williams considered humanitarian impulses, noting that in order to understand completely the impact of one nation on another, these too must be examined if there is to be any hope of "transform[ing] ... tragedy into a new beginning."[4]

Highlighting avowedly progressive dimensions of Japan's imperialist agenda reminds us that empires were popularly imagined and lived as well as conquered and constructed. Not only did soldiers, diplomats, and officials commit themselves to Japan's imperial cause, but so did civilians. Settler colonialism was as inherent in Japanese imperial projects as in any other modern empire.[5] Studies of the British imperial experience in China, moreover, suggest that a study of the nation most invested in China after the United Kingdom is warranted.[6] Indeed, before the outbreak of war in 1937, more Japanese civilians lived in China than any other group of foreign nationals. Even in Shanghai, the 26,460 Japanese more than doubled the roughly 10,300 Britons present.[7]

This study began as a local history investigating the various communities present in the city of Changchun but came to focus on the Japanese creation of an imperialist enclave and identities imagined in the process. Because of its focus on Japanese perspectives and experiences, discussion of other experiences within this imperialist project is necessarily limited, although their exploration shows promise. Yet a narrow focus on the evolving Japanese presence in Manchuria in advance of the disastrous wars at mid-century is instructive. A key component of Japan's empire, Manchuria was embedded in the pre-war Japanese imaginary in multiple, significant ways and remains so, as current publications and public interest attest. For example, a 2002 quarterly journal issue focusing on Manchuria, including work by non-Japanese, caused such a stir that it was expanded into a 2006 book.[8] Meanwhile, symposiums beginning in Changchun in 1992 led to a 2008 book, in collaboration with Chinese scholars and published also in Chinese, on the era in which Japan tightly controlled the region, followed by another collaborative volume in Japanese in 2014.[9]

This study builds on previous analyses of the Japanese built environment in Changchun and Manchuria, pioneered by Koshizawa Akira on urban planning[10] and Fujimori Terunobu on architecture.[11] Nishizawa Yasuhiko has examined buildings, architects, and the construction industry as modern institutions and more systemically as means of imperialist domination.[12]

English-language studies followed, by David Buck, David Tucker, Qinghua Guo, and myself.[13] This study differs from the above by considering civilians within the built environment more broadly. In addition to being creators of urban milieux, planners, architects, and officials were also members of communities residing in or visiting these milieux as lived space – something people walked, sensed, and contemplated. Henri Lefebvre recognized professionals' various roles in the three types of space he identified: perceived, conceived, and lived.[14] Non-professionals, however, also perceive space as a social product, and interactions with and within built environments can influence popular perceptions, including issues of identity. The loss of physical space also influences views – consider postwar repatriates seeking compensation for lost assets, despite having served the policies of the empire, in the process contributing to fostering a "victim consciousness" in postwar Japan.[15]

Examining this community over the length of Japan's occupation enables a consideration of the evolving nature and significance of civilian activities. The first chapter introduces Manchuria and Changchun, sketching their evolving significance for pre-war Japanese. Ensuing chapters explore aspects of the Japanese experience there and how they changed over time with respect to urban planning, architecture, the economy, and settler society. The concluding chapter recounts Japanese repatriation and reflects on the significance of experiences in these various areas. As Japanese activities in Changchun before 1931 were more or less in line with those of other imperialists, Japanese generally identified with other imperialists, despite intensifying imperialist rivalries and emerging challenges to the imperialist system. After 1931, Japanese ostensibly sought to create a new order in Manchuria, one superior to anything offered by rivals, but Japanese activities indicate an incomplete commitment to new ideals. Since 1945, Japanese have had to consider these efforts along with the destruction and chaos of the war and immediate postwar eras, yet have renewed contacts with Chinese in Changchun and elsewhere. Unlike the grand narratives of the two pre-war eras, however, postwar views of this experience are varied and conflicted, indicating instabilities in the social imaginary that problematize views of earlier eras.

The sources for this study are primarily Japanese, but Chinese, American, and European contemporaries offer useful perspectives. Although individual agendas are not always easy to assess, some, such as those of journalists, are discussed in scholarly literature.[16] Japanese terms are transliterated according to the modified Hepburn system and Chinese according to pinyin, though common English exceptions appear such as *Tokyo, Sun Yat-sen,* and *Chiang*

Kai-shek. The abbreviations *Ch* and *Jp* are provided if a word's origins are unclear from the context. Transliterated Japanese names for which no contemporary pronunciations were obtained follow the National Diet Library online database, alternate databases (e.g., CiNii), previous transliterations, or my own judgment. Unless otherwise noted, translations are my own. The value of the yen shifted over the period of this study, but before 1931 was US$0.50. Plunging to US$0.21 at the end of 1932, it rose toward US$0.30 until the outbreak of the Pacific War in 1941, when it plunged again.[17]

The name *Manchuria* has a contested past. Chinese today call the region *Dongbei* (Northeast), and some suggest that using *Manchuria* implies a false autonomy rendering the region separable from the People's Republic. Noting weaker historical linkages, however, Prasenjit Duara used *Manchuria* for the period this study addresses, since its denouement was then "an open-ended historical situation," though not all non-Chinese scholars agree.[18] This study follows Duara, among others, given that Japanese and other foreigners at the time typically referred to the region with the word referencing its Manchu forebears, and the focus herein is on that era and their views. This is also despite the erroneous inclusion of eastern Mongolian territories and omission of territories north of the Amur and east of the Ussuri Rivers.[19] The conventional transliteration of *Manchukuo* (country of the Manchus) is used rather than the official but less common *Manchoukuo* or *Manchoutikuo* or a more exact transliteration (Ch, Manzhouguo; Jp, Manshūkoku). For expediency, the common Chinese and Japanese practice of prefacing *Manchukuo* with the terms *wei* (Jp, *gi*), meaning "bogus" or "sham" is not followed, because the state's fictional nature is universally accepted. The state's nature is also evident in the common attribution *puppet state* (Ch, *kuilei zhengquan;* Jp, *kairai kokka*) often ascribed to Manchukuo, as Japanese ruled it through intermediaries, despite the ambiguities the term presents.[20]

Sources typically refer to Changchun before the twentieth century as *Kuanchengzi.* In the present study, *Changchun* refers to the walled Chinese settlement once called Kuanchengzi or the adjacent Japanese railway town, and *Kuanchengzi* refers to the town built around the Russian railway station northwest of Changchun. In March 1932, Changchun became Xinjing, at the time transliterated as *Hsinking.* Although citations use the language of the work to refer to places of publication, the Chinese term appears in the text rather than Japanese *Shinkyō* because, despite Japanese control, its population was mainly Chinese and, as in their use of *Manchukuo,* Japanese intended a Chinese veneer. Similarly, the Chinese pronunciation of *Dalian* is used rather than Japanese *Dairen* for the city the Russians once called Dalny. Jilin City is identified as such to distinguish it from the province of the same name. For consistency, I use *Fengtian* for the provincial name, rather than alternating it with *Liaoning.* Given the alternations in its capital's name, *Shenyang* is used rather than *Fengtian* – to distinguish the city from the province – or *Mukden* (Ch, Shengjing), the Manchu name by which foreigners (including Japanese) typically recognized it. Contemporary Chinese called it *Shenyang,* a term in use since the Yuan Dynasty and again today. *Andong* is used rather than *Dandong,* since that was its contemporary name, *Lüshun* rather than *Port Arthur,* and *Beijing* rather than *Beiping* for consistency despite the name change of the last city between 1928 and 1949. *Kantōgun,* rather than *Kwantung* or *Guandong Army,* is used for the Japanese garrison because it was a Japanese military formation.

Portions of this work have been published previously, but are revised and updated here.[21] Along the way, this study benefited from the insight and advice of many, beginning with my graduate supervisors: Bill Wray, Diana Lary, Bob Kubicek, Don Price, Kwang-ching Liu, and Earl Kinmonth. In Japan I profited from the sage advice of Nishizawa Yasuhiko, Imura Tetsuo, Liu Jianhui, and Nakai Yoshifumi. Along the way I received valuable counsel from Douglas Reynolds, David Buck, John Stephan, Terry McGee, David Edgington, David Tucker, Owen Griffiths, Norman Smith, John Van Sant, Jay Carter, Robert Perrins, Shinji Takagaki, Norio Ota, Kirrily Freeman, Sun Xiaoping, Miyuki Arai, and Alec Soucy. In the final stages I benefited from the useful comments of two anonymous readers contacted by UBC Press. I am grateful to Randy Schmidt and Megan Brand at UBC Press for their guidance and assistance, and to Barbara Tessman for meticulous copy-editing. I also wish to acknowledge the aid of resourceful librarians at the University of Tokyo, Waseda University, the International Research Center for Japanese Studies, Tokyo University of Foreign Studies, Changchun Municipal Library, Jilin Provincial Archives, Jilin Provincial Library, Academia Sinica, the Asian Library of the University of British Columbia, the Hoover Institution, the Northeast Asia Reading Room at the University of Hawai'i, and Saint Mary's University's Patrick Power Library. I also acknowledge with gratitude financial assistance provided by the Social Sciences and Humanities Research Council of Canada, the Japan Association for International Education (Nihon kokusai kyōiku kyōkai), the University of British Columbia, Saint Mary's University, and the Awards to Scholarly Publications Program. This study could not have been completed without the aid of these individuals and organizations. Naturally, any errors in fact or judgment despite this assistance reflect my abilities alone.

Beyond the academy, I thank my family for their enduring support. Without my wife's patient optimism, my daughter's cheerful understanding, my mother's unflinching encouragement, and decades of bantering about history and politics with my late father, this would have been a far less rewarding project. This book is dedicated to them.

Abbreviations

Bōsan	Manchuria Home Construction (Manshū bōsan kabushiki kaisha)
CCB	Capital Construction Bureau
CCP	Chinese Communist Party
CER	China Eastern Railway
CIA	Central Intelligence Agency
Daitoku	Daitoku Real Estate (Daitoku fudōsan)
Denden	Manchuria Telegraph and Telephone Corporation (Manshū denshin denwa kabushiki kaisha)
IJA	Imperial Japanese Army
Man'ei	Manchuria Film Association (Manshū Eiga Kyōkai)
Mangyō	Manchuria Heavy Industries (Manshū jūkōgyō kaihatsu kabushiki kaisha)
Mantetsu	South Manchuria Railway (Minami Manshū tetsudō kabushiki kaisha)
MKZ	*Manshū kenchiku zasshi* (*Journal of Manchurian Architecture*) – published as the *Manshū kenchiku kyōkai zasshi* (*Journal of Manchurian Architectural Association*) 1921–33
MNNS	*Manshū nichi nichi shinbun* (*Manchuria Daily News*) – published as *Manshū nippō* (*Manchuria Daily*) 1927–35, and *Manshū Shinbun* 1944–45
STKH	*Shinkyō toshi kensetsu hōsaku* (*Plans for the Construction of Shinkyō*)
TK	*Toshi kōron* (*Urban Review*)
Tōdai	Tokyo Imperial University (Tōkyō teikoku daigaku, Univers)

Constructing Empire

Map 1 Manchuria and Manchukuo.

Sources: Adapted from "Manchurian Railways," 1:6,336,000, in *Manchurian Railways and the Opening of China: An International History*, ed. Bruce A. Elleman and Stephen Kotkin (Armonk, NY: ME Sharpe, 2010), xx, and "Manchuria and Environs in the 1930s," 1:11,088,000, cartography by Dana Lombardy with graphic assistance from Bruce Weigle and Judy Tart, in Alvin D. Coox, *Nomonhan: Japan against Russia, 1939* (Stanford: Stanford University Press, 1985), inside cover; ESRI Data and Maps (World Oceans, World Administrative), scale varies, Environmental Systems Research Institute, 2005; GADM Global Administrative Areas Database, Level 0, Level 1, and Level 2, various contributors, 2015–11; V6 Time Series Prefecture Polygons, scale varies Harvard Dataverse v2, 2016–12–21. ETOPO2 v2, 2', National Geophysical Data Center, 2006; VMAP Level 0 (Watercourses, Inland Water Areas, Railroads), 1:1,000,000, National Imagery and Mapping Agency, 2000; Getty Thesaurus of Geographic Names, Getty Research Institute, 2017; World Geocoder, scale varies, Environmental Systems Research Institute, 2017. Cartography by Greg Baker, 2017.

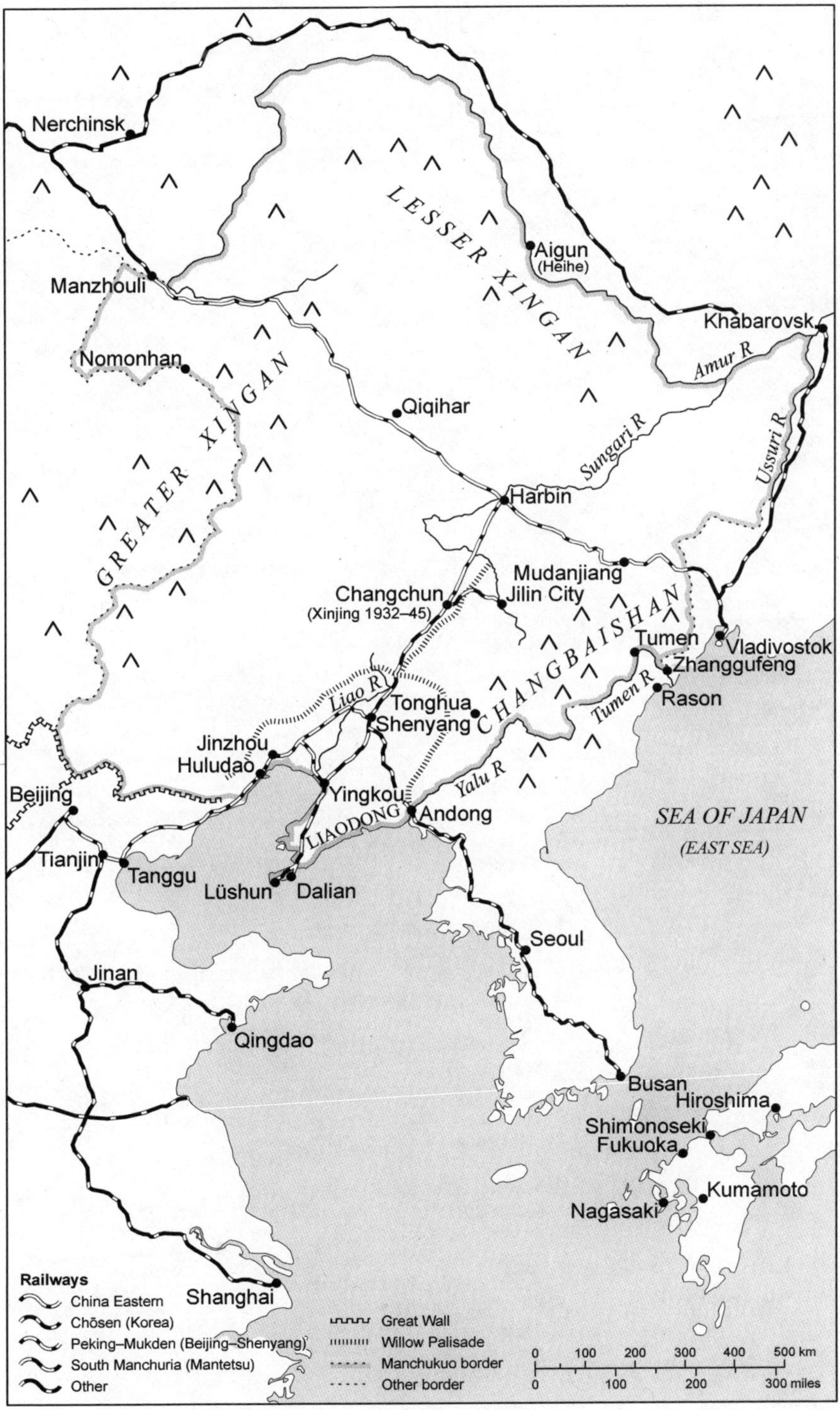
Nerchinsk
LESSER XINGAN
Aigun
(Heihe)
Manzhouli
Khabarovsk
Nomonhan
Amur R
GREATER XINGAN
Qiqihar
Sungari R
Ussuri R
Harbin
Mudanjiang
Changchun
(Xinjing 1932–45)
Jilin City
CHANGBAISHAN
Tumen
Vladivostok
Zhanggufeng
Rason
Liao R
Tonghua
Shenyang
Tumen R
Jinzhou
Huludao
Yingkou
Yalu R
Beijing
Andong
SEA OF JAPAN
(EAST SEA)
LIAODONG
Tianjin
Tanggu
Lüshun
Dalian
Seoul
Jinan
Qingdao
Busan
Hiroshima
Shimonoseki
Fukuoka
Kumamoto
Nagasaki
Shanghai
Railways
China Eastern
Chōsen (Korea)
Peking–Mukden (Beijing–Shenyang)
South Manchuria (Mantetsu)
Other
Great Wall
Willow Palisade
Manchukuo border
Other border
0 100 200 300 400 500 km
0 100 200 300 miles

Map 2 Changchun in the 1920s

Sources: Adapted from "Shinkyō," in Tanaka Shūsaku, *Shin Manshūkoku chishi* (Tokyo: Kokon shoin, 1932), 371; Landsat 7 Scene p118 r030, 15m, United States Geological Survey, 2000–10–20. Cartography by Greg Baker, 2017.

1 Changchun Railway Station
2 Mantetsu offices
3 Yamato Hotel
4 North Corner (later East) Plaza
5 Police station
6 Bank of Korea (Chōsen)
7 West Plaza
8 East (later South) Plaza
9 Post office
10 Changchun Telephone Company
11 East Park
12 Mantetsu Hospital
13 Mitsui Bussan
14 Shinto shrine
15 Schools
16 New Chinese Administration offices
17 West (later Kodama) Park
18 Japanese consulate
19 Damalu (Dama Road)
20 North Gate
21 Mahao Gate

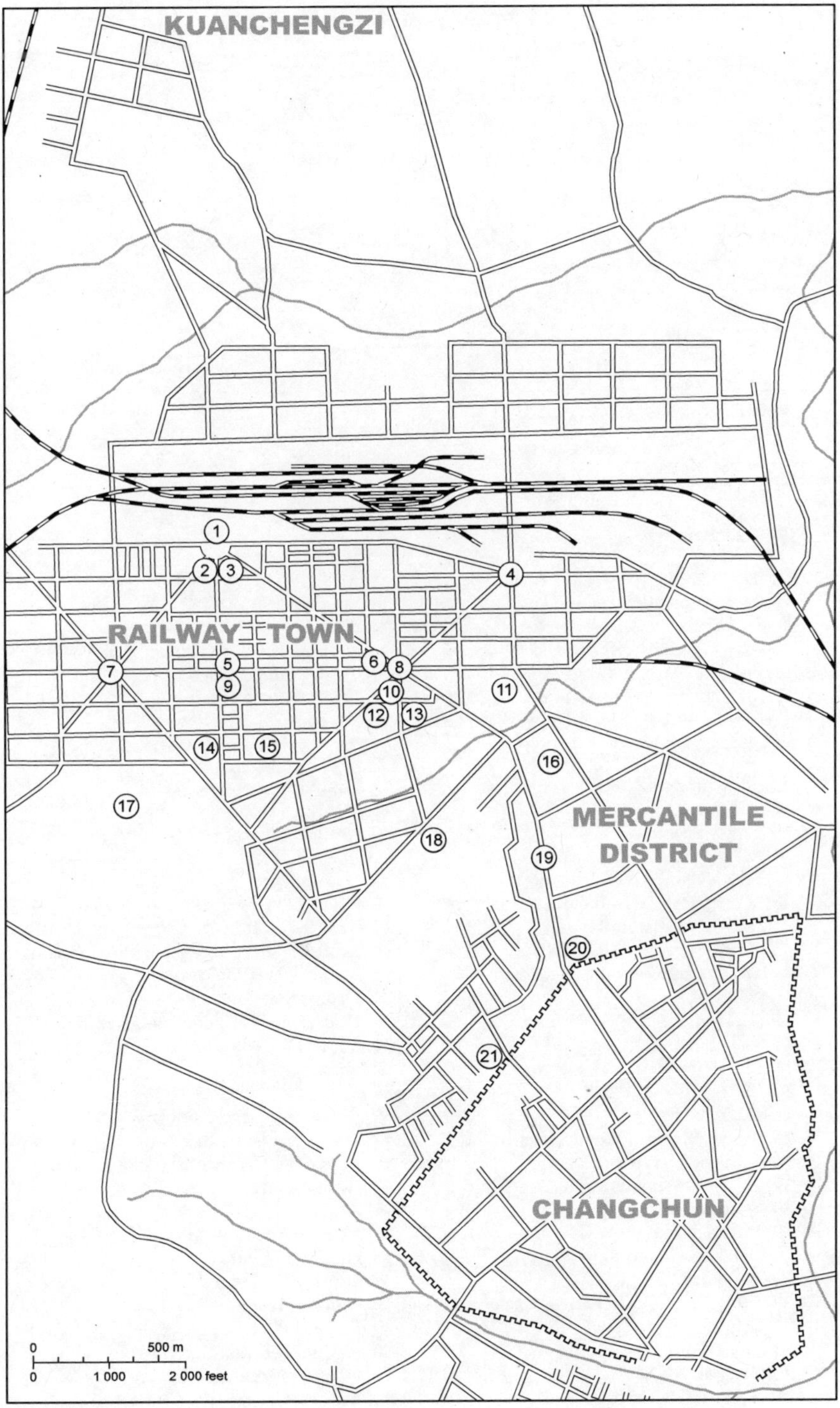
KUANCHENGZI
RAILWAY TOWN
MERCANTILE DISTRICT
CHANGCHUN
1
2
3
4
5
6
7
8
9
10
11
12
13
14
15
16
17
18
19
20
21
0
500 m
0
1 000
2 000 feet

Map 3 Planning Xinjing (not all shown was constructed).

Sources: Adapted from "Kokuto kensetsu keikaku yōtochiiki bunpai narabini jigyō daiichiji shikō kuiki zu," 1:60,000, in Shinkyō tokubetsushi kōsho, *Shinkyō shisei gaiyō* (Shinkyō: Shinkyō tokubetsushi kōsho, 1934); "Kokuto kensetsu keikaku zu," 1942, in Koshizawa Akira, *Manshūkoku no shuto keikaku: Tōkyō no genzai to mirai o tou* (Tokyo: Nihon keizai hyōronsha, 1988), 173; Landsat 7 Scene p118 r030, 15m, United States Geological Survey, 2000–10–20; Satō Akira, *Manshū zōen shi* (Tokyo: Nihon zōen shūkei kyōkai, 1985): 80. Cartography by Greg Baker, 2017.

1 Changchun station
2 Airport
3 Puyi's Residence
4 West Plaza
5 South Plaza
6 West (later Kodama) Park
7 Japanese consulate
8 Kantōgun Headquarters
9 Guandong Government office building
10 Monument to the War Dead
11 Daikō Building
12 Horse track
13 Golf course
14 Kangde Hall
15 Tokyo Maritime Insurance Building
16 Minakai Department Store
17 Oriental Development Company
18 Foreign Ministry
19 Prime minister's residence
20 Bank of Manchukuo
21 Banruosi Temple
22 Manchuria Telegraph and Telephone
23 Datong Plaza
24 Palace and gardens site
25 Baishan Park
26 Second Government Building
27 First Government Building
28 Guandi Temple
29 Mudan Park
30 Jinmuden
31 Datong Park
32 South Station site
33 Xingren Dalu
34 Ministry of Public Security/Manchukuo Military Headquarters
35 Hall of State
36 Department of People's Livelihood
37 Shuntian Park
38 Shuntian Dajie
39 Ministry of Justice
40 Ertong Park and Zoo
41 Sports fields
42 Ministry of Transportation
43 Anmin Plaza
44 Supreme Court
45 Xiehe (Concordia) Plaza
46 Huanglong Park
47 South Lake Park
48 Datong Academy
49 Jianguo Plaza
50 National Foundation Shrine
51 Nanling Memorial Tower
52 Jianguo University

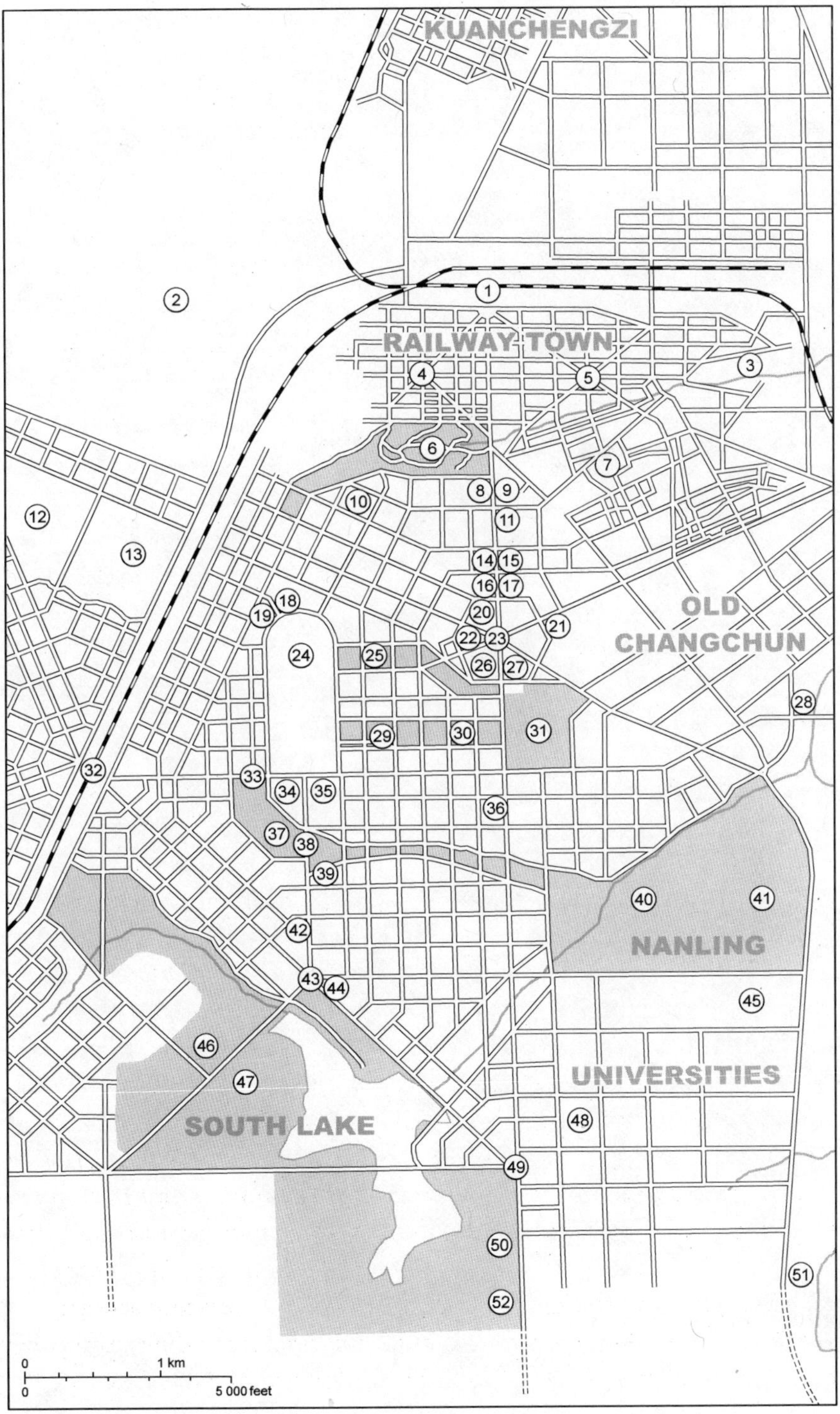
KUANCHENGZI
RAILWAY TOWN
OLD CHANGCHUN
NANLING
UNIVERSITIES
SOUTH LAKE
0
1 km
0
5 000 feet
1
2
3
4
5
6
7
8
9
10
11
12
13
14
15
16
17
18
19
20
21
22
23
24
25
26
27
28
29
30
31
32
33
34
35
36
37
38
39
40
41
42
43
44
45
46
47
48
49
50
51
52

Introduction

The city of Changchun, capital of the landlocked northeastern province of Jilin, might seem an odd place in which to explore Japan's pre-war empire. Just over fifteen hundred kilometres from Tokyo, Changchun is not quite as far away as the Okinawan capital, Naha, but lies inland more than six hundred kilometres north of Dalian and Seoul and five hundred kilometres west of Vladivostok. Cooler and drier than Japan, its continental climate compounds its remoteness by making it, for Japanese, a different kind of place. Changchun, moreover, has rarely graced international headlines in recent years, given Jilin's economic development's lagging behind the coastal provinces, though the city did host the 2007 Asian Winter Games. In the twentieth century's first half, however, Changchun figured prominently. The Russo-Japanese War resulted in its becoming the boundary between the Russian and Japanese spheres of influence in northeast China and a transfer point for travel between Europe and Asia. The terminus of the broad-gauge Russian railroad track required a physical transfer to different trains, and, before 1917, a twenty-three-minute difference between Harbin and Dalian time zones required travellers to reset their watches.[1] Following Japan's seizure of Manchuria, Changchun, renamed Xinjing, became the capital of the puppet state of Manchukuo, recognized by the Axis powers and a partner in Japan's Greater East Asia Co-Prosperity Sphere. In 1945, Manchukuo bore the brunt of the Soviet assault on Japan, with its capital a primary objective, and following Japan's surrender Soviet troops remained. Upon their withdrawal, forces of the Chinese Nationalist (Guomindang) and Chinese Communist Parties contested the city, resulting in its changing hands several times.

In addition to soldiers and diplomats, Chinese, Japanese, Korean, Russian, and other civilians sought to inscribe Manchurian territory as theirs, either directly through claiming land and building structures or indirectly through work and daily affairs in communities with others of similar linguistic and social backgrounds. Constructing empire was a mundane and popularly imagined affair as well as a diplomatic, political, and military one. Studies often focus on elite decisions or actions, but the popular dimension must also be considered to grasp fully empire's nature. A growing body of scholars of Manchuria recognizes this.[2] Using chiefly Japanese materials, this study explores aspects of the Japanese experience in Changchun/Xinjing to examine civilian contributions to empire. No single motivation is apparent, as some Japanese embraced imperial expansion as a patriotic cause while others saw different idealistic or personal opportunities. Some were motivated by a desire to facilitate change in Japan, while others acted in response to several motives simultaneously. For many, if not most, their actions were no passing fancy – Manchuria posed peril as well as opportunity.

Contextualizing Japanese activities in Changchun, this introductory chapter sketches Manchuria's geostrategic significance to indicate the region's importance for Japanese. The chapter then considers the Japanese administrative and corporate presence in Manchuria with which civilians interacted, and provides an overview of Changchun's history to which later chapters relate.

Japan's Northeast Asian Cauldron

Founded in 1869, Tokyo's Yasukuni Shrine enshrines the spirits of almost two and a half million war dead, most perishing in the Asia-Pacific War. Of the eleven conflicts recognized at Yasukuni as including active duty – required for eligibility for enshrining – four witnessed fighting in Manchuria: the First Sino-Japanese War, the Russo-Japanese War, the Manchurian Incident (also known as the September 18th, Mukden, or Liutiaohu Incident), and the Asia-Pacific War. Three of the eleven conflicts occurred in Japan and Taiwan between 1868 and 1877, but the remaining four were fought near Manchuria and were not unconnected with the region's fate: the Boxer Expedition, the First World War (including what Japanese call the Japan-Germany War, fought on China's Shandong Peninsula), the Jinan Incident, and the Second Sino-Japanese War. Recurring strife in Manchuria ensured Japanese attention and was reinforced by continuing speculation about other potential conflicts in the region given that Manchurian issues contributed to broader tensions. These were exacerbated by Manchukuo's founding, as it represented a possible launch pad for a Japanese invasion of the Soviet Union.

Manchuria's significance for the imperial Japanese state developed inadvertently yet inexorably. Following the 1868 Meiji Restoration, officials sought control of nearby islands; only after their consolidation did they seek hegemony over one part of the mainland – Korea. This meant removing Chinese influence from that country, which was achieved in the first Sino-Japanese War. In the 1895 Treaty of Shimonoseki, which ended that war, China not only recognized Korean autonomy but also ceded to Japan in perpetuity Manchuria's Liaodong Peninsula, where some of the fighting took place, including everything south of a line extending from Yingkou (Niuzhuang) to Haicheng, fifty kilometres northeast, to the Anping River, fifty kilometres northeast of Andong. Acquiring this region would have buffered Korea and secured Japanese access to north China and central Manchuria, but the governments of Russia, Germany, and France immediately demanded a Japanese retrocession. Japan acquiesced – in exchange for a larger indemnity – but Japanese generally perceived this "Triple Intervention" as a national insult.[3]

Imperialist competition over Manchuria intensified in the following decade, resulting initially in Russian hegemony – unsurprising, given long-standing Russian interest. Although forcibly excluded from that territory by a 1689 treaty signed in Nerchinsk, Russia, following the Crimean War, compelled a weakened Qing Dynasty to cede lands north of the Amur and east of the Ussuri by treaties signed at Aigun (1858) and Beijing (1860), as well as to allow a Russian presence south of these areas (Map 1). Responding to the Treaty of Shimonoseki, Russia provided loans to the Qing, acquired the right to build a trans-Manchurian railway from Manzhouli to Vladivostok with a southern spur to Lüshun – the China Eastern Railway (CER) – and leased the southern tip of the Liaodong Peninsula, the Guandong Leased Territory.[4] Protecting these investments, Russian troops occupied Manchuria during the 1900–1 Boxer War, which followed the 1897–99 "scramble for concessions," when many thought China was about to be divided by the Great Powers. Americans responded by calling for an "Open Door" in China to preserve trade opportunities, but Russia's unwillingness to withdraw from Manchuria prompted Japan to launch what became the Russo-Japanese War. When that war ended, with the September 1905 Treaty of Portsmouth, Russia recognized Japanese predominance in Korea and in Manchuria south of Changchun. The Qing acknowledged this by the Treaty of Beijing that December, agreeing also not to build any parallel lines that might compete with the now Japanese railway. In November, Japanese officials compelled Korean acceptance of protectorate status, although Korean resistance resulted in annexation in 1910. The Japanese government-general in Korea thereafter pursued Korean guerrillas into eastern Manchuria, where Korean migrants had established communities, and the Japanese Foreign Ministry insisted on Chinese cooperation in subduing them.[5]

Dominating Korea initially drew Japanese into Manchuria, but opportunities and new rivalries turned securing southern Manchuria into a fixation. The Imperial Japanese Army (IJA) designated a garrison force, the Kantōgun, to defend Japan's new sphere of influence.[6] Many anticipated a Russian war of revenge for losses suffered in 1905, but Japanese and Russian diplomats proved able to mend fences and establish a working relationship by the start of the First World War. In a series of treaties beginning in 1907, diplomats agreed not only to respective Russian and Japanese spheres in northern and southern Manchuria, but also western and eastern spheres in Inner Mongolia, divided at the Beijing meridian. Just prior to the Russian Revolution, the tsarist government even agreed to sell to Japan the rail line connecting Changchun and Harbin.[7] Spurring this reconciliation was a new rival – the United States. Along with issues of race and immigration, newfound American interests in Manchuria after 1905 led to a rapid deterioration in American relations with Japan, sparking alarm in both countries.[8] The First World War pushed this enmity aside, and in 1917 US Secretary of State Robert Lansing acknowledged that "Japan has special interests in China, particularly in the part to which her possessions are contiguous," which the United States would respect as long as China's territorial sovereignty was not threatened. Seeking to restrain Japan's expansion, the United States abrogated Lansing's recognition in 1923, but that did not prevent some Japanese officials from using the agreement in the meantime to imply American support in compelling the acquiescence of Chinese officials in Manchuria to local demands.[9]

Improved relations with the United States helped stabilize Japan's sphere of influence in southern Manchuria, but the Russian Revolution destabilized the north. While the Kerensky government recognized the railway sale, the Bolsheviks did not. Concerned also for war supplies warehoused in Vladivostok and the potential for a rival's seizing eastern Siberia, troops from Japan, the United States, Canada, and other powers occupied that city as well as railways in eastern Siberia in 1918. This provoked dissent in Japan. Japanese troops did not withdraw when the allies did in 1920, although, having also occupied railways in northern Manchuria, the government did cancel plans to reinforce its presence there. Eventually, the Red Army compelled the capitulation of anti-Bolshevik forces in the region. Withdrawing in September 1922 – from northern Sakhalin in 1925 – Japan managed to salvage only fishing, oil, and other rights in recompense for the loss of life and tsarist debts when it grudgingly recognized the Soviet Union in 1925.[10]

In claiming Siberia, Soviet forces not only established a Communist presence on the Korean border but also installed a Mongolian client regime to Manchuria's west in 1921. The solidifying Soviet grasp contrasted with developments to the south. Disorganized after the 1911 revolution, China was vulnerable to Japanese pressure. In 1915, Japanese diplomats presented a list of "Twenty-One Demands" to the Chinese Republic; among the fifteen ultimately accepted were seven expanding Japanese privileges in Manchuria. In 1917, Nishihara Kamezō organized a series of loans on Tokyo's behalf that sought to secure Japanese financial hegemony in Manchuria, Inner Mongolia, and China while expanding Korean industry and the reach of the Bank of Korea. A military agreement signed the following year was in support of the Siberian intervention, but also aimed to expand Japanese influence in China.[11]

These schemes not only ultimately failed, but they provoked suspicions among Japan's wartime allies and contributed to China's continuing dissolution into warlordism, prompting further intervention and frustration. As warlordism in China developed, all imperialist powers had to make arrangements with local strongmen to retain influence, but these men used foreign connections to further their own ambitions. Attracted to modern weaponry and systems, these warlords built rapacious regional administrations that, in vying for power, painfully disrupted Chinese society while experimenting with new modes of civic organization. In Manchuria, Zhang Zuolin achieved hegemony with modernizing civic officials and Japanese aid. Yet he proved an uncertain collaborator for both, more committed to solidifying his authority and developing a national role than to narrowly managing Manchuria as his advisers prescribed, although his occupying north China may have been an effort to become more fiscally autonomous. Japanese defended Zhang from rivals, but Kantōgun officers, acting on their own authority, assassinated him in 1928.[12] Zhang's son and successor, Zhang Xueliang, however, also proved a challenge to Japan; by the end of that year, he had agreed to cooperate with the Nationalist government established in Nanjing by Chiang Kai-shek in 1927. His decision was, in part, a consequence of regime insecurity, but he also sought to develop Manchuria and achieve greater autonomy from Japan.[13] He supported building rival railways and attempted to reclaim the CER from the USSR in 1929, provoking a Soviet military incursion.[14] His government also orchestrated an effort to weaken Japanese influence in Manchuria by trying to "drive the yen out of circulation" in the first half of 1931, an effort that followed "a decade of stagnation for Japanese commerce in Manchuria."[15] In June of that year, his troops executed a Captain Nakamura Shintarō in western Manchuria, causing

Kantōgun concerns to flare. Although Nakamura had been on a covert reconnaissance mission, his death infuriated Japanese officers and weakened Japanese Foreign Ministry efforts at negotiation.[16]

Japanese diplomacy endeavoured to separate Manchuria from China south of the Great Wall to assure the region's peaceful development with Japanese assistance. Yet, in addition to flying the Nationalist flag in Manchuria, Zhang intervened in support of the Nationalists – against Japanese advice – when warlord allies rebelled in 1930.[17] Edgar Snow reported that Zhang even tried to compel Japanese diplomats to discuss Manchurian matters with the Nationalist government.[18] Nationalist connections were unacceptable to Japanese, given the former's anti-imperialist agenda and efforts to end China's "unequal" treaty relationship with the Great Powers. Indeed, many Japanese dismissed the Nationalists as leftists in league with the Soviet Union, which also remained a threat to Japanese.[19] That the Nationalists were engaged in a civil war with Chinese Communists did not dispel this view, and the latter's arrival in Yan'an in 1936 only increased concerns for communism's threat to North China and Manchuria.

Chinese civilians in Manchuria were also of concern to Japanese. The anti-imperialist May Fourth and May Thirtieth Incidents of 1919 and 1925 were not without repercussions in Manchuria.[20] In addition, Chinese merchants posed economic challenges to Japanese interests. As well as participating in boycotts of Japanese goods, many competed favourably with Japanese merchants, forcing some Japanese firms in Dalian to close in the 1920s.[21] That same decade, Chinese-made cotton cloth challenged the Japanese monopoly.[22] In 1919, a foreign observer noted that Chinese were "a greater competitor to fear than the European or American":

> The wealthy merchants down to the humble peasants, have also cast covetous eyes upon Manchuria, and it will be hard indeed for Japan to keep them out of that country or to best them in the struggle for the trade or the rich soil itself. The success of European enterprise in China has largely been due to the fact that the merchants have combined or co-operated with the Chinese; but the Japanese seem to be following the plan of competing with them. The result will be that they will fail, as to a large extent they have already, in their big undertakings. One has only to glance at Lüshun (Port Arthur) and Dalian to see that they are a long way from being as prosperous as such a treaty port as Tianjin is, or even as they were themselves when held by the Russians.[23]

Encouraged by the Zhang regime, Chinese immigration was substantial, surpassing one million each year between 1927 and 1929.[24] Japanese Foreign Ministry officials sought to counter this by encouraging Korean immigration into the region, which, in effect, expanded Japanese influence, as the annexation of Korea had transformed all Koreans into Japanese subjects. Korean immigration was not to the liking of Kantōgun officers, however, and also provoked Chinese protests. Sino-Korean antagonisms boiled over near Changchun at Wanbaoshan in the summer of 1931, when Chinese vigilantes contested water rights with Korean farmers. Anti-Korean – by implication, anti-Japanese – riots spread quickly, and Koreans responded with anti-Chinese riots in Korea. These were not the first such incidents – feuding had occurred previously near Andong – nor were they the last. Chinese troops assaulted Korean civilians across Manchuria following the Manchurian Incident.[25] Nor was this the only recurring violence – plaguing all was China's swelling banditry. Japanese estimated that there were fifty thousand bandits in Manchuria in 1930 and expended ¥20 million annually on soldiers and police in the railway zone, although the accuracy of their estimate is questionable, given that inflated numbers could have been used to justify a stronger military presence.[26]

Officers of the Kantōgun launched what became known as the Manchurian Incident on 18 September 1931. Driving them to execute the takeover of Manchuria on their own initiative were the concerns identified above and the view that the Japanese government could not address them. Quickly reinforced with support from Korea – in violation of proper chain of command – the Kantōgun pushed Zhang's forces into north China and later detached the province of Rehe, strategically useful for further expansion into Inner or Outer Mongolia or North China.[27] Busy with a fourth anti-Communist campaign in southern China, the Nationalists had little choice but to acquiesce and agree to a truce negotiated at Tanggu in 1933, delineating the border at the Great Wall, agreeing to an unarmed neutral zone immediately south, and eventually re-establishing rail and postal connections.[28] Nationalist China did not officially recognize Manchukuo – established 1 March 1932 and recognized by Japan in September – but the Kantōgun and other Japanese went about constructing it as a modern yet dependent client state, developing Manchurian resources in preparation for a future conflict. Aware of concerns in Japan about their actions, Kantōgun officers engaged in a media campaign defending themselves, intimating the kind of society they would build – one excluding exploitative capitalists and "degenerate" politicians.[29] Recruiting local Chinese elites and inventing new national symbols, Manchukuo officials presented the state to Japanese as an ally, as well as a solution to China's and Japan's ills, giving cause for Japanese to believe the empire was reaching out to disaffected Asian brethren.

Many Japanese viewed the Manchurian Incident and the creation of Manchukuo favourably from the start. Japanese immigrants in Davao, in the southern Philippines, began referring to their community as "Dabao-kuo," and Manchukuo later served as a model for new wartime governments in the Philippines and Burma.[30] Many condemned the League of Nations' censure of Japan for the incident.[31] Contemporary observers reported activities like Japanese civilians buying warplanes for the services through public subscription, while some ten thousand Japanese marching in Shenyang protested "League interference."[32] When Japan withdrew from the league in 1933, it seemed to many in that country that Japan had acted to preserve hard-won privileges in a vital region. This was an enduring perspective – a decade later the editor of the *Mainichi Shinbun* identified China as Japan's "Near West," asserting Japanese actions there were not unlike European actions in the Near East.[33]

The Manchurian Incident was of enormous consequence. It emboldened Japanese officers to make similar efforts in north China and Inner Mongolia, despite provoking rifts within the army. Such actions ultimately led to conflict: in the summer of 1937, Japan became enmeshed in a war with China that proved impossible to conclude swiftly.[34] The incident also galvanized Chinese, especially given continuing Japanese encroachment.[35] In exposing the League of Nations' limitations, the incident also encouraged German and Italian unilateralism. Japan's subsequent tilting toward the Axis states in signing the 1936 Anti-Comintern Pact reflected diplomatic *realpolitik* as well as growing interest in revising the international order by all three governments and pundits in each country.[36] Although Germany did not do so until 1938, fourteen countries and the Vatican eventually recognized Manchukuo, heralding a new era for those seeking a Fascist International.[37]

The incident proved a boon to Soviet diplomats, enabling them to end their country's isolation by obtaining recognition from Nationalist China in 1932 and the United States in 1933 as well as admittance to the League of Nations on 18 September 1934. Given previous Japanese interest in acquiring the CER, in March 1935 Soviet officials agreed to sell the railway to Manchukuo, averting any potential incident. The Red Army then reinforced its eastern flank, more than doubling troops in the region over the 1930s, adding long-range bombers that could reach Tokyo, and briefly occupying

Xinjiang, in western China, to forestall any Japanese advance there. The government also double-tracked the Trans-Siberian Railway and promoted settlement, building the new industrial city of Komsomolsk on the Amur River.[38] To this growing infrastructure, Soviet officials added an active defence – leading to border conflicts with the Kantōgun at Zhanggufeng in 1938 and Nomonhan in 1939 – and began shipping arms to China after signing a non-aggression pact less than seven weeks after the Marco Polo Bridge Incident inaugurated the Second Sino-Japanese War in 1937. Unable to match the Soviet buildup, Manchukuo resorted to fortifying the border with Maginot Line–type defences, though the Kantōgun continued planning to attack the Soviet Union.[39]

The United States responded to the Manchurian Incident by edging closer to the countries threatened by Japan, electing even to participate for the first time in a League of Nations council session. With the extension of hostilities between China and Japan to Shanghai in 1932, moreover, Secretary of State Henry Stimson mused publicly about Japan's possibly having violated treaties signed in Washington in 1922, which meant that the United States might not consider itself bound by concurrent naval arms limitations. In reality, economic difficulties constrained options, especially because Manchuria was not critical to the American economy. Although the Americans, British, and French continued to consider opportunities in Manchukuo, American policy could but pointedly refused to recognize the new state.[40] A US consulate in Shenyang, opened in 1904, remained, but relations continued to be tense, intensifying as the Second Sino-Japanese War erupted, and Japanese operations expanded to compel China's capitulation. American policy inclined increasingly toward support of China, and, with Japanese and American negotiators unable to find any common ground, Japanese forces launched the attacks of 7–8 December 1941. Still a thorn in Japanese-American relations, Manchuria may have played a small role in Japanese supporting the decision for the Asia-Pacific War: some – not Prime Minister Tōjō Hideki – interpreted Secretary of State Cordell Hull's 26 November 1941 note to Japan as demanding a withdrawal from the region as well as from China south of the Great Wall.[41]

Imperial Infrastructure and Incentives

Tensions surrounding Manchuria were enduring – in forwarding a consular report in 1928, the British envoy in Beijing warned London's Foreign Office that a railway issue had reached a point where it "appeared likely that Japan was about to take strong measures and possibly utilize the incident in order to bring to a head the various railway and other questions outstanding in her relations with Manchuria."[42] Earlier that year, the British consul general in Shenyang reasoned that, given Japanese economic interests in Manchuria, Chinese efforts to assert sovereignty over the region, and fears that Chinese military confrontations could extend to Manchuria, "Japan may find herself committed to action which may involve the occupation by Japanese troops of the territory."[43] That same year an American political scientist labelled Manchuria "one of the danger spots in the Far East," as Japanese sought to maintain their position in the region while Chinese feared losing sovereignty.[44] Noting that Japanese railway investments in Manchuria exceeded ¥1.5 billion (more than US$750 million), a Columbia University professor warned in 1930 that "the security of Japanese industry could be assured only with the occupation of Manchuria by Japan and the annexation of the territory as part of the Empire."[45] Following the Manchurian Incident, an American commerce official observed that Manchurian resources represented "the difference between the present order tenuously sustained by the trade and resources of Manchuria, and a possible chaos superinduced by the famine that would result from their relinquishment." He concluded that "for Japan there is no military or diplomatic retreat, because there is no economic retreat."[46] Nor did foreigners universally denounce Japan for its ambitions in Manchuria. In 1932, George Woodhead – a British journalist and founding editor of the *China Year Book* (a journal often thought to be favourable toward Japan) – reported the takeover "was not unexpected by the foreign communities [in Manchuria] nor was it viewed with disfavor ... [even if they were] skeptical as to the exact pretexts used to justify the occupation of Shenyang and the extension of Japanese military activities to other parts of Manchuria."[47] For their own reasons, British Shanghailanders supported Japan's takeover.[48] British historian Zara Steiner notes that even the UK "Foreign Office believed that Japan had a strong case in Manchuria."[49] The Manchurian Incident was more than a simple land grab.

Manchuria's significance for Japanese involved more than opportunity, China's disorganization, and geographic proximity. In the years prior to the Manchurian Incident, many Japanese had taken to calling Manchuria a "lifeline" (*seimeisen*), a view that was understandable given Japan's battering by economic and social uncertainties, beginning with the 1927 failure of the Bank of Taiwan even before the global depression.[50] Manchurian resources were valuable to Japan's industrializing society, and Manchurian fields promised opportunity for settlers: the region was not densely inhabited and its area was larger than the entire empire's – four times larger than Japan's main islands. Despite long-standing connections, moreover, Manchuria was not continuously integrated with China south of the Great Wall, although expanding trade and migration in the twentieth century meant the region was becoming more linked.[51] Although southern Manchuria often lay within imperial Chinese jurisdiction, and Chinese settlement expanded during the Ming and Qing Dynasties, the Qing limited migration beyond that by erecting a fence, the Willow Palisade. This was to preserve their ancestral homeland, though after about 1750 the palisade's functioning as a barrier deteriorated.[52] Nineteenth-century imperialist threats also prodded the court to reverse this policy and encourage Chinese immigration in order to retain sovereignty, and Japan's arrival prompted a 1907 administrative reorganization to enhance Manchu authority. This included incorporating Changchun into China's telegraphy network by the end of 1906.[53] Nevertheless, the region remained relatively sparsely populated at the dawn of the twentieth century, enabling images of an uninhabited Manchuria to figure prominently in Japanese media.[54]

The Japanese presence in Manchuria is often considered an example of "informal empire," meaning that Japanese had limited rights and needed to respect Chinese sovereignty and the interests of other nations with treaty privileges in China. Japan was only one of the foreign states participating in the "unequal" treaty system, gaining privileges through military conflict or other forms of pressure. As a result, China as a whole was not colonized, but Chinese resentment toward foreign influence and the piecemeal colonization of their country understandably grew. After joining this system in 1895 and expanding the scope of privileges shared by all, Japanese rationalized growing tensions as well as their growing presence with an array of self-serving justifications.[55]

Given its wartime foundation, the Japanese presence in Manchuria was initially under military authority. Accepting the transfer of Russian privileges to Japan in a December 1905 treaty signed in Beijing, China acknowledged Japanese authority over all Russian leases in southern Manchuria. This included the 3,400-square-kilometre Guandong (Kwantung) Leased Territory – about 13 percent of the roughly 26,000 square kilometres Japan won briefly in 1895 – and the 700-kilometre railway running between Dalian and Changchun. Also included was a 233-square-kilometre railway zone of "attached lands" (Ch, *fushudi;* Jp, *fuzokuchi*) consisting of the rail line, a thirty-metre strip along either of side of it, and town concessions. In addition, China accepted a 275-kilometre railway connecting Andong with Shenyang built by Japanese during the war, new Shenyang–Xinmintun and Changchun–Jilin City branch lines, and Japan's stationing up to fifteen railway guards for every kilometre of track.[56] With peace, the military retained authority over the Guandong Leased Territory, and Foreign Ministry officials assumed responsibility elsewhere, a problematic situation should the two differ over current or future visions. A third entity added in 1919, the Guandong Government-General, responsible to the Ministry of Colonial Affairs in Tokyo, took over civilian administration on the leased territory. Even though the Foreign Ministry endeavoured generally to work within the international treaty system, its officials also pressed to expand Japanese interests and deter imperialist rivals.[57]

To see to mundane matters in the Guandong Leasehold and railway zone, in 1906 the Japanese government created the South Manchuria Railway Company, abbreviated in Japanese as Mantetsu. A private corporation in which the government owned 51 percent of the stock and appointed senior officials, Mantetsu represented a compromise between the IJA, the Foreign Ministry, and other government arms.[58] Despite contradictory pulls, Mantetsu developed into Japan's largest pre-war corporation in terms of paid-in capital, orchestrating much of the Manchurian economy. After replacing the broad Russian railway gauge with standard gauge and double tracking the entire line, Mantetsu shifted to not only hauling passengers and freight but also developing and managing ports, coal mines, power-generation facilities, factories, experimental farms, and railway-zone towns, initially with personnel with experience in Taiwan. Collecting taxes, Mantetsu saw to municipal administration in Japan's railway towns. It was also committed to technological innovation and efficient administration, establishing a research arm and publishing house exploring issues in Manchuria and beyond. Mantetsu recruited from Japan's top universities and celebrated Manchurian achievements prominently in Japan. The company marked Japan's twentieth year in Manchuria, for example, with a public exhibition in Tokyo.[59] Befitting its modern image, Mantetsu built sleek new headquarters in 1936 athwart the southern entrance to Tokyo's Kasumigaseki district, the heart of Japan's national bureaucracy. Yasui Takeo, a 1910 Tōdai (Tokyo Imperial University) graduate who later accepted positions at Waseda and Kyoto Imperial Universities, designed the stepped silhouette of the Mantetsu Biru. The building was built by Ōkura, one of the smaller *zaibatsu* (financial combines) but one with a strong presence in Manchuria and Korea, particularly in coal mining and iron manufacturing.[60] Another landmark connected with Mantetsu was Tokyo Station (1914). Designed by Tatsuno Kingo, one of Japan's first modern architects, the station sold tickets to destinations across the empire, including Manchuria, and beyond. Travel from Tokyo to Paris in 1940 via Mantetsu took just sixteen days.

Although Mantetsu was a means of exploiting Manchuria, Japanese justified it because of the benefit it also brought non-Japanese. Seki Hajime, for example, noted how Mantetsu contributed to the "collective economic interest," benefiting Chinese too. In dominating Manchurian trade, however, Mantetsu used its growing assets to discourage rivals, making it difficult for new Chinese railways to emerge. Through discounts, Mantetsu also ensured Manchurian commodities' export through Japanese-dominated Dalian or Korea, rather than Russian Harbin and Vladivostok or Yingkou, opened by the 1858 Treaty of Tianjin and home to British and other merchants.[61] Yet Mantetsu was only one component of the Japanese presence in Manchuria. Financing investments were institutions like the Yokohama Specie Bank (founded 1880) and Mitsui Bussan. Having opened branches in Chinese coastal regions prior to the Russo-Japanese War, each soon opened inland branches in Manchurian railway towns. The Bank of Korea (1910) followed, collaborating in Manchuria with the Bank of Taiwan (1897) and the Industrial Bank of Japan (1902).[62] The Bank of Korea replaced the Yokohama Specie Bank – which had helped fund Mantetsu's early development – as the main Japanese bank in Manchuria in December 1917, the same year the Oriental Development (Colonization) Company (Tōyō takushoku or Tōtaku), founded in 1908, extended operations from Korea into Manchuria.[63]

Manchurian resources, including coal, timber, fish, and arable land, enticed these ventures. Soybeans proved especially valuable, as a food source, fertilizer, and oilseed for industry. Fifty-two percent of the value of Manchuria's exports in 1930 consisted of soybeans, soybean cake, and soybean oil, followed distantly by millet, sorghum, and other cereals.[64] The dominance of soy and its derivatives did not change until the onset of military-enforced industrialization.[65] Long exported by Chinese from Yingkou, soybeans had garnered increased attention during the Russo-Japanese War. By 1909, Manchurian soybeans constituted 90 percent of the global market, and Japanese experimental farms investigated varietals. In 1931, the region still produced about 75 percent of the global total, with another 12 percent in Korea and Japan. Not only did a rapidly urbanizing Japanese population grow dependent upon soy, but so did Japanese shipping and, to some extent, industry.[66]

Manchuria beckoned also because of popular Japanese concerns about a presumed "surplus" population, especially because Korea and other colonies could not accommodate large numbers of Japanese, and immigration restrictions had emerged in Australia, Canada, the United States, and eventually Brazil. However, while both Mantetsu and Manchukuo encouraged rural immigration, efforts never succeeded to the extent Japanese officials hoped. Instead, most Japanese in Manchuria were urbanites, typically literate and organized. Mark Peattie noted that "most [Japanese in China] arrived not as despairing tenant farmers, impoverished laborers, or racially suspect immigrants, but as members of an ambitious, profit-seeking, and generally privileged class." They formed self-governing local residents' associations, linked to local consuls.[67] This inclination was more than a by-product of empire; Kamishima Jirō reported that such local organizing was common in Japan, noting that transplanted Japanese were able to cooperate as a new village within new urban locales.[68] Underscoring both observations is Sandra Wilson's that Japan's emerging Great Power discourse "was a resolutely urban-centred one."[69]

A sense of shared proprietorship over southern Manchuria quickly emerged among resident Japanese. In the early years, zealous police, railway employees, military authorities, and postal officers, for example, allegedly engaged in surveillance and harassment of rival imperialists in Manchuria, opening mail and losing or damaging goods. Although the decline in American exports was due to natural fluctuations, Mantetsu and the IJA were also accused of obstructing trade.[70] Japanese officials denied it, yet Tokyo ordered restraint.[71] Hayashi Tadasu, foreign minister in the first Saionji cabinet, acknowledged that "boastful and aggressive" Japanese troops alienated Chinese, Europeans, and Americans, although he suggested that American trade declined more because of superior Japanese trading methods.[72] Toyokichi Iyenaga, a University of Chicago professor of political science, exemplified attitudes by acknowledging some discrimination under the military administration, chiefly due to language and cultural differences, and that government rebate practices to corporations amounted to unfair trading practices. He suggested, however, that Americans benefited from high tariff walls at home and concluded that Japan was naturally concerned of being "deprived of the fruits of war secured at such enormous cost," and that "an American commercial campaign in Manchuria" was politically motivated and thus "neither wise nor just."[73]

Empire proved popular in Japan, engendering nationalism and imbuing Japanese with a sense of greatness. The sense of inferiority often present in the early Meiji period diminished as Japanese came to see themselves as citizens of a great nation, one of the Great Powers, defined in civilizational as well as military terms.[74] Apparent in the First Sino-Japanese War, this perspective intensified during the Russo-Japanese War as Japan became the first non-European state to defeat a major European military.[75] Anger at the Liaodong retrocession paled against the rioting over the Portsmouth Treaty. Many deemed Japan insufficiently rewarded, and the anger eventually toppled the wartime government of Katsura Tarō.[76] Since the war with Russia resulted in one hundred thousand casualties (including wounded) and cost ¥2 billion, many opined that Japan should never abandon anything won so dearly. Ironically, the Japanese press vilified Japan's chief negotiator at Portsmouth, Foreign Minister Komura Jutarō, even though he sought more than the government demanded. Fearing for his safety, the government assigned extra security upon his unpublicized return to Japan.[77] Views explicitly citing the losses in 1904–5 re-emerged in the 1930s.[78]

Celebrating Japan's military, the media published photographic collections and organized postwar tours of battlegrounds – another activity with echoes in the 1930s – and Mantetsu arranged for artists and writers to tour Manchuria.[79] Individuals gained public recognition for wartime actions. Some held high rank, such as Fukushima Yasumasa, who, in addition to serving in the Sino-Japanese and Russo-Japanese Wars and carrying out individual reconnaissance missions in peacetime, was also the first to oversee the military administration of Manchurian cities under Japanese control. He was elevated to the peerage, and his name remained public posthumously: a stone monument dedicated to the faithful who died in battle (*chūkonhi*) in his calligraphy can be found at Yamanashioka Shrine, Fuefuki City, in Yamanashi, and his ashes are buried near those of other famous people in Tokyo's Aoyama Cemetery, a new kind of commemorative site.[80] More humble Japanese were also celebrated, such as the courageous soldiers lauded as "human bullets" (*nikudan*), a term coined in the battle for Lüshun.[81] Following the Manchurian Incident, the media fanned the flames of war fever again.[82] Although it is impossible to know what consumers of popular media thought, that this orientation was broadly shared indicates that editors deemed such views would be readily consumed. Japanese "red journalism" functioned much like American "yellow journalism."

More was involved than simple jingoism: the media often justified such views with civilizational rhetoric. The victories of 1894–95 and 1904–5 provided opportunities to assert a sense of equality with the major powers and, in the 1930s, a sense of superiority over these states. This was evident in many venues, including even innocuous events like beauty pageants.[83] Many Japanese thought it was their presence that stabilized Manchuria under the capricious rule of Zhang Zuolin.[84] Such views were not government-mandated; the state did not attempt to "radically" mobilize the media until after war's outbreak in 1937, having "no power to compel" media support in the early 1930s.[85] Government censors instead tended to limit inflammatory views of the Manchurian Incident rather than suppress criticism of the government, as the incident "both reinforced and extended some exclusivist types of Japanese nationalism." As was apparent during the late Meiji, "the strongest views – the hard line – often came from outside the government."[86] And militancy was also apparent among some favouring cooperation with the "West."[87]

Noting that this war fever waned, Sandra Wilson contends that the Manchurian Incident was a "discrete episode" and not the start of a "Fifteen-Year War" or the inauguration of a decade of militarism.[88] In contrast, Louise Young notes broader complicity. Building Manchukuo was a modern act, as "industrial capitalism and other revolutions of the modern age" rendered nineteenth- and twentieth-century empires "multidimensional, mass-mobilizing, and all-encompassing." Manchukuo became a "total empire" involving all of society, given that it "took more than ministers and generals to make an empire."[89] Following Young's and Barak Kushner's distinction, active "unofficial" propaganda emerged as intellectuals, artists, and academics used the media and new forms of communication to support "official" efforts.[90] Scientists and engineers too not only contributed to fostering Japanese science and technology but also supported imperial expansion and eventual social renovation in Japan.[91] This was more true for government planners and the engineers and technicians in their employ, but all shared a similar interest in building powerful modern systems at home and overseas. Citing Tak Matsusaka and David Wittner, Daqing Yang notes the role of what can be called "techno-imperialism" in the development of Japan's empire, and Janis Mimura underscores this inherent modernism among certain bureaucrats by terming their efforts "techno-fascism."[92] Indeed, despite their suspicions of the military, Mantetsu research personnel found they could continue their work under military rule, as initially the Kantōgun required Mantetsu assistance in running Manchukuo, and later in north China. The Manchurian Incident resulted in Mantetsu gaining a wealth of new responsibilities, increasing its purview dramatically and expanding civilians' roles in this corner of the empire. The outbreak of fighting in China and the Pacific, however, inescapably heightened tensions between the military and civilians in Manchuria, perhaps especially intellectuals.[93]

This specialist and multifaceted nature of Japanese imperialism was present at the outset. Nishizawa Yasuhiko notes that, in addition to the military means by which Japan began colonial regimes in Taiwan, Korea, and Manchuria, Japanese pursued economic programs in these regions as well. These entailed the creation of infrastructure, requiring local construction and banking industries in addition to facilitating the development of organizations like Mantetsu, the Oriental Development Company, and newspapers. Construction projects and the systems they represented thus reflected Japanese dominance. Reinforced with hospitals, schools for Japanese and others (to train non-Japanese to be able to work with Japanese), and public buildings paid by public expense – Mantetsu in effect collected taxes – and administered by graduates of top universities, the Japanese empire proceeded on a broad front.[94]

The views above place the role of empire at the heart of national discourse and identity, something to which Andre Schmid calls attention – in his case for the significance of Korea in pre-war Japanese history.[95] Perceiving empires this way is akin to history "from below." Yoshimi Yoshiaki wrote of "grassroots imperialism" in his 1987 study of popular attitudes in the Asia-Pacific War.[96] Jung-sun Han goes so far as to suggest that "the Japanese populace actively participated in the construction of imperialist ideology and culture. In other words, the creation of Japanese will to empire was facilitated by the cooperation of the populace."[97] In part this was because prewar Japanese typically perceived themselves positively as members of a multi-ethnic empire, as Oguma Eiji reminds us.[98] Growing Japanese interest in Pan-Asianism functioned as a mobilizing ideology and identity for prewar Japanese, as Eri Hotta has shown.[99]

Ideological influence is difficult to assess. While many think the state and media influence public opinion, some note the abiding strength of private individuals' impacts. James Huffman found that, in the Meiji era, "the press may have created a public, but it was that public ... that gave the press its sense of direction."[100] James Dorsey problematizes the nature of influence by suggesting a "looping" pattern from state to public to state that binds the public to the state ever more closely.[101] Charles Taylor has observed that "what the public sphere does is enable the society to come to a common mind, without the mediation of the political sphere, in a discourse of reason outside power, which nevertheless is normative for power."[102] However described, Japanese society was more involved in Japan's imperial project than is often acknowledged. Exploring a colonial enclave, especially one as central to the Japanese imperial project as Manchuria, helps bring this participation to light.

Changchun and Xinjing

Constructing Japan's informal empire in Manchuria and the puppet state of Manchukuo required civilian participation. Although military, government, and corporate officials outlined policies and organized infrastructure, constructing empire on the ground could not have been done without broader participation. Moreover, even if individual motives differed and did not align with official or even other civilians' goals, individual Japanese in Manchuria, unless they were actively sabotaging communal efforts, could not help but contribute to constructing empire. Many did so unconsciously by simply relocating and participating in the daily affairs of colonial society, but others did so deliberately by contributing to the creation of something new. This dynamic was equally true in the puppet state of Manchukuo because, as in the decade following the Russo-Japanese War, the 1930s witnessed a surge in popular support for more assertive policies. Both eras also witnessed spikes in Japanese immigration to the region.

Japanese urban planners, architects, bureaucrats, and business people found opportunities in places like Manchuria, initially creating treaty port towns not too different from those of other imperialists in China. This did not reflect simple imitation, but was instead another example of Japanese digesting foreign forms.[103] The government played a key role in this, seeing embracing foreign disciplines as central to reforming the state after the 1868 Meiji Restoration. Under the supervision of the Ministry of Public Works (Kōbushō), founded in 1870, the ministry's Imperial College of Engineering (1873) joined with the architectural section of the liberal arts college Kaisei Gakkō (1868) and other schools in 1877 to form Japan's prestigious first university – Tokyo University, Tokyo Imperial University until 1947 (Tōdai). Planners, architects, and other professionals who trained there and at other emerging institutions served an important bridging function, importing foreign techniques and adapting them to Japanese needs. For example, Japanese considered modern architecture a discipline of engineering, demanding technological competency.[104] In addition to learning to design structures using steel and reinforced concrete, Japanese architects learned also to adapt foreign construction techniques to meet Japanese realities, including earthquakes.[105]

While planners, architects, bureaucrats, and business people shaped and interacted with Changchun's built environment to varying extents, all Japanese present contributed as well. Professionals designed town features, but non-professionals peopled towns and brought them to life. Although individual impacts were small, the influence of organized individuals was larger. When acting in concert, either simultaneously or over time, citizens exemplified broader trends. Henri Lefebvre contends that producing urban or any space reflects capitalism's inherent contradictions and environmental limitations, but others see roles for collective human agency in modifying lived space.[106] At its outset, Japanese society in Changchun naturally reflected its Meiji origins, and later arrivals ensured continuing links with Taishō and early Shōwa Japan. Many Japanese "carried the state with them," in Tamanoi's phrasing, projecting attitudes learned at home upon colonial milieux and peoples.[107] This was true even for some with reputations for pacifism and anti-militarism.[108] Andrew Gordon recommends perceiving Japan's pre-war democracy as a particular kind – an imperial democracy – with particular assumptions.[109] Central was membership in an imperial community, or "family-state" (*kazoku kokka*), even among those more progressively inclined.[110] These attitudes and assumptions defined the social imaginary, the "sense of the normal expectations" most Japanese had for one another or "the kind of common understanding" that enabled them to function as a society, even if they included self-serving fictions.[111] They accompanied Japanese overseas. Emer O'Dwyer has shown imperial attitudes present in Dalian, leading her to advocate a shifting of focus from imperialism to "imperial history."[112] It is reasonable to assume similar perceptions were held among Japanese in other railway towns: even if they varied in size and nature, treaty ports were on territories conceded by the Chinese government and thus were predisposed to tensions between natives and imperialists. Marjorie Dryburgh and Joshua Fogel have shown how strategic and cultural tensions affected Japanese settlers' views of Chinese and the Japanese state in Tianjin and Shanghai.[113] Jun Uchida and Todd Henry have identified tensions among Japanese in Korea with regard to Koreans, the colonial government, and colonial Seoul.[114] Japanese were also critical of official Japanese policy at times and were not the only colonial settlers in China so affected. Robert Bickers has shown that British Shanghailanders also developed distinct and multilayered identities, sometimes disagreeing vehemently with official policy, such as officials' willingness to return unequal privileges to the Nationalist government.[115] Chinese also experienced tensions in appropriating some of the urban forms and practices of imperialist societies, whether they resided in cities with concessions or not.[116] Even if not overtly imperialist, Japanese in Changchun through their presence and daily affairs were complicit in the imperialist project and furthering these kinds of tensions and more – some of which became manifest in the built environment. Any Japanese returning to Japan, moreover, would have done so with acquired experiences and attitudes, in effect carrying the empire with them home, to paraphrase Tamanoi.

Chinese constructed Changchun's first cityscape on grassland originally belonging to the Mongolian Front Gorlos Banner. In 1791, the banner headman became the first to rent Mongolian land to Chinese settlers in defiance of Qing prohibitions, later petitioning the throne to accept the tenants' presence. The Qing acceded, likely because the Jilin garrison commander reported in 1799 that the Changchun walled village (*pao*) on the right bank of the Yitong River exceeded 3,330 households farming forty thousand acres. Given that there were too many settlers to remove forcibly – and that Chinese domination of Manchurian towns was already becoming the norm – the Qing attempted to confine them the following year by establishing Changchun sub-prefecture (*ting*), outside of which farming was forbidden. The court also placed Changchun under the jurisdiction of the Manchu military governor of Jilin, shifting provincial boundaries.[117] In 1825, Qing officials transferred from the Changchun Gate in the Willow Palisade brought imperial authority and a new name to the town that until then had been called Kuanchengzi.[118]

Changchun prospered with continued immigration, trade supplementing farming, and became recognizably Chinese. In 1825, the sub-prefectural offices moved west across the river, and the district as a whole shifted north. In 1864, in response to bandit raids but without official permission, residents dug a moat and raised sixteen-foot-high brick walls stretching twenty *li* (about ten kilometres), although a British visitor in December 1886 described the works as no more than "a ditch and a low mud wall, with a rusty gun on a worm-eaten carriage mounted at each gateway." He also reported that, like just about all Manchurian towns, the city had a regular grid plan with a main north-south street running almost three miles. Although most buildings were single-storey and brick, the main street was "really a splendid thoroughfare – a bewildering vista of sign-posts, and obelisks, and gilt inscriptions, and lamps. The four cross streets are also prettily decorated." The Guanyin Temple near the East Gate was impressive, "the only piece of modern ecclesiastical architecture we noticed worth looking at in Manchuria." He concluded his description by noting he expected to find Mongolians but was "disappointed. It is a Chinese town, pure and simple." The Willow Palisade between Changchun and Jilin City, moreover, "had so utterly disappeared that we did not even notice it."[119] Growth and foreign encroachment prodded continuing administrative reorganization. Changchun became a prefectural capital in 1889. On 14 January 1907, the government officially opened Changchun to foreigners, that fall appointing Manchuria's first governor general, Xu Shichang, to deal with emerging issues. On the eve of the 1911 Revolution, Changchun was the headquarters of one of Jilin Province's four intendancies, with jurisdiction over two prefectures, two sub-prefectures (one independent), and seven districts. In 1912, the new government made Changchun prefecture a county (*xian*) and in 1925 the city a municipality (*shizheng*).[120]

The Japanese presence in central Manchuria unfolded in a series of waves, overlapping with arriving Europeans. The first Japanese in Manchuria after 1868 arrived in Yingkou in 1872 but did not travel north of Shenyang.[121] One of the first visiting Changchun, in the winter of 1899, was IJA captain Hanada Nakanosuke, who, masquerading as a Buddhist priest, gathered intelligence across Manchuria, Mongolia, and eastern Siberia.[122] Changchun's earliest European visitors were members of religious societies (discussed in Chapter 4), but Hanada was more interested in imperial agents, especially Russians who began building a CER maintenance yard in 1898 at Kuanchengzi, a kilometre northwest of Changchun, in violation of an agreement to stay twenty versts (twenty-one kilometres) away from urban centres. Other Japanese likely passed through at that time, given that Japanese labourers and peddlers contributed to constructing Russian railways.[123] Working from opposite ends, Russians completed the CER just south of this yard on 18 July 1901, enabling the line to commence operations that fall before officially opening on 1 July 1903, though the *Yomiuri shinbun* incorrectly reported that the line passed through Jilin City.[124] Delaying the official opening of the railroad was the Boxer uprising, resulting in some 2,500 Russian troops occupying Changchun and Jilin City until the Russo-Japanese War.[125] Any Japanese present would likely have withdrawn for the war's duration, but many returned to live in Mantetsu's growing new railway towns.

A Russian presence endured at Kuanchengzi, the station town providing Japanese accommodations if pressed for housing in Changchun, although the town failed to develop. The town stagnated, despite its gaining a branch of the Russo-Chinese Bank in 1900, only two years after branches opened in

Harbin and Dalian. Initially focusing on financing railway construction and bribing Manchu officials when necessary, the bank quickly shifted to tea in exchange for Russian kerosene and textiles.[126] Kuanchengzi was not much more than a train stop in 1902, however, and did not thrive after 1905.[127] Economic difficulties in Russia made it difficult to administer Harbin, let alone smaller towns.[128] The town gained a consulate in 1907 and an Orthodox church in 1908, but immigrants were few. Although some five million of the tsar's subjects immigrated to Siberia between 1891 and 1910, few journeyed as far as Kuanchengzi, despite support offered by the railway.[129] A French missionary reported in 1908 that there was "nothing remarkable" about the settlement except the post office.[130] A 1913 Japanese travel guide described it as only "an isolated spot with scarcely any buildings except a few belonging to the station," and there was little change in the 1920 edition.[131]

Russian Kuanchengzi's failure to thrive was due in part to Japan's arrival in Changchun, a strategically important locale. Located on the northwestern side of the foothills of the Changbaishan range, Changchun facilitated Japan's access to the central Manchurian plain. Changchun was also prosperous. Writing in 1905, British China Hand Bertram Lenox Simpson (writing as Putnam Weale) described it as "the most important entrepot for trade in the whole of Manchuria, containing a quarter of a million inhabitants." He opined, "The occupation of Jilin [City] will be strategically far more important than the occupation of Shenyang because the headwaters of the great river the Sungari will be reached and a base provided for further important operations ... [Changchun] will provision the Japanese armies from its vast granaries."[132]

Histories of the Russo-Japanese War typically conclude discussing the land campaign with the Battle of Shenyang, where a half million troops collided. These analyses, moreover, note the poor condition of Japanese forces after facing the larger Russian foe, suggesting that another large battle may not have ended in Japan's favour. One British observer even thought Japan's war plans originally did not consider proceeding beyond Tieling or Shenyang, and lacked meaningful reconnaissance in the north.[133] Changchun and Jilin City's allure, however, likely galvanized Japanese. War's end found the two armies facing one another more than a hundred kilometres to the southwest, but Japanese cavalry raids, sometimes joined by Chinese irregulars, stalked the Changchun region, threatening Russian supply lines.[134] The *Yomiuri* reported a secondary Russian defensive line at Changchun only a month after Shenyang, describing the area's topography as well as a rumoured advance toward Changchun and a weakening enemy.[135] During the Portsmouth negotiations four months later, an unidentified Japanese reported that imperial forces "are within striking distance of [Changchun], the greatest trade market in Manchuria."[136] Some expected a Japanese occupation of Changchun, or reported it as a fait accompli.[137] Hearing the treaty's terms, some in the Russian field headquarters at Guojiadian (Godzyadani) wondered if Russia had been "outwitted" at the bargaining table, because making Changchun the boundary meant losing control of Jilin Province, source of Russian foodstuffs and coal for the previous six months.[138] Japanese journalists quickly spotted opportunities and reported on preparations to occupy Changchun.[139]

By the Treaty of Portsmouth, Russian diplomats agreed to transfer to Japan that section of the railway "south of Changchun," but determining exactly where jurisdiction changed resulted in dispute. Japanese took the treaty to mean Kuanchengzi, the station nearest Changchun, as was reported in Mantetsu's *Manshū nichi nichi shinbun* (*Manchuria Daily News*), which began publishing on 3 November 1907, initially calling Kuanchengzi "West Kuanchengzi," part of Changchun. Not until January were the two separated, the *Yomiuri* reporting on negotiations in Japan.[140] After briefly sharing facilities, Japanese opted to build a new town on land that was primarily sorghum fields – the site of the future Yokohama Specie Bank was a field where rabbits were hunted – and home to scattered farmers. Cossacks were quartered near the old town, and so Japanese had to oversee their transfer as well as claims from landowners. Mitsui arranged these land purchases, although ultimately some bribery proved necessary.[141]

The Qing officially opened Changchun and other northern towns on 14 January 1907.[142] The new Japanese settlement emerged between the walled city of Changchun and the Russian station at Kuanchengzi, integrating more with the former than the latter. A road soon linked the new town's train station with old Changchun's North Gate, only two kilometres distant, and the town's central southern boulevard curved southeast to the Mahao Gate. Just inside this gate were the offices of the Daotai and other officials.[143] A mercantile district (Ch, *shangbu;* Jp, *shōfuchi*) between the Japanese settlement and Chinese Changchun further integrated the two.[144] These activities were not novel – Japan's first urban enclave on the Asian mainland was at Busan in 1876. The Chinese response – to constrain the Japanese town, the government encouraged the mercantile district's expansion – was evident in other similar situations.[145] Ultimately both towns grew, a testament to the region's economic dynamism. This lured Japanese civilians, though such immigration paled in comparison with Chinese settlement (see Chapter 4). The British naturalist Arthur de C. Sowerby observed in 1919 that "the Japanese areas of Shenyang and Changchun are pitifully lifeless when compared to the neighboring Chinese quarters of these towns, or with the Russian sections of Harbin." Ominously, he concluded that "however much the Japanese may strive against it, it is almost certain that Manchuria is doomed to be settled and populated by Chinese, whoever gains the political control of that country."[146]

Anticipating Chinese numerical dominance and with prior experience in Taiwan, Mantetsu's first president, Gotō Shinpei, championed a modernizing presence for Japanese in places like Changchun. Specifically, this meant administering "scientific policies" based on "biological principles" – meaning studying native practices in order to understand colonized peoples and encouraging their gradual participation in Japanese empire building, eventually assimilating them. At the same time, Gotō sought to subtly secure Japan's position through a policy of "military preparedness in civilian clothing," ensuring real strength was never far away, while encouraging acceptance of Japanese through colonial development and the demonstration of Japanese leadership in scientific and urban infrastructure. Gotō returned to Japan in 1908, but as a senior official, including stints as home minister, foreign minister, and Tokyo's mayor, he continued to influence policy on planning and the built environment across the empire.[147]

Changchun stood for a quarter century as the northernmost outpost of Mantetsu's string of railway towns, altering its built environment in a manner reflecting the evolving nature of Japanese society, including what it meant to be modern.[148] The Manchurian Incident challenged the railway's domination of the town, however, and shifted some of the ways Japanese defined urban modernism. This shift was especially evident in Changchun, renamed Xinjing (New Capital; Jp, Shinkyō) on 14 March 1932. Jeffry Frieden has observed a higher incidence of military takeover of regions having greater investment in primary production for export, notably the extractive industries and agriculture.[149] Manchuria's seizure seems to belong to this category, but Manchukuo involved more than resource extraction. Rather than a new colony, Kantōgun officers created a notional country, replete with currency, ceremonies, and symbols. Seeking to accommodate Chinese nationalism, Kantōgun officers also sought a quick reversion of the railway zone to Manchukuo sovereignty – though resistance delayed this until 1 December 1937. In relinquishing extraterritorial privileges, returning railway towns to local authorities, and withdrawing Japanese police, Japan did not give up control. From the outset, beneath the national fig leaf, Japanese directed the country via a strategy called "internal guidance" (*naimen shidō*), pairing Manchukuo's leaders with Japanese advisers and having the Kantōgun supervise Japanese bureaucrats. The Kantōgun commander also served simultaneously as the Japanese ambassador – though the Japanese consulate continued to operate – and it was Japanese who managed Manchukuo's foreign affairs.[150] The ubiquitous presence of Japanese advisers amid Xinjing's tight security at Manchukuo's declaration of independence on 9 March 1932 led some foreign observers even then to call the new state "Manikinchuria" or "Japanchukuo."[151]

Similarly noting Japanese minders, Peter Fleming – Ian Fleming's brother – a special correspondent for the *Times* of London, ruminated in 1933 on Manchukuo's rhetoric. He wrote of "Propaganda Elbow" – that is, of being weighed down by voluminous documents one could not easily dispose of and, given a lack of taxis, had to carry. Its regularity prompted him to wonder "why this perpetual guilding [*sic*] of the lily? Why these everlasting and redundant attempts to pass off a policy of enlightened exploitation as a piece of disinterested rescue-work? This parading of non-existent virtues, this interminable process of self-vindication breeds doubt and scepticism in the foreign observer."[152] Citing Homi Bhabha and Mary Louise Pratt, Annika Culver suggests such activities are central to how new states establish themselves and can reflect imperialist attitudes.[153] Fleming was also responding to the hyperbolic nature of the rhetoric, in particular to the "Principle of Benevolent Rule" (Ch, *wangdao;* Jp, *ōdō*), also translated as "kingly way," a term derived from the Confucian tradition and meaning ethical rule. Revitalized by Sun Yat-sen and reaffirmed by some left-leaning members of the Nationalist Party, the term was promoted by some Japanese civilians seeking a new state even before the Manchurian Incident. Fleming noticed other "portenteous phraseology," perhaps referring to the utopian promises of Manchukuo's becoming a "paradise" (*rakudo*) and an "ideal state" (*risō kokka*) offering "ethnic harmony" (*minzoku kyōwa*). Specifically this was "five races' harmony" (*gozoku kyōwa*) for the Chinese, Manchu, Mongolian, Korean, and Japanese inhabitants.[154]

To co-opt Chinese support, Manchukuo's architects gleaned what they could from China's heritage and the Nationalist regime, and wrapped what they used in a Pan-Asianist flag.[155] The regime later also invoked the "spirit of national foundation" (Ch, *jianguo jingshen;* Jp, *kenkoku seishin*), a phrase gaining currency in Japan. The government-published pamphlet *Fundamentals of Our National Polity* (1937), for example, sought to define Japan's own "national essence" (*kokutai*) in this manner and presented Manchukuo's founding as an extension of prehistoric Japan's own imperial unification. Invoking this in Manchukuo, however, may have represented a shift from initially emphasizing civilizational ideals to the needs of state building.[156]

More than slogans, these mantras represented efforts to distinguish Manchukuo from previous and rival forms of government.[157] Under these banners, Xinjing became a stage for the military and its supporters to put an acceptable face on their activities, often with much pomp and circumstance. The capital's first mayor, for example, was the Manchu prince Jin Bidong. His lineage was close to the Qing throne – there was even some support for Jin's becoming Manchukuo's leader, and some Japanese had earlier supported an independent Manchuria under Jin's father Shanqi (Prince Su).[158] Jin himself ultimately supported his clansman Puyi, the Kantōgun's choice, helping his sister Kawashima Yoshiko (Jin Bihui) smuggle Puyi's wife out of Tianjin in 1932.[159] Puyi – the last emperor of the Qing Dynasty, whose ancestors supposedly once lived northeast of Xinjing at Shitouchengzi[160] – became Manchukuo's head of state (Ch. *Zhizheng;* Jp. *Shissei*) that year. This was not an imperial title, but Manchukuo's calendar acknowledged Puyi's authority as regent by instituting the era-name *Datong* (Great Community), a phrase referring to Confucius' utopia. Allowed to be named emperor in 1934, Puyi inaugurated a second era, *Kangde* (Abundant Virtue) – *kang* being the first character of the era name of one of the greatest Manchu rulers, the Kangxi Emperor, and *de* the first character of the temple name (*miaohao*) of the Guangxu Emperor, Puyi's uncle. The Kangde Emperor celebrated his elevation by announcing his accession at a makeshift Altar of Heaven in Xinjing, wearing the robes of the Guangxu Emperor as a symbol of a Qing Restoration rather than the military uniform required by the Kantōgun for his enthronement.[161] Reportedly, fifty thousand troops flanked the seven-kilometre route of his procession.[162] Puyi embodied not only the Manchu and Chinese traditions, though – his lineage also included Genghis Khan, imbuing him with broader significance.[163] Puyi's lack of children, however, elevated his younger brother Pujie's importance. In 1937, Pujie married into the Japanese imperial clan, and Puyi worried that a successor could come of this union.[164] Manipulated and insecure, Puyi grew desperate to stabilize his throne, resorting even to enshrining Amaterasu, the Japanese Sun Goddess, in the palace's new National Foundation Temple in 1940, despite issues that raised among Chinese. To do so, Puyi visited Japan that year, leaving and returning to Xinjing with much fanfare. Japanese officials encouraged this visit, enabling Puyi to be part of the lavish celebrations that year recognizing the 2,600th year since the empire's founding, something also to be marked by Tokyo's hosting the Summer Olympics.[165] Although war caused the games' cancellation, under Puyi's "patronage ... 50,000 youths representing Japan, Manchukuo, and China" assembled on the capital's Datong Plaza on 19 September 1940 to mark the empire's anniversary. Later that month, Manchukuo's largest games to date were held at the capital, with thirteen hundred participants.[166]

Although Puyi recalled a warm reception upon arriving in Changchun in 1932, opposition to his selection and elevation emerged from the outset among both Japanese and Chinese who saw him and the position of emperor as symbols of a bygone era. Peter Zarrow has observed that, after 1911, Chinese "mainstream elite imagination no longer conceived of the state as based on an emperor," and Puyi's moving out of the Forbidden City in 1924 allowed for the "complete museumification" of that space.[167] Selecting Puyi and the puppet state's structure reflected Kantōgun priorities, but ultimately neither helped the Kantōgun govern.[168] Japanese constituted a tiny minority in Manchukuo, so officials needed at least the tacit support of non-Japanese to govern and complete their various construction and economic projects. Ultimately, the Japanese relied on the use of force or its threat to maintain order. Although widespread collaboration was unavoidable, instances of Chinese "collaborationism" – meaning ideological identification with Japan – were few.[169] This was significant, because the puppet state expected to elicit non-Japanese support, and some thought it possible. The problems inherent in Zhang rule had left many Chinese open to an alternative arrangement, and Japanese rule in Taiwan succeeded in eliciting Chinese support there.[170] Japanese promoted economic growth and modern practices in Manchuria, and, even if they did so primarily for their own profit, others would benefit too. Noting the advantages of currency stabilization and the expansion of transportation infrastructure, Edgar Snow thought some Chinese willing to collaborate with imperial Japan, including those seeking a Confucian revival as well as those merely seeking profits.[171] Despite finding "little enthusiasm," George Woodhead reported general Chinese acquiescence in 1932, noting Zhang regime corruption and that "millions ... have emigrated to Manchuria ... to escape the oppression and misrule" of the warlords in the south. He described Chinese peasants as "potential neutrals," but cautioned that there could be "passive, if not active resistance," elsewhere, especially among "merchants, politicians, and the old militarists."[172] On the other hand,

Manchus and Mongolians apparently had reason to support the new state, as did many Koreans following the Wanbaoshan Incident.[173]

Some noteworthy Chinese elites offered public support. One was the monarchist Zheng Xiaoxu, Manchukuo's first prime minister. Educated in Japan, Zheng advised Puyi after 1923 and encouraged him to trust Japan, although soon after Manchukuo's founding he reconsidered Japan's reliability.[174] Perhaps written with a defensive eye, in his diary he was critical of Puyi, the Japanese, and the new regime, as well as Chiang Kai-shek and Zhang Xueliang, whom he called "mice, not men" for their reactions to the Japanese takeover.[175] More supportive were men such as Zhao Xinbo, a lawyer educated at Meiji University who favoured a constitutional republic but helped draft Manchukuo's declaration of independence and served as the first president of Manchukuo's Legislative Yuan and first mayor of Shenyang after the takeover.[176] A Kantōgun legal adviser at the time of the Manchurian Incident, Zhao objected to Zhang Xueliang's opposition to Japan – a 1934 British consular report called him a "pro-Japanese opportunist of notorious reputation."[177] The terms Manchukuo and Xinjing are sometimes attributed to Zhao.[178]

A frontier town on the Mongolian prairie, Changchun experienced extensive changes in the twentieth century with the additions of a treaty port and an imperial capital. The Japanese-built urban environment and local economy and the society associated with them reflected the varying motive forces present in Japanese society at home as well as in Manchuria. These transformations ultimately paved the way for Changchun's becoming Jilin's provincial capital after 1945, usurping Jilin City's role despite the latter's longer history. Even if much of Changchun's pre-war built environment is today rapidly disappearing, its contemporary influence remains.

1 City Planning

Japanese built two different urban environments in Changchun. The first was a railway town, designed and maintained by Mantetsu personnel, and the second an imperial capital, planned jointly by Mantetsu and the Kantōgun. Representing different eras in Japan's empire, the two cityscapes reveal divergent imaginings of Japan's colonial project. Yet each was rooted in contemporary Japanese conceptions of urban space and imperial society, indelibly stamping them as products of Japanese imaginations at particular points in time. Each spoke to issues evident in Japanese, as well as Manchurian, society. After considering the planning of the Japanese railway town at Changchun, the imperial capital of Xinjing is examined. Although the capital represented efforts to affirm state power, it also exhibited modernist concerns, an endeavour consistent with Japanese efforts in the railway town before the Manchurian Incident.

Treaty Port

Home to one of Mantetsu's eight branch offices established October 1907, Changchun was important for the Japanese from the start. After the railway towns at Shenyang and Liaoyang, Changchun's was the third largest in area, larger even than Chinese Changchun.[1] Prominent Japanese such as the war minister and chairman of the Mantetsu board of directors, Terauchi Masatake, as well as Mantetsu president Gotō Shinpei, were involved in determining the railway town's location and size. Gotō, who toured Changchun and other northern towns in November 1907, doubled its initial size, making it larger than Russian Kuanchengzi.[2]

Laid out in a roughly rectangular grid, the town repeated some Russian practices in Manchuria (Map 2). According to Changchun's first planner, Katō Yonokichi, an 1894 Tokyo Imperial University (Tōdai) civil engineering graduate and head of Mantetsu's civil engineering section from 1914 to 1923, this approach was typical of modern urban planning. It was also practical.

Level ground allowed him to focus the town on the railroad by putting it at the centre of the northern edge. The town nestled snugly within the site's topography: two creek beds draining east and three rail lines connecting the city with points east, north, and south. While the northern creek helped separate the Japanese and Russian towns, the southern became a park, still in use today.[3]

Katō's first survey trips were in July 1907 – one at least was reported in the *Manshū nichi nichi shinbun* (*Manchuria Daily News* [*MNNS*]). His 1908 plans included almost four square kilometres for the town and 1.27 square kilometres for the railway's needs. Not including space allocated for the railway and trees, by 1922 this plan translated into 15 percent residential use, 33 percent commercial, 31 percent stables and fodder (primarily for horses), 9 percent public parks, and 11 percent public works. The northern third of the railway town, north of the station, was given over to the railway, storehouses, and stables, though warehouses were also located east of North Corner (later East) Plaza. Offices and government buildings clustered around the town centre immediately south of the station. The remainder of the railway town was split between residential in the west and commercial in the east.[4]

With broad avenues and city blocks generally measuring 218 by 109 metres, the town south of the station measured roughly nine blocks east to west and seven blocks north to south. Diagonal streets bisected the grid, creating large plazas (Ch, *guangchang;* Jp, *hiroba*). The largest was North Plaza, directly before Changchun station, measuring 91 metres across. Nishizawa has suggested that railway plazas like this served larger purposes, as they enabled people to gather or make connections within Japanese-controlled space.[5] From North Plaza radiated the town's three main boulevards. About five blocks down either of the streets running diagonally from it could be found two other large plazas, East (later South) and West Plazas. For Katō, this created a "grand" (*kōsō*) street plan with sufficient public space to let citizens gather, as in all "magnificent" (*idai*) cities.[6] The convergence of streets at these plazas allowed for eight lots facing East and West Plazas and five facing the North, and made possible distant views in multiple directions. Clustered around North Plaza would soon stand the major railway buildings, including the local Mantetsu office and the railway's Yamato Hotel. Banks would front East Plaza, and nearby would be the Japanese consulate (established in 1911).

There were six classes of roads, the widest of which was 36.3 metres across and the narrowest 10.9 metres. All but the smallest had sidewalks. Changchun Boulevard (Ch, Changchun Dajie; Jp, Chōshun Taikai), the wide road running due south from the station, was a class-one street. The two broad streets heading southwest and southeast from the station, West Diagonal Boulevard (Ch, Xixiejie; Jp, Seishakai) and East Diagonal Boulevard (Ch, Dongxiejie; Jp, Tōshakai), were class-two streets, 27.3 metres wide. Most streets in the residential area were either class five (14.52 metres wide) or six (10.9 metres). Streets running north-south were class five and numbered in order from Changchun Boulevard, beginning with West First Street (Ch, Xiyitiaotong; Jp, Sei'ichijō Dōri), which ran parallel to the central boulevard one block west. Streets running east-west varied in size, the ones closer to the periphery being class two but others class six. East-west street names followed Japanese practices: *i-ro-ha* sequencing in the western half, *hi-fu-mi* in the eastern – starting with Izumi and Rogatsu on the west and Fuji and Mikasa in the east. Later additions followed the *a-i-u-e-o* syllabary.[7] Japanese paved these streets with macadam and coal tar. Paving was necessary, as horse carts' four-centimetre-wide wooden wheels could quickly sink to their axles when the streets were wet and muddy. Despite the paving, Chinese horse carts, some as heavy as two tons, posed problems. Fearing damage, Katō initially planned to limit the use of horse carts. Gotō Shinpei, however, overruled him, allowing carts and widening roads, indicating that Japanese recognized that they had to adapt themselves to Chinese practices.[8]

Designating creeks and otherwise unusable lands as parks, Katō helped avoid flooding of built-up areas and created urban green space. The railway town's main park was West Park, the creek bed within emptying into the Yitong River to the east. Designed by Tōdai professor Shirasawa Yasumi, the park had space for athletics, rental boats, and flowerbeds as well as a merry-go-round, a small zoo, and other children's amusements. It also featured a memorial stele to those who died fighting Russia.[9] Woodhead described the park in 1932 as "comparing favorably" to any in Shanghai, forested, and open to all residents.[10] Initially it was the intended site of a Shinto shrine, but that was built a little to the north.[11] Higher than West Park and not situated on a creek was East Park. At the south end of East Diagonal Boulevard, it was originally the site of a copse of old trees that gradually diminished as wood was appropriated for construction.[12] In it stood two "grotesque" animal statues and a tablet commemorating the slain statesman Itō Hirobumi.[13]

Town construction began soon after finalizing land purchases in September 1907.[14] Initially reliant on water from the Yitong River, Japanese began drilling wells in February 1908.[15] Mantetsu controlled construction through zoning and loan policies, meaning that urban zoning laws appeared in

Changchun a decade earlier than Japan's national code. Enabling tighter control of space, zoning appealed to colonial administrators, and it was easier to implement in a colonial setting.[16] Mantetsu put a halt to "cramped Chinese construction" at least as early as March 1908.[17] The early work followed Gotō Shinpei's priorities: infrastructure, schools, and hospitals (Table 1.1). Housing was less a priority, given space to rent in Russian Kuanchengzi and Chinese Changchun – one resident recalled living in a temporary hut.[18] Among the first buildings constructed were the post office, police office, Mantetsu office, and Yamato Hotel. While the latter two sat across from the train station on either side of Changchun Boulevard, the former pair fronted that boulevard on the east side three blocks south. Construction on Changchun's new station began in August 1910, replacing a temporary structure that commenced operations 1 December 1908. Built even before the one in Shenyang, this was one of Mantetsu's five most important stations and served as Japan's gateway to the north. Securing the town was a barracks and parade ground for the Changchun garrison built in the town's western corner, adjacent to West Park, in 1906, and a Kenpeitai (military police) facility between the police station and West Plaza built by 1913. All of Japan's colonial outposts, of course, began under military occupation.[19]

Table 1.1
Changchun railway town expenses through April 1911, in yen

	1908	1909	1910	Total (with 1911)
Roads and drainage	1,829,335	138,487,756	278,163,876	842,980,337
Markets	–	4,077,987	–	4,077,987
Parks	–	2,107,666	1,361,000	3,468,666
Cemetery, crematorium	–	1,427,282	–	1,427,282
Hospital	2,617,030	37,657,973	44,670,000	158,905,113
Elementary school	42,300,954	7,954,427	1,107,516	76,692,947
Sanitation	–	2,369,925	–	2,369,925
Apartment housing	1,418,800	–	–	1,418,800
Office construction	–	–	58,451,850	59,109,650
Totals (¥)	47,877,189	194,084,016	383,753,242	1,160,614,487

Note: "*Totals*" row numbers in original source are incorrect and do not add up.
Source: Izumi Renji, *Chōshun jijō* (Chōshun: Chōshun Nihōsha, 1912), 8–9.

In addition to granting Japan sixteen railway towns, the Treaty of Beijing allowed foreigners to acquire the right to use land in the mercantile districts where China retained sovereignty. Located between the railway town and the Chinese city's North Gate, Changchun's mercantile area opened in 1908. Complaints about muddy roads prompted calls for work that fall.[20] The magistrate of the Chinese city, Yan Shiqing, ordered road construction connecting old Changchun with the railway town as well as new offices (*yamen*) in a Western-inspired style and a police station in the mercantile district's north end in 1910, adjacent to the consulate site. His successor, Meng Xian'i, further encouraged development in that zone by organizing a local consortium to construct stores, parks, theatres, and brothels in 1911–12, especially along the main north-south street, Damalu (Dama Road), running from the city's North Gate. A 1940 publication noted that construction of a Chinese-style "pleasure quarter" in the area had contributed to rapid development on this road, along which could be found a row of "grand buildings" (*taika kōrō*). Although Chinese construction did not benefit from the same largesse as Japanese, it helped affirm a developing sense of Chinese pride.[21] The growth of Japanese and Chinese Changchun, moreover, stimulated Chinese construction in the surrounding countryside.[22]

A rising sense of Japanese patriotism was evident in the built environment, especially in names inscribing the town as Japanese. Maps show that, by 1927, Changchun Boulevard had become Chūō Dōri (Central Avenue), and the boulevard that ran diagonally across the east side of the railway town was Nihonbashi Dōri (Bridge of Japan Avenue), the name of a bridge in downtown Tokyo from which distances in Japan were measured. West Diagonal Boulevard became Shikishima Dōri.[23] Shikishima (islands that are spread out) is a traditional appellation for Japan and was the name of a British-built Japanese battleship that served prominently in the Russo-Japanese War. Along with the familiar Japanese means of organizing streets, these changes illustrated the marginalization of colonized peoples inherent in the imperialist process. Although Gotō Shinpei intended the railway town's features to integrate Japanese and Chinese communities, later officials were apparently less concerned with doing so.[24]

Japanese reports praised the new railway town. A 1908 *MNNS* article described the new town streetscape as "ideal."[25] In the 1920s, a Mantetsu researcher suggested the town had finally joined the modern world, a view echoed by journalist Yamada Hisetarō and a mimeographed Kantōgun report noting Changchun had entered a "different age."[26] The *MNNS* reported electric lighting by then was on until 11:00 p.m. in the summer.[27] This kind of view fulfilled earlier prophecies of Manchuria's "inevitable development" and "final destiny."[28] Photographs of Changchun, moreover, circulated alongside photos of Dalian, Shenyang, and other Manchurian enclaves in books, journals, and newspapers in both Manchuria and Japan, testifying that paved streets, sidewalks, and Western-inspired architecture were appearing across Japanese-controlled Manchuria. Albeit propaganda, reports like these defined Japanese efforts as building civilization where before there was nothing. Hard on the heels of battlefield sacrifice, this was a narrative that took hold in the Japanese imaginary.

Japan's reading public would likely have been receptive to perspectives like these, since they replicated recent transformations in Japan's own urban environment. Not only did contemporary planners share common educational backgrounds, but Gotō Shinpei helped cultivate attitudes and values through the Urban Studies Association (Toshi kenkyūkai), established in 1917 when Gotō was home minister, and publisher of the influential *Toshi kōron* (*Urban Review* [*TK*]).[29] An editorial in an early issue intoned that urban development was key to national progress.[30] Gotō himself declared that planning was fundamental to all Great Powers, and that the mission of urban planners was to help usher in a "new age in urban life."[31] Expressing the opinions of planners in academia and government, the journal dealt with pressing concerns in Japanese cities, offering occasional reports on urban conditions in Manchuria, other parts of China, the United States, and Europe.[32] The journal thus linked urban planning in Japan to developments elsewhere, helping justify changes. It contributed to a view of urban planning that comprised not only improving urban conditions but also creating a modern society, and by extension a new national identity.[33]

Exemplifying this, the jurist Hozumi Shigetō suggested constructing "internationally attuned cities" as transportation hubs as well as centres of moral and spiritual development.[34] Others focused on parks and green space, given their previous lack in urban Japan. Reporting from the United States in 1919, the planner Takei Takashirō examined seven kinds of parks in Europe and America with reference to Japan, observing that foreign cities invested heavily in their construction, with few complaints about expense given the "rational[ity]" of the endeavour.[35] Shigenaga Hisomu, a planner active in Kyoto in the 1920s, called for space for youth to exercise and be entertained, as such activities were healthy and helped decrease crime.[36] Others suggested parks were hallmarks of the future.[37] Planners wanted Japan's cities to be not only more efficient and livable but also accommodating of expanding populations. Architecture, transportation, regional planning, and coping with natural disasters were different aspects of a broad endeavour. Arguing this integrated approach explicitly was frequent *TK* contributor Sano Riki (Toshikata), a 1904 Tōdai graduate, a long-time associate of Gotō Shinpei, and a Tōdai professor who helped pioneer Japanese earthquake engineering.[38] Accomplishing this vision, another Gotō assistant suggested, secured national pride and dignity.[39] Of course, planners encountered difficulties in achieving their visions, as corporations, developers, and the state had other goals.[40] Yet, backed by the authority of the colonial state, planners had a freer hand in places like Manchuria and were able to present towns like Changchun as modern imperial outposts.

Planning Mantetsu's towns meant crafting cityscapes conducive to business and attractive to settlers, but it was also a means of expressing national identity, distinguishing Japan as a Great Power equal to other imperialists. These concerns endured even as the urban planning discipline evolved. Although Japanese planners remained interested in overseas examples, especially in England, Italy, Germany, and the United States, in the 1920s there emerged a marked and mutually reinforcing tendency toward more radical solutions relying more on theoretical principles than precedents elsewhere.[41] Inclinations toward the abstract were also apparent in reconsidering state roles and societal efficiency, inspiring new ways to represent the state and its bureaucratic components in the built environment. Globally, the most influential proponent of this vision was perhaps Le Corbusier, but Japanese planners gravitated similarly.[42] In 1932, some Japanese planners enjoyed the opportunity to endow one city with what they thought were the most modern amenities. This city, in turn, was to invigorate an entire society in moving toward a new social vision, one ostensibly designed to be superior to anything offered by the West. This city was Changchun, reborn as Xinjing.

Imperial Capital

With similarities to other foreign concessions in China, Japan's Manchurian towns before the Manchurian Incident reflected internationalist inclinations. In 1932, Japanese struck out on a different path, intending the new capital to express a Pan-Asian identity that would surpass the West. Planners did so by invoking elements of the Chinese tradition in modernist forms. Ultimately, Pan-Asian commitments were secondary to state power and authority, and behind the carrots of Asian harmony and material progress lay a menacing administrative stick.

Xinjing's propaganda role did not prevent foreign approval of the city. A University of Chicago geographer visiting Changchun in 1947 could not help praising Japanese construction. He found the city to have "wide boulevards and elm-lined streets; parks dot the city and its suburbs; large modern buildings of brick, concrete and stone rise from what was the site of soy bean farms." For him, the city constituted "a tragic tribute to the aspirations of the Japanese in East Asia."[43] Despite its service as a puppet capital, it appealed to this American academic because it was not altogether foreign. Likewise, Étienne Dennery, then a professor at the elite École libre des science politiques and a postwar director general of the Bibliothèque nationale in Paris, observed that one of Manchukuo's two biggest successes was in city building, "especially that of the capital."[44] This approval stemmed from recognizing technological capabilities and the aesthetic appeal achieved by Japanese planners through combining Pan-Asian ideals with lessons learned in the interwar-era debate on the urban milieu. A statement of identity and a continuing laboratory for Japanese urban planners, Xinjing was not simply a wartime contrivance. Under the direct control of the Manchukuo government, planners presumed other cities would follow the capital's lead.

Designated one of only two "special municipalities" to assure direct control by the new "national" government, the new capital and its environs constituted a separate administrative zone outside provincial jurisdiction (Map 3). The designation granted the municipality broad taxation powers, and the mayor reported directly to the prime minister.[45] Supervising Xinjing's construction was a special agency, the Capital Construction Bureau (CCB), including men from Mantetsu and the Kantōgun. This small group represented a wealth of experience, as detailed in the June 1932 issue of *Manshū kenchiku zasshi* (*Journal of Manchurian Architecture* [*MKZ*]) devoted to the new capital.[46] Nishizawa notes that Japanese began this new venture as they had development elsewhere after the Russo-Japanese War, recruiting experienced personnel from across the empire.[47] The small number involved ensured that Xinjing came close to fulfilling official goals faithfully, but military supervision entailed restrictions. Mantetsu's Aiga Kensuke, who served as head architect, later recalled having to submit decisions to military authority, resulting in some "confusion."[48] That said, military officials were willing to compromise more in developing Xinjing than in places nearer the Soviet border.[49]

Under a Chinese figurehead, the CCB general affairs manager was Yūki Seitarō (sometimes transliterated Kiyotarō), a graduate of Tōdai Law School and a former head of general affairs at Mantetsu who promoted Manchuria's reorganization prior to 1931.[50] Most of his staff were young, in their forties, and many would later achieve prominence in Japan. Some who were to play leading roles, such as Sano Riki, were already prominent. Most were Tōdai graduates, though some were graduates of Kyoto or Waseda Universities. Many were experienced. Mizoe Satsuki, a 1916 graduate of Hokkaido University who also studied at the Universities of Wisconsin and Chicago, worked in the Osaka municipal government before becoming chairman of the Shenyang Government Construction Office. Another was Kondō Yasukichi, a 1916 Tōdai graduate who worked on the reconstruction of Tokyo.[51] Some were members of the association that published the *MKZ* – the CCB requested five men from that association in November 1932.[52] Mantetsu's delegation included Shenyang railway department vice-chairman Gomibuchi Hajime, a 1912 Tōdai graduate and postwar mayor of Yokote, Aichi Prefecture, and Orishita Yoshinobu, a former parks section head in the Tokyo reconstruction bureau. Orishita was invited to Manchuria at the behest of Sogō Shinji, then a Mantetsu employee but also a 1909 Tōdai graduate, a long-time associate of Gotō Shinpei, and the "father" of the postwar bullet train.[53] A later member was Sekiya Teizō, an Oxford and Tōdai Law School graduate who was the son of a Mantetsu employee as well as one himself. Following completion of the city's first five-year plan, he took over as CCB head while serving as the city's deputy mayor from 1937 to 1940, later serving as deputy minister in the Manchukuo Welfare Ministry from 1943 to 1945. After the war, he published positive views of Manchukuo and designing Xinjing, and in 1959 was a Liberal Democratic Party candidate for Japan's House of Councillors.[54]

Officially, Kantōgun officers began inspecting Changchun in February 1932 and Mantetsu representatives the following month, after Manchukuo was proclaimed on 1 March and Changchun was named the capital 10 March. The CCB began meeting that month, although Aiga Kensuke recalled being sent to investigate Shenyang and Changchun earlier – only one week after the Manchurian Incident.[55] Some urgency was apparent – until agreeing on Xinjing's new forms, urban projects elsewhere were on hold. Aiga recalled living like "canned goods" and working often from seven in the morning until two at night, and sometimes all night.[56] Sano Riki reported that the plan's outlines were decided by summer 1932.[57] The CCB completed its plan in

December, submitting it to the prime minister in January 1933. Manchukuo's State Council ratified the plan in January and promulgated it as law in April.[58]

Transcripts of fall 1932 inter-agency meetings were published in 1935 as *Shinkyō toshi kensetsu hōsaku* (*Plans for the Construction of Shinkyō* [*STKH*]), one in a series of publications on planning for Shenyang, Harbin, Tumen, Beian, and Mudanjiang.[59] Planners agreed that the new capital would be modern and rational but also more than simply a capital. On one hand, constructing Xinjing meant seeing to the economy, public peace, and air defence. On the other, it meant creating a space for a unified government for Manchukuo's thirty million people, requiring that planners create a "grand appearance" for the new executive.[60] More than a capital, Xinjing was a city on a hill. To provide a firm economic foundation for its future population, Kantōgun planners indicated Xinjing should grow from around 150,000 to 500,000 within twenty years. This was a minimum size for capital cities around the world, observed Yūki Seitarō, who justified several decisions for Xinjing's future on comparisons with Tokyo and Washington, DC.[61] (Others expected the population to soar to one or one and a half million.[62]) At the crossroads of seven major highways, the capital's hub role was also recognized. Revealing an anti-capitalist disdain, the military wanted growth to occur in "an orderly fashion" and under "municipally unified supervision."[63] Representing Mantetsu, Gomibuchi Hajime agreed Xinjing would be the "capital of a rising Manchukuo" and a "modern, civilized city" where growth was "controlled," but, given the experience of other political cities, Mantetsu planners expected more vigorous growth than did the military.[64] Gomibuchi also concurred with the military that Xinjing be built according to five-year plans, and also agreed, perhaps more genuinely, about the need for zoning control.[65] Gomibuchi accepted that the ultimate goal be an "ideally planned region" – a perspective rapidly gaining currency.[66] Although it was evident that Mantetsu's position was inferior to that of the military, some goals coincided, allowing agreement between the two groups.

Planners endowed Xinjing with a spacious two hundred square kilometres. Aiga reported that only farmhouses were present in the designated area, and mentioned some resistance among those who lost farmland. Indeed, a woman committed suicide rather than surrender land farmed by her family for two centuries.[67] The generous size was to avoid the "cancers" apparent in other large cities, as planners expected the imminent arrival of more than 100,000 people.[68] Planners also agreed to proceed gradually, reserving half of the designated area for the future. The first five-year plan (1932–37) focused on

Table 1.2
Xinjing construction in the initial five-year plan (km²)

Palace and administration	2.0	Residential	6.5
Public facilities	1.5	Commercial	2.0
Parks	2.0	Industrial	1.0
Roads	4.5	Agriculture and livestock	0.5

Source: Minami Manshū tetsudō kabushiki kaisha keizai chōsakai, *Shinkyō toshi kensetsu hōsaku* (Dairen: Minami Manshū tetsudō, 1935), 9.

only twenty square kilometres, ten each for public and private use, though the total area ultimately planned for development in the first five-year plan came to just over twenty-one square kilometres (Table 1.2).[69] In comparison, the old city of Changchun encompassed about eight square kilometres, the Japanese railway town five, the mercantile district four, and the Russian railway town at Kuanchengzi four. At the time, Tokyo itself comprised only eighty square kilometres. For Sano Riki, the large-scale construction reminded him of the rebuilding of Tokyo after the 1923 earthquake.[70]

Eight months of negotiations saw the CCB incline toward the military's proposal for the remaining 179 square kilometres (Table 1.3).[71] Generally, the military wanted more land for government offices, industry, and their own use, while Mantetsu representatives wanted more land for commerce, parks, and infrastructure. Different recommendations reflected different priorities, the military's being official and military and Mantetsu's the issues apparent in the *TK* and the *MKZ*. Gomibuchi suggested learning from Tokyo's experience and providing the best possible modern infrastructure, including roads, water, sewage, electricity, telephones, and gas. This was "holistic planning."[72] CCB general affairs manager Yūki later suggested Xinjing could manage with a smaller economy than Mantetsu recommended. Both Tokyo and Washington, DC, he noted, were large capital cities that allowed nearby cities like Osaka and New York to dominate commerce.[73] An official CCB publication repeated this assertion, saying that Anshan and Fushun could do for Xinjing as Osaka and Kitakyūshū served Tokyo.[74] Yūki also reasoned that Xinjing would mature into a city for all Asians (*Tōyōjin*), in much the same way that Edo had become Tokyo for all Japanese, given that Xinjing would presumably attract banks and other institutions.[75]

Open space was a key feature attracting Japanese to Manchuria, and planners ensured Xinjing maintained this allure. The CCB noted that, while the density of Tokyo and Osaka was 37 and 80 m² per person, respectively, the

Table 1.3
Proposed and actual land use in Xinjing (%)

	Kantōgun Plan	Mantetsu Plan 1	Mantetsu Plan 2	Mantetsu Plan 3	First 5-Year Plan
Palace and administration	6.5	4.43	5.07	6.56	11.0
Military	9.0	3.44	3.68	2.55	–
Residential	27.0	35.75	40.50	39.20	28.0
Commercial	8.0	10.80	9.78	9.71	11.0
Industrial	6.0	4.79	5.00	4.97	6.0
Parks	7.0	8.68	10.00	9.95	13.0
Public facilities	3.5	4.76	5.00	6.22	–
Communications	–	10.10	10.25	10.18	–
Agriculture and livestock	12.0	–	–	–	–
Roadways	21.0	–	–	–	22.0
Undesignated	–	17.25	10.72	10.66	–

Note: The unaccounted 9 percent in the final column is listed as "other."
Source: Minami Manshū tetsudō kabushiki kaisha keizai chōsakai, *STKH,* 8–10, 21–22; Nagami Ken'ichi, "Manshūkoku sandai toshi no kōen sonota," *Kōen ryokuchi* 3, nos. 4/5 (1939): 31.

Changchun railway town provided 126 m^2 and the mercantile district 179 m^2. At 86 m^2, even the Chinese city of Changchun was less dense than either Tokyo and Osaka. Looking further, the CCB noted that contemporary Paris allowed 27 m^2, London 67 m^2 (Greater London 237 m^2), Boston 166 m^2, and New York 138 m^2. The figures for Beijing and Tianjin were 63 and 46 m^2, respectively. Gomibuchi suggested Xinjing's goal should be 150 m^2 per person, accomplished through parks, streets, and an encircling greenbelt.[76] A Kyūshū University professor reported that this figure rose to 200 m^2, roughly double the space of most Japanese big cities.[77] In addition to being roomy, Xinjing was orderly, something Gomibuchi thought sound economic development depended on.[78] Laid out in a grid pattern, Xinjing's city blocks were larger than those of the railway town, though broad, diagonal streets radiating from large, circular plazas again crossed the city. Planners also continued to incorporate creeks south of the railway town emptying into the Yitong River by transforming them into parks.

Several issues proved contentious, one involving financing. While the military initially recommended a budget for the first five-year plan of ¥31,595,000, Mantetsu recommended a budget of ¥43 million, with a plan to borrow the difference overseas. The military demurred, suggesting that borrowing was like building official structures in a Western style: it was not in keeping with the spirit of Manchukuo's "kingly way." At the same time, Manchukuo officials were negotiating with French investors to give lip service to the Open Door and perhaps secure French recognition of Manchukuo. For some, the issue was a matter of retaining control, fearing that loans might make it possible for creditors to compel the adoption of different plans, but Yūki wanted to avoid foreign loans in order to emphasize Japanese leadership in Asia.[79] The military's position was again adopted, although a 1939 report predicted the cost of the new city's construction would eventually total ¥100 million. The first five-year plan's budget was ultimately ¥30,596,000, with some ¥5 million borrowed from the Bank of Manchukuo to complete land purchases.[80]

There were also divergent opinions expressed over Manchukuo state offices and Puyi's palace, recognizing their central roles and that they constituted the "foundation of national reverence" (*kokumin sūhei no kongen*). Two of Mantetsu's three proposed plans envisioned a European kind of palace, including gardens and vistas, but the topography and location of other structures required that the palace not face south, traditional in Chinese capital planning. These planners eventually relented, conceding that their plans connected the palace with the existing city poorly and that putting the palace in the southwest would render it freer of smoke from the city centre (predominant winds being from the southwest). Because construction halted on the palace in 1942, however, this debate proved moot.[81] Puyi's new palace gardens were ultimately also smaller than what Mantetsu suggested, sitting enclosed, north of the new palace, just as the private imperial courtyard did in Beijing. On Puyi's order, however, the gardens were in a Japanese, not a Chinese, style, in the manner of Tokyo's Akasaka Detached Palace – perhaps another effort to shore up his position by linking himself to Japan.[82]

Situating the new palace was significant. Beijing's Forbidden City occupied a central, axial location in relation to the city's walls and temples. Xinjing only partially replicated this – lacking any walls or Beijing's roughly rectangular shape, Puyi's palace was to be "near the centre of the city."[83] It also repeated some of the Forbidden City's relationships. Due south of Beijing's Forbidden City lay the "outer court," the offices of the imperial bureaucracy; the "inner court" north of Tiananmen was the domain of the imperial family and their servants. Physically, the outer court combined two rectangular courts in the shape of a "T": an east-west "front court" (Ch, *qianchao;* Jp, *zenchō*[84]) capping a north-south "Thousand-Pace Corridor" (Ch, *qianbu lang;* Jp, *senbu rō*) along which offices of the imperial bureaucracy faced. South of Xinjing's palace lay the 35,000-square-metre Shuntian (Heaven's Will) Plaza, corresponding roughly to Beijing's "front court." Crossing the "T" at Shuntian Dajie was Xingren (Rising Benevolence) Dalu, an east-west avenue running from the future South Train Station to Datong Dajie, where it changed names.

Manchukuo government offices eventually occupied space corresponding to that of Beijing's outer court, but instead of a walled, hidden enclave, the sixty-metre-wide, tree-lined Shuntian Avenue descended south from the palace site. On the eastern side of the street, at the northern end nearest the palace, would sit the Hall of State (Ch, Guowuyuan; Jp, Kokumuin) and its annex to the south. This housed Manchukuo's top executive, the State Council. Across Shuntian Avenue sat the Ministry of Public Security, which in 1943 became the headquarters of the Manchukuo military. Other major ministerial offices sat along Shuntian Avenue, ending in a traffic circle at Anmin Plaza. Beyond it lay South Lake Park, including the artificial South Lake. In addition to offering recreation, the lake, as well as other parks' creeks, was useful for retaining beneficial *qi* according to Chinese geomancy (*fengshui*).

In Beijing, commoners and marketplaces were relegated to the northern areas of the city. In Xinjing, the railway town and Chinese Changchun, home to most Chinese in the area, lay northeast of the palace. New residences appeared across the city, including in the southern districts, but there was also expansion northwest of the palace on the other side of the railway. So perhaps Xinjing generally replicated Beijing in this respect, but, unbounded by walls, the capital's population also sprawled into the surrounding countryside. A closer similarity to traditional planning involved locating the palace with respect to temples. In Beijing, the Forbidden City sat roughly equidistant between the Temples of Heaven and Earth in the south and north, and the Temples of the Sun and Moon in the east and west. All were Ming Dynasty creations, but the Qing refurbished them and continued religious observances at them. Xinjing quickly raised its own altars in three of the four cardinal directions and incorporated a few others, but planners did not rigorously adhere to traditional principles of location. North of the palace was the Monument to the War Dead (Ch, Zhonglingta; Jp, Chūreitō), completed in 1934. Southeast of South Lake stood the National Foundation Shrine (Ch, Jianguo zhonglingmiao; Jp, Kenkoku chūreibyō), opened on 18 September 1940 and modelled on Tokyo's Yasukuni Shrine. Like the capital's diagonal boulevards, it was oriented at roughly 45 degrees, roughly in the direction of Japan's Ise Shrine. Enshrining the twenty-four thousand Manchurian and

Japanese lives given in Manchukuo's service, it was built with labour and materials from across Manchukuo on a sprawling 450,000 square metres. The Monument to the War Dead was more modern in inspiration, serving the needs of a nation-state by recalling the sacrifice of those killed in its establishment. Its 120,000-square-metre plaza provided space for public rallies. With Asian roofs, the two were intended to mobilize Manchukuo society.[85] Puyi visited them under security and enforced fanfare. Less accessible to the public, within the new palace grounds would eventually also be found an Altar to Heaven, built in 1934 for Puyi's ascension, and a National Foundation Temple (Ch, Jianguo shenmiao; Jp, Kenkoku shinbyō) erected at his temporary residence in 1940. In a Japanese style, this was Puyi's personal shrine commemorating Amaterasu, the Japanese Sun Goddess, inspired by Japan's Ise Shrine. Anyone walking past it or one of the similarly named ones built later across Manchukuo was expected to make a formal "ninety-degree bow" or be "punished for 'disrespect.'"[86]

East of the palace near the Yitong River sat a Guandi temple (Ch, Guandimiao; Jp, Kanteibyō). Established around 1800, it served a local protective function for early Chinese settlers.[87] Near Datong Plaza was Changchun's largest Buddhist temple, Banruosi, relocated from old Changchun in 1932. Named after the temple of the sixth-century monk Huisi, in 1934 it was renamed Huguo (Protect the Nation) Banruosi. South a few blocks was the Dutiful Son Mound (Ch, Xiaozifen; Jp, Kōshitsuka). Planners were going to demolish it and the elm tree under which it stood, since they obstructed the projected Datong Dajie, but a public outcry ensued, including reports of miracles.[88]

Traditional Chinese capital planning located the palace and temples so as to ensure imperial ceremonies were in harmony with the cosmos. The correct orientation of the imperial seat ensured stability in the empire – and the universe – through exact rituals in proper locations. Imperial authority issued southwards from the throne, past temples and halls replicating cosmological actors on earth, through the city's gates, and into the world.[89] This was not the case in Xinjing, where modern inspirations were more important. Those emphasizing the significance of the south facing of the palace and the use of traditional principles like geomancy overstate the degree to which planners embraced traditional Chinese urban planning.[90] Mantetsu accepted the importance of using "ancient practices" (*kojitsu*) in locating the new palace only after debate, and at the same time continued to affirm the importance of seeking the advice of specialists in constructing this "rising country" (*shinkō kokka*).[91] Neither did the military suggest that a southern orientation was necessary in their earliest report in the *STKH.*[92] In calling attention to the preference for a southern facing of the palace, moreover, the CCB did not defend that choice through recourse to the Chinese tradition.[93] Thus, although some desired a south-facing palace from the outset, that eventuality was perhaps less certain.

Planning Xinjing entailed an imperial dimension, but traditional patterns of urban planning were evident only in certain sections of the city. Adjoining two existing towns, the new city was more fundamentally modern, with intended but only incidental invocations of tradition. Like Japanese support for Puyi, Xinjing's fidelity to Pan-Asianism was superficial.

Modern Capital

Xinjing's planning involved the needs of the modern state, including amenities, infrastructure, and order. Zoning and five-year plans organized its construction, a process that ensured an ideological expression. Suspicions about capitalism, for example, resulted in real estate brokers not being permitted to operate within the capital.[94] Selective adoption of elements from the Chinese urban planning tradition was to give the city a Chinese flavour rather than resurrect traditional values, as Xinjing's planners were more inspired by modernism. The capital, for example, was considered with respect to regional transportation and economic concerns.[95] This commitment to modernity was also evident in Xinjing's infrastructure, including mass transit, electrical power, water supply, sewage disposal, garbage incineration, and other amenities, offering solutions to problems that had been raised in journals like the *TK*. Likewise, planners wanted to confine light industry north of the railway town and east of Kuanchengzi or, along with heavy industry, north of Xinjing's East Station on the line to Jilin City, so that the prevailing winds carried pollution away. These locations were also convenient to rail and river transport. For the same reason, planners confined railroad expansion to the north of Changchun station.[96] Other areas of the city emerged as centres dedicated to other purposes, such as an education district east of South Lake and an area dedicated to sports on the east side of Nanling (see Map 3). Japanese commentators praised this organization, one noting that the city developed as an "organism."[97]

Road construction proceeded quickly, and by December 1937 included 312 kilometres, equivalent to the distance from the capital to Shenyang.[98] The central avenue was the fifty-four-metre-wide Datong Dajie (Datong

Boulevard), extending south from Chūō Dōri in the railway town to a "civic centre" (Jp, *shipiggu sentā*) on Datong Plaza, the centre a common topic among contributors to the June 1932 issue of the *MKZ* focusing on the new capital, several of whom were inspired by the work of Le Corbusier.[99] Mutō Tomio remembered the plaza being a thirty-minute walk from the train station.[100] Japanese guides noted that, excepting the Dutiful Son Mound, Datong Dajie continued south unbroken for five kilometres.[101] While the significance of terms like *Datong* (Great Community) may have helped imbue the capital with a sense of a shared Asian past, the plaza articulated state power. Located at the centre of the city atop a small plateau a little more than a kilometre northeast of the site of the new palace, the plaza had broad avenues radiating out from it, linking it to all quadrants of the city.[102] The plaza was the first constructed space of the new city, and the site of the Bank of Manchukuo, the Manchuria Telegraph and Telephone Corporation, Public Security, and the CCB itself. A large hotel was also planned for the site.[103] Each of these institutions occupied an entire block between two of the six avenues, and planners endowed each with a striking architectural form. Although reminiscent of the Russian circular interchanges in Dalian and Shenyang, Datong Plaza was larger. Three hundred metres across and covering some seventy thousand square metres (including streets), the plaza allowed frontages of over one hundred metres for the six sites facing it. The park within spanned 187.6 metres, a memorial tablet to the city's founding at its centre.[104] Listing forty-four sites within the capital he thought required imposing size, Gomibuchi thought sites like these would endow Xinjing with the proper "dignity" of a national capital.[105]

Not only were Xinjing's boulevards unusually wide for Asian streets, they were lined with paved sidewalks and trees.[106] To Kitakōji Ken, raised in Dalian and later a teacher there, Xinjing's spaciousness contrasted markedly with the southern port. Intriguingly, Kitakōji considered Dalian very – perhaps too – Japanese.[107] Xinjing's large city blocks and broad avenues, however, contributed to a need for mass transit, to connect residents with other parts of the city as well as the golf course, horse track, and airfield. Planners originally called for a subway, after excluding an above-ground railway "in view of the noise and disfiguring effects created by tramways and their vulnerability to air raids."[108] In the end, costs required that the city settle for a bus system and light rail. By 1937, eight bus routes served the city, six more connecting it with the surrounding countryside from the bus terminal four blocks northeast of Datong Plaza.[109] By 1942, eleven routes ran within the city, and thirteen outside of it, along with sightseeing buses conducting tours in Japanese and Chinese. Transportation employed eleven hundred people. A fixed rail system that began in 1941 expanded the following year to average seventeen electric trams plying the city's four tracks, totalling 186 kilometres daily.[110] Although taxis and other vehicles appeared, traditional horse carts, as well as rickshaws and similar vehicles remained. In 1941, the capital was home to roughly 11,000 horse carts and 752 three-wheeled vehicles; rickshaws averaged 1,444 between 1939 and 1941.[111] Xinjing's traffic was a mix of old and new.

More unambiguously modern was the commitment to urban green space – almost unknown in Asian cities, it was ubiquitous in Xinjing. There were no parks in Chinese Changchun until 1907, when a park covering seventeen thousand square metres was situated on the grounds of a former Muslim cemetery outside the city's West Gate.[112] Both Mantetsu and the military stressed the need for civic green space in Xinjing, and their concerns for sanitation, health, public peace, and municipal beauty led them to create parks, athletic fields, racetracks, and other places of leisure. For Gomibuchi, trees and water soothed the nervousness inherent in civilization's progress, and "picturesque scenery" (*keiryō*) near the residences and offices of foreign officials would maximize the impact of Xinjing's greenery on foreign opinion.[113] The *MNNS* celebrated the anticipated parks as a blessing for all, including children.[114] While the *STKH* had noted that green space provided water reservoirs for combatting fire and obstructing poison gas, one *TK* contributor noted that it also played a role in a city's defence, as wide avenues and fields reduced the impact of aerial attacks.[115] In that journal, Colonel Kuwabara Shirō suggested that planners endow cities with many small parks rather than a few large ones in order to reduce potential damage and provide refuge. Noting also that a dispersed city without tall buildings was the opposite of industrially oriented urban planning, Kuwabara urged a general rethinking of urban planning concepts.[116] Following the Marco Polo Bridge Incident, Japan adopted a new air defence law on 1 October 1937 that Manchukuo used, and German air defence preparations appeared in the puppet state two months later.[117]

Xinjing's extensive green space and modern amenities eventually included eight large parks and a variety of fields (Table 1.4). Three parks ran east from the palace as far as Datong Dajie along intermittent creek beds emptying into the Yitong River. Beginning at the palace grounds, Baishan (White Mountain) Park and Mudan (Peony) Park led to Datong Park, just southeast of Datong Plaza. Datong Park offered a pool and locker rooms, and five provisional wells helped initially provide the city with water.[118] Shuntian Park began at a lake southwest of the palace and led to Ertong (Children's) Park. In addition to these parks was a planned athletic complex at Nanling, with fields amounting to some 1,440,000 square metres.[119] Almost complete in 1937, this facility offered space for soccer, baseball, track, hockey, bicycling, basketball, and horsemanship. It hosted large events like the "Continental" and Japanese-Chinese-Manchukuoan competitions of 1940 in preparation for the (cancelled) Tokyo Olympics. Equipped with electricity and a loudspeaker system, it was a modern athletic complex.[120] To the west, there was also the enormous Xinjing Zoo and Botanical Garden, encompassing 780,000 square metres. Opened partially in 1940 and planned by zoo directors in Japan, it featured open enclosures without bars. It too was modern, and intentionally unlike zoos in Japan.[121] Mangyō president Takasaki Tatsunosuke helped promote the zoo and donated funds to support its expansion.[122]

Beyond these sites, planners embedded greenery in Xinjing's streetscapes, using Kentucky bluegrass as ground cover.[123] Nearly eleven thousand trees, mostly willows, occupied more than 120,000 square metres throughout the

Table 1.4
Xinjing's parks, 1939

Name	Area (m^2)	Water (%)	Cost (¥)	Completion
Datong Park	273,975	12.3	256,890	3/1933
Baishan Park	166,333	0.4	86,721	4/1934
Mudan Park	138,171	0.3	100,491	3/1934
Shuntian Park	560,000	12.1	186,750	7/1934
Heshun Park	136,474	42.9	8,575	4/1934
Huanglong Park	1,286,000	37.7	201,844	10/1936
Xi Park (West Park)	276,333	–	753,167	4/1914
Wumalu Park	17,387	–	–	1907
Total	2,854,673			

Notes: Heshun Park sat on the east side of the Yitong River south of the East Station. Wumalu Park was built on a Muslim graveyard in the old city. West Park now included expansion to the southwest.

Sources: Satō Akira, Eguchi Hidematsu, and Toyoshima Masayoshi, "Shinkyō tokubetsushi no rokuchi keikaku ni tsuite," *Kōen ryokuchi* 3, nos. 4/5 (1939): 9–11. Percentages for water area are from Nagami, although he provides different total areas for some parks. Nagami Ken'ichi, "Manshūkoku sandai toshi no kōen sonota," *Kōen ryokuchi* 3, nos. 4/5 (1939): 33–34.

Table 1.5
Xinjing's plazas, 1940

Name	Area (m²)	Name	Area (m²)
Datong Plaza	27,648	Shuntian Plaza	120,758
Anmin Plaza	16,875	Zhonglingtaqian Plaza	9,964
Xing'an Plaza	11,340	Xing'A Plaza	12,106
Jianguo Plaza	2,700	Xiehe Plaza	366,640
South Plaza	1,662	*Total*	569,657

Source: Satō Akira, *Manshū zōen shi* (Tokyo: Nihon zōen shūkei kyōkai, 1985), 94.

city, prompting a postwar publication's description of Xinjing as a "city of groves."[124] Trees lined the major arteries or appeared in traffic strips separating vehicular and horse-drawn traffic. Traffic circles at the city's six largest intersections were landscaped, providing another 6,353 square metres of green space. Along Shuntian and Xing'an Boulevards ran "street parks" (Ch, *jieyuan;* Jp, *kai'en*), adding, respectively, another 26,946 and 1,560 square metres of green space.[125] Other green space surrounded landmarks such as the Jianguo and Zhonglingtaqian Plazas fronting the two national monuments (Table 1.5). South of the zoo, Xiehe (Concordia) Plaza provided room for 150,000 to assemble.[126] Small parks, a golf course (330,000 m²), a horse track (also 330,000 m²), two plant nurseries to the southeast, cemeteries, and small tracts among residential neighbourhoods rounded out Xinjing's green inventory, though the zoo and sports complex awaited the second five-year plan.[127] Plans to celebrate Manchukuo's tenth year inspired the creation of even more public green space, including on former warlord government offices and the battlegrounds of the Manchurian Incident. There was also a small forest in nearby Jingyuetan, where a new reservoir for the capital was built.[128]

In comparison with North America and Europe, Asian cities traditionally offered little green space. Xinjing's total park space, shown in Table 1.4, meant that a population of 500,000 would have 1,751.5 people per Xinjing park hectare, something planners reckoned put Xinjing on about par with many European and older American cities and rendered it far superior to Japanese urban areas.[129] Japanese had bemoaned the paucity of natural beauty in their cities and promoted the benefits of parks and the utility of leisure.[130] This view imbued urban green space with an ideological role, and creating sufficient green space was a key concern among the contributors to the June 1932 issue of the *MKZ*. To one reporter, Xinjing's green space surpassed anything in

Table 1.6
Total green space in Xinjing, 1940 (m^2)

Parks	6,100,591
Zoos	716,627
Recreational facilities	778,132
Plazas	202,647
Along streets	228,184
Nurseries	1,751,935
Cemeteries and gardens	3,877,097
Total	13,655,213

Source: Manshū teikoku rinji kokuto kensetsu kyoku, *Kokuto kensetsu ni tsuite* (n.p.: Manshū teikoku rinji kokuto kensetsu kyoku, 1940), 45. These figures are larger than the 10,876,000 m^2 in Satō, *Manshū zōen shi*, 74, 77. The city's own figures shift from 10,769,894 m^2 in 1940 to 13,123,355 m^2 in 1942 in Shinkyō tokubetsushi shichōkanbō shomuka, *Kokuto Shinkyō* (Shinkyō: Manshū jijō annaijo, 1940), 105–6, and Shinkyō tokubetsushi shichōkanbō shomuka, *Kokuto Shinkyō: Kenkoku jūshūnen kinan* (Shinkyō: Shinkyō tokubetsushi kōsho, 1942), 199–201.

Japan and offered the appearance of "great-natural-park-ism" (*dai shizen kōen shugi*). It was also a means of defining modern civilization. This same reporter thought Xinjing's parks were "progressive."[131] After the war, Satō Akira, a Xinjing official, described the city parks as "civilized" because of the technical expertise involved in their engineering. Moreover, Satō thought that such work overseas was more significant than anything in Japan. This was because Japanese in Manchukuo were attempting – literally, "groping" – to create a new culture. Satō did not regard this effort as an act of pure benevolence: it was a means of invigorating Asian culture as a whole against that of the West. To that end, Oka Ōji, head of the Architecture Department within the Manchukuo bureaucracy, was developing a new Chinese style for the palace's outer gardens when the war ended. Although the details are not known, this effort too meant somehow reviving traditional forms.[132] After the war, Satō reflected proudly that Xinjing's total green space in 1940 (Table 1.6) reached the level of Europe and North America, about 453 people per hectare, and this did not include the enormous green belt encircling the city. Even if his estimate is inaccurate, it is revealing that his point of reference is Europe and America.[133] A 1940 publication noted that every resident enjoyed 22.7 square metres of green space, slightly more than Satō's figure.[134]

Publications extolled Xinjing's green space as helping cultivate the city's beauty.[135] They also praised the high-quality facilities for recreation and

Table 1.7
Xinjing's parks, 1944

Name	Area (m^2)	Name	Area (m^2)
Kodama (West) Park	276,331	Wumalu Park	17,388
Nihonbashi (Ribenqiao) Park	6,186	Cuihua Park	7,144
Datong Park	391,109	Andajie Park	7,109
Baishan Park	166,214	Shuntian Park	566,262
Mudan Park	161,212	South Lake Park	2,242,954
Heshun Park	136,475	Huanglong Park	1,170,000
Monument to the War Dead (*Zhonglingta*) Outer Garden	34,888	Huanxiling Park	304,804

Note: Cuihua Park was built in the old city section in 1939. Huanglong Park sat northwest of the triangular South Lake Park.
Source: Satō, *Manshū zōen shi*, 80–81.

relaxation designed by experienced professionals whom planners had summoned from across Japan.[136] One such professional was Orishimo Yoshinobu, the designer of the outer areas of Tokyo's Meiji Shrine.[137] Another was Numata Soyao, a Tōdai and Nihon University professor who became Harbin's chief planner in 1933 and Xinjing's after 1940, contributing several articles on Manchuria to the journal *Kōen ryokuchi* (*Parks and Open Space*).[138] Professional designs allowed planners to present their parks as "oases" for recreation as well as refuge in emergencies.[139] Green space remained significant in Xinjing's second five-year plan, as planners added 4.6 square kilometres of green space (Table 1.7). More was still available along the Yitong River and in the surrounding countryside to which the population could escape.[140] Eventually, this surrounding area fell within Xinjing's jurisdiction.[141]

As evident in its parks, Xinjing's modern infrastructure often involved aesthetic dimensions. An early law forbade the use of unsightly above-ground power lines – all had to be buried. Nor were there telephone poles: telegraph and telephone lines all were placed underground, as some thought was done in major cities in the West. The capital's rapidly expanding water supply system also ran underground.[142] More than 30,000 metres of piping for the city were completed by the end of 1932, able to provide 340 cubic metres of water daily. Another 1,000 cubic metres of supply was anticipated, with 8,535 metres of piping being built in 1933 and another 8,535 metres planned for 1934.[143] Receiving much attention was the new reservoir at Jingyuetan, a few kilometres southeast of the city, given its size and recreational atmosphere. Begun in April 1934, it began providing the city with 40,000 cubic metres of water daily in January 1936. Covering seventy-eight square kilometres, the reservoir contained enough water to supply a half million people, and with wells and the nearby Yinma River there was enough for a million.[144]

Constructing Xinjing was one aspect of a "national" policy, as the city in turn served as a "model city" for the rest of Manchukuo.[145] The urban planning law of June 1936 – thought by at least one observer generally more progressive than Japan's – adopted one year before the second five-year plan's inauguration, indicated that, thereafter, attention was to shift to other cities and towns.[146] The CCB assumed planning responsibilities for other Mantetsu railway towns as well as towns along the former CER the following year.[147] By 1940, forty locales were using an urban planning law based on Xinjing's, including inspectors. Xinjing's planning was evident also in the "greenification" (*midorika*) of Manchukuo's towns and cities, involving the construction of flowerbeds and other public green spaces as well as occasionally incorporating natural settings into residential neighbourhoods.[148] Urban planning in Korea also included references to the new capital. Not only were urban planning laws in Japan and Korea similar, but CCB personnel attended academic conferences with colleagues working in Korea and China, where discussions of Xinjing figured prominently.[149]

Xinjing was planned as grand, green, and modern. Japanese reports showed a new city arising on a virtual *tabula rasa*, and the creation of a modern city the equal of anything in the West excited many.[150] Muroi Osamu, a Shenyang architect and frequent *MKZ* contributor, called it a "city of modern ideals."[151] Sano Riki effused about its size and spaciousness in articles in the prominent journals *Toshi mondai* (*Urban Issues*) and *Kenchiku zasshi* (*Architecture Journal*). Manchukuo itself, after all, was almost twice the size of the Japanese islands and deserving of an appropriately sized capital. Moreover, as a stage for Japanese development, Sano thought it demonstrated Japan's power to the world.[152]

But perhaps Xinjing illustrated Japan's power too well. In emulating elements of Beijing, Japanese planners attempted to legitimate their efforts, but a close comparison is revealing. Both cities were planned capitals, but the vision coordinating Beijing was more logically consistent. As built space, the Forbidden City emphasized dynastic rulers as the heads of a coherent state. Xinjing marginalized Puyi, thereby emphasizing only the power of the state. Excepting Shuntian Dajie (Shuntian Boulevard), Xinjing's long streets and large city blocks did not focus attention on any consistently identifiable objects, in contrast to the Forbidden City or other landmarks. Broad streets, spacious parks, and zoning reflected rationally inspired goals, but, while technically competent, the vision Xinjing's design represented was rather empty. It encouraged patriotism without a genuine nation-state, celebrating instead a broader Asia. Although CCB general manager Yūki Seitarō suggested in 1934 that, just as Tokyo emerged from Edo, so too would Xinjing transform itself into an "Oriental city" (*Tōyōjin no machi*) capable of organizing the region, even he acknowledged that a strong and continuing military presence was necessary.[153]

At the same time, Japanese used Xinjing to glorify their leadership. The built environment could do so pointedly, as can be seen in the renaming of West Park on 3 November 1938 in honour of General Kodama Gentarō (today Victory Park) or, more subtly, through Xinjing's planning.[154] The unspoken implication was that, if Japanese could be trusted with the physical creation of a new city, then they could also be trusted with the creation of a new country and society.[155] This strategy ultimately failed, because, in Xinjing as well as in Manchukuo at large, the facade mattered more than the content for Japanese. This is to say that, while Xinjing had the appearance of a magnificent city, superimposing an Asian veneer on a modern city failed to address power relations. Despite Xinjing's rapid growth, almost half of the population continued to live in the old city, rendering access to new parks and other modern features problematic (Table 1.8). Another large residential concentration emerged east of the Yitong River, where planners concentrated the capital's industrial facilities. The two districts there (Heshun, Dongrong), together with the two districts constituting old Changchun (Changchun, Datong), included two-thirds of the population of the capital's inner ten districts, and over half of the city's entire population. Chinese constituted the majority in the outer six districts, although the government sponsored around one hundred Japanese colonist households who arrived between 1937 and 1941.[156]

In August 1940, the Xinjing mayor's office published a short pamphlet that depicted the city at what was perhaps its zenith – *The Grand Appearance of a Rapidly Progressing National Capital* (*Yukushin kokuto no iyō*). Xinjing's "grand appearance" was defined variously, but in lauding certain factors the pamphlet chiefly portrayed the city as progressive. Xinjing was a "modern city," providing its half million residents with water, electricity, and roadways.

Table 1.8
Population distribution in Xinjing, 1942

		Area (km^2)	Households (*N*)	Population
Inner districts	Shikishima	4.96	12,234	67,033
	Kuanchengzi	11.90	3,956	19,565
	Changchun	3.96	24,372	136,518
	Datong	3.57	19,069	107,137
	Shuntian	8.64	12,943	60,962
	Anmin	21.7	2,637	10,199
	Xiyang	18.26	918	4,861
	Dongguang	15.62	4,359	19,811
	Heshun	10.32	15,054	79,824
	Dongrong	8.52	8,625	40,175
	Total of ten inner districts	107.45	104,167	546,085
Outer districts	Jingyue	124.01	2,579	15,753
	Nanhedong	50.76	1,557	11,565
	Beihedong	38.31	1,412	8,899
	Helong	39.31	6,295	35,787
	Dacun	34.23	2,638	15,564
	Shuangde	50.12	2,050	11,523
	Total of six outer districts	336.74	16,531	99,081
Total		444.19	120,698	645,166

Note: Xinjing was divided into sixteen districts (Ch, *qu;* Jp, *ku*) in January 1942. Shikishima corresponded roughly to the old railway town, Kuanchengzi to the former Russian railway town plus land to the east. Changchun included the mercantile district and northwestern part of the old city, and Datong the southeastern half of the old city. Shuntian included the vicinity of the new palace and government offices, Anmin the southwest of that, and Xiyang west of the railway. Much of Xiyang, Anmin, and Kuanchengzi were not yet developed. Dongguang district was east of Datong Dajie but south of the old city and west of the Yitong River. Heshun designated the new development east of the Yitong River along the road to Jilin, and Dongrong the area north of Heshun. The outer six districts encompassed the capital's green belt and the watershed for the Jingyue resevoir. Each district had its own mayor and administration.
Source: Shinkyō tokubetsushi shichōkanbō shomuka, *Kokuto Shinkyō* (1942), 56–57, 66–68. Slightly different population figures for 1942 are in *Shinkyō no gaikyō* (Shinkyō: Shinkyō shōkō kōkai, 1942), 16–19.

By 1939, more than 366 kilometres of roads – almost 30 percent of which were paved – integrated the city, and two separate networks for waste water ensured that sewage went in one direction while rain water entered a storm system that led to low-lying depressions in the city's various parks.[157]

Municipal administration was rationally organized under the direct supervision of the prime minister and the national bureaucracy.[158] The central one hundred square kilometres was subdivided into eight sections, or wards. The city was large: the area that it encompassed was more than 70 percent as large as Tokyo and a little less than one and a half times the size of London, although much of this was rural. The pamphlet categorized its 440 square kilometres as municipal (21 km^2), commercial (79 km^2), and agricultural (340 km^2).[159]

The Grand Appearance of a Rapidly Progressing National Capital declared Xinjing a "livable capital city" (*sumiyoi miyako*). It suggested that, of all Manchukuo's cities, Xinjing had made the most "rapid development" and had come to function as Manchukuo's "heart" for politics, economics, culture, and just about every field of endeavour. Xinjing was also aesthetically pleasing: in new areas, utility lines were buried, houses were separated by four metres of open space, and height restrictions on buildings ensured no skyscrapers marred the horizon. The height limit of twenty-three metres was judged to be about the same as the ten-storey limit apparent in much of Europe and North America. Transportation was organized around a network of buses, and a subway was planned. Streets were labelled rationally, exhibiting the "great ideal" implicit in "founding the state," as north-south arteries were consistently labelled as *gai* (Ch, *jie*), while those running east-west were *ro* (Ch, *lu*). All boulevards wider than thirty metres merited the prefix *dai* (Ch, *da*). The abundant ponds and streams functioned as both "oases" as well as places of refuge in case of emergency. "In short, creating a 'livable capital city' meant ensuring that residents did not suffer from any lack in services with regard to disaster prevention, health care, transportation, safe havens, self-cultivation (lit., 'cultivating sentiments'), and the like."[160]

Generous funding – more than 21 million yuan between 1934 and 1940 – facilitated the construction of hospitals, schools, universities, markets, housing, roads, a sewage system, an electrical power grid, and other modern amenities.[161] Given that local taxes – amounting to 6,418,607 yuan by 1940 – accounted for less than a third of the total expenses, the role of outside investment was clear. Japan's role was crucial, and authors like those of *The Grand Appearance of a Rapidly Progressing National Capital* championed it. Such projects were part of Japan's "holy work of reviving Asia" (*kyōA no daishōgyō*). In return, the city's "three great duties" of construction, maintenance, and development meant Xinjing had to serve as a base of operations for reforming Japan and Manchukuo. There was, however, room for improvement, as the pamphlet noted problems of supply, pricing, production, and mobilization in Xinjing.[162] Such problems were understandable, given the ambitious agenda and the flagging funding following the Marco Polo Bridge Incident as war exigencies required reducing resources to the capital. Yet construction continued. In a November 1942 article, Tōdai architecture professor Kishida Hideto – who had helped rebuild Tōdai, notably Yasuda Hall, in the 1920s – stated that of all the significant changes he saw upon returning to Manchukuo, the capital city was the most changed. Not only had it grown tremendously in size but an "ideal city plan" had been realized.[163]

Views like this can be dismissed as propaganda, but the new capital also impressed a British intelligence officer. He thought Changchun in 1920 a "filthy, unimposing, uninteresting-looking Chinese town," but, taken to the top of the new Justice Ministry in the spring of 1934, he observed that the Japanese "are certainly showing extraordinary vigour and enterprise, laying out magnificent wide asphalted roads and boulevards, parks, and even a golf course, and fine big buildings going up apace. Two consecutive five-year plans are to be carried out and a really fine city should be the outcome." Nor was he alone in this view: a colleague reported the previous December that "magnificent new buildings [are] going up in Changchun and elsewhere, excellent roads being laid in the leading towns and cities and constructed in all directions."[164] Even if it catered to the needs of the Japanese military, the new capital was a project to which Japanese civilians contributed with pride. It represented the creation of a new civilizational order, including rational state planning, mass mobilization, and Japanese leadership in Asia.

Japanese authority, however, eclipsed Pan-Asian rhetoric, and the capital's planning shows its commitment to Asian ideals as only skin deep. Japanese walking Xinjing's streets could take greater pride in the city's more ubiquitous modernity than in its nods to tradition. Estela Duque has suggested that in American planning for the Philippines, militarization "expose[d] a difference between intentions and action, a distinction parallel to Lefebvre's abstract and real spaces." Although Manila's original plan posited particular ideals, the military's efforts to control elements of the built environment in the name of efficiency demonstrated how power was used and resisted.[165] Xinjing's denouement was similar. With the city born out of military action and a continuing sense of emergency, the chance that genuine Pan-Asianists might actually lead was slight indeed.

2 Imperialist and Imperial Facades

Helping flesh out Changchun's and Xinjing's new urban environments were architects trained at Japan's most prestigious institutions, who articulated themes and issues meaningful to Japanese society at large. Like urban planners, they sought to showcase empire appropriately for audiences foreign and domestic, but their concerns were more than simply imperialist or mundane. Emerging as part of a wider discourse on the built environment, the city's facades reflected divergent Japanese modernist impulses in a colonial setting. Architectural discourse gives tangible expression to issues of communal identity, something Lewis Mumford thought especially true during periods "of rapid social crystallization ... when the community acquires, through critical inquiry and self-conscious re-orientation, a firm collective insight into its own purposes and a passionate faith in the possibility of a new attitude and a profound societal change." Moreover, while "in an age of social disintegration and unrelated specialism ... architecture loses most of its essential character: in an age of social synthesis and construction, it steps forward once more as the essential commanding art."[1] For the Changchun railway town and the "national capital" of Xinjing, both built from scratch and systematically planned, these insights are particularly apt. They encapsulate the heady years of two momentous periods in Japanese history. After exploring the treaty port's evolving cityscape in relation to developments in Japan, this chapter addresses the capital's imperial, Pan-Asianist structures and their modernist foundations. As evident in Xinjing's planning, modernist inclinations proved more consistent among architects as well.

Japanese Concession

Architects were part of the Japanese empire-building project from the outset. In 1910, about 13 percent of the members of the Japan Association of Architects (Nihon kenchiku gakkai), established in 1886, indicated residency in Korea, Taiwan, or China. This figure climbed to 20 percent in 1942 and included Koreans and Chinese.[2] Nishizawa Yasuhiko calls these men "architect adventurers," an adaptation of British "merchant adventurers." Although they did not create or staff empire, Nishizawa sees their creations reflecting empire's evolving assumptions and goals.[3] He identifies Maeda Matsuoto as the first "architect adventurer," arriving in Dalian in September 1904 two months after graduating from Tōdai and seven months after the outbreak of the Russo-Japanese War. During the war, Maeda oversaw construction of supply depots in Yingkou and Liaoyang. With the end of hostilities, Maeda returned to Dalian to work with Okada Tokitarō, an associate of Tatsuno Kingo, the designer of Tokyo Station. Maeda soon joined the Guandong Government-General's Civil Engineering Department and helped define the face of Japan's budding empire in Manchuria and determine industry standards before becoming a Tokyo Higher Engineering School (later University) professor in 1907.[4]

Japanese construction in Changchun emerged as part of a national discussion on the built environment. Architects were educated public citizens committed to improving society by physically altering the built environment. They discussed their work in journals like *Kenchiku zasshi* (*Architecture Journal*), Japan's oldest architectural journal, which began publishing in 1887, or *Manshū kenchiku zasshi* (*Journal of Manchurian Architecture* [*MKZ*]), which began in 1921. A congruence of vision emerged, due not only to a common education and membership in a professional organization like the Japan Association of Architects but also to a common client base, as government ministries and large corporations demanded similar kinds of structures. These realities were also present in Manchuria, rendering Japanese articulations of the built environment even in places like Changchun illustrative of particular moments in Japanese history. At the same time, Changchun's evolving built environment reflected international trends, as Japanese architects introduced concepts from overseas while interacting with regional vocabularies. This continued in the 1930s, and problematically, for the creation of a new Asian style then was balanced by continuing to build also in international styles, even as architects in other countries continued to distance themselves from their traditions.

Illustrating the state's role in Japan's empire, Mantetsu, in overseeing the development of Changchun, built public structures first. Two of the first in the Changchun railway town were the post office and the police headquarters. Begun respectively in 1907 and 1908 and completed in 1910, they were designed by Matsumuro Shigemitsu, an 1897 Tōdai graduate and Maeda's successor in the Guandong Government-General. Matsumuro was a busy architect, designing public structures across Manchuria and later in Japan.[5] He was also an active contributor to the *MKZ*, exhorting Japanese to improve lifestyles through alterations to education and patterns of daily life.[6]

Constructed with stone facades, the Changchun post office and police headquarters would have been instantly recognizable by Europeans as products of their architectural tradition. The engaged Tuscan columns on the post office and the Gothic turret on the police headquarters might have tempted a passerby to wonder why European expressions appeared in an inland Japanese colonial outpost in Manchuria. An answer requires understanding that these facades reflected particular functions and attitudes, as the systems housed within these buildings were modern and represented the degree to which Japanese embraced these organizations and made them their own. Like much of Meiji Japan, these institutions were based on foreign models, though not imported wholesale. Japanese saw these systems as modern but pragmatically adapted what they adopted. The same was true for the architectural style of the buildings housing these systems, referred to as historical eclecticism.

Perhaps the most famous Japanese example of this style is Tokyo Station (1914) – "a temple to progress and a monument to empire" – although earlier buildings in this style include Japan's Law Courts (1896) and Ministry of Justice (1895).[7] Japanese deemed this style appropriate because of its recent emergence and popularity in Europe and North America. Prior to that, a building's function in Europe generally determined its style, such as classical or Renaissance for commerce and Gothic or Romanesque for churches. New styles emerged, however, such as Gothic Revival, which reasserted idealized Christian values and cultural heritage. A more imperial style was evident in Vienna's Ringstrasse (1860s–90s) and the reconstruction of Paris after the Franco-Prussian War. Applied to new kinds of structures, like railway stations, these new styles diminished the correlation of style and function. The Gothic style spread from religious to secular structures such as London's Houses of Parliament (1838–68) and Law Courts (1868–82). Technological change also influenced these changes. Although the Gothic Revival celebrated the virtues and piousness of medieval craftsmen, cast iron and steel framing enabled construction of larger buildings, transforming structural elements into decorative motifs. Rendered ornamental, styles became easier to combine, especially as increasingly larger buildings provided architects the room to transition smoothly from one style to another on a single surface. The Queen Anne style of the 1870s and 1880s completed the ornamentalization of the Victorian High Gothic, rendering it a motif.[8]

Ornamentalizing architectural elements changed their meanings for Europeans by eliminating symbolic linkages, rendering them more vague recollections of historicized pasts that could be put in the service of new agendas. Greek forms became simply classical and Baroque more broadly European. Gothic Revivalism evolved from fundamentalist to nationalist significance. Once embraced by secularizing Victorian society and carried overseas by British architects, it became also an overtly imperialist style – although it returned to England with Byzantine and other variations for Britons to reabsorb.[9] Britain's power and grandeur in turn kindled Japanese interest in British styles, particularly Gothic Revivalism. From the bronze decorations of mythical beasts on the Nihonbashi (1911), the symbolic centre of Japan's transportation network, elements of the style appeared across the empire, even to the Gothic turret on a police station in far-off Changchun.[10] Although Gothic Revivalism entailed an imperial dimension for Japanese architects, they perceived it as simply a modern, European style.

When Japanese first sought tutoring in European architecture, they invited eminent architects to Japan. The first choice was 1876 Soane medalist Josiah Conder, briefly an employee of William Burges, another noteworthy Gothic Revivalist. Conder arrived in Japan in 1877 to find European architects already at work, but found most early structures were hybrids true to neither Japanese nor foreign traditions, including "pseudo-Western style" (*giyōfu*) structures like the Tsukiji Hotel (1867–68). Within two decades, many of these were deemed awkward and torn down.[11] Conder encouraged Japanese to build in more coherent styles. His own architectural legacy served as a guide, as his more than seventy structures included important buildings in the Marunouchi business district, including the Rokumeikan, the St. Nicholas Cathedral, a number of elite mansions, and the building that eventually became the Tokyo Imperial Museum at Ueno, designed in a Hindu-Saracenic style. All were historical, and all were true to one era. Not as antiquarian as Burges but teaching primarily European styles, Conder applied such styles to Japanese structures based on their functions, thereby instilling in Japan's first generation of architects a strong sense of historicized significance.[12]

Until 1888, Conder taught the first architecture classes at Tōdai. His first class of four graduated in 1879, and within a decade his students were designing important structures. They did not do so, however, based solely on his teaching. Japanese architects were keen to continue learning architecture as an international medium, and many travelled overseas. One of Conder's first four graduates was Tatsuno Kingo. Before becoming a Tōdai professor in 1884, he studied in England and dreamed of developing a uniquely Japanese modern style. Tatsuno succeeded Conder as head of Tōdai's Department of Architecture.[13] Another was Katayama Tōkuma, designer of the Akasaka Detached Palace and the Imperial Museums at Nara and Kyoto. Before attempting such structures, he too studied in Europe, focusing particularly on European palaces. In the Akasaka Detached Palace, his artistic skill was matched by his technical competency – the palace suffered no damage during the 1923 Kantō earthquake.[14]

Japan's first generation of modern architects learned to work in a variety of styles. The Ministry of Education adopted the French Classical Revivalist style of the first Napoleonic Empire as its more or less official style. The Second Empire became popular among graduates of Tōdai's College of Engineering, understandable given that the Second Empire's neo-baroque was then becoming a preferred means of expressing state power around the world.[15] Nothing championed neo-classicism more than Tsumaki Yorinaka's new Nihonbashi, modelled perhaps on the Alexander III Bridge across the Seine, built for the 1900 Paris Exposition. Tatsuno's Bank of Japan (1896) also demonstrated neo-classicism, but his design for Tōdai's new engineering building on the Hongō campus (1888) exhibited the melding of neo-classicism and Gothicism.[16] Historical eclecticism gained popularity in Japan hard on the heels of its popularity in Europe, though Meiji Japanese architects initially shunned using historical Japanese motifs.[17] Purely European forms were the order of the day, as was the use of foreign technology, and architects used Tokyo's evolving cityscape to demonstrate progress.[18] Meiji Tokyo's built environment favoured symmetry, historical eclecticism, and the use of brick, especially red, something that became emblematic of the era. Through devices such as these, Japan's new architects provided more than a new style for modern Japan. In taming foreign architectural idioms and mastering new methods of construction, they succeeded in making a statement about modern civilization and articulating it as an aspect of Japanese identity.

The students of Conder and his colleagues designed much, if not most, of the architecture of Japan's empire, which explains its consistency. An influential postwar history even suggested Japanese structures in Manchuria were in an English style.[19] Ichida (after 1925 Aoki) Kikujirō, a 1906 Tōdai graduate, designed the three prominent structures greeting visitors arriving in Changchun. Facing North Plaza were the station, the railway's regional offices, and Mantetsu's Yamato Hotel. Standing on the northern edge of the square and facing south, the station was in the Renaissance style (Figure 2.1). Completed

Figure 2.1 Changchun station. *Source:* Henry Walsworth Kinney, *Modern Manchuria* (Dairen: Japanese Advertiser Press, 1929).

in 1914, its symmetrical wings flanked a central gabled roof supported by a row of columns.[20] While Dalian and Shenyang had to make do with temporary structures, the nearby Russian presence prompted Japanese to build Changchun's station quickly.[21] The long, two-storey structure dwarfed the Russian station at Kuanchengzi, and 1926 renovations maintained a fresh facade.[22] It contrasted with other major stations, especially Shenyang's more ornate station (1910) in what was becoming known as the "Tatsuno style." Across the plaza on the southwest corner stood the Mantetsu regional office. Completed in 1910, it was a massive, symmetrical, three-storey structure capped on either end with gothic spires.[23] The third building, the Yamato Hotel, Changchun's pre-eminent hotel, was begun in September 1907 and completed in 1909 (Figure 2.2). Its role was to shelter important bureaucrats and foreign dignitaries in a suitable manner. It did so with modern conveniences and a modern flourish, its style being the natural progression from historical eclecticism – art nouveau. One pamphlet described the hotel as the city's "representative Western-style hotel" (*daihyōteki yōshiki ryokan*).[24] Rejecting increasingly meaningless historical styles, art nouveau derived organic, flowing motifs from biology and gained popularity as a modern form. Although Russian architects in Dalian had worked in historical eclecticism, those in Harbin chose art nouveau for the train station and associated railway offices. Founded in 1898, Harbin developed rapidly into an important transportation hub that defined itself by its novelty and freedom from pre-existing

Figure 2.2 Yamato Hotel. *Source:* Minami Manshū Tetsudō Kabushiki Kaisha, *Manchuria, Land of Opportunities* (New York: South Manchuria Railway, 1922).

constraints.[25] Some Chinese architects also adopted art nouveau, most notably in Qingdao and Jinan.[26]

The Yamato Hotel in Changchun was the only Mantetsu hotel built in the art nouveau style, although Japanese architects in other parts of Manchuria did occasionally use this style, notably Maeda in the Dalian fire station (1907).[27] Completed six years after the first art nouveau structure in Japan, the hotel was a two-storey brick building with a sleek facade and careful attention to the interior.[28] The decision to build Mantetsu's first new hotel, as well as one of the earliest and most significant structures of the Changchun railway town, in this style is instructive. According to Nakamura Zekō, Gotō Shinpei's successor as Mantetsu president, constructing the railway town occurred in a context of responding to Russian intimations that, despite military victory in 1905, Japanese were culturally backwards.[29] As Japan's prestige depended in part on conducting diplomatic negotiations in suitable halls, architects leapt to the challenge, with the new hotel demonstrating that Japanese could use any style the Russians – or other Europeans – used. Nishizawa claims that Harbin, which lay only a few hours north of Changchun by train, influenced Japanese structures more in Manchuria than in Japan.[30] This is reasonable – art nouveau did not captivate Japanese architects as it did Europeans, given that the former were not inspired by its rebelliousness and were more interested in demonstrating technical competency. In the first issue of the *MKZ*, for example, one-time Columbia University student Ono

Takeo called for the use of art nouveau in Manchuria simply because it reflected global trends.[31] In Japan, architects worked mostly in historical styles because Japanese were more concerned with joining Europeans than in overthrowing European aesthetics. The Changchun elementary school (1908), identical to one in Shenyang, was a single-storey brick neo-Gothic structure with a spire at either end and a bell tower in the middle, a style in keeping with many schools in Japan. Due to the cold, however, these buildings included more indoor space than in Japan, though an outdoor garden served as a skating rink.[32] The *Yomiuri* reported a whopping −36°C temperature during the first winter Japanese were living in Changchun.[33]

A consistency of styles was apparent in many of the Mantetsu railway towns, unsurprising given the similar training of most Japanese architects and the fact that company architects oversaw much of the construction. For example, the new office of the Jilin–Changchun railway line, completed in Changchun in 1924, was reminiscent of Changchun station.[34] Similarly, the Changchun Hospital complex, built between 1909 and 1911, displayed striking stepped gables throughout its associated structures, consistent with hospitals elsewhere in Manchuria in the "Mantetsu hospital style," many designed by Onogi Takaharu.[35] Perhaps the exaggerated gables were intended to draw viewers' attention upwards so as to evoke humility or passivity in those entering. Although Mantetsu architects did not design all new construction, other structures in Manchuria were consistent with their vision. Between 1909 and 1912, for example, the Foreign Ministry had one man, Mihashi Shirō, design consulates in Changchun, Shenyang, Jilin, Yingkou, and elsewhere, as well as oversee the restoration of the consulate in Andong.[36] All construction had to meet building codes, extracts of which appeared in the *MKZ*.[37] Yet some diversity was apparent. Matsumuro Shigemitsu designed Changchun's stock exchange, completed in 1918 in a flamboyant Renaissance style. From Seoul, Nakamura Yoshihei, a former Tatsuno aide, designed and built banks and other structures across the empire. While the Changchun branch of the Yokohama Specie Bank (1922) was solidly neo-classical, the Bank of Korea (1920) was a more streamlined version of the late Meiji style (Figure 2.3). Like Maeda Matsuoto and Okada Tokitarō, Nakamura returned to work in Japan having established his career overseas.[38]

The relatively clean lines of the Bank of Korea foretold an important development. Henry-Russell Hitchcock and Philip Johnson brashly declared in 1932 that a wholly new style had emerged around the world, an "international style" that was identifiably modern. Three principles characterized

Figure 2.3 Bank of Korea

it: a concern for creating volume and not simply mass, regularity in line and form rather than simple symmetry, and the use of construction materials themselves as decorative facades rather than adding frivolous ornamentation. Although Hitchcock and Johnson included only one example of Japanese architecture in 1932, in a later preface they admitted that more Japanese projects could have been cited.[39] Japanese architects in the 1920s similarly expanded interior volumes and rejected ornamentation, perspectives apparent in the *MKZ*. For example, Shimada Fuji, an architect and 1918 Tōdai graduate associated with the City Beautiful movement in Japan, wrote in 1925 that he thought many of the decorations on buildings he saw in Europe were ostentatious.[40] Three years later, an anonymous writer used foreign examples to suggest not only that modern industrial architecture was scientific and economic, but also that it was inspired by notions of beauty, just as Hitchcock and Johnson were to assert.[41]

Although it exhibited a reflexive symmetry in its windows and buttress-like projections, Changchun's Bank of Korea branch eliminated historicized ornamentation and expanded the workspace within. Similar was the dormitory of Changchun Commercial School.[42] Representing the emerging international style in Changchun more than any other structure were the offices

Figure 2.4 Changchun Telephone Company

of the Changchun Telephone Company (1930), near the Bank of Korea (Figure 2.4).[43] Designed by the Guandong Government's Civil Engineering Department and described in the *MKZ* as simply "modern," it was a graceful three-storey structure with rounded corners and an off-centre elevator tower. Six "beehive" profile windows near the tower may have reminded viewers of Ishimoto Kikuji's Asahi Newspaper offices (1927) in Tokyo, itself suggestive of earlier German and Dutch art nouveau. Ishimoto and others, after all, had in 1920 founded Japan's first modern architecture society, and Ishimoto later studied under Walter Gropius.[44] A similar structure was the office of the Changchun Mantetsu Consumers Cooperative, designed by Mantetsu's Construction Department and built on West Plaza in 1930. Also labelled "modern," but more boxy and ornamented, was Mantetsu's Changchun Library (1931). Plainer was the Changchun branch of the Japan Tourist Bureau, although a row of multiple arches on the ground floor suggested a Central Asian flavour.[45] The latter was not the only structure within the railway town's modern streetscape offering a nod to traditional vocabularies. Religious structures remained more traditional, evident in the Shinto shrine and Pure Land Buddhist Temple.

Like planners, Japanese architects in Manchuria were participating in an international debate about their craft, exploring different ways to create modern forms. Another modernist project involving these architects concerned reforming society by altering patterns in daily life. Some articles in the *MKZ* recommended new technologies, but others considered improving living conditions. In the first issue of the *MKZ*, for example, Munekata Shuichi argued that Japanese home construction, having inherited bad practices, needed a laboratory like Manchuria to create more efficient and practical styles. For Munekata, the goal was more than learning to deal with a new climate – it involved a fundamental reorientation of daily life.[46] Matsumuro Shigemitsu, the Mantetsu architect busy in Changchun and elsewhere, called for a revolution in daily life through the creation of new structures using modern technology. This meant warmer buildings and more sanitary conditions.[47] Such buildings could facilitate the emergence of a new "cultural lifestyle" that integrated the physical and the mental aspects of existence, as another article postulated.[48] Nor was the topic merely academic, as articles on modern sanitation and home construction appeared in Manchurian newspapers from the start of the Japanese presence.[49]

Practically speaking, new practices could emerge only with time. In the early years of the Changchun railway town, Japanese found accommodations in the old town or in temporary structures. Mantetsu sheltered many of its first workers in Changchun in a company dormitory, building dorms initially in only three cities – Dalian, Shenyang, and Changchun. Built between 1908 and 1909, Changchun's used brick and provided three rooms to each apartment. Rooms had "Japanese ceilings" and used the traditional Japanese means of defining floor space: tatami mats. For heating, apartments included a Korean-style *ondul* (heated floorboards) on the ground floor and a Russian *pechka,* a large ceramic stove, on the second.[50] Mantetsu eventually built rental apartments of five grades, the highest two built of Japanese brick, the next two of Chinese brick, and the lowest built of wood. Rents varied accordingly, between 1.5 and 0.6 yen per *tsubo* (about 3.3 square metres).[51] The Buddhist Higashi Honganji added a lodging house in 1908.[52]

Heating was a major concern. Changchun's average lows in December and January were between −20 and −25°C. Even the summers could be cool, with lows ranging between 15 and 20°C.[53] As a result, architects paid great attention to window sizes and placement, building materials, and foreign techniques. The *ondul* and the *pechka* were only two adoptions, and practical technologies like these furthered the debate on revolutionizing daily life. As Mantetsu architect and later chairman of the Manchurian Architects' Society

Onogi Takaharu observed in 1922, much of the Japanese development of Manchuria was based on Russian foundations.[54]

Discussing the value of foreign influences was actually a long-standing debate. Although Japanese often evinced a mania for things foreign in the 1870s and 1880s, attitudes shifted to a more nationalist assessment of borrowing by the turn of the century. This debate continued in the twenties, with architects suggesting that there was still much to learn from overseas. Some argued that, in proceeding intelligently, architects could contribute to a more modern society that did not displace all things Japanese. This line of thinking was in keeping with the underlying premises of "Taishō Democracy." Matsumuro Shigemitsu framed this debate in an eight-part series in the *MKZ,* explaining why he thought Japanese architects stood at a "fork in the road." Matsumuro recognized that, in addition to being public officials, architects were technologists capable of devising a more modern society. Responding to criticism regarding his unapologetic use of Western forms and technology, Matsumuro argued that Japan as a society had the choice of being either isolated, insular, and conservative or cosmopolitan and progressive. Because Western forms remained superior, he argued, it was still important to learn from them, although ultimately Japanese needed to find some sort of a compromise. Cultural mixing was already a well-established Japanese path, he thought, and now it was up to architects to help lead the way to a more modern society.[55] Referring to improvements in residential housing, Tanabe Toshiaki reinforced the need for continued compromise as preparation for a culture of the future. Specifically, Tanabe wanted a "Japan–West compromise style" (*wayō setchū shiki*).[56] Soon after, an anonymous four-part *MKZ* editorial predicted that, among other changes, Japanese homes in the future would have chairs and specialized rooms, and rooms would be taller and wider. Doors and walls would be thicker, and homes would be safer from fire.[57] Another writer envisioned new residential suburbs in the countryside that, given their locations, would be cheaper and more sanitary. At the same time, he too recommended learning from foreigners, especially Russians, Germans, and even Chinese.[58] The changes these writers recommended affected Japanese lifestyles directly, not only at home but also in schools, hospitals, libraries, stock exchanges, and other areas of the built environment. Together, architects used both architectural styles and new technologies to identify Japanese society as being as culturally and technically sophisticated as any other power.

In enhancing Japan's status and revolutionizing living conditions, architects presented themselves as progressive and cosmopolitan, and they were zealous in seizing all opportunities to advance their ideas. The Kantō earthquake, for example, resulted in renewing motivations to improve the urban environment.[59] Nine years later, the establishment of Manchukuo provided a similar impetus, though by then the context of the debate had changed. Still, looking back from what he thought to be a splendid and comfortable new capital city in 1942, a later president of the association that published the *MKZ* could not help but be grateful to the likes of Maeda Matsuoto, Onogi Takaharu, Matsumuro Shigemitsu, and others for their free experimentation and willingness to explore new paths. He was also cognizant of the role experimentation in Taiwan and Korea played, as well as the guidance Russian creations in Dalian and Lüshun offered, in developing Manchurian architecture.[60]

Osaka mayor Seki Hajime once suggested that there were only two types of cities: those that developed historically and those that were more idealized.[61] While Chinese Changchun exemplified the former, the Japanese railway town began as the latter but shifts and accommodations were already evident in its short history. The new capital was an even more strident example of an idealized city: in articulating Manchukuo's pretensions most cogently, Xinjing's Asian-inspired structures especially were more striking than anything in the railway town.

Imperial City

In planning Xinjing, the Capital Construction Bureau (CCB) sought to affirm the state's authority through technical proficiency and the use of space while appealing to Asian sentimentality. The capital's architecture had similar political implications, and, despite the use of architectural expressions derived from Asian traditions, Xinjing's architectural orientation was fundamentally modern. The integration of traditional motifs within modern styles served two important purposes. Most obviously, it attempted to encourage Chinese and other Asians to embrace a novel form of national organization and cooperate with Japanese. A second, subtler goal was to reorient Asians toward a new conception of civilization, one superior to that in Europe and North America. Yet, in contrast to contemporary Chinese Nationalist and postwar Communist architecture, which similarly revived Chinese traditions, the Japanese effort failed, in that the capital's new style did not appear elsewhere in the puppet state in any significant fashion, despite the accolades it received. It failed also because appropriating culturally and ethnically identifying characteristics had more to do with attempting to legitimize Japanese imperialist efforts than responding to popular sentiment. This likely problematized the new style for Asians other than Japanese, rendering it unlikely to elicit popular support. Yet Japanese also tended to disregard the new style because it conflicted with their assumptions about the world. Modernity's inherently cosmopolitan perspective was difficult to reconcile with purely national or even cultural boundaries.[62]

The use of Asian motifs was the trait in Manchukuo's official architecture most celebrated in the Japanese media. It represented Pan-Asianism, a concept long part of the Japanese ideological landscape, expressed by writers such as Ōkawa Shūmei, a one-time Mantetsu researcher. But Japanese did not uniformly agree on what the term meant in practice. In essence, Pan-Asianism reversed Fukuzawa Yukichi's famous "Leaving Asia" (*datsu-A*) thesis to recast Japan as an Asian society. For many, this meant a renewed commitment to a Japanese version of *la mission civilisatrice,* legitimizing Japan's leadership in place of Western colonialism. The philosopher Miki Kiyoshi explained to foreign readers that the Manchurian Incident did much to spur "Japanism," as well as a growing disdain for Western liberalism.[63] Promoting Japanese spirit and leadership in Asia, however, led to other tensions between Japanese nationalism and perspectives more inclusive of allied Asian groups.[64] Architects in Xinjing seem to exemplify this paradox because they simply – perhaps arrogantly – assumed that reviving traditional Chinese motifs and forms would appeal to Chinese.

Many architects embraced Japanese leadership in the 1930s, identifying national attributes. In 1936, Oka Ōji, a 1912 Tōdai graduate and, after 1925, a professor at the South Manchurian College of Engineering, lamented that modern architecture in Japan was only "limping" along, and creations like Tokyo's celebrated Maru Biru (1923) were examples of only occasional bursts of progressive activity. Looking to continuing traditional wood construction, however, Oka concluded that, while Japanese society was "enterprising and progressive," it retained sufficient traditional components to advance while retaining "the true nature of the spirit of the Japanese race" and was unlikely to be overwhelmed by modernism.[65] In 1937, *MKZ* editor Naitō Tairō observed that, despite absorbing much from China, Japanese retained a separate culture, indicating the "strength of the Japanese race." Rendered more powerful by mastering modern science, this strength was being woven into Manchukuo's fabric, apparent in a new architectural style reflecting the "spirit of ethnic harmony."[66] Naitō's view represented a shift from views like those of Matsumuro Shigemitsu, the designer of the post office and police station in the Changchun railway town. In 1924, Matsumuro argued that, in coming to Manchuria, Japanese were working with Chinese, Koreans, Europeans, and Americans to develop a new, more genuinely internationalist culture, one that would eventually include a new architectural style.[67] He was not alone.[68]

The Manchurian Incident provided architects the opportunity to change direction, and many perceived it as the dawn of a new age – a view common to articles about the capital published in the *MKZ* in 1932 and 1933. Many Japanese architects rushed to Manchuria, some settling in Xinjing.[69] There was much work, and some found Mantetsu's thirty years' experience to be of little value, given now outdated designs primarily of brick and reinforced concrete.[70] Not all agreed – one insisted that, with regard to residential construction, Mantetsu's experience and stable of some twenty companies remained useful.[71] Makino Masami, head of Xinjing's Architecture Department in 1942, suggested that it was only Manchukuo's sudden establishment that made Mantetsu's experience difficult to utilize. Indeed, he thought the lack of recognition for Mantetsu in books like Tokutomi Sohō's *Manshū kenkoku tokuhon* (*A Guide to the Foundation of Manchukuo*) (1940) was a glaring omission.[72]

Despite such lingering sentiments, Mantetsu and the ideals of the previous era were clearly being eclipsed. Mantetsu had built only three structures in a non-Western style before the Manchurian Incident; now, in rethinking the built environment there was a renewed effort to appeal to Chinese.[73] Recounting his role in the design of Manchukuo's new Hall of State, Ishii Tatsurō, an associate of Sano Riki's, recalled visiting Beijing in the fall of 1933 within a few months of arriving in Manchukuo, as a Chinese style of architecture had been decided upon for the new capital.[74] Global perspectives also remained important, as indicated by Aiga Kensuke, head of the CCB's Department of Architecture and later head of the Bureau of Court Construction. In September 1936, he set off to examine palaces around the world. Returning in May 1937, he felt that, through studying Europe's past, the "direction in which America was heading," and Japan's "development," he had acquired a "global viewpoint from which to proceed."[75]

Onogi Takaharu, chair of the association that published the *MKZ*, demonstrated Asianist views even before the Manchurian Incident when he observed that, despite the sharing and universalization of styles and customs brought about by the development of international transportation and trade, national variations in modern architectural styles were increasingly apparent. He was confident that Japanese architects embracing "special characteristics" would emerge. At the same time, it seemed to Onogi that, because cities like Shanghai were internationally attuned, no national style was emerging in China. In contrast, in Manchuria, industrial development facilitated the emergence of modern cities and a local style.[76] In 1932, he concluded that the Manchurian Incident had paved the way for a certain style – an "internationally rising style based on Asian architecture" – in addition to practical zoning measures and tall buildings in the new capital.[77] Oka Ōji, Onogi's vice-chair and eventual successor, echoed this view, calling for a blending of science, rationality, revivalism, and uniquely Asian traits.[78] Yumoto Saburō, chair of Mantetsu's Civil Engineering Department in Dalian, went further. Since modern technology and materials rendered purely Chinese styles obsolete and planners did not want to simply replicate Western or Japanese styles, a "local style" (*rōkarukarā*) was necessary.[79]

The June 1932 issue of the *MKZ* focused almost exclusively on Xinjing. In addition to agreeing that the new capital should be aesthetically distinctive, the contributors insisted its style be economical and practical – a natural expression of the times rather than a fanciful Xanadu.[80] Many thought it imperative to go beyond outmoded Western forms, several citing Le Corbusier and Walter Gropius. Two explicitly suggested avoiding Western mistakes. Former Mantetsu personal secretary Ueda Kyōsuke suggested avoiding "Yankee style" (*Yankii shiki*) construction, with buildings on every corner. Murata Jirō wanted to avoid American- and European-style realism and suggested learning from experiences in Taiwan.[81] Only one contributor suggested adopting a Japanese style, while another recommended avoiding the ills of other modern cities.[82]

Xinjing's significance was not lost on its designers. Oka Ōji noted that Manchukuo and Xinjing were to be "models" and the "light of East Asia" (*tōA no hikari*).[83] Aiga Kensuke, whose team designed Xinjing's major public buildings, later recalled the goal was to create "architecture for the government offices of an ideal country's national capital." Specifically, he wanted something that would "show a Chinese style flavoured with a modern style," meaning a "new style inextricably woven with an Asian style."[84] Aiga's reminiscences agreed with an early CCB publication foretelling grand buildings that combined "ancient elegance" and "modern clarity."[85] In 1942, Makino Masami, head of the municipal Department of Architecture, deemed Manchukuo's "architectural culture" without parallel, and claimed that it was the only country in the world based on ethnic harmony. He thought many of the small countries born after the First World War were consumed with international styles, but that none of these styles affirmed any heritage. Manchukuo's uniqueness was especially providential, as in turn it could stimulate Japanese culture.[86] Possibly Makino referred here to the debate surrounding Japan's new Diet building. Completed in 1936, though begun in 1920, the structure was considered modern, but its rather bland, designed-by-committee facade encouraged some to call for more clearly Japanese sensibilities. Ironically, the new Diet building had been intended to project Japan among the ranks of great builders.[87]

Construction on the capital's first two major structures, the First and Second Government Buildings on Datong Plaza, began in 1932 and finished in May and June of 1933. Pictures and brief descriptions of the buildings appeared in the November 1933 issue of the *MKZ*. Each was symmetrical, two storeyed, and had a square, twenty-eight-metre tower projecting from its centre. Although the *MKZ* labelled both as "Manchurian" in style, their facades differed markedly. The first, which housed the CCB, had little adornment and flat roofs, but the second was more identifiably Asian. Joining the central tower of the second were four single-storey towers, two at either end and two over the entry. Sloping, tiled roofs supported by engaged columns capped all five towers. The parapet was similarly sloping and tiled, sporting the mythical animals common to traditional Chinese roof decorations. Located upon either side of Datong Dajie on the southern side of Datong Plaza, the two offices faced the distant railway station like sentinels, reflecting the Western and Eastern elements of Manchukuo's architectural heritage.

Aiga designed both. He had been uncertain about the second and feared criticism arising from its Asian design, yet ultimately this style pleased officials.[88] It may also have reflected a trend in Japan. The 1917–18 competition for the new Diet building resulted in one design offering a traditional Japanese roof. Although not built, it provided a name for subsequent buildings emulating the "imperial crown" style (*teikan yōshiki*), sometimes called *yane no aru* (having a [Japanese-style] roof). The first was the ferroconcrete Homotsuden (Treasury, 1921) at the Meiji Shrine, replicating the eighth-century Shōshōin in Nara. The style became more notable in the 1930s. Like the Homotsuden, the ornamental roof of Tokyo's Imperial Museum (1937) ran the building's length. Others offered portions of a neo-traditional roof on buildings four or five storeys tall, such as the Kanagawa Prefectural Offices (1926), Tokyo's Gunjin Kaikan (Soldiers' Hall; today Kudan Kaikan, 1934), and the Aichi

Prefectural Offices (1938). Competitions generally called for these buildings to be of "Japanese taste" (*Nihon shumi*). Maekawa Kunio challenged this style with something more modern for the Imperial Household Museum in 1931, but in vain.[89] Elements of the Japanese architectural tradition began emerging in Manchuria and Korea in the 1920s as well.[90]

These efforts were part of a broader goal of creating architectural statements that were modern and native at the same time. In Nanjing, architects invoked a neo-classical tradition as a means of asserting social stability.[91] In Japan, the tension between indigenous and foreign played out also in the folk art (*mingei*) revival of the 1920s and 1930s. Under the encouragement of intellectuals such as Suzuki Daisetsu and Nishida Kitarō, these efforts produced a self-orientalizing view that would ultimately be mobilized as part of a "Japanese fascist experiment" applicable to a variety of wartime issues.[92]

To cloak modernist programs, colonial administrators exploited native vocabularies, both in Manchukuo and elsewhere.[93] The planning of New Delhi, for example, represented an effort to redefine British-Indian relations within the continuing assertion of British rule, even if one historian thought the "use of Indic features ... while innovative, reflected the loss of imperial self-confidence."[94] Mantetsu reached out to Chinese in Jilin City with a 1923 hospital featuring a central, circular Chinese roof.[95] In Xinjing, Japanese architects sought simultaneously to speak to Japanese, Chinese, and other Asian identities. Xinjing's Second Government Building differed from the "imperial crown" style in that it was lower, busier, and in a more Chinese style. It also mixed styles by grafting more than blending, reminiscent of early Meiji hybrid structures, and was more awkward than later structures. Viewers could not mistake it for traditional construction.

Makino Masami thought Xinjing's first buildings were the product of a period of chaos.[96] In contrast, the buildings south of the palace lining Shuntian Dajie represented the best effort to create a new style, which Koshizawa Akira refers to as the "Asian Revival" (*kōA*) or "Asianism" (*Ajia shugi*) style, linking it to Sano Riki and others.[97] While Sano played a role in its creation, many were receptive to it, or something like it. A 1939 *MKZ* contributor reported that a "new and revived Asian culture" (*atarashii kōA bunka*) was present in the capital, and noted a need to establish a "theory for revived Asian architecture" (*kōA kenchiku riron*).[98] Makino described the buildings lining Shuntian Dajie as *yane no aru kenbutsu* (buildings having a [Japanese-style] roof), appropriating the Japanese term, or in the "Manchukuo bureaucratic building style" (*Manshūkoku kanchō kenchiku yōshiki*), which is probably

Figure 2.5 Hall of State

more apt. Nishizawa notes that, because not all buildings were in this style, it could not be called an official style.[99]

The term *kōA* ("Asian Revival," "Raise Asia," or "Revive Asia") had been around since the Meiji era, used by those looking to stand with Asian brethren against the Europeans and Americans. A KōA Society, founded in 1880, endeavoured to put such views into action, with branch offices in Korea and China.[100] Manchukuo provided the opportunity to represent this shifting and nebulous goal in stone. The political centrepiece was the Fifth Government Building, the Hall of State, begun in 1934 and completed in 1936 (Figure 2.5), designed by Ishii Tatsurō.[101] Recognizing that it was to represent the entire country as the chief government offices, Aiga Kensuke recalled the need to design it appropriately.[102] Significantly, a painting at the turn of its central stairs showed five women skipping hand in hand, an idealized representation of Manchukuo's harmony of five races appearing in publications and postage.[103] Although evoking the "imperial crown" style, the roof of the Hall of State differed from that standard in key ways. Most noticeably, it sported a pagoda-like roof atop a central tower and two similar caps at either end of the building's central section. A sloped, Asian-style parapet graced the remainder of the roofline. Even though it did not include mythical figures, the roof was more similar to the Second Government Building on Datong Plaza than to anything in Japan. The Hall of State, however, was a more mature expression: the caps at either end of the central section were better integrated into the overall structure than the four turrets scattered

Figure 2.6 Postage stamp. Manchukuo stamps often featured state iconography, sometimes overprinted with new messages. This 1936 three-fen stamp depicting the Hall of State was put in circulation after the first anniversary of the outbreak of the Pacific War, the overprint noting that Asia's revival (*kōA*) began 8 December 1941.

atop the Second Government Building, and their pagoda-like roofs were less fanciful. Images of the Hall of State appeared frequently in government publications, as well as on the five-yuan note and some postage stamps (Figure 2.6).

Beneath those caps reared free-standing columnular entryways with wings extended to either side, further differentiating the Hall of State from the other government buildings. The First and Second Government Buildings were basically long hallways culminating at either end in expanded, square footprints, but in the Hall of State those expansions were transformed into arms jutting before and behind the central section, creating a sprawling H-shaped footprint. It was also monumental, as the central section stood five storeys tall and the wings four. A massive, three-storey, columned porte cochère stood in front, the columns of which served as a uniting motif: four columns appeared on each side of the central tower, as well as below the front face of the tower and above the porte cochère. Four large columns also graced the entryways at either end of the central section. More prominent than the engaged columns of the Second Government Building, the free-standing columns were also more striking than the columnular effects produced by the use of stone in the Aichi Prefectural Offices and the Kanagawa Prefectural Offices. Overall, the repetitive effect of the columns enhanced a sense of verticality. Many of the footprints for structures with "imperial crowns" were square, fitting each into an identifiable city block. Sitting upon a much larger city block amid trees and lawns, the Hall of State spanned more

Figure 2.7 Ministry of Justice

space, emphasizing state power. However, the Hall of State was similar to other "imperial crown" style buildings, including the four in Japan, in that the floor of the central section below the roof line was set back, thus giving the roof a more traditional, cantilevered effect.[104] This style did not occur in the wings, which repeated instead the windows and surfacing found in the central section so as to integrate the building's elements.

Nishizawa suggests that, given the need to appear authentic, the new architecture was inspired more by Chinese Revivalism than anything in Japan.[105] Horizontality in traditional Chinese lore expressed sedateness and harmony. A long roof represented the sky.[106] In incorporating these elements into the Hall of State, Japanese architects sought to associate Manchukuo's government with traditional symbols and values. The structure most similar to the Hall of State sat several blocks south. This was the Seventh Government Building, housing the Ministry of Justice, begun in 1935 and completed in 1936 (Figure 2.7).[107] Not as large as the Hall of State, it was perhaps a more successful application of the new style, though Nishizawa reports internal criticism against this and later structures.[108] The roof's materials and decorative ridges were distinctly Chinese, while its windows and colouration endowed it with a sense of balance.

Three other buildings in the capital helped define the new style. Across from the Hall of State sat the massive, four-storey Ministry of Public Security (Figure 2.8). Built in 1935, in 1943 it became the headquarters of the Manchukuo military. It was not discussed in the *MKZ*, but, with its face toward the new palace grounds, it could not be missed. The central section

Figure 2.8 Ministry of Public Security

Figure 2.9 Ministry of Transportation

was capped with a sloping tiled roof with an exposed gable, similar to Tokyo's Soldiers' Hall. Decorative frieze work along the fourth floor interrupted an otherwise smooth facade of brick and windows. Government Building Number Eight (1937) housed the Ministry of Transportation (Figure 2.9), described

Figure 2.10 Manchukuo Supreme Court

in the *MKZ* as in the "rising Manchurian style" (*shinkō Manshū shiki*).[109] Like all the buildings on Shuntian Dajie, this was a long rectangular building, three storeys high, but its roofline was more innovative. Except for the centremost section housing the central stairway, the entire roof was a crenelated parapet, a motif that reappeared on the porte cochère. The centremost section, by contrast, featured a traditional exposed gable roof, but, instead of a gable, the external wall continued. The design and ornamentation of the central staircase and the landings to which it led also echoed other structures. Sitting at the foot of Shuntian Dajie, southeast of Anmin Plaza, Manchukuo's Supreme Court offered another variation (Figure 2.10).[110] Completed in 1938, its footprint included long wings almost the same length of the central section, but rounded corners and the oblique angles in which the wings extended gave the building a more expansive appearance. Another wing extended behind the building from the central section housing the actual courts. Makino determined the architectural requirements of the Manchukuo legal system, including the building's internal space, by comparing Xinjing's needs with other facilities elsewhere in Manchuria and Japan.[111]

These five buildings were the most noteworthy efforts to create a new style. Several others on Shuntian Dajie, though similar, were comparatively unremarkable, such as the Ministry of the Economy.[112] Another group on Datong Dajie about a kilometre east of the Hall of State presented more hybridized facades. A good example was the Third Government Building (1937), housing

Figure 2.11 Department of People's Livelihood

the Department of People's Livelihood (Figure 2.11).[113] This was a simple, two-storey structure with a squat, square, pitched roof over the central section. Five columns supported the roof in front. Across the street was the Ministry of Finance, a similar structure. Perhaps the most arresting building in this sector stood adjacent to the Third Government Building, the Bureau of Mongolian Affairs (1936) on the corner of Xingren Dalu and Datong Dajie.[114] Its embedded columns and white stone quoining gave it an almost Renaissance air, but a small, insignificant tower and a single decorative gable rendered the design of this building perhaps the least coordinated in the new capital.

There were other buildings in the revivalist style, but the media most often featured the ones discussed above, with the exception of those involved with security or the military. All were symmetrical, perhaps a reaction to the asymmetricality of the international style but likely also reflecting a desire to demonstrate harmony and balance. This approach would have reinforced Japanese propaganda as well as traditional Chinese building practices – as noted by perhaps Japan's most famous pre-war architectural historian, Itō Chūta.[115] Also supporting Japanese propaganda was the scale of these buildings. Several were large, with prominent central towers. Their mass demonstrated state power by compelling viewers to look up, implicitly asserting power and authority – a construction stratagem employed by Japanese in Taiwan and Korea as well.[116] A third similarity involved roofs, but the incorporation of some form of an Asian roofline was more than simply a repeating motif serving to unite the various structures. It affirmed an Asian taming of foreign forms. Situating modern organizations under recognizably Asian roofs was an effort to showcase modernity in an Asian guise so as to make it more palatable to Asian viewers. It was also an effort to revitalize Asian traditions by blending aspects of those traditions physically with the capabilities and concerns of a new era.[117]

For some Japanese, these structures were as significant as those in Japan with "imperial crowns." Fueki Hideo, chief engineer at the Manchuria Civil Engineering and Architecture Society, thought that the "Eastern flavour" evident in Xinjing's bureaucratic offices, as well as in the Aichi Prefectural Offices and the Kanagawa Prefectural Offices, displayed Japanese leadership. To him, structures like these helped pave the way for a new era, as capitalism was presumably in its final days. Indeed, a new era deserved new nomenclature. The leadership of individuals such as Sano Riki led some to suggest replacing outdated terms like *internationalism* and *rationalism* with *Sano-ism* (*Sanoizumu*), given how frequently he judged competitions.[118] Despite the hyperbole, Xinjing's style was not entirely novel. Below the Asian-inspired roofs, plainer surfaces dominated, reflecting the international style's emphasis on materials in their natural state rather than painting or glazing. Implying solidity and permanence, exposed brick and especially stone subtly expressed power and authority. Differences in external facades, moreover, did not translate into differences in internal spatial organization. All of these were office buildings, and luxury was tempered but ubiquitous. In addition to symmetricality and the use of central staircases, usually marble, meeting rooms offered plush interiors, and electric lighting illuminated marbled halls, as pictures in the *MKZ* attest.

Some public monuments in Xinjing echoed this revivalism. The Monument to the War Dead was one of nine such monuments in Manchukuo dedicated to Japanese who died during the Manchurian Incident (Figure 2.12). Designed by the military, it affirmed the indivisibility of Japan and Manchukuo.[119] Begun in April 1934, it was completed in December of that year. The monument, standing five storeys, was a mammoth stone tower with a pointed, tile roof and four echoing eaves below. The government staged mass rallies at the site, as in 1938 on the first anniversary of the China Incident.[120] The monument contrasted markedly with earlier war memorial monuments in Dalian and Shenyang, which were smaller and stylized without Asian references.[121]

Xinjing's National Foundation Shrine (1940) also offered Asian features. The *MKZ* published photographs of a model in 1937 and again in 1941 along with sketches and actual photos, including a photo of the main shrine – a

Figure 2.12 Monument to the War Dead. *Source:* Postcard, International Research Center for Japanese Studies, Kyoto.

lone tower set amid low walls. The tower could be reached through two large gateways between which sat a square compound including two gateways on either side. Encircling trees and a nearby river confirmed Xinjing's embrace of nature. Its overall style was mixed, the result of negotiations beginning in 1935 that included the art historian Murata Jirō.[122] Although roofed in a Chinese fashion, the open veranda surrounding the square courtyard was reminiscent of structures in more southern climes. The stylized pillars, ornamental support beams, and balustrades were more in keeping with international style. The main shrine, a stocky, square tower with a double roof, echoed Manchukuo's bureaucratic style with symmetry, massive verticality, and a traditional roof.[123]

A monument that was never built helps define Xinjing's bureaucratic style. Judges, including Sano Riki, Naitō Tairō, Oka Ōji, and Xinjing mayor Wei Yunjie, entertained 200 submissions from Japan and 74 from Manchuria (67 Japanese and 7 "Manchurians") for a monument commemorating Puyi's first state visit to Japan. The winning design was reminiscent of the "imperial crown" of Tokyo's Soldiers' Hall and would have been a free-standing section of a massive Chinese city wall surmounted by a small central keep and Chinese roof. The monument was to represent the "spirit of Japan-Manchukuo harmony" and be located just south of Anmin Plaza, due south of the palace at the end of Shuntian Dajie, facing north. Its Asian features were anticipated, as judges had asked that entries be in an "Eastern style" (*Tōyōfū*). Runners-up were more streamlined but similarly retained a central tower.[124]

Not all Xinjing monuments, however, reflected the new style. Two monuments recognized battles in the suburbs of Nanling and Kuanchengzi, but they similarly evinced a streamlined and blunt verticality, without any Asian reference.[125] With the outbreak of war in China in 1937, a wave of similar monuments appeared across Japan, showing commitment to the war effort, some favouring modernist and others more Japanese styles.[126] A 1937 competition for a Xinjing monument celebrating Mantetsu's achievements in education did not require an Asian component. Although the monument was never built, first place was awarded to a rectangular obelisk with a recessed alcove in which sat a Renaissance figure holding a book. Above the figure was the inscription "Kyōikutō" (Education Tower), and above that the Mantetsu insignia.[127]

Manchukuo's architects presented their creations in architectural exhibitions, such as one at Xinjing's Nikkei Gallery on Datong Dajie, held on 21–23 September 1937 and featuring some of the capital's latest structures. A commemorative medal featured the exhibition's title and a burly labourer carrying large stone blocks in either hand toward buildings reminiscent of those on Shuntian Dajie.[128] Another, larger exhibition was in Datong Park in 1942 with examples from across Manchukuo and the world.[129]

Admiration for these structures sometimes noted their significance for Japan. Matsuki Genjirō, an architect employed by Showa Steel in Anshan, reported in the *MKZ* that architects in Japan were impressed.[130] On a return visit in 1942 as part of Manchukuo's tenth anniversary celebrations, Maeda Matsuoto, Nishizawa's first "architect adventurer," found Xinjing's tall buildings affirming a distinctly Eastern, beautiful style, one he called a "Xinjing style," though in an addendum he described them as "East Asian." More pointedly, he commented that, while Japan itself could not escape lingering European and American influences, Xinjing shone "purely and clearly," radiating an "Eastern urban beauty."[131] Nor was Maeda alone in perceiving architecture in Japan as dated. At a Tokyo public forum in the fall of 1939, later published in an article in the popular magazine *Gendai kenchiku* (*Modern Architecture*), Sakakura Junzō, an architect who studied in France with Le Corbusier, stated that Xinjing greatly impressed him and that it had advanced beyond what was possible in Japan. Indeed, Sakakura thought Xinjing could influence Tokyo. Horiguchi Sutemi, another pioneer modernist, agreed.[132] Often bridling against older architects interested in Japanese motifs that reflected older, often Chinese-inspired ways, modernists such as Sakakura and Horiguchi preferred updating Japanese motifs through blending with international styles, a practice that became evident in wartime construction.[133]

On 30 August 1939, the SōA kenchiku renmei (Create Asia Architecture Federation), an organization including contributors to the *MKZ,* such as Muroi Osamu and Hideshima Tsutomu (Kan), sponsored Kishida Hideto, a Tōdai professor of engineering, and Sakakura to talk to twenty-two members of their organization at the Xinjing Central Bank Club. Kishida, having visited Changchun in the mid-1920s and again in the summer following the Manchurian Incident, saw extraordinary changes in the scale and nature of construction. Kishida suggested this meant that Manchukuo was capable of leading architectural change. His sponsors agreed, offering two rationales. One involved Manchukuo society, as each of the five races of the multi-ethnic state was allowed to develop its own unique architectural style in response to technological advances. They also suggested that architectural innovation could flourish, given that there was less government oversight in Manchukuo than in Japan.[134] A summary of this discussion appeared in *Gendai kenchiku* in January 1940. The ten authors agreed that 1932 marked the beginning of a revolution initiated in Xinjing, since the capital, reflecting a new social and ethnic constellation, was now the centre of a new style and culture focused on constructing the future. The presence of Tungusic tribes, Chinese settlers, and Russian planners before 1932 had meant a reliance on traditional means of shaping the built environment; by contrast, they thought that, after 1932, Manchurian architecture assumed novel forms. This was especially true in the new capital, where an independent architectural style served the purpose of an "ethnically diverse country." Yet this new style was a reflection of more than simply the region's ethnic diversity. As architecture reflects the nature of society, received architecture reflected the development of capitalism. Manchurian architecture was breaking free of such constraints, thanks to comprehensive planning, and Xinjing was planned through 1955.[135] In this respect, they believed that Manchukuo was leading Japan.

Some architects referred to overseas criticisms of Xinjing's forms, although without identifying them. Makino Masami insisted that such critics lacked vision and did not understand what was transpiring. Japanese technology and tastes, unused to the conditions on the mainland, were adapting Chinese forms so as to be able to lead Manchurians.[136] Kishida defended the new style in a Dalian public lecture, calling narrow the foreign complaints that Manchurian architecture was somehow worse than Soviet. To him, foreigners simply could not understand the revolutionary changes Xinjing's official buildings represented. Moreover, the expansive style fit well with Manchurian geography and the use of brick reflected local customs, despite a Japanese preference for wood. It also allowed young Japanese architects the opportunity to practise their craft so that they might one day lead the regeneration of China. As a result, Kishida thought Manchurian architecture was greater than the sum of its Japanese, Chinese, and Western components.[137]

Like urban planning, architecture in Manchukuo consciously expressed modernity and state authority, both perceived in a global context. The November 1939 issue of the *MKZ,* for example, reproduced pictures of contemporary Italian Fascist and Soviet monuments featuring large flags and enormous statues atop high pedestals. To the anonymous editorialist, these seemed similar to each other as well as to recent structures in the Third Reich.[138] The SōA kenchiku renmei discussants disparaged these designs. Kishida thought Nazi architecture "boring" (*aji mo sokke mo nai*). Sakakura Junzō suggested that political control stunted the natural expression and growth of those countries' architecture. Others noted that, while Japanese ideas helped form a new Manchurian style, Manchuria's emptiness – its blank slate – allowed for completely new and vigorous expressions.[139] Makino thought Nazi efforts to reinvigorate Germany with medieval motifs were backward. In Manchukuo, the focus was on the new.[140] Even the translator disparaged Nazi nostalgia in an excerpted translation of *Das Bauen im Neuen Reich* by Gerdy Troost, a favourite of Hitler's.[141] This was despite the fact that National Socialist architecture loosely met the criteria for Manchukuo's new style. Although Nazi structures were similarly symmetrical, massive, and made use of historical elements, these Japanese architects perceived them as archaic.

Other Japanese praised new German policies. For example, the *Toshi kōron* (*TK*) included a three-part series commending Nazi actions regarding social security, public health, and highway creation, as well as the use of nationalism in motivating people and encouraging support for eventual expansion.[142] Japanese architects' views differed because they were more fundamentally modern. The Nazis considered modern architecture not only decadent but foreign, implying Jewish or Bolshevik connections. The public buildings and fora of the Third Reich sought to invoke a pre-modern conception of community untouched by undesirable traits. Expansionary goals and theories of racial purity inevitably became manifest architecturally.[143] While Japanese imperialism included a racial component, it did not manifest as an attempt to recreate courtly Japan or China. Instead, Japanese focused more on energizing the Asian tradition so that the empire could move on to a new, presumably more evolved state. Although Japanese could admire policies seeking national strength and power, architects could criticize Nazis for holding too strongly to an idealized past.[144]

Japanese architects were ideologues imposing empire-builders' notions on a foreign populace. Their structures served ideological purposes, and their discourse revealed political concerns. This could be overt, as when Oka Ōji used his annual *MKZ* address to promote the "construction of a new East Asia" and the 2,601st anniversary of Emperor Jinmu's accession in the midst of the current "holy war."[145] More subtly, Japanese architects designed Xinjing to impress and mobilize populations both colonial and Japanese. As Anthony King has suggested, "the extensive relations of colonialism must themselves be seen not only as a particular mode of production but also a space of production, affecting cultural practices and products in the metropole as much as the colonies, whether these are literary texts or building forms."[146] Xinjing's new architecture was monumental and mixed, designed to impress viewers with a sense of grandeur, power, and technical innovation. Using architectural vocabulary Chinese would understand, it nonetheless fundamentally remained modern, employing techniques emphasizing verticality, size, and expanse. Whether it demonstrated cultural innovation is another question. Despite Japanese insistence of the contrary, the new style was essentially a hybrid. Raiding the historical treasury, the new style provided cover for Japanese imperialism.

Publicly, Japanese applauded the new style and what it represented. Upon his retirement, Aiga Kensuke was decorated for his work.[147] Paradoxically, however, despite the avowed pretenses made about the new style's leadership, only a few structures elsewhere in Manchuria were in keeping with it. The closest published approximations were the train stations in Dongjing, Jiamusi, and Chengde, though 1935 railway offices in Jilin City featured Chinese-roofed towers at either end of a three-storey building.[148] Of course, the outbreak of war limited funding for later projects, but most new structures in the capital and Manchukuo continued to be like structures outside Asia. Some structures, notably Shenyang's central police station and Dalian's Manchuria Medical College, both completed in 1929, even anticipated some of what later became Xinjing's bureaucratic style. The photos that appeared in the *MKZ* showed large, symmetrically balanced structures with wide wings, portes cochères, and central "keeps" strikingly similar to what later appeared on Shuntian Dajie.[149] Even Xinjing's national monuments were reminiscent of earlier structures, such as the stepped Chūreitō monuments in Dalian and Shenyang and the simpler but still vertically imposing monument to lost miners in Fushun.[150] All that was missing were stylized Asian motifs, confirming that the new Asian style was essentially a modern style.

Modern Centre

The conclusion that Xinjing's Asian-inspired architecture was more fundamentally modern than traditional is reinforced by examining the city's other structures, the vast majority of which were unambiguously modern and in keeping with new construction in Europe and North America. Xinjing's modernism, moreover, impressed some foreigners. One reported that "the building boom in Xinjing is giving Manchukuo a modern and attractive capital city," concluding that "Datong Circle will present an imposing appearance; for the park is laid out on a broad scale and the new government buildings are modern and substantial."[151] Kasahara Toshirō, a 1907 Tōdai doctorate in engineering who helped Sano Riki with Tokyo's reconstruction before becoming a professor at Nihon University and later coming to Manchukuo, defended the use of European forms at a public lecture in Xinjing in September 1938. Kasahara reminded readers that, with the absorption of northern Manchuria and the China Eastern Railway, Manchukuo's roots included European architectural traditions, especially those of imperial Russia. Even if Manchukuo's official architectural style began with Chinese features, it seemed reasonable to include other technologies and forms.[152]

The *MKZ* included photos and floor plans of other buildings, although they were published with little accompanying discussion. Structures drawing particular attention were in Datong Plaza's new "civic centre." Matsuki Genjirō was especially approving of these, as they demonstrated something new could be achieved without Asian roofs.[153] Perhaps most conspicuous were the offices of the Bank of Manchukuo (Figure 2.13). This enormous structure, completed in 1938 and lavishly finished in marble, occupied thirty thousand square metres.[154] Its large columns replicated those of other banks in the empire.[155] Its progressive and modern features, both technical and architectural, were hailed at a public round table (*zadankai*) at the bank's private club in July 1938 as "new architecture" (*shinkōsha shinchiku*) for "new people" (*atarashii hitotachi*). Although designed by Tokyo's Nishimura Construction, bank personnel and members of the CCB were also involved.[156] Southwest was the headquarters of the Manchuria Telegraph and Telephone Corporation (Denden; Figure 2.14). Completed in 1935, it was similarly modern.[157]

Like buildings in the Manchukuo bureaucratic style, the Bank of Manchukuo and Denden headquarters were symmetrical and large. Neither, however, featured Asian motifs, though Denden repeated the bureaucratic style in four other ways. It had a central tower, though subdued, and repeated stylized columns in the porte cochère and centremost section. The trim

Figure 2.13 Bank of Manchukuo

Figure 2.14 Manchuria Telegraph and Telephone Corporation

Figure 2.15 *Qilin* in front of the Manchuria Telegraph and Telephone Corporation

Figure 2.16 Tokyo Maritime Insurance Building

running below the topmost floor was reminiscent of the cantilevered look on the Hall of State. Lastly, stone sculptures of *qilin* (Jp, *kirin*) stood on either side of the porte cochère, a nod to Chinese tradition. Denden's *qilin*, however, were not traditional. Smooth and stylized, they were modern versions of traditional statuary (Figure 2.15).[158]

Figure 2.17 Daikō Building

Most buildings in the new capital were modern in inspiration, such as those just north of Datong Plaza, including the offices of the Oriental Development Company and the Tokyo Maritime Insurance Company (1939, Figure 2.16).[159] The most prominent building in this area was the Daikō Building (1937; Figure 2.17), the head office of the Manchuria Industrial Bank. Designed by Nakamura Yoshihei, who designed the Bank of Manchukuo, it sat upon a busy street corner and had stylized pillars rising over a corner entry.[160] Another modern structure was the new Mantetsu office building, completed in 1936 on the same plot as the original across from the station.[161] Along with other new structures appearing across Manchukuo and Japan, these were unapologetically modern and point to a continuing interest in international trends.

In designing modern buildings, architects occasionally employed elements of the Japanese tradition. One such building was the Jinmuden (Jinmu Hall, 1940), named after Japan's legendary first emperor. It was a low structure built of reinforced concrete rather than wood (Figure 2.18). It was in a "Japanese style" (*Nihon shiki*), likely because of its martial purpose.[162] On a large (920-metre) site located in Mudan Park, the hall had an enclosure for fencing, judo, and archery.[163] As in the previous era, religious structures also retained traditional elements, such as the Higashi Honganji Temple north of Datong Plaza.

Other structures were more inventive. One striking building appropriated the "imperial crown" style, the Kantōgun Headquarters and the office of Japan's ambassador to Manchukuo, the Kantōgun commander, built in 1935.[164]

Figure 2.18 Jinmuden

This was a sprawling, three-storey structure with three crowns, each reminiscent of the upper reaches of a Japanese castle. Two were at either end of the central section and a larger, three-storey crown sat atop the central keep. Fueki Hideo thought it cut a "grand appearance," something that helped ameliorate the area's troubled past (just south of the building had been an execution ground – a spot where Japanese built bachelor's quarters).[165]

The Kantōgun Headquarters must be considered with the sprawling building across Datong Dajie immediately east, the Guandong Government (Kantōkyoku) and Kenpeitai headquarters (1934), also housing much of the embassy staff. It was more modern than the Kantōgun building, though a 1935 ceremony marked the exterior affixing of an imperial chrysanthemum crest, the Kenpeitai emblem.[166] Both it and the Kantōgun Headquarters faced south with addresses on Xinfalu, but their grounds each occupied an entire block of Xinjing's central avenue. Moreover, their flanking positions in the transition zone between the railway town and the new civic centre ensured that anyone travelling between the train station and Datong Plaza would pass between large structures representing two of the chief sources of Japanese authority in Manchuria. One foreign journalist called them "the two most imposing structures in Xinjing."[167]

Another structure reminiscent of the "imperial crown" style but with a more Asian than Japanese roof was the prominent Kangde Hall (Jp, Kōtoku kaikan, 1935), built in partnership with Mitsubishi and adopting Puyi's reign name.[168] Located on Datong Dajie across from Tokyo Maritime Insurance and north of a modern department store, this office building was a smooth structure, originally four storeys, with a single slender tower standing over the entryway (Figure 2.19). The addition of an Asian roof to the tower gave it an "imperial crown," but, unlike many other buildings in the style, it lacked a porte cochère. Instead the entryways were outlined with extensions resembling European castle gates at the sidewalk (Figure 2.20). Below the tower, crenellations ringed the roof. The Kangde Hall was not the only structure demonstrating European affinities. The residence of the Kantōgun commander (1933), west of the Kantōgun Headquarters, appropriated elements of a European manor (Figure 2.21).[169] Except for the tower, the nearby Japan-Manchukuo Soldier's Hall was similar.[170] The curious mix of styles evident in these three buildings associated with the military suggests an effort to distinguish the military from the Manchukuo bureaucracy architecturally, while the Kangde Hall stylistically bridged the various Japanese institutions present in Xinjing.

Only one of Manchukuo's official residences – that of the prime minister – expressed aspects of Asian heritage other than Japanese. Situated just northwest of the new palace site, this sprawling mansion, built in 1936, included steeply pitched tile roofs in a Chinese style.[171] All other official residences in the city were closer to the international style, including those of the governor of the Bank of Manchukuo and the chief Japanese civilian

Figure 2.19 Kangde Hall

Figure 2.20 Kangde Hall entrance

Figure 2.21 Residence of the Kantōgun commander

administrator of Manchukuo, the director of general affairs for the State Council (Manshūkoku kokumuin sōmuchō chōkan). These were large, two-storey structures that would not have looked out of place in Europe or North America. The general affairs director's residence exhibited motifs that would have been in keeping with Frank Lloyd Wright's Imperial Hotel in Tokyo. Other official residences elsewhere in Manchuria were similar, such as that for the Guandong Peninsula's chief bureaucrat.[172]

Two significant buildings in Xinjing were eclectic. One was the headquarters for the Concordia Association (Kyōwakai, discussed below). Located just south of the First Government Building on Datong Dajie, its green-tiled roof perhaps suggested an Asian heritage, but the roofline did not. Arched windows and entrances made for a busy style. Another unique structure was the Foreign Ministry building, built in 1936 north of the prime minister's residence. Designed by a French firm, Brossard-Mopin, it was the only major structure in Xinjing designed by a foreign firm, although the company hoped for more. This "rambling and asymmetrical" building was modern, but it was not in keeping with the Manchukuo official style and did not influence other structures.[173]

The vast majority of Xinjing's buildings revealed similarities to structures overseas, both in Japan and Europe. Two examples were the new theatre (1935) and the Manchurian Information Association, the latter located on Chūō Dōri in the railway town.[174] Both not only looked like buildings found overseas but emphasized their presence with windows outlined in contemporary bold trims, the theatre's highlighting its horizontal dimensions and the Information Association building its vertical lines. A prize-winning structure on Datong Dajie near the Kangde Hall was the Hōyū (Friendship) Building. Boldly designed with circular windows and broad horizontal trim, it was labelled "modern" by the *MKZ*.[175] Japanese continued to plan other buildings even after the outbreak of the China Incident.[176] Of course, not all structures were eye-catching; some were more functional than distinctive, such as the Shuntian Dajie telephone exchange and the Xinjing Engineering College, but all reflected international rather than Asian trends.[177]

Residential construction in Xinjing after 1932 similarly showcased modernism.[178] Although it built primarily in rural areas, the Oriental Development Company also built 150 houses in Xinjing for Japanese, having begun by building modern "culture houses" in Dalian and Korea.[179] Fujii Sadamu thought that the technology and science Japanese used in creating new residential quarters overseas showed Japanese ingenuity at its best, especially given Manchukuo's housing shortage.[180] Redefining daily activities, however, remained a widely shared goal of housing construction, as evidenced by Zheng Bingwen, a CCB housing bureau architect. He thought the "feudal extended family system," in which large families lived together under one roof for economy and protection, was a natural but antiquated practice. With society becoming less agricultural and more urban, new residential forms facilitated "emancipated lives." By 1941, new housing for Chinese ("Manchurians") in Xinjing increased to fifty-one thousand dwellings, leaving a shortage of only three thousand. Improvements in housing technology, sanitation, and supply, moreover, improved the quality of life.[181] Fujii agreed with Zheng, emphasizing the capital's role in improving Manchurians' lives through technological advances such as electric lighting, gas, and running water.[182]

Oka Ōji thought residences and office buildings were key to reforming society, but while new offices were exemplars of innovation in Japan it was new residential construction that illustrated innovation in Manchuria.[183] Adapting to a different climate, Japanese architects had by Manchukuo's founding long studied Chinese and Russian residential construction.[184] Other Japanese promoted new technologies in Manchuria – given the climate, heating was of particular interest.[185]

The government arranged new housing, initially through an office in the Bank of Manchukuo and later through a special firm organized by the bank in April 1934: the Daitoku Real Estate Corporation. Capitalized at 3 million yuan, Daitoku oversaw the building and management of residences, for which it received a commission of 3 percent of the building costs. In the event that this rate did not provide adequate return, the government agreed to compensate Daitoku, thus ensuring its solvency.[186] Daitoku built a number of apartment complexes for Manchukuo's bureaucracy east of the offices on Shuntian Dajie. Officials began moving into the 390 apartments of the first government residential complex by the end of 1934. Although equipped with flush toilets, the apartment block initially lacked vegetation or anything else to make it homey, but within ten years it included a post office, a clinic, and a police *kōban* (neighbourhood office). This led Fujii to suggest that new forms of community like this required at least ten years to mature.[187] A second complex emerged a kilometre to the south in 1935, comprising 184 apartments and 39 bachelors' quarters, and a third in 1936 with 208 apartments. Architects considered all of these units "Japanese" (*Nikkei*) in style. A fourth complex, built in 1937 just west of the third and north of the Xinjing Central Courthouse, provided an additional 308 units of which 82 were described in the *MKZ* as "Manchurian" (*Mankei*), although it is not clear what this label meant. Daitoku's construction in Xinjing amounted to 1,090 Japanese-style apartments, 83 Manchurian-style apartments, 79 bachelors' quarters, 24 Japanese-style houses, and 9 bachelors' houses.[188]

Some corporations saw to the construction of housing for their own workers. The central bank organized residences for its employees in a strip northeast of the palace.[189] The government assigned other corporations their own sections on which to build.[190] A 1941 map indicates space encompassing several blocks for housing, both for government officials as well as corporations like Denden, the Bank of Manchukuo, Mangyō, Manchuria Electric, and Manchuria Mining, much of it south of Jilin Dalu between Shuntian Dajie and the sports complex.[191] To accelerate construction, in March 1938 the government founded a special corporation, Manchuria Home Construction (Tokubetsu kaisha Manshū bōsan kabushiki kaisha, hereafter Bōsan), which absorbed Daitoku. While Daitoku had focused on complexes in Xinjing and one in Harbin, Bōsan was active in ten cities in 1938 and sixteen in 1939. These cities were primarily in northern Manchuria, where there was a larger housing shortage for Japanese, as few had resided there before the Manchurian Incident. By mid-1942, Bōsan's construction totalled more than 16,000 units across Manchukuo. Over 6,000 of these were in Xinjing, including 2,526 Japanese-style apartments, 148 Manchurian-style apartments, 699 bachelors' quarters, 2,390 Japanese-style houses, and 317 bachelors' houses. Construction was apparently rapid – many of Xinjing's bureaucrats gained a reputation for short stays as renters in the railway town, derisively earning the nickname "stay for one hour people." Large endowments made such rapid construction possible – Daitoku's and Bōsan's combined expenditures amounted to almost ¥45 million in less than nine years. Each was also the affiliate of a specific bank, Daitoku with the Bank of Manchukuo and Bōsan with Manchuria Development Bank, established in December 1936, though Bōsan was also linked to the Oriental Development Company.[192]

Daitoku and Bōsan focused mainly on Japanese needs. For others, the situation was worse. Makeshift accommodations appeared northeast of the city, and planners eventually designated space for new Chinese accommodations east of the Yitong River.[193] Other such accommodations were pulled down. Makino Masami, chairman of Xinjing's Architecture Department in 1942, was pleased to report the complete removal of what he called a "slum" (*suramu*), referring to dark buildings of Russian construction, and their replacement by a "bright and cheerful" residential space.[194] There was also new construction in the old railway town, but these buildings were not likely for Chinese.[195] Notably, the capital's new apartment complexes included more rooms in a Japanese (*Nikkei*) than in a Manchurian (*Mankei*), or Chinese, style, and an apartheid-like system was apparent in the distribution of housing.[196]

Japanese officials lauded new residential construction. Yamazaki Tadao of the central bank suggested that new, smaller, and modern houses especially were advancing society, enabling a fusion of East and West.[197] In later articles written with the bank's Hamada Yoshio, Yamazaki explored how modern science and architecture improved health.[198] Architects exhibited modernist inclinations in a 1943 "national housing" (*kokumin jūtaku*) competition. They hoped that experimentation in Manchukuo would improve conditions in Japan, although, intriguingly, one of the winners observed that, despite differences in traditions, modern families in Japan and the West lived in essentially the same conditions. Another suggested eliminating tatami mats in Manchurian construction.[199]

Architects echoed Japan's wartime discourse, such as Oka Ōji's celebration in the *MKZ* of the "construction of a new East Asia" and the alliance with Germany and Italy.[200] Still, wartime altered priorities, the head of Xinjing's residential construction department admitting that housing worsened after 1937.[201] New concerns appeared in the *MKZ*, with references to camouflage, aerial bombardment, shelters, and other ways of accommodating to war conditions.[202] Some mused about mobilizing Manchukuo scientists for the war effort and reorganizing residential life to create a new order in wartime.[203] New rationalization measures went into effect in April 1944, impacting new residences.[204] Revisions to the urban planning law in 1943 took into consideration aerial bombardment and national planning.[205] In early 1945, Makino acknowledged that 1944 had been a terrible year and that 1945 could be worse. Still, he exhorted readers to endure, reminding them of achievements like the 1944 mausoleum for Genghis Khan in western Manchukuo.[206] Late wartime construction, however, tended to be more functional than inspiring, such as Xinjing's warehouse-like new movie theatre.[207]

Providing the concrete face of urban renewal, architects are central to creating new notions of civic space. In the late nineteenth and first half of the twentieth century, architects throughout the world supported imperialism by defining colonial urban spaces in manners befitting imperial powers. In keeping with that tradition, a 1935 contributor to the *MKZ* suggested that Japan's "special characteristic" was to make appearances more beautiful, whether the object was food or housing.[208] Japanese architects in Manchuria, however, confronted issues of substance as well as appearance. Before 1932, Japanese architectural expressions in Manchuria reflected those found in Japan, Europe, and North America. These expressions included a nationalist and eventually Asianist turn from emotionally hollow modernism, yet the resulting bureaucratic style, newly fabricated and imposed by fiat, also proved empty. Few structures that were outside of the CCB's administrative reach adopted it. What was more, the capital's own officials turned away from it. The Fourteenth Government Building, for example, immediately south of the Hall of State, was a two-storey structure with distinctly modern lines.[209]

In his study of Thai architecture, Clarence Aasen concluded that, "while Thailand adopted many of the underpinnings of modernism and internationalism, nevertheless the cultural distinctiveness and diversity of the nation and its peoples remained and were continually reconstituted. As in previous periods, what was involved was not so much a wholesale and mindless adoption of inappropriate foreign models, although clearly this did sometimes occur, as strategically selective appropriations."[210] Japanese made similar "strategically selective appropriations" in the first half of the twentieth century. Although the Manchukuo bureaucratic style gained approval in the media, the more genuine modern style, truer to the needs and goals of society, enjoyed greater popularity. This was because Japanese architecture was more identifiably modern than was Thai, and because Japanese architects as a group cleaved more to the modern than to folk traditions.

A consideration of the styles of buildings in Xinjing reinforces the view that Manchukuo's bureaucratic style would see limited use. Before the 1930s, Japanese architects showed themselves to be of a mind similar to architects in Europe and North America, and were successful in helping foster popular perceptions that Japan was a modern society and one of the Great Powers. Celebrating Japanese successes through the creation of new cityscapes imbued those styles with connotations of modernity, and removing historical significance from the architectural palette made it difficult, if not impossible, to reinject structures with historicized content. This is to say, while the international style favoured physical accomplishment, the subsequent creation of an explicitly nationalist style could not help being semantically weaker. Once negated, tradition could not be resurrected in any significant way for political ends. Reasserting traditional elements while endowing Manchukuo with modern attributes were contradictory efforts. Ultimately, the traditional aspects could not help but become secondary to the more cosmopolitan and modern core. A major postwar study by many involved in Manchuria unintentionally confirmed this in their assertion that Manchurian architecture consisted of only Chinese architecture of the kind existing before imperialists arrived, "European-style Russian architecture," and "Western-style Japanese architecture." This judgment either ignores the Manchukuo bureaucratic style or accepts it as a kind of "Western-style Japanese architecture."[211]

The bureaucratic style was perhaps also internally conflicted. The tranquility associated with horizontality in traditional Chinese architecture clashed with the verticality of modern architecture, which typically expresses monumentality and power. Attempting to blend these efforts was a contradictory endeavour, requiring Japanese to take one as paramount. Given that designing Manchukuo's capital involved not only innovative techniques but also a desire to impress and intimidate non-Japanese, it should be unsurprising that concerns for the modern would dominate. Given Japanese authorship, moreover, it is also difficult to imagine that those other than Japanese might share in perceiving this Asianist architecture as a nationalist expression, especially given Manchukuo's social structure (discussed in Chapter 4).

New architectural forms were contradictory in a more general sense as well. Replacing traditional expressions of the built environment with a sleek functionality displaying prowess in engineering made modern architecture doubly modern. Technically developed, it was also internationally cosmopolitan. New structures attempting to be faithful to both a resurrected tradition and modern cosmopolitanism ultimately failed – they were hybrids having more in common with the clumsy efforts of the 1870s than the creation of new architectural vocabulary. Related to this was the failure to appropriately house Puyi, who theoretically should have played a prominent role in the new city and state but did not. In 1937, he "continue[d] to reside in the moderate-sized old building formerly used by the salt administration. With dozens of fine new buildings being constructed, the Emperor is still without a palace."[212] This began to change in 1938, when work commenced on a new palace, to be built over eight years. All buildings associated with it were to be "'elegant structures of the old Oriental style,' but fireproof and with modern equipment."[213] Puyi never actually lived in this complex, however, as construction lapsed in 1943. Similarly, Kantōgun engineers began building an air defence shelter in the imperial garden but completed only a portion of it by war's end.[214] Puyi remained in the renovated but drafty offices of the former salt gabelle – today a museum dedicated to the puppet state – north of the old town (Map 3), a place he described with some understatement as "far from being the grandest house in the city."[215]

3 Economic Development

Connected to distant markets, Changchun had emerged as a regional trade hub before the arrival of foreign empire builders. This drew foreign attention and enabled the exploitation of the town and region for the Japanese empire. Chinese continued to power economic development – subsequent growth could occur only with Chinese input – but Japanese were in positions to shape and profit from it. Despite Xinjing's not industrializing like other Manchurian cities, the economy continued to grow after the Manchurian Incident, albeit in a different manner. After surveying Changchun's commercialization during the Qing, this chapter addresses how Japanese integrated the town's economy into the empire's and, in so doing, transformed the urban landscape. As with planning and architecture, economic expansion in the railway town and imperial capital reflected local and even international issues as well as individual mindsets. Ultimately, though, Japanese attitudes not only influenced how economic development materialized within the city's built environments but simultaneously both spurred and constrained it.

Frontier Outpost

Seventeenth- and eighteenth-century Jesuits generally described Mongolian lands as poor but attested to a vibrant long-distance luxury trade in Manchuria. Changchun emerged at the end of this era to sit astride defined and policed road and river routes already in use.[1] Jilin City lay just to the east, and trade between Shenyang and Qiqihar passed through Changchun on a route running west of the Willow Palisade's northern spur. From Shenyang, roads also led to Yingkou, Beijing, and Korea. From Qiqihar, headquarters of the Heilongjiang garrison, lesser roads continued north.

A traveller in 1886 described Manchuria as "a very fertile plain, somewhat broken up by watercourses, resembling a piece of the Tapi valley" in central India.[2] Manchurian rivers were relatively shallow, so traders travelled overland, despite poor conditions. Roads often out of repair left carts stuck for hours at a time, and this same traveller reported seeing one cart upset "in a lake of black mud" just outside Jilin City's north gate, a situation common even in Beijing.[3] Horses sometimes even drowned in deep mud.[4] Three decades later, another traveller reported, "The roads, if one may use the term, were excessively bad, and we had considerable difficulty in making headway. We had not gone far when one cart was overturned into a deep pool beside the road, and its whole contents soaked. At one place we had to cross a treacherous ... swamp ... one in which the soft black ooze is closely dotted with peculiar tussocks of grass. In summer the long grass hides everything, with the result that in trying to cross the swamp one encounters a series of pitfalls, as one's feet miss the tussocks and plunge into the ooze, often up to the waist."[5]

Bandits compounded such troubles, but trade grew, initially in ginseng and sable.[6] Another commodity was timber: before China's forced opening, Chinese south of the Great Wall imported lumber from Manchuria and Korea (albeit "small trees" from the former).[7] A missionary reported just after 1900 that "native [Chinese] lumber ... is scarce and often small and crooked," and that better, more expensive lumber was available from Oregon.[8] Jilin City was the traditional centre of the timber trade, a riverine garrison and port. Its streets were reportedly "paved with wooden blocks" and enclosed by fifteen-foot-high walls except along the river, where great wooden doors were closed at night.[9] Manchuria also exported grain as well as coal, gold, and iron ore. The manufactured goods most evident to travellers were soybean oil and alcohol, the latter made from surplus millet and "maize," likely sorghum.[10]

Manchuria's distinguishing crop was soy, introduced as an export crop but also found useful to restore depleted soil. Chinese south of the Great Wall, especially in the Yangzi River delta, used Manchurian soy fertilizer, and, by the end of the nineteenth century, so did farmers in Southeast Asia.[11] Some ten thousand Fujianese households in southern Manchuria were involved in the trade as early as 1791.[12] By 1909, Manchuria provided 90 percent of global soy exports, 75 percent in the mid 1930s. By then, soybeans grew on a quarter of Manchuria's cultivated land, and soy products typically accounted for more than half the value of the region's exports.[13] Changchun took part in this trade from early on, despite its inland location. Before the advent of rail traffic, the city lay only fifteen days from Yingkou in the winter and twenty-one in the rainy season, though perhaps three to four weeks was more typical.[14] Ultimately, soil depletion in southern Manchuria rendered land around Changchun more attractive.[15]

Growing trade encouraged the cultivation of new crops, like cotton.[16]

Another was opium, which became an important cash crop especially once legalized in 1890. Per capita usage of the drug in Manchuria was already high in 1889.[17] On the eve of the Russo-Japanese War, a Briton found he could travel from Jilin City to Changchun fastest by "opium mule."[18] Although by 1920 opium was grown primarily in Heilongjiang, Changchun was its "chief mart ... [although] so extensively smuggled as hardly to appear in the customs returns."[19]

Increasing trade facilitated immigration. Chinese immigrants in the early Qing were few, and many arrived due to banishment. For example, the court exiled descendants of some of the followers of Wu Sangui from Yunnan to along the Nonni River, north of the Sungari. Ordered to maintain roads and horses for postal service, this small group established a trade network across northwest Manchuria connected with more populous centres, apparently via Changchun.[20] Another kind of network involved Chinese "liaison stores" (*lianhao*), run by local managers but financed by investors receiving income according to their capital or labour contributions, detailed in contracts. These continued to prosper in Manchuria despite the growing imperialist presence, and some managed to extend activities to Japan. A network centred on a Shenyang silk store established two stores in Changchun around 1900.[21] Chinese immigration ultimately transformed Manchuria's economy by expanding export production, stimulating import demand, and integrating the labour market with north China.[22] The idiom *chuang Guandong* (rush east of the pass [at Shanhaiguan]) illustrates popular Chinese recognition of Manchuria's potential.

Foreign travellers on the Shenyang–Jilin City highway bypassed Changchun.[23] Those visiting were impressed. One described "the great town of [Changchun]" in 1869 as "the centre of the trade in Eastern Mongolia, and the ruling market for pulse, indigo, and opium." As for the town,

> the streets are full of shops of all kinds, but the shops are not fine, and are evidently places where men are intent on making money rather than spending it on external decorations. The population is large, say 60,000 or 80,000. There is no regular wall, only an attempt at a mud fortification; the gates are made of wooden planks, and are not formidable; but one huge cannon lay looking out of the north gate.[24]

Others bear out this description. An Irish missionary reported Changchun "a commercial town ... larger and more populous than Jilin City" and suspected it would be easy to found a church there.[25] A member of the Bombay Civil Service called the town "the most important commercial city in Manchuria, containing about 100,000 inhabitants. The cold weather traffic had begun, and there was as much life and bustle as in the city of London." Heading south to Shenyang, he counted more than nine hundred carts one day, many pulled by eight or nine mules or ponies.[26] Estimating the size at 120,000 in 1896, then British consul in Yingkou (Niuzhuang) Alexander Hosie called Changchun "the most important commercial mart of Manchuria," given its regional roles in distribution and indigo and felt manufacture, as well as "the chief market" for opium in the province.[27] A few years later, French missionaries opened a mission in Changchun, having determined it to be the "most commercial" town of all northern Manchuria and the junction for carts meeting from north and south.[28] Its role as a commercial entrepôt was likely the reason that, as a Japanese guidebook noted, Changchun's roads were broader than elsewhere in the region.[29]

On the eve of the Russo-Japanese War, Putnam Weale described Changchun as "a mighty place." Recalling the 1896 British estimate of the population to be 120,000, he was inclined to believe Chinese claims that were closer to 250,000. The main street ran ten *li* (about five kilometres), lined with caravanserais, pawnbrokers, and warehouses full of goods from across Manchuria as well as ponies from Mongolia and merchandise from Yingkou. He ascribed the mud wall and old city gates to a Chinese preference to investing in commerce, and, indeed, the road between Jilin City and Shenyang via Changchun was a hundred feet wide in places.[30] At the same time, Weale mourned a passing era: "Though in ancient days horsemen armed with bows and lances could sweep like a tornado over the land, leveling everything save the walled cities, in the nineteenth century such methods had become impossible. Mongolia and Manchuria had also ceased to be inexhaustible reservoirs of warlike men; the more adjacent portions had become commercialized; whilst the outer regions had sunk to depopulated graziers' lands."[31]

Central Manchuria's economic dynamism provoked a scramble among provincial administrators in the final years of the Qing. While Fengtian acquired much of eastern Mongolia, Jilin gained Changchun. This dynamism also brought foreigners, further destabilizing the region. Noting that the China Eastern Railway (CER) did not stop in any major city except near Shenyang – three to five kilometres away at that – a French observer predicted that major cities not on the line would decline and new boomtowns along it would emerge.[32]

Railway Town

To encourage Changchun's economic development, Japanese investigated opportunities and integrated new endeavours into an emerging commercial network, something Japanese reporting exemplified as progress. This initiative involved working with the local Chinese community – in the old city and the new mercantile district – and navigating international competition, initially Russian. The first Imperial Russian Geographical Society expedition reaching the Changchun area following the Treaty of Aigun arrived in Jilin City by steamship in 1864.[33] In addition to spreading civilization and Christianity, Russia sought to expand trade in Manchuria, especially with the CER's founding in 1897. The railroad's completion in 1901 reduced travel time between Dalian and St. Petersburg to thirteen and a half days – eighteen between Shanghai and London – at a time when travelling between Shanghai and London by ship or crossing Canada required thirty-one days.[34] Losing the railway south of Changchun in 1905 naturally reduced trade potential, and few Russians remained in Kuanchengzi when the army withdrew. Noting Japanese competition, a 1909 report indicated that the Russian railway station at Kuangchengzi was "practically idle,"[35] despite the CER's reconnecting with the South Manchuria Railway (Mantetsu) in September 1907 and the expansion of connecting infrastructure in February 1909.[36] The Russians who remained in the area dealt chiefly in textiles, winter clothing, and tobacco, eventually joined in this trade by some Japanese.[37] Of the 1,553 present in Kuangchengzi in 1922, 18 were Japanese and 642 were Chinese; most of the remainder were presumably Russian.[38]

Japanese reporting on Manchurian resources – including those in Changchun – was already evident during the Russo-Japanese War.[39] Yet the Japanese railway town also initially grew slowly: a 1913 railway guide noted the town still had "spaces not yet filled in" and that many Japanese and Russians "still" maintained stores in the Chinese town. Although all the streets were paved ("macadamised"), West Park had only recently been laid out, as had a vegetable garden. After the "modern" Yamato Hotel, the guide recommended two "second-class" hotels in "half Japanese, half European style," one near the station and the other outside the old town's West Gate.[40] The town developed more quickly thereafter, the Russian link proving useful after the outbreak of war in Europe in 1914, which spurred rail traffic through Changchun.[41]

Via Mantetsu and its growing network, Japanese promoted economic growth across Manchuria but, before the Manchurian Incident, did not alter the region's reliance on agriculture, resource extraction, and light industry. Despite the distance from Japan, central Manchurian goods remained profitable, in part because Mantetsu kept transport fees low.[42] Low fees also helped Japanese penetrate northern Manchuria. Although much soy ended up in Russian ships leaving Vladivostok for ports in Korea, China, and Japan, many farmers found better prices in Changchun.[43] The British Foreign Office identified Changchun in 1920 as "the principal centre of the internal trade of Manchuria" as well as "the principal centre for the sale and purchase of horses in Manchuria."[44] The Siberian Intervention furthered Japanese penetration by enabling acquisition of much of the soy production transported to Harbin and enabling Japanese to gain awareness of northern Manchuria's potential.[45] A 1922 agreement with the Soviet Union to allow Mantetsu to transport soybeans along the CER ensured continued access to the northern part of the region.[46] Expanded service supported this growth – by 1926, there were five trains each way daily between Dalian and Changchun, departing every three or four hours. The trip normally required around twenty hours, though the express only twelve.[47] (The trip between Changchun and Harbin took around seven hours, with CER officials adding cars in 1926 to meet demand.[48]) Aggressively expanding infrastructure enabled Japan to dominate Manchurian trade, in 1929 receiving more than two-thirds of all exports from the port of Dalian.[49] Although Manchuria's expanding soy production reached Europe, the Japanese empire consumed the lion's share.

Japanese dominated regional investment as well. A 1929 study showed Japanese investment in Manchuria to be almost triple that of the next six major sources combined.[50] Another calculated Japanese investment to be 70.45 percent of the region's total in 1935, with Soviet investment at 25.71 percent. The CER accounted for three-quarters of Soviet investment (¥450 million of ¥590 million), a value likely inflated. What remained was "mainly of a commercial nature, including oil, tobacco and match distribution, and also banking facilities and a British bondholder's interest in the Beijing-Shenyang Railway." At the time, only 10 percent of Japanese investment was in north Manchuria.[51]

Japanese investment took many forms, but before 1932 most was by Mantetsu. Although the railway and its associated industries received the largest share, Mantetsu's towns were also beneficiaries. Total Mantetsu investments in towns along the railway amounted to ¥131 million by 1929, ¥200 million if the various waterworks, electric plants, and tramway systems turned over to private interests are included.[52] A breakdown of investments on the eve of the Manchurian Incident shows how substantial municipal endeavours were in relation to other areas of investment (Table 3.1). Investment in municipalities included moneys for daily operations – Mantetsu covered most of the expenses for public services within the railway zone that

Table 3.1
Summary of Mantetsu investments (as of 31 March 1931)

	(¥)	(%)
Railways	270,230,960	36
Harbours	83,200,948	11
Railway workshops	6,465,032	1
Coal mines	117,871,977	16
Iron works	27,716,716	4
Oil shale plants	8,824,461	1
Municipalities	146,125,530	20
Sanitation	15,842,006	2
Education	14,304,671	2
Other	51,486,905	7
Total	742,069,206	100

Note: Percentages do not align due to rounding.
Source: South Manchuria Railway, *Third Progress Report on Manchuria, 1907–32* (Dairen: Mantetsu, 1932), 48.

Table 3.2
Railway town budgets and Mantetsu aid, 1907–33 (yen)

Years	Income	Expenditures	Aid (deficit covered by Mantetsu)
1907–8	120,794	251,006	130,212
1912–13	633,211	1,401,012	767,800
1917–18	1,930,284	3,538,709	1,267,560
1922–23	3,995,249	10,831,659	6,836,410
1927–28	6,098,234	19,104,447	13,006,210
1928–29	6,230,083	19,425,207	13,195,124
1929–30	4,689,833	18,288,336	13,598,503
1930–31	4,586,369	15,305,429	10,719,060
1931–32	4,488,883	15,366,294	10,877,411
1932–33	4,824,183	16,511,465	11,687,222

Source: South Manchuria Railway, *Fourth Report on Progress in Manchuria to 1934* (Dairen: Mantetsu, 1934), 165.

were not paid for by fees and rents the towns received (Table 3.2). Public expenditures in the Changchun railway town soared from ¥9,452 in 1908 to ¥60,214 in 1912 to ¥408,024 in 1921, about half of which was paid by local revenues and the other half by Mantetsu or loans. These figures did not include all construction projects and expenses; the Changchun regional office's total expenses amounted to ¥17,480,477 in 1921 alone. About 43 percent of this sum was paid with bank loans and just over 4 percent by Mantetsu.[53] Sustained investments in municipalities and servicing municipal debt indicate that town building was more than window dressing.

Japan's expanding infrastructure managed this investment. Mitsui Bussan and the Yokohama Specie Bank opened branches on Changchun's east side in 1907, Mitsui just southeast of South Plaza. Telephone service came the next year – Changchun was one of fourteen towns with Mantetsu-maintained telephone systems by 1920.[54] The North Manchuria Bank and the Bank of Korea established themselves in 1912 and 1913, as did two private banks in 1918, but other foreign interest was negligible.[55] Indicative of relative interests, the only consulate in Changchun before 1932 was Japanese. The nearest non-Japanese consulates were in Shenyang and Harbin.[56] Reporting on Changchun's economy was Mantetsu's *Manshū nichi nichi shinbun* (*Manchuria Daily News* [*MNNS*]), with a weekly Changchun section on Wednesdays as well as other reports. One early example claimed the soil around and south of the town was some of Manchuria's most fertile.[57] Other publications repeated positive views. A 1910 report praising the potential for soybeans throughout Manchuria described Changchun in particular as a substantial market attracting agricultural products from its surrounding environs, especially from its northwest.[58] Another noted mineral resources available to the southeast.[59]

Fuelled by soybeans, the economy of the Changchun area – including the railway town, the mercantile district, and the old city and its environs – grew rapidly. The following discussion reflects this growing integration. Although the 1907 harvest was poor, exports quadrupled between 1907 and 1911, and Changchun initially led Manchurian soy production.[60] Good land outside the town as well as in nearby Gongzhuling and Sipingjie could produce more soybeans per hectare than comparable land further south.[61] A 1919 Shenyang consular district report listed Changchun as the major source for soybeans, shipping 706,000 tons that year. A distant second was Kaiyuan at 178,050 tons.[62] Gongzhuling, which lay only sixty kilometres southwest of Changchun, also increasingly figured in soy exports (Table 3.3). This reflected

Table 3.3
Manchuria soy exports (tons), five-year averages, 1911–25

	1911–15 (%)	1916–20 (%)	1921–25 (%)
Changchun	195,114 (26.1)	423,106 (31.8)	101,860 (6.0)
Kaiyuan	168,300 (22.5)	234,896 (17.7)	214,191 (12.6)
Gongzhuling	83,106 (11.1)	79,341 (6.0)	100,639 (5.9)
Changchun-Jilin Railway	–	62,682 (4.7)	224,234 (13.2)
CER	34,898 (4.7)	141,893 (10.7)	565,781 (33.2)
Other major towns	266,406 (35.6)	387,168 (29.1)	496,266 (29.1)
Totals	747,824	1,329,086	1,702,971

Source: Mantetsu keizai chōsakakai, "Manshū kōtsū tōkei shūsei" (1935), as cited in Ishida Takehiko, "Chūgoku tōhoku ni okeru ryōsan no dōkō: Manshū jihen mae ni okeru," *Hokkaidō daigaku keizaigaku kenkyū* 24, no. 1 (1974): 152.

a northern shift in soy production. By 1931, the total area under cultivation was greater in both Jilin (54,813 km^2) and Heilongjiang (55,103 km^2) than in Fengtian (40,212 km^2).[63] Agricultural expansion consumed both forest and grasslands, and the Songnen plain north and west of Changchun was intensively converted to crops.[64] Better conditions in the north, expanding overseas demand, and a growing labour supply sparked a boom in soybean production and other exports, though rising prices soon meant Chinese south of the Great Wall were unable to purchase Manchurian soy fertilizer because of higher prices.[65] Supported by chambers of commerce and other related business organizations, Changchun trade ended up not only in Manchuria but also in Korea and every Japanese prefecture by the time of the Manchurian Incident.[66]

At the same time, Changchun did not ship only soy products, something evident from the outset. Between October 1907 and March 1908, for example, 55,000 of the 176,000 tons (31 percent) of goods shipped from Dalian came from or via Changchun.[67] Noting the city's status as a growing hub, one Mantetsu report called Changchun "one of Manchuria's most important cities."[68] Some called Changchun the "entryway" (*genkan*) to northern Manchuria, and Changchun station the "entry station" (*genkaneki*).[69]

Changchun's built environment reflected the city's moniker "Bean Town" (Ch, *Doudu;* Jp, *Mame no to*), most obviously in the growth of warehouses, offices, and accommodations associated with the soy trade.[70] Photographs of mounds of soybeans and soy cakes in Changchun seem to appear in virtually every contemporary account of Manchuria in Japanese. Yet Changchun was more than a depot. Agricultural research was conducted in Changchun's southern outskirts.[71] Japanese experimental farms developed improved soy strains, and the one developed at Changchun in 1928 allegedly doubled or, according to some sources, even quadrupled harvests.[72] Changchun's merchants also engaged in soy processing, expanding soybean oil production between 1925 and 1929 and raising the region's share of all Manchurian production from 2 to 3 percent. Izumi Renji reported twenty-five processing plants in 1912, with a mix of machine and horse-powered presses, only two in the railway town. Although output grew, mechanization reduced the number of processors: by 1934, there were three large processors – one Japanese and two Chinese – and nine smaller plants.[73] Supporting this expansion was the founding of exchanges for the sale of staples. Changchun's opened in 1916, only three years after Dalian's and four years before Shenyang's. At the end of 1929, Changchun's exchange had forty-five brokers, the same as in Shenyang, although this was a fraction of Dalian's 156.[74]

Changchun's regional economy did not depend only on soy. Sorghum and millet passed through the city, their combined totals sometimes exceeding that for soy.[75] For example, while soybeans accounted for 30 percent of all agricultural exports in 1921, sorghum accounted for 25 percent, millet 20 percent, and wheat 10 percent.[76] Millet channelled through Changchun in 1921–22 provided between one-quarter and one-third of the total amount exported through Dalian, and about one-fifth of all Manchurian millet exports.[77] Japanese tested the potential of other crops as well, including flax – grown on Changchun's experimental farm – herbs, vegetables, and sugar beets.[78] Perhaps 10 or 15 percent of the sugar produced in Manchuria grew near Changchun.[79] Changchun was also known for animal husbandry, especially for horses and mules.[80] A 1936 *MNNS* article extolled in particular the virtues of the region around the capital and to the north for horses.[81] In addition, fresh and dried marine products, especially fish, passed through Changchun in growing quantities, moving north from the Guandong peninsula but also south from the Amur basin. This trade likely encouraged the appearance of local fish merchants in Changchun: by 1917, there were three Japanese and four Chinese shops, and five of each by 1920. After 1920, the number of Chinese fish merchants continued to grow while the number of Japanese shops declined, a reflection of the lower labour costs that enabled Chinese merchants to keep prices low.[82]

Light industry emerging in Changchun depended on local resources and demand but expanded steadily, primarily in the Chinese sections. A 1910 report noted that Manchuria's industrial growth in the late Qing began along the southern coast, although Russians built a second industrial centre in Harbin. Other industrial zones followed, typically developing around the processing of local agricultural goods.[83] Changchun was no exception, and Chinese manufacturers produced soybean oil and sorghum liquor prior to such production in the treaty ports. Chinese Changchun had three distilleries when the Japanese arrived.[84] With the development of the railway town, Changchun was soon home to seven new distilleries and a bone-manure plant, and Japanese added a soy sauce factory.[85] There were nine distilleries in 1932, producing more than 1.1 million litres of sorghum liquor.[86] A 1928 report indicated the presence of six Japanese lumber mills and two textile plants, along with a flour mill, a brick plant, an oil refinery, a match-making factory, a soap-making plant, and an agricultural products (*nōboku*) producer, in addition to the railway and power-generation facilities and not including another fifteen unnamed plants on the town's outskirts.[87] A 1934 report listed the following production facilities in the railway town and city in addition to those involved in the soy industry: flour milling (wheat and corn), match making, lumber, electricity, gas (*gasu*), rice polishing, textiles, *shōchū* (rice liquor) distilling, brick making, soap making, printing, and ironworking. The same report also listed a variety of cottage industries, producing candles, hats, shoes, tiles, socks, and garters.[88] Some 260 handicraft producers worked in Changchun in 1931, a greater number than in Shenyang (174), Andong (42), Harbin (36), Yingkou (27), or Tieling (253).[89]

Construction supplies constituted an important industry.[90] Changchun produced tile, glass, and wood – a 1930 report listed forty-four woodworkers in the railway town and the mercantile district.[91] Initially, lumber was milled in Changchun, but as local wood supply diminished the city served more as a hub for the lumber trade. By 1930, Andong and Jilin City were the largest regional collection points for lumber, followed by Shenyang, Dalian, Changchun, and Harbin.[92] Brick making in Changchun surged during the First World War era, reaching a high of 130 producers in 1921, after which numbers declined until a second surge occurred with the construction of Xinjing.[93]

Changes in foreign competition had a profound effect on some industries. Many developed or expanded in response to opportunities provided by the First World War, when foreign competition was limited. Although, prior to the war, Russian imports posed a challenge, the disappearance of European competition buoyed both Japanese imports and local producers. Foreign competition returned after the war, including American lumber and Canadian flour, the latter imported via Harbin.[94] A good example of Changchun's interaction with international trade involves textiles. By the time of the Manchurian Incident, two Japanese and nine Chinese plants used Indian hemp bought in Dalian to supply Manchuria with sacks.[95] Changchun, however, relied on local sources of cotton and quickly became the most important market north of Shenyang for the gathering and spinning of cotton, producing more than ten thousand bales of thread a year.[96] Changchun's first cotton cloth mill appeared in 1913, but 1915 was pivotal, due to growing trade with Japan and the war in Europe.[97] Factories in Changchun were soon exporting cotton thread and cloth to Dalian, Shenyang, Shanghai, and Japan, although concerns for cotton's viability in Manchuria endured, given American competition.[98] Nonetheless, Manchurian cotton supplied the local knitted goods industry; four factories appeared in the old city and the mercantile district between 1921 and 1925, though Changchun trailed Dalian, Shenyang, and Andong in production.[99] A 1931 publication noted three cotton-thread factories in Changchun and four producing cotton cloth.[100] Textile manufacturing also involved an extensive cottage industry producing clothes and bedding for domestic consumption. It too was subject to the vagaries of the international market. Although by 1918, the city had 700 locations using 2,600 looms for weaving, that number declined to only 90 locations and 320 looms in 1920 as pre-war competition returned. Rebounding to 250 locations by 1925, only 100 were in operation after the onset of the Great Depression. However, rising demand and greater security following the Manchurian Incident appear to have helped this industry, as Japanese claimed the value of production leaped from ¥1,246,500 in 1931 to ¥2,045,000 in 1932. By 1934, Xinjing had five cotton cloth factories and some 300 smaller workshops, contributing to the total of 1,300 businesses producing woven fabric in the city.[101]

Although Japanese contributed to this economic growth in private and public capacities, Chinese labour produced most of it, even if sources do not always acknowledge it. In the important business of warehousing – central to Changchun's economic role before 1931 – a 1934 publication noted that three Japanese firms in addition to Mantetsu provided these services, "outside of those on the Manchurian side."[102] This kind of reporting, typical of Japanese publications, was misleading. Although under-reported, Chinese economic activity, especially outside the railway town, was significant.[103] Chinese outnumbered Japanese on Changchun's foodstuffs exchange, as they did in all Manchurian cities. When the exchange opened in 1916, there were 6 Japanese and 28 Chinese, according to a 1928 report. In the peak years of 1920 and 1921, there were 32 Japanese and 52 Chinese, and 34 and 47, respectively, in 1922. These dropped to 18 and 26 in 1927.[104] Flour milling was similarly dominated by Chinese, beginning in Changchun in 1913 by a firm branching out from Tieling, although other Chinese mills were established during the war era, three in Kuanchengzi alone. In contrast, Japanese and Koreans dominated the rice-polishing industry, which expanded rapidly after 1921. By 1933 there were five Japanese, five Korean, one Korean-Japanese, and two Chinese rice-polishing plants in the city.[105]

Manchuria's economic success depended on Chinese demand as well as labour. For example, Changchun's five soap makers, including a Japanese plant, produced largely for the Manchurian market. While the Japanese factory – founded in 1923 – specialized in cosmetic soaps, the Chinese produced primarily laundry soap as well as candles. Most was either consumed locally or sold along the railway, but some detergents and candles were exported. Another example of an industry serving the Chinese market is soy sauce and bean paste production. In 1934, the new capital had two Japanese soy-processing shops, which began production in 1919 and 1932, along with ten Chinese shops, the largest two producing for more distant markets.[106]

Chinese capital was also present in Changchun, but was more limited. A Manchuria-wide network of over three hundred private associations (*hang*) provided financial services by 1910. Izumi Renji listed twenty-nine in Changchun in 1912, dividing them into three grades, as well as other financial establishments.[107] Chinese also appear to have rallied in response to the arrival of the Japanese, organizing a new Chamber of Commerce in 1908, the year after Changchun's opening to Japan. The fact that the first Chinese-owned power-generating facility in Changchun was capitalized by a bank in Jilin City, the provincial capital, and not Changchun, however, points to a relative scarcity in local Chinese investment capital.[108]

Changchun played a considerable role in the development of Manchuria's economy before 1931, Japanese both abetting and exploiting Chinese economic growth. Such development drew many Japanese to the region, but the creation of Manchukuo created new economic opportunities in the city, attracting increasing numbers of Japanese, including more civilians. At the same time, Japanese officials limited such opportunities, while, ironically, representing such policies as progressive.

National Centre

Shortly after the Manchurian Incident, a member of the Xinjing Economic Friendship Society, perhaps a local businessman, suggested that, even as a "political city," Xinjing must also develop as a "commercial and industrial city." Such economic development would be in keeping with the pattern of Tokyo's development, and, moreover, Xinjing's future size and population required goods and people to look after those whose work was political. He urged reforms to stimulate the economy – sponsoring projects, expanding roads, establishing faster rail connections via Korea, recognizing trademarks, standardizing weights and measures, developing tourism, and building industry – noting contributions to military airplane production in the capital.[109] Ideologically, the Imperial Japanese Army officers directing Manchukuo inclined more to state planning than unfettered capitalism, but, realizing their own limitations, they eventually agreed with some of these recommendations and the utility of recruiting professionals. One of these recruits was Nissan head Ayukawa Yoshisuke, who arrived in Xinjing in 1937 to take over Manchuria Heavy Industries (Mangyō), with its modern headquarters on Datong Dajie just north of Shuntian Park. Manchukuo's capitalism, however, remained guided. Although desiring growth, officials continued to constrain economic activities so as to conform with "ideal" state principles, to the chagrin of Ayukawa and others like him.[110]

Manchukuo, however, was challenged from the start, as the Manchurian Incident provoked the withdrawal of non-Japanese capital.[111] Until war in the south redirected resources after 1937, Japanese investment made up for this shortfall, though the road was rough. To stabilize prices, in May 1932 the government instituted a system of bonded warehouses (*hozei sōko*), beginning with three in Xinjing, although low-value goods were distributed privately. This system helped bring inflation under control by early 1933, with wholesale prices levelling off at around 140 percent of fall 1932 prices. Compensating for a loss of imports from Shanghai and Tianjin, Japanese exports to the city almost quadrupled from 1931 to 1932. The high value of silver – backing the Manchukuo yuan until 1935 – rendered Japanese imports more affordable, including items of daily use. This stability encouraged grocers, restaurateurs, innkeepers, and the like catering to a rapidly growing bureaucracy to relocate to Xinjing. Insufficient supplies of some goods, such as soy sauce, also spurred production.[112]

Compounding matters, exports declined following the Manchurian Incident, leaving investment to drive Manchukuo's economy.[113] By 1936, Japanese investments in Manchukuo totalled ¥800 million, on top of the ¥1.7 billion invested before the incident. Much of this sum was in loans, though Mantetsu – which remained Japan's principal economic actor in Manchuria

– almost doubled its capitalization between 1932 and 1934.[114] Former Mantetsu director Ōkura Kinmochi bragged that, by the end of 1939, Japanese investment exceeded ¥3 billion. A postwar American estimate of all Japanese investments in Manchuria as of June 1945 was ¥11 billion.[115] Xinjing received much of this. For example, the city received more than 12 percent of the total spent by Mantetsu on local administration in 1937, third behind Shenyang and Dalian, despite the change in focus to developing Manchukuo's cities outside the capital with the second five-year plan.[116]

Much of this investment in Xinjing went into construction. Manchukuo's expenses for new construction and renovations increased from ¥2.5 million in 1932 to ¥9.3 million in 1937 and ¥21.6 million in 1939.[117] Xinjing's share was large, averaging about 18 percent of the total between 1932 and 1938. In contrast, Shenyang received about 13 percent of all official construction expenses and Dalian about 10 percent (see the investment totals in construction in Table 3.4). A 1940 publication gives an overview of Xinjing's official construction projects, but does not include corporate offices that relocated or opened branch offices in Xinjing (Table 3.5).[118] Firms representing every major industry from mining and metalworking to chemicals and textiles eventually opened in Xinjing.[119] Others, like the Manchuria Development Agency (Manshū takushoku kōsha, or Mantaku), founded in 1937 with the assets of a Japanese private firm established the year before, were semi-official concerns promoting development. From its headquarters near Shuntian Dajie, Mantaku supervised Japanese and Korean immigration across Manchuria, especially in the north but also in new towns near the capital.[120]

Japanese construction firms profited from empire. Before the Manchurian Incident, firms like Nakamura Yoshihei's built banks across Manchuria, while others enjoyed more modest roles, such as the Sawai Gumi, builder of Changchun's Yamato Hotel. Building Manchukuo's capital, however, provided added opportunities for Japanese companies. A widely used postwar account lists the following Japanese firms as active in Changchun and Xinjing: Fukui-Takanashi, Hasegawa, Hoshino, Maruyama, Mase Engineering, Nishimatsu, Ōbayashi, Ōkura, Takaoka, Tatsumura, Zenitaka, and Shimizu.[121] This was only a partial list, though, as the 1936 annual report of Shimizu's Manchuria branch listed 108 Japanese competitors across Manchuria, 57 in Xinjing alone.[122] Supplying these were firms like Onoda Cement, which, despite adding plants in Harbin and Mudanjiang, continued to import from Korea to meet demand that year.[123]

Table 3.4
Municipal construction in Manchukuo, 1932–38 (yuan)

	1932	1933	1934	1935	1936	1937	1938	Total
Xinjing	6,796,000	16,309,800	33,265,490	48,941,332	24,840,000	29,223,000	38,227,000	197,602,622
Dalian	2,815,000	13,239,150	17,589,960	19,710,564	18,580,000	14,605,000	17,471,000	104,010,674
Mukden	5,796,000	14,412,940	20,522,589	18,328,014	10,038,000	21,774,000	45,600,000	136,471,543
Mudanjiang	–	–	–	–	10,545,000	6,116,000	6,319,000	–
Anshan	300,000	3,627,900	6,133,147	2,099,454	2,617,000	4,464,000	17,673,000	36,914,501
Fushun	553,000	1,291,830	2,353,755	5,505,247	5,594,000	5,748,000	9,841,000	30,886,832
Harbin	–	3,665,940	11,249,233	17,764,572	6,550,000	4,296,000	10,008,000	53,533,745
Qiqihar	–	2,476,190	5,434,919	9,660,402	4,751,000	2,178,000	3,039,000	27,539,511
Jilin	–	–	–	–	1,110,000	1,642,000	2,307,000	–
Jinxian	–	–	–	–	2,233,000	1,019,000	3,306,000	–
Andong	621,000	1,447,140	954,042	2,389,707	1,292,000	843,000	966,000	8,512,889
Others	40,784,500	46,609,020	57,129,693	25,472,138	47,524,000	70,075,000	138,072,000	–
Totals	57,566,500	104,074,010	154,632,828	149,871,432	135,674,000	161,982,000	292,829,000	1,056,629,770

Sources: Figures for 1932–35 are from Shimizu gumi Manshū shiten, *Nenkan* (n.p.: Shimizu gumi Manshū shiten, 1936), 36, and for 1936–38 from South Manchuria Railway, *Report on Progress in Manchuria to 1939* (Tokyo: Herald Press), 107.

Table 3.5
Official construction projects in Xinjing, 1933–37

	1933	1934	1935	1936	1937	Total
State offices (buildings)	5	2	5	2	3	17
Other offices (buildings)	2	9	7	68	3	89
Special residences (units)	547	971	1,225	258	–	3,001
General (units)	160	795	1,325	1,342	1,928	5,550
Rental (units)	–	185	538	344	–	1,067

Note: A missing figure for certain categories means that for that year the count for that category was merged into the general category.
Source: Shinkyō tokubetsushi shichōkanbō shomuka, *Kokuto Shinkyō* (Shinkyō: Manshū jijō annaijo, 1940), 14–15.

One construction firm active in the empire was Shimizu Construction, founded in 1804. Initially a traditional construction firm, having worked on Edo castle in 1838, Shimizu began experimenting with foreign techniques and styles as early as 1861. Working often with Mitsui, Shimizu was involved in a variety of innovative building projects, such as Mitsui House (1871), an early hybrid structure. Over the next half-century, Shimizu built banks, hotels, mansions, bridges, and factories, as well as railway and subway stations and lines across Japan. Many are noteworthy, such as Tatsuno Kingo's Bank of Japan, Tōdai's Yasuda Hall (1925), and the Gunjin Kaikan (Soldier's Hall) built with an "imperial crown." Shimizu also expanded with empire, building in Korea, Taiwan, and Manchuria, opening a Dalian office in 1915, and erecting factories, offices, hospitals, and other infrastructure. In 1932, the corporation renamed the Dalian office the "Manchurian" branch office. It opened new offices in Xinjing in 1934, ultimately making it their head Manchuria office in 1938. With the outbreak of war, Shimizu opened offices in in Shanghai (1938), Nanjing (1942), and Hankou (1942).[124] Shimizu's more prominent structures in Xinjing included the Manchukuo Ministry of the Economy and the offices of the Oriental Development Company. In addition to supervising a new water supply system for the Guandong Peninsula, Shimizu aimed to be involved in railways, which were anticipated in 1936 to expand by ten thousand kilometres, including north China.[125] Shimizu's success involved important connections. None other than Sano Riki became one of the firm's executives, recommended by the influential Shibusawa Eiichi. Joining the company at one of Shimizu's most difficult economic periods, owing to the global depression, Sano reorganized personnel, promoting "rationalism," and secured government contracts, particularly with the Home Ministry.[126] The latter connection proved invaluable as far as the company's activities in Manchuria were concerned, as members of the ministry were especially well represented in Manchukuo's administration.[127]

Xinjing's construction energized smaller, local firms. There were five lumberyards in the new capital in 1934, and nine in 1935. The local production of bricks jumped from 15 million red and 35 million black bricks annually before 1931 to 170 million red and almost 80 million black bricks a year after the Manchurian Incident. In 1933, this industry included eighteen Japanese, fifty-two Manchurian, and fifteen jointly run firms. Local mines around Xinjing and Jilin supplied aggregate, and a twenty-five-kilometre light railway hauled quarried stone. Fifty-four percent of Shimizu's 1935 total purchases of tile – worth ¥8,571 – by the Manchurian office came from Xinjing Jiancaishe (Building Materials). Some manufactured goods had still to be imported for construction, but the quick development of local sources is significant.[128] As elsewhere, the speedy energizing of the local economy not only attracted immigration and helped support a growing population but spurred commercialization and helped transform the local economy.[129]

Other industries experiencing rapid growth after the Manchurian Incident included those serving the expanding bureaucracy that occupied Xinjing's newly constructed office space. One was the hospitality industry, although statistics for restaurants, prostitutes, and other components of this industry are elusive. Nevertheless, the creation of the puppet state likely gave new hope to local vendors. For example, following declines in the 1920s, fourteen fish markets could soon be found in Yoshinomachi, the railway town's chief shopping district, which ran east from the central boulevard, just north of the police station.[130] In 1933, Xinjing offered two premier hotels as well as ten first-class, eight second-class, and eight third-class, but more were planned.[131] The demand for alcohol increased, as evident in the expansion of rice wine production.[132] Beer brewing took place only in Harbin and Shenyang, at least before 1938.[133] Other industries serving the bureaucracy included the furniture industry, involving both Chinese and Japanese producers. In 1933, Xinjing's twenty-one workshops produced furniture worth ¥1,313,027, a figure higher that than for soybean cake and oil combined that year.[134] Publishing was another growing industry, although government orders had still to be placed with Mantetsu publishers in Dalian and Shenyang, as local printers evidently could not keep up.

While Xinjing's growth could not help but spur some industries, ideology limited other development. In keeping with the capital's political role, the regime initially favoured only light, consumer-oriented production, minimizing the possibility of pollution or labour disruption. As a result, Xinjing's 14 cotton textile factories in 1933 did not increase through at least 1941. In comparison, in 1941 Shenyang had 69 mills, Yingkou 46, and Andong 40.[135] The announcement of a five-year plan in 1936 signalling that the government was retaining Shenyang as Manchukuo's industrial centre resulted in a surge in that city's population: hovering around 400,000 in the early 1930s, the population jumped to 711,674 in 1937 and 1,044,182 in 1939, including 110,000 Japanese.[136] Xinjing did gain a cigarette factory, with production climbing quickly from 1,638 tons in 1933 to 4,355 tons in 1936.[137] Flour milling expanded, from 1,101,000 bags in 1934 to 4,934,000 bags in 1936.[138] With northern Manchuria under Japanese control, the empire also hoped to expand soy oil processing in Xinjing in order to export more to Japan via Korea, and to Europe via Dalian. Small-scale industries also began to emerge, including steel, tool, and graphite producers, and metalworks.[139] By 1935, Xinjing's scattered output nevertheless constituted more than one-fifth of the Manchukuo industrial total.[140] With the securing of adequate water supply, official planners agreed to an expansion of the city's industrial base, designating a six-square-kilometre district east of the Yitong River as an industrial sector.[141] By 1942, the city employed 3,200 people in heavy industry and 87,133 in light.[142]

Despite constraining heavy industry, officials ensured that Xinjing continued to serve as a regional centre. Along with border ports, the capital had a customs house (as did Shenyang and Harbin).[143] Not only did Changchun's hinterlands commercialize and develop, but Mantetsu and Manchukuo planners extended the city's reach by expanding rail and road networks, connecting the city with the rest of Manchuria and beyond.[144] The railway connecting the capital with Tumen and the Korean port of Rason (Jp, Rashin) received much attention, for in connecting northern Manchuria with Japan's undeveloped Sea of Japan, planners hoped to develop both regions.[145] One publication described the international character of Xinjing's railway role as the knot tying together European and Asian trade.[146]

Communications is central to any hub, and the capital's communication infrastructure was top notch. Japanese endowed it with one of the first wireless transmitting facilities in Manchuria.[147] Manchuria Telegraph and Telephone's

Denden hundred-kilowatt radio station in Xinjing, constructed in 1934 for ¥3 million, was the "largest in East Asia," capable of reaching Japan and North China. Assuming control over telecommunications and telegraphy facilities, the company built radio receivers at a Shenyang plant and constructed telegraph stations across Manchukuo, ensuring that members of the growing Japanese population were not incommunicado, no matter where they settled.[148] Wireless telephone service between Japan and Manchukuo began on 1 August 1934, and, at an expense of almost ¥44 million, an advanced Japan–Manchukuo telephone cable was laid in 1935–39, connecting Xinjing and Tokyo directly – eventually with scramblers for security.[149]

With an eye on international developments – Charles Lindbergh had crossed the Atlantic in 1927 and the Pacific in 1931 – Japanese pursued the development of air transport in Manchuria. One of the first Japanese to fly to Changchun was the aviation pioneer Itō Otojirō, who landed in the eastern end of Changchun's West Park in December 1926.[150] Developments in aviation supported postal services, including parcels and remittances, which increased substantially for both Japanese and Chinese.[151] Regular airmail service between Osaka and Dalian began in 1926, and air travel between Tokyo and Dalian in 1929. With the extension of the London–Paris–Berlin–Moscow air route as far as Irkutsk in 1930, Changchun briefly became a relay station for airmail between Europe and Asia.[152] Regular airmail between Xinjing and Japan began in November 1933, the capital's airport by that time lying west of the train station just across the railway line.[153]

Connecting Manchukuo's cities with Japan and the Soviet Union, Manchuria Airways began operations in 1932 with capital from Manchukuo, Mantetsu, Mitsui, Mitsubishi, Sumitomo, and others. By 1935, it offered an air network three times that of Japan's, and military routes were opened to business people.[154] Seats on six-passenger planes were cheaper than first-class rail tickets and were reportedly available to all, though subject to military requisitioning.[155] Ten routes were in operation in 1934, with frequent flights.[156] Seven flights a week linked Xinjing with Dalian, stopping in Shenyang, carrying cargo as well as passengers.[157] These routes predated foreign competition – the maiden run of Pan-American Airlines' *China Clipper* between San Francisco and Manila was not until November 1935, although a Soviet route between Moscow and Vladivostok began in 1931.[158] By July 1937, travel between Xinjing and Dalian required only four or five hours.[159] Although travel time by air between Tokyo and Xinjing in 1932 was initially 52.5 hours, a year later the express route between the two cities – via Shenyang, Seoul, and Fukuoka –

was less than 10.[160] Direct air routes connected Xinjing with Beijing in February 1939, with Seoul in October of that year, and with Tokyo in April 1941.[161]

The development of Japanese civilian aviation entailed strategic considerations. Manchuria Airways was an offshoot of the Japan Air Transport Corporation, established in 1928 when the Ministry of Communications combined three private firms. It established the first air routes linking Japan with Dalian, Korea, and Taiwan and, after war broke out in China, with Beijing.[162] Following the signing of the Anti-Comintern Pact in 1936, German and Japanese aviation planners endeavoured to establish a Berlin–Tokyo air route via Xinjing, Inner Mongolia, western China, and the Middle East. The route was to be operational by the 1940 Tokyo Olympics but was set aside after fighting broke out in China in 1937.[163] In 1941, on the eve of the Pacific War, Japanese air routes reached Bangkok and East Timor, and Japanese were exploring other routes of strategic rather than commercial value in the south Pacific.[164] Military concerns were likewise evident. Manchukuo's first military air unit was based in Xinjing, and some of the Manchuria Airways fleet – including Junker 86s and Messerschmitt 108s – provided air support for military action.[165]

Another strategic, though not novel, industry was banking. Headquartered in the capital, the Bank of Manchukuo was organized in a similar manner to the government – that is, Chinese directors were balanced with Japanese advisers.[166] By 1942, there were 130 branches and agents across Manchuria, including branches in all major cities.[167] By 1936, eleven private Japanese and ten Manchurian banks could also be found in Xinjing, though some originated before the Manchurian Incident.[168] As a point of comparison, in 1930 only one Japanese bank was headquartered in Changchun, although branches of three other Japanese banks served the city. Only one Chinese bank had its headquarters in Changchun, the Yitong Commercial Bank, with branches in Harbin and Shanghai, but branches of five Chinese banks also served the city before 1931.[169] By 1942, two new banks joined the Yitong Commercial Bank.[170] These were in addition to special banks such as the Manchuria Industrial Bank, established in 1936.[171]

A new industry promoted by the government in Xinjing was film. West of Huanglong Park sat the offices of the Manchukuo-sponsored Manchuria Film Association (Manshū Eiga Kyōkai, or Man'ei). Its first president was the Manchu prince Jin Bidong, Xinjing's first mayor. Man'ei produced newsreels such as the *Manchuria News* (*Manshū nyūsu eiga*) series, which relayed highlights of official ceremonies, visits of foreign officials, public rallies, and sports events, many of which occurred in Xinjing.[172] Man'ei also produced movies, perhaps the best-known featuring Yamaguchi Yoshiko. Making her debut in 1938, the year after Man'ei's founding, Yamaguchi was born of Japanese parents in China and took the Chinese name Li Xianglan (Jp, Ri Kōran). She embodied Pan-Asianism on screen, or at least this was what film executives hoped.[173] Organizationally, the Japanese and Manchukuo film industry was linked with German and Italian precedents, and was modelled on Italian laws.[174]

Film was only one industry demonstrating growing Axis connections. Germany began actively considering linkages with Manchukuo in 1935, culminating in a mission arriving in Xinjing in December and a trade agreement in 1936, which led to a German trade commissioner being stationed in Xinjing.[175] Manchukuo's relations with other states varied. Trade missions from Poland and Czechoslovakia, for example, showed interest, which was apparently reciprocated. French and British financiers also showed interest and proved able to sign agreements, such as one leading to the French construction of the Foreign Ministry in Xinjing.[176] Some Chinese capital also returned. Although most of the 5 million to 7 million yuan invested in Shenyang withdrew to North China after the Manchurian Incident, some 2 million yuan returned by 1935.[177]

Manchukuo had an unfriendly attitude toward other foreign firms, and compelled some to leave. For example, while two of Changchun's four match factories were Japanese, established in 1927, two older and larger firms – Jilin Matches and Japan-Qing Matches – fell on hard times and in 1924 came under the control of Swedish investors. Both of these were originally Chinese, though Japan-Qing Matches had been acquired by a Japanese firm in 1920. Manchukuo announced a nationalization of the match industry in 1937, compelling the Swedes to sell controlling interests in these firms to Japanese companies in 1934. Given that, by 1935, factories in Changchun and Jilin City accounted for 44 percent of the matches produced in Manchuria, this was a lucrative industry, and Swedish competition – labelled a "Swedish *zaibatsu*" in one publication – apparently long irritated the Japanese.[178] Another example involved oil: until 1935 when Manchukuo instituted a government monopoly, foreign companies "almost entirely" distributed oil in Manchuria.[179] The Great Depression prompted Japan Petroleum's Hashimoto Keizaburō to reorganize this strategic industry, founding Manchuria Petroleum in 1934 and Chōsen Petroleum in 1935, announcing the former from Xinjing.[180] Yet Manchukuo continued to offer some opportunities to foreigners, as American exports to the state generally grew, including petroleum products, typically re-exported from Japan so that the puppet state recognized them as Japanese.[181] Other foreign firms similarly managed to find new roles. Anglo-American mining interests reportedly obtained rights to mine gold in Korea, Rehe, and northeast Manchuria, and the British-American Tobacco Company built a new factory in Liaoyang, incorporating under new laws and paying taxes to Xinjing. However, this firm's market in China faced new Japanese competition when Manchuria Tobacco followed Japanese forces south of the wall after the outbreak of war, transferring Japanese machinery from Xinjing to Tianjin.[182] Japanese featured Manchukuo prominently in Japan's new "bloc" economy. Foreign Minister Arita Hachirō defended this policy in noting that the United Kingdom and the United States had abandoned free trade in the 1930s and that bloc economies were natural economic units.[183] With the outbreak of war, Manchuria's significance to the empire escalated, as Japanese expected Manchukuo's factories, mines, and fields to replace other overseas sources.[184] Officials also aimed to expand agricultural production to make Manchukuo "the foodstuff supply base for Japan" and "Japan's 'blood transfusion' ally."[185] This goal did not materialize, however, given shipping losses and Manchukuo's own demands. Ultimately, more food resources were available in Xinjing than Tokyo, especially as the war drew to a close. After the war, one former bureaucrat recalled his garden in Xinjing fondly, as vegetables grew so easily there – all he needed do was plant the seeds.[186]

The war effort inexorably consumed materials and men, sidelining construction and even maintenance. While many Xinjing corporations took part in extending Japanese authority over China, including Manchuria Airways and Denden, shortages problematized daily affairs in Xinjing. Some benefitted, like Taiwan tea makers, since diminished trade with Southeast Asia assured them greater market share in the empire.[187] For most, the war was more gruelling. Officials organized "neighborhood factories" to mobilize unused domestic labour, assigning quotas for crops such as castor beans – useful for aircraft lubricant – planted in parks and along Xinjing's streets.[188] With the onset of American bombing of Manchuria in July 1944 – though not of Xinjing – Kantōgun officials began dispersing production, against the wishes of Mangyō president Takasaki Tatsunosuke. Like his predecessor, Ayukawa Yoshisuke, Takasaki complained of interference by the military and Manchukuo bureaucracy in rational business decisions.[189] Despite the bombing, officials discussed the possibility of relocating some Japanese industry to Manchuria to save factories from the greater threat of aerial bombardment in Japan as well as to save the expense of shipping finished goods from Japan made of raw materials gathered in Manchuria.[190]

Arriving in Changchun on the heels of victory in 1905, Japanese officials and civilians had set about incorporating the town and its hinterland into an imperial economy, chiefly through exploiting natural resources. After securing control of the region through military action in 1931–32, Japanese officials and civilians expanded those efforts while adding, eventually, an industrial base. Even if tardy, this base helped put the city at the forefront of development and provided impetus to develop its technological infrastructure. After a brief visit to Xinjing, Washio Kenzō, an editor of the *Manshū kenchiku zasshi* (*Journal of Manchurian Architecture*) and instructor at the South Manchuria Technical School in Dalian, wrote in early 1939 that both Xinjing and Shenyang surpassed Dalian as centres of innovation, demonstrating rapid scientific advances that revolutionized life. Washio claimed that these cities were setting Japanese on a progressive, new path, one that would lead the cultural development of all East Asia. He even warned that Dalian might relinquish its leading role for Manchuria and the North China region.[191] Xinjing's surge, however, diminished and came to a standstill, the imperial economy never fully reaping what Japanese endeavoured to sow.

4 Colonial Society

Building overseas enclaves in places like Changchun involved Japanese from diverse walks of life. Although durations of stay varied, all those present contributed to the railway town and capital through their presence and actions. After considering demographic change and the arrival of European missions, this chapter considers Japanese society in Changchun and Xinjing for indications as to how residents arranged and perceived their environs and how their actions within and concerns for the town helped form a local imaginary in Changchun and similar locales. Even in remote Manchuria, Japanese recreated much of the lifestyle that characterized contemporary Japan, demonstrating a closer allegiance to Japanese customs and society than to anything broadly Pan-Asian.

Demographic Change

Chinese, Japanese, and Koreans

Christopher Isett estimates Manchuria's population at around 2 million in 1800 and 14 million in 1900.[1] Economic opportunity and the court's promoting Chinese immigration as a means of maintaining sovereignty propelled this growth. With similar encouragement from the Zhang and Nationalist governments, the population reached roughly 33 million in 1930 and, under Manchukuo, 43 million in 1940.[2] At the same time, labour shortages prompted Japanese to promote migration by raising wages and establishing recruiting offices elsewhere in China.[3] One American reported that Chinese wages in Manchuria were higher than in the south as early as 1921.[4] Constructing Manchukuo provided further stimulus – some 3,613,000 Chinese were employed in construction in Manchukuo in 1933.[5]

Chinese immigration to Manchuria for employment was often temporary in nature. Initially, most Chinese found agricultural work, arriving in the spring and returning in the fall, but about two-thirds stayed between one and four years. Early immigrants tended to be owner-cultivators, but after around

Table 4.1
Population growth in Manchurian railway towns by ethnic group, 1907–37

Year	Chinese	Japanese	Korean	Foreign	Total
1907	12,256	13,436	–	7	25,699
1910	25,807	24,676	–	9	50,492
1915	57,554	33,816	252	162	91,784
1920	102,415	64,682	1,614	359	169,070
1925	179,954	82,433	8,636	1,456	272,479
1930	235,016	99,411	15,901	1,769	352,097
1935	258,385	190,508	31,415	1,088	481,396
1937	310,136	216,513	30,388	917	557,954

Source: Minami Manshū tetsudō kabushiki kaisha sōseishitsu chihōbu zanmuseiri iinkai, *Mantetsu fuzokuchi keiei enkaku zenshi* (Tokyo: Ryūkei shosha, 1977), 1: 152–53.

1907 soy farming increasingly attracted poorer tenant farmers and wage labourers.[6] Opting to work in territory subject to Japanese influence was a difficult decision, but many were motivated by economic difficulties at home.[7] Improved communications and the ability to send remittances, even after 1931, helped make the decision to relocate easier – 94.3 percent of Manchuria's international post in 1926 went to China, remitting $10 million to China in 1934.[8] Highlighting Chinese sojourning was its gender imbalance, typical of frontier societies. Between 1932 and 1940, gender ratios among Chinese in Manchukuo ranged between 119.9 and 123.4 men for every 100 women. The 1940 census indicated that, in Manchukuo's seventeen cities with populations greater than fifty thousand, the ratio of men to women was even more skewed – an average of 167 to 100, which roughly reflected the proportions in Xinjing.[9] Gender ratios were equal in densely inhabited rural areas that had been longer inhabited by Chinese, although rural-to-urban migration was also apparent, given that women outnumbered men in the three counties adjacent to large cities in Fengtian. Already by 1906, there were perhaps twice as many men as women in Shenyang.[10]

As shown in Tables 4.1 and 4.2, Chinese gravitated to Mantetsu's towns. Destinations included Changchun, where they outnumbered Japanese before 1931. The imbalance in the ethnic makeup of this area becomes more evident when old Changchun is included. Contrary to foreign estimates of Changchun's population cited in the previous chapter, Japanese reported 82,151 Chinese in old Changchun in 1916 and 87,319 in 1926.[11] About 80 percent

Table 4.2
Population growth in the Changchun railway town by ethnic group, 1907–37

Year	Chinese	Japanese	Korean	Foreign	Total
1907	566	687	–	2	1,255
1912	5,052	2,728	–	29	7,809
1917	11,525	4,781	–	185	16,491
1922	15,058	7,668	217	353	23,296
1927	21,050	8,938	774	608	31,370
1932	22,162	15,627	2,494	446	40,729
1937	27,448	34,115	3,180	280	65,023

Sources: Minami Manshū tetsudō kabushiki kaisha chihōbu, *Chihō keiei tōkei nenpō* (Dairen: Minami Manshū tetsudō chihōbu, 1938), 40–41; Manshikai, ed., *Manshū kaihatsu yonjūnenshi* (Tokyo: Manshū kaihatsu yonjūnenshi kankōkai, 1965), 3:66; Minami Manshū tetsudō kabushiki kaisha sōseishitsu chihōbu zanmuseiri iinkai, *Mantetsu fuzokuchi keiei enkaku zenshi,* 1:151, 156–57, 3:340–41. Slightly higher numbers appear in Gaimushō tsūshōkyoku, *Chōshun no jijō* (n.p.: Gaimushō, 1929), 59.

of the 150,000 people in the Changchun area in 1930 were Chinese. One report indicates that there were 20,157 Chinese, 10,161 Japanese, 1,807 Koreans, and 446 foreigners in the railway town, and 101,156 Chinese, 1,397 Japanese, 1,700 Koreans, and 51 foreigners in old Changchun and the mercantile district. Chinese presumably also constituted the majority of the 2,700 in Kuanchengzi and 4,000 nearby.[12] Although Japanese eventually outnumbered other ethnic groups in the railway town, Chinese far outnumbered other groups in Xinjing (Table 4.3).

The number of Japanese in Manchuria also increased rapidly. Only 16,000 in 1906, the total civilian population exceeded 200,000 by 1930 and 1 million by 1940 (Table 4.4). (Census data consider military personnel in Manchuria as resident in Japan, but they numbered around 12,000 before the Manchurian Incident and upwards of a half million after.[13]) These numbers were less than anticipated: while Manchukuo officials succeeded in recruiting 300,000 rural settlers, they aimed for 5 million.[14] Nonetheless, Manchukuo proved the most popular Japanese emigration destination in the 1930s, accounting for 376,036 of the 997,115 Japanese residents abroad in 1936, the second largest being Brazil (193,057).[15] Many arrived from overseas communities like Hawaii, where the government advertised Manchuria as a destination.[16] Manchuria's inherent instability, however, deterred many, as did the acceptance by local Chinese and Koreans of lower standards of living, discouraging the migration of working-class Japanese.[17] Chinese workers lived on less than

Table 4.3
Population growth in Xinjing area by ethnic group, 1931–40

Year	Chinese	Japanese	Korean	Other	Total
1931	114,354	10,630	1,837	731	127,552
1935	249,295	54,637	6,764	825	311,521
1937	261,691	65,222	7,045	734	334,692
1938	285,147	82,146	10,115	971	378,379
1940	359,869	114,503	14,818	1,063	490,253

Sources: Manshū teikoku rinji kokuto kensetsukyoku, *Kokuto kensetsu ni tsuite* (n.p.: Manshū teikoku rinji kokuto kensetsu kyoku, 1940), 11; Kokumuin sōmuchō tōkeisho, *Manshū teikoku genjū kokō tōkei* (Shinkyō: Kokumuin sōmuchō, 1936), 1–10; South Manchuria Railway, *Report on Progress to 1936* (Tokyo: Herald Press, 1936), 51; South Manchuria Railway, *Report on Progress to 1939* (Tokyo: Herald Press, 1939), 146; *Manshū teikoku genjū kokō tōkei* (Shinkyō: Chianbu keimushi, 1939), 8–11; *Manshū teikoku genjū jinkō tōkei: Kōtoku shichinen jūgatsu tsuitachi genzai* (Shinkyō: Kokumuin sōmuchō tōkeisho, Kokumuin chianbu keimushi, 1942), 10–11.

half the minimum monthly budgets of Japanese, and Koreans lived on a third less than Chinese.[18] As in the Chinese population, Japanese men outnumbered women, more so in periods of tension. Visiting in the spring of 1928, for example, the poet and author Yosano Akiko commented on the scarcity of Japanese women, reporting that Mantetsu had evacuated "all Japanese women residents."[19]

Xinjing grew rapidly after the Manchurian Incident. A Chinese publication stated that there were 600,000 residents in 1942, and a postwar American estimate of the 1943 population was 750,000.[20] In 1933, a projection of annual growth of 30,000 people underestimated the reality, for the most part (Table 4.3).[21] In exceeding this figure, Xinjing reflected the trend of regional urbanization. More than 10 percent of Manchukuo's population was urban by 1940, with Xinjing accounting for 12 percent of the urban and 1.3 percent of the entire population, despite ranking eleventh in density.[22] Only 2.1 percent of Manchukuo's 1940 population, Japanese accounted for 12.7 percent of all urban population in the region. Similar to rates in Taiwan (65.6 percent) and Korea (56.5 percent), 65.3 percent of Japanese lived in cities.[23] Japan itself was increasingly urban – by 1940, almost a third of that country's population lived in cities of more than 100,000.[24] Xinjing's 1940 population made it the tenth largest city in Japan's empire.[25] It was also one of the most Japanese cities overseas, with Japanese constituting 23.4 percent of the population, up from 8.3 percent in 1931. Shenyang's Japanese were about as numerous (110,000) but constituted only 11 percent of that city's population, and the

Table 4.4
Japanese civilians in Manchuria, 1906–40

Year	Guandong Peninsula	Railway towns	Elsewhere	Total
1906	12,792	3,821	–	16,613
1910	36,668	25,266	14,407	76,341
1915	50,176	34,396	16,993	101,565
1920	73,894	61,576	24,590	160,060
1925	90,542	83,620	13,826	187,988
1930	116,052	99,411	18,368	233,749
1935	159,749	190,508	144,451	494,708
1940	202,827	–	862,245	1,065,072

Source: Manshikai, ed., *Manshū kaihastu yonjūnenshi,* vol. 1 (Tokyo: Manshū kaihatsu yonjūnenshi kankōkai, 1964), 84.

167,000 in rapidly industrializing Seoul constituted 15 percent in 1942, down from 28 percent (113,000) in 1935.[26] Fewer Japanese resided in Taibei (Taipei) in 1940, but they constituted 28 percent of the population of that city (91,550 of 326,407).[27] As for Dalian, Japan's pre-eminent Manchurian city since 1905, Japanese continued to reside there in greater numbers, but its growing Chinese workforce meant that, by 1942, Japanese lived in about the same concentration as in Xinjing.[28]

Tables 4.1 and 4.2 indicate that few Koreans settled in urban Manchuria initially, but over the 1920s they became Changchun's third-largest group. Their numbers grew more quickly after 1931, as more than 200,000 Koreans immigrated to Manchukuo over the ensuing four years, with the government hoping to attract another million.[29] By 1940, Koreans accounted for 3.2 percent of Manchukuo's population, a higher proportion than the Japanese (1.99 percent).[30] A 1943 plan aimed for 50,000 Koreans to immigrate every year for five years, and perhaps 2 million Koreans were in Manchukuo by 1945.[31] In 1936, ManSen (SenMan) Takushoku was established to support Korean immigration to Manchukuo; in 1941, its offices sat on Xingren Dalu, just three blocks east of the new palace site.[32] Indicating growing job opportunities (Table 4.5) – though still relatively few – the number of Koreans in Xinjing in 1940 was more than eight times the number present in the area in 1931.

Manchukuo's Pan-Asianism gave reason for other Asians to reside in Xinjing.[33] At the end of 1939, the capital was home to 405 Mongolians and

Table 4.5
Occupational distribution of the population of Xinjing by ethnicity, 1940 (percent)

	Chinese	Japanese	Korean	Others	Total
Agriculture, forestry, and husbandry	18.4	0.5	9.1	0.4	14.1
Fishing	0.04	0.06	0.0	0.0	0.04
Mining	0.2	2.1	0.6	0.0	0.64
Industry	24.1	13.5	19.8	6.2	21.6
Commerce	21.3	20.6	16.0	27.1	21.0
Transportation	3.4	6.8	7.0	3.9	4.3
Civil service and professional	16.0	35.8	27.3	32.0	20.7
Household service	4.3	6.8	6.0	4.2	4.9
Other	12.3	13.8	14.1	26.2	12.7

Source: Manshū teikoku genju jinkō tōkei (Shinkyō: Manshū teikoku chianbu keimushi, 1940), 4, 10–11.

4,958 Muslims.[34] Most Mongolians in Manchukuo lived in the west, where Japanese appealed to them by halting further Chinese encroachment.[35] A Danish anthropologist seeking to enter that region thought Xinjing's Bureau of Mongolian Affairs "impressive," reporting also "friendly helpfulness and understanding ... on all sides." He thought the Mongolians he encountered in the west benefited from Japanese rule, noting that "the advent of the Japanese meant the salvation of the Mongols from complete annihilation." Of course, he was likely accompanied by Japanese minders when he wrote these words.[36] Muslims had also long resided in Changchun. A mosque outside the town's North Gate "with a three-storied pagoda as a minaret" dated from 1861. Painted on its door in the 1880s was a 1694 decree by the Kangxi Emperor proclaiming Islam's toleration. In 1934, the mosque reportedly served seven thousand and had an attached school.[37] Construction in Xinjing required the transfer of a Muslim cemetery to outside Chinese Changchun's West Gate. The Capital Construction Bureau summoned a converted Muslim, Kawamura Kyōdō, to see to the details, ultimately organizing compensation, commemorative markers, and links to the local community that contributed to organizing Muslims across Manchukuo.[38] Other groups, such as Manchus, were present in smaller numbers, although statistics often do not list them – presumably including them with Chinese as "Manchurians." Only eleven or twelve Chinese from Taiwan lived in Changchun in 1926, but more arrived after closer sea links between Manchuria, Taiwan, and south China were established that year.[39] In 1940, 342 Taiwanese (233 males, 109 females) lived in Xinjing.[40] Twenty-nine Taiwanese eventually graduated from Datong Academy (discussed below), finding administrative positions in Manchukuo, though some had also studied in Japan.[41]

Europeans and North Americans

Europeans and Americans were few in the area. In 1900, Kuanchengzi was home to a Russian railway engineer, a bank representative, a doctor, a military officer, and soldiers – a traveller encountered a small detachment of Cossacks on the highway five or six kilometres south of the old town.[42] Few remained after 1905, although Russian consulates opened in Kuanchengzi and other southern Manchurian towns in 1907.[43] Twenty years later, Kuanchengzi was home to 900 Russians and 1,600 Chinese. At that time, most of the 504 foreigners in the Changchun railway town were also Russian, primarily labourers, restaurateurs, and general goods merchants.[44] Perhaps as many as half of these were actually Ukrainian, something Japanese did not widely recognize until 1934. Ukrainians were initially associated with the China Eastern Railway (CER) and its derivatives, but some established independent workshops or became farmers along the railway.[45] Foreigners were also guests at the region's hotels, although their numbers varied. Figures for guests at Changchun's Yamato Hotel, for example, give a sense for its evolving clientele. In 1917, 16 percent of the guests were Japanese, 18 percent Chinese, and 66 percent foreign. This shifted in 1926 to 57 percent Japanese, 19 percent Chinese, and 24 percent foreign.[46]

Arriving in the region before the Russians were Christian missionaries, although the earliest did not linger. The first vicar apostolic of the Archdiocese of Manchuria (established 1838), Emmanuel Verroles of the Société des missions étrangères de Paris, founded a woman's order with a school at Xiaobajiazi, about thirty-five kilometres northwest of Changchun, in 1868.[47] Irish Presbyterians began visiting in 1875, opening a Changchun mission in 1886, having taken charge of all Protestant activities north and west of the Liao River in 1869. As of 1886, the Changchun mission – "a humble mud house" – was the most northerly Protestant mission in Manchuria.[48] A Chinese priest founded Changchun's first Catholic church in 1897, under the supervision of a Belgian priest who soon joined him, adding a hospital and schools for girls and boys by 1900.[49] Danish Lutherans arrived thereafter, as did Franciscan sisters in 1910 – gaining access to Changchun's prison in

1923 – and Seventh-Day Adventists in 1916. These missions were more active in Chinese Changchun than in the railway town, opening smaller missions in the surrounding countryside.[50] All reported success, the Presbyterian community numbering 392 in 1900 and 1,590 in 1920.[51] Roman Catholics reported 116 converts in 1904 and 746 in 1913.[52] Work was occasionally dangerous, as missionaries were subject to attacks by Chinese troops and bandits, and all fled during the Boxer insurgency. There were occasional confrontations with Japanese too. Before the Manchurian Incident, the worst occurred in 1918, when Japanese railway guards in Changchun beat an Irish missionary named Florence Crawford for trespassing. The Japanese government recalled the battalion commander, donated ten thousand gold yen to the local mission, and offered an apology, which the British government accepted.[53]

The Manchurian Incident precipitated a shift in the non-Asian foreign population of the region. On the eve of the incident, 2,850 Russians resided in Changchun. However, the city had only 52 other European and American residents – fewer than in Harbin, Shenyang, Qiqihar, Manzhouli, Yingkou, or Andong.[54] By the end of 1939, though, that figure had increased to 971, and Xinjing accounted for the bulk of Americans and other Europeans (that is, other than Russians or Poles) in the puppet state.[55] This number rose to 1,063 in 1940, with most engaged in commerce or in consular or missionary work (Table 4.5).[56] Notably, this demographic group was the only one in the city with more women than men, a reflection of the number of women involved in missionary work and the relative success of missionaries in Manchukuo.[57]

The Manchurian Incident may also have had an impact on missionary work: Catholics reported more baptisms than usual the following year, perhaps a reflection of Chinese seeking security under a foreign church.[58] Manchukuo officials encouraged missions to remain, and the puppet state's recognition of mission school diplomas increased enrolments.[59] The construction of Xinjing even provided opportunities to expand. Catholic missionaries completed a Gothic-style cathedral, Sainte Thérèse de l'Enfant-Jésus, in 1932 on the east side of the old mercantile district a kilometre southwest of the mosque and a kilometre southeast of the Protestant church built after the turn of the century. One of the two vicars was Korean, and his main task was to serve the local Korean community. Catholics built churches in the new part of the city for Japanese – one being the Changping Church west of the new palace site – and another south of the old town for Chinese and a large new school for the regime's elite.[60] The Augustinian Fathers of the Assumption, supported by the Société des missions étrangères de Paris, completed a seminary in 1940.[61]

Although missionaries were often not overly concerned by Japan's 1931 takeover, attitudes shifted as Japanese sought to augment their authority.[62] Railway discounts previously granted missionaries were reduced in the late 1930s and terminated in 1941.[63] Missionaries eventually needed police permits to travel, and often were unable to obtain them.[64] Japanese officials began intimidating missionaries and coercing Chinese into disassociating from them.[65] Japanese censored correspondence, making it unsafe to communicate criticisms of the regime.[66] Nor were missionaries the only foreigners treated roughly. A British diplomat noted during a visit in 1934–35 that "most of the Japanese officials and soldiers in Manchukuo adopt an overbearing attitude towards foreigners, certainly towards British and Americans, in great contrast to the uniform courtesy shown in Japan itself."[67] In 1941, American consular officials reported various issues, including the detention of three American missionaries, requiring negotiation with Xinjing authorities; "police interference with the Consulate" in Dalian; Americans encountering difficulties leaving Manchukuo with cash and personal effects; and even Japanese postal employees' "tampering" with official mail in Tokyo. Consular officials were advised to present themselves to the Japanese embassy in Xinjing with an itemization of their household effects.[68] Japanese eventually sought to reorganize religious bodies by purging them of foreign leaders and funding and training Chinese leaders in Japan.[69] Later they required popular worship at Shinto shrines across the empire, sanctifying what until then had been considered a civil act.[70] Missionaries sought to accommodate themselves but eventually agreed to close schools after 1942, sell property, and leave. Those who did not were interned soon after 8 December 1941 and sent to Japan in June 1942 to await repatriation. Some left the following spring, but others interned with missionaries based in Japan did not leave until after the war.[71] Approximately forty-six Protestant missionaries, among other Europeans and North Americans, were on the outskirts of Nagasaki in August 1945, including five from Manchuria.[72]

Railway Outpost

Many of the first Japanese to reside in Changchun for any duration were prostitutes: in 1902, prostitutes arriving via Vladivostok composed more than half of the forty-three Japanese in the town.[73] These were *karayuki,* women "going to China" to earn a living, though some ventured as far as Russia, in response to the Russian government's authorization of brothels in colonizing Siberia. *Karayuki* were often the largest contingent in overseas Japanese communities, something Japanese Foreign Ministry officials, growing concerned for Japan's reputation, strived to correct after 1897.[74] *Karayuki* in Manchuria left with war's outbreak in 1904, but with peace returned in the thousands, reinforced with new recruits. Some 360 Japanese resided in the Changchun area at the end of 1906, before any Japanese construction.[75] Of the 314 identified who can be identified, 202 were *shakufu* (barmaids), many of whom were prostitutes.[76] Licensed prostitution remained legal in the pre-war Japanese empire, albeit with age restrictions and mandatory medical examinations. Perhaps as a result of such regulation, statistics reported in 1926 that Japanese soldiers suffered lower rates of venereal disease than sailors, lower even than a global average.[77] Private efforts to end the trade beginning in 1880 were unsuccessful, but in the 1930s some women were retrained for other professions, such as housemaids for Japanese in Manchuria. Yet others in Manchuria celebrated brothels: a newspaper write-in poll in the winter of 1910–11 produced a list of Manchuria's top ten, including Changchun's Yachiyokan.[78]

Changchun's social composition shifted quickly as soldiers departed and the railway arrived. Of the 1,086 Japanese fully employed in February 1908, the largest group remained barmaids (143) – plus another 42 female entertainers – followed by those working in the town's 39 restaurants (70 men, 63 women). The next largest categories included those employed in the town's thirty general stores (89) and carpentry firms (44).[79] By the spring, the number of Japanese had grown to 1,218, of whom almost half (541) were from Kyushu. Of the 493 women, 249 were from Kyushu, 163 of these from Kumamoto and Nagasaki prefectures, which were the origin of most *karayuki*.[80] By June, only 31 barmaids remained, and the largest groups were Mantetsu employees (133), carpenters (102), railway porters (62), and civil engineers (55). In comparison, most Chinese employed in the town were labourers (331 of 658), followed by workers in inns (68) and restaurants (47) and on the railway (40).[81] Many were seasonal workers, as their numbers dropped from 1,344 in October 1907 to 343 in December.[82]

Over time, Japanese society in the town diversified, some developing new niches (Table 4.6). Shimotoku Naosuke, for example, opened a currency exchange and small-goods store in Changchun station in 1907. He soldiered on despite being robbed two years later. Having learned Chinese and served

Table 4.6
Japanese employment in Changchun, June 1926

		(%)			(%)
Mantetsu employees	525	23	Restaurant and bar workers	178	8
Merchants and shopkeepers	416	18	Post office, telegraph, and telephone workers	120	5
Bank employees	335	15			
Students	292	13	Construction and engineering workers	109	5
Government officials	279	12			

Note: There were 2,803 men but only 518 women employed in the railway town. Including the 321 Japanese outside the railway town, the total Japanese population in the Changchun area was 9,432.
Source: "Fuzokuchi no hōnin kyūsen yomyō," *Manshū nichi nichi shinbun*, 25 August 1926, 4.

as an army interpreter, Wato Ryōkichi opened a store on Changchun's East Diagonal Boulevard selling electrical and construction supplies, later opening branches across Manchuria, including Harbin.[83] Some became long-term residents – 288 Japanese in Changchun in 1926 had been there twenty years.[84] Rapid population growth, however, meant that Japanese, like Chinese, were more often sojourners. In 1920, more than 60 percent had been in Manchuria less than five years; in 1930, the figure was still around 45 percent.[85] Some maintained household registration (*koseki*) in Japan.[86] Before 1931, most Japanese in Changchun were from western Japan, though relatively impoverished Nagano was also well represented.[87] Many sent remittances home – more than ¥20 million from all Manchuria in 1925.[88]

Although economic reasons for Japanese coming to Changchun are evident, migration patterns suggest other motivations as well. Chinese immigration responded to conflict, declining in 1932 and 1937 but peaking in 1927–28 and 1939–40.[89] Japanese immigration spiked following the Russo-Japanese War and the Manchurian Incident, suggesting immigration expanded with newly won opportunities. Given that some theorists downplay simple economic rationales and emphasize historical and social contexts, it is reasonable to conclude that Japanese came to Manchuria not simply with economic aims.[90] Although Yanagisawa Asobu notes that many Japanese aimed to get rich quick in Manchuria, he is sensitive to incentives influencing migration in addition to the financial.[91] Some Japanese reinvented themselves in Manchuria, such as former Bank of Taiwan president Shimada Shigeru, who took the helm of Manshū Seikatsu Hitsujuhin (Manchuria Daily Necessities), with offices on Datong Dajie, after being cleared of corruption charges in

1937 after the thirty-month Teijin trial.[92] Economic motives inevitably met reality. Tsukase Susumu notes three groups: military and Mantetsu administrators; merchants and traders; and shopkeepers and tradesmen catering to other Japanese. Unable to compete with Chinese over wages, unskilled Japanese were few. Japanese merchants and shopkeepers faced Chinese boycotts and competition and sometimes European and American imports, although European or American merchants were few in Manchuria and there were none in the Changchun area other than some Russians.[93] Merchants' and shopkeepers' motives in immigrating, moreover, cannot be simply construed as following the flag. Although their position in the war years grew precarious even in Japan, Earl Kinmonth found "little ... enthusiasm" for Manchukuo or militarism among small business owners.[94]

Encouraged by Foreign Ministry officials, Japanese society in Changchun was organized. Military supervision of the Changchun concession shifted to the Shenyang consul-general in 1906, and a Changchun consulate opened in 1907 under Shibata Yōjirō. The consulate in turn helped establish a Changchun Local Residents' Association as a private corporation in June 1908. Resident associations were common in overseas communities, providing a kind of local self-government. With the consulate providing advice, Changchun residents determined twelve councillors and paid dues. One early association budget indicates that a third went to office expenses, a third to medical (including an isolation unit in response to a plague outbreak), 15 percent to sanitation, 6 percent to education, and 4 percent to local relief efforts. Employers collected dues from transitory workers like geisha, *maiko* (apprentice geisha), and barmaids.[95] This system continued after Manchukuo's establishment, presumably with decreasing consular involvement. Contributions to local expenses continued – in 1935, more than half of the Xinjing Residents' Association's dues went to health and sanitation, a little more than a third to the care of children, and a little less than a fifth to office expenses.[96]

Nishizawa points to the significance of public infrastructure, paid for in part by residents' associations, as helping establish a Japanese presence and making colonial life more pleasant. Libraries located near Mantetsu offices, for example, were intended to support Mantetsu personnel, but in Changchun's case they were open to residents too.[97] Mantetsu worked with consuls and residents' associations to manage Changchun, a shared means of governance found in all Mantetsu towns. Sharing residents' concerns for health, Mantetsu built modern facilities. Changchun's first Japanese clinic, established in 1907, was a branch of Mantetsu's Dalian hospital. Located southwest of East Plaza, it became Changchun Hospital in 1912 with its own branch clinic in Chinese Changchun in 1910. A missionary called the hospital "splendid."[98] In 1932, it became Xinjing Hospital, despite continuing references to it as the "Mantetsu Hospital."[99] Japanese were not alone in introducing modern medicine. By 1922, there were ten private Chinese clinics, French and "English" (likely Irish Presbyterian) missionary clinics in old Changchun, and a Soviet clinic in the mercantile district outside the North Gate, all vying for Chinese patients.[100]

Education was also a priority. Supported by donations, Mantetsu built an elementary school in 1908 east of the central boulevard on the town's southern side, a year before Shenyang's.[101] Before that school opened, a temporary elementary school housed inside the consulate began in April, with fees paid by the residents' association.[102] A kindergarten followed in 1911, a Chinese public school in 1912, and a Japanese girls' school in 1913.[103] Supplementing these were a girls' high school that opened in 1923, another Japanese elementary school in 1925, and a junior high and a high school adjacent to the first elementary school.[104] A business school began in 1910 in the Mantetsu offices; by 1916, it offered courses in Japanese, Chinese, English, Russian, mathematics, engineering, architecture, machinery, geography, and history.[105] This became the Changchun Commercial School in 1920, offering instruction in the English, Russian, Chinese, and Mongolian languages.[106] Supporting these educational institutions was the Mantetsu-built library (1910) across from the Shinto shine, rebuilt in 1931 and renamed the Xinjing Municipal Library in 1933.[107] With local bookstores on the commercial streets of Yoshinomachi and Nihonbashi Dōri, the library sponsored a November 1926 "reading day" (*tokusho dē*) in Changchun.[108]

Religious institutions, many including schools, were also present. Mantetsu built Changchun's Shinto shrine in 1912. In 1916, this was one of sixteen in Manchuria and one of twenty-nine Japanese Shinto shrines overseas.[109] A school attached to it opened in 1916. There were also four schools attached to Buddhist temples – which opened in 1908, 1915, and two in 1916 – and two more Christian schools built in 1916 and 1921.[110] Serving Japanese constituencies, Buddhist establishments included sects belonging to Honpa (Nishi) Honganji (1908), Sōtō Zen (1913), Ōtani (Higashi) Honganji (1915), Shingon (1916), Nichiren (1917), and Pure Land (1919). Joining these were the so-called "new religions" – Tenrikyō (1909, 1929), Tensokyō (1912), the Shinto sect Konkōkyō (1918) – and Japanese Christian establishments (1916,

1921, 1931). A prominent Japanese Christian church was on Chūō Dōri a block south of the Mantetsu offices.[111]

Changchun's growing Korean community followed a similar pattern. The Changchun Korean Residents' Association, founded in 1919, jointly ran a school with Mantetsu that opened near the first Japanese school in 1922, and a night school opened for Koreans in 1933 in Nanling.[112] Acknowledging local Koreans, a small memorial at the Shinto shrine honoured Emperor Sunjong on his passing.[113] By contrast, Chinese society was more on its own. The Qing and later the Zhang regime encouraged the growth of Chinese schools but, out of necessity, left their development to local governments and communities. Recognizing the importance of education and enabled by growing incomes, many Chinese contributed, even in rural areas, inspired by foreign models and a mounting sense of nationalism.[114] In 1922, the old city and the mercantile district offered the Chinese population nine elementary schools, a provincial middle school, two girls' schools, a teachers' school, and by 1929 a "self-strengthening" (*ziqiang*) school.[115]

The presence of modern schools underscores a key characteristic of Japanese colonial society – it was literate. Moreover, a common education helped shape popular views. While Mantetsu's education system nurtured patriotism, it may not have turned militaristic until after the Manchurian Incident.[116] Any such views would likely have been reinforced by Japanese-language publications affirming community identification and perceived differences with Chinese.[117] The major Japanese newspaper in Manchuria was Mantetsu's *Manshū nichi nichi shinbun* (*Manchuria Daily News* [*MNNS*]), which included local reports from each of the major railway towns, identifying issues journalists thought – or were asked to think – were newsworthy. Although newspapers cannot indicate what readers thought, they do identify some of the contours of public discourse. A focus on the years 1906–8 and 1926 along with other contemporary reports provides insight into issues present at the town's outset and in the era prior to the Manchurian Incident. The built environment, for example, was a common topic. Articles on new construction advertised the town's modernity, as did those on the town's progress, some featuring Changchun.[118] The paper also covered major projects elsewhere in the region, such as the new Yalu River Bridge or Dalian's sleek, new train station (1937), the latter resembling Tokyo's Ueno Station.[119] A variety of publications billed the Shuifeng Dam on the Yalu as the world's largest upon its completion in 1942.[120] The *MNNS* also reported concern for increasing third-class flophouses for less affluent – presumably not Japanese – workers.[121]

The *MNNS* often reported on local sports. West Park's baseball diamond opened in 1923, used by a recreational league and a town team formed in 1926 with jerseys bearing the letter "C."[122] The latter played against the two teams in the Manchurian professional league founded in Dalian in 1927 – one representing Mantetsu (Mantetsu Kurabu or Manku) and the other representing other companies – as well as visiting teams, such as one sponsored by the Korean railway.[123] Japanese later added a Manchuria-wide league with teams from the major railway towns. One-time Osaka Tigers star pitcher Nishimura Yukio, whose wife was of Japanese ancestry from Hawaii, later played for Xinjing's Manchuria Telegraph and Telephone team, Shinkyō Denden.[124] More than a pastime, baseball helped link Manchurian towns with the imperial homeland.

In addition to baseball, West Park offered a four-hundred-metre track near the baseball diamond along the more elevated north edge of the park.[125] Changchun held its first track meet there in October 1926, including a ten-kilometre race looping through Kuanchengzi and the railway town from West Park. An elementary school and the girls' high school apparently also held regular meets.[126] Other sports demanded less space. Changchun's Mantetsu-built judo hall held its second city tournament in 1926.[127] The *MNNS* frequently reported *sumō* meets in railway towns.[128] Military units organized fencing (*kendō*) and other martial competitions.[129] The tennis star Ōta Yoshiro visited in the fall of 1926.[130] University teams from Japan competed across Manchuria in diverse sports. Outdoor activities like hiking and hunting took place in the city's outskirts, sometimes as activities of school clubs.[131] In addition to ping-pong and billiards competitions in Changchun, there were also archery, marksmanship, and fencing events across Manchuria.[132] Some took to auto racing.[133] The Changchun swimming pool opened in 1926.[134] West Park offered fishing and boating in summer, skating in winter.[135] These activities were less reported than baseball, but they too helped integrate Manchurian towns with the imperial homeland by promoting a shared culture of recreation and leisure.

The *MNNS* covered diverse social events, typically of local import but sometimes of national significance. A prominent social fixture was the Mantetsu Employees' Club, fronting West Plaza.[136] Built in 1912 near the Mantetsu offices, it boasted over a thousand members by 1933. In addition to relaxation and parties, it hosted visiting dignitaries, though others visited soon after Changchun's opening. For example, Mantetsu's first president Gotō Shinpei and Andō Sadayoshi, commander of the 10th Division of the

Imperial Japanese Army (IJA), which played an important role in the Russo-Japanese War, visited in 1908.[137] Although Prince Kan'in ventured only as far north as Shenyang when he toured Manchuria in 1926, former prime minister Kiyoura Keigo visited Changchun that year and, like most VIPs, stayed in the Yamato Hotel. After touring Manchuria, Kiyoura met with Puyi in Tianjin.[138] Even less prominent visitors were mentioned in the press, such as a Lt. Colonel Suzuki and Captain Kurosawa stopping en route to Harbin.[139] The *MNNS* also announced Mantetsu personnel changes and farewell parties,[140] as well as Mantetsu-organized celebrations such as on the town's first birthday on the central plaza in front of the station.[141] Some announcements were for private functions, such as for women's groups or to learn Chinese.[142] The paper noted shopkeepers' and professional trade associations, including a Manchurian medical association.[143] Coverage of song and handicrafts competitions brought Changchun Japanese in touch with others in Manchuria.[144] The *MNNS* even reported on people relaxing in the evenings in the small gardens at West Park and near the Yamato Hotel and on organized dances at the hotel.[145]

Unsurprisingly, some activities reported in the *MNNS* involved the military, including Army and Navy Day celebrations. Changchun's army reserve unit emerged in 1911, and a youth brigade in 1927.[146] Across Manchuria, reservists numbered twenty thousand in 1926.[147] The Boy Scouts of Japan, founded in 1922, soon came to the colonies. Gotō Shinpei was its first president, and Seki Hajime supported its growth in Osaka – both men left their marks on Changchun's built environment. Manchuria was home to at least five scout troops at the time of the Manchurian Incident, and some mobilized in support of the Kantōgun. Contacted by local military headquarters, the Changchun troop mustered to transport bullets and provisions, care for the injured, and serve as couriers. In the wake of the incident a new group, called the Manchurian Little Boys' Troop, was organized for non-Japanese. Puyi served as its president and the troop visited Japan.[148]

Another link with Japan was provided through entertainment, such as Mantetsu's Chōshunza (1920) theatre, located one block northwest of East Plaza. The modern dancer Ishii Baku performed there in February 1926.[149] Changchun's first Western music concert was held in April, and the haiku master Iwaya Sazanami visited in July.[150] Two public halls southeast of the Yamato Hotel also served the railway town, completed in 1922 and 1925.[151] The first was the Changchun (later Xinjing) Memorial Hall, honouring the tenth year of the Taishō Emperor, which offered facilities for chess, billiards, and lectures as well as a cafeteria.[152] The silent German film *The Light of Asia* (1925) about the life of the Buddha, discussed several times in the *MNNS*, played two days at the Memorial Hall in July 1926, sparking interest in a foreign film society, and Charlie Chaplin's *The Gold Rush* (1925) played there in the fall.[153] Recognizing the popularity of film, Mantetsu announced the production of a documentary history of Manchuria and Mongolia from ancient times to the present.[154]

Changchun's retail districts advertised in the *MNNS*. The railway town's main shopping and entertaining street was initially East Diagonal Boulevard, later called Nihonbashi Dōri, but Yoshinomachi quickly became popular and another commercial area – Damalu – emerged between the Japanese and Chinese towns. Nine of the fifteen restaurants listed in a 1908 *MNNS* advertisement were listed as "outside the North Gate." Four were in the railway town and one in old Changchun. That same page also noted two foreign goods store, a liquor store, a timepiece store, and a hotel outside the North Gate.[155] Many shops listed telephone numbers in the *MNNS*.[156] Japanese in Changchun initially found Chinese goods most commonly available, along with Russian alcohol and cigarettes.[157] Japanese goods gradually became accessible, including clothing, pharmaceuticals, toiletries, and housewares current in Japan. The Kintai Yōkō department store anchored Yoshinomachi at Nihonbashi Dōri, and to the west could be found restaurants, groceries, clothing, housewares, barbers, and more. The shops on Nihonbashi Dōri northwest of South Plaza were mostly Japanese, but around a third were Chinese and 10 percent were Russian.[158] One advertisement showed three outlets in Changchun in 1927 that sold the Nipponophone record player – made by Nihon Chikuonki Shōkai, founded in 1910 – just below an advertisement for a Japanese translation of H.G. Wells' *The Outline of History* (1920).[159] The *MNNS* also noted that retailers raised funds to renovate Yoshinomachi in 1926 and organized display window competitions.[160]

Media like the *MNNS* helped define Japanese identity as modern and imperial. It did so also through discussions of Japan's place in the world and the publication of historical fiction like *Sengoku mitsudan* (*Secret Tales of the Warring States Period*), a long-running series in 1926. The paper also reported on local events that were likely to reinforce the link with Japan. For example, it covered the raising of a stele in West Park honouring Japanese civil servants killed in the line of duty in or near Changchun.[161] The paper's reporting on holidays and other events would have reinforced connections to Japan. For example, the *MNNS* noted events at Changchun Shrine that marked Empire Day and other imperial holidays.[162] (The imperial birthday was celebrated in Changchun soon after its 1907 founding.[163]) Other events reflected municipal rhythms similar to those in Japan: school began in April and carp streamers flew in May; graduations occurred in late February or March, and local dignitaries attended ceremonies at postsecondary institutions. The *MNNS* reported, for example, that a Mantetsu president attended the spring 1926 Changchun Commercial School graduation of its second class, which included fourteen men from the Chinese language department, five from the Russian, and twelve from the English.[164] The newspaper noted that a youth group had been established on the Taishō Emperor's birthday in 1919, though it disbanded the same day in 1926 in the Mantetsu Club.[165] In 1926, the shrine observed the Meiji Emperor's birthday, and beginning in November the shrine held services praying for the recovery of the Taishō Emperor, and in December for his passing.[166]

In discussing these kinds of issues and events, the *MNNS* conveyed not only a sense of pride and empire, but also a sense of normalcy, portraying Japanese society in Changchun as much like Japanese communities elsewhere. Despite the colony's distance from Tokyo, the content of the *MNNS* suggests that Changchun Japanese could even aspire to middle-class lifestyles and that conditions were perhaps not as dire as some anecdotal sources suggested. (One observer opined in 1929 that "the only solace for employees at [Railway] Zone stations is mahjong."[167]) Changchun's location meant inevitable delays in communications, of course, but the *MNNS* reinforced the normalcy of Japanese living and working there – and that is how most Japanese perceived their presence in places like Changchun. Yet the newspaper also provided information that was a cause for concern among Changchun Japanese. Some issues, like the weather, were inescapable. Summer rains collapsed buildings, closed the rail line temporarily, or fell by as much as an inch at a time.[168] Summer heat could be intense.[169] Snowfall could be more than in much of Japan, including a blizzard in 1926.[170] Winter and spring brought blinding yellow dust borne upon Mongolian winds.[171] Less predictable were the fires reported in the paper. A November 1926 fire in Chinese Changchun killed one, having begun in a second-floor *ondul*, and a larger fire the following January affected twenty-seven buildings and seventy-seven households.[172] The railway town also suffered, as a fire broke out in a flophouse in November 1926.[173] That year, the paper reported that the Changchun railway town ranked fifth in the number of fires reported by Mantetsu (25 of the 314, or 8 percent) and fourth in damage (¥92,115 out of ¥764,244, or 12 percent).[174] All Mantetsu towns had fire crews – established in 1918, Changchun's included a pump truck (*sokutō jidōsha*), three Japanese and twenty Chinese firefighters, with another twenty-three available from Changchun station.[175]

Threats from fire were accompanied by sometimes dire health threats, which enabled Japanese officials to put medical technology to use and expanded their authority, much as they did in Tianjin.[176] In the winter of 1910–11, pneumonic plague killed 60,000 across Manchuria, 6,000 in Changchun alone, where a newspaper reported "one hundred deaths daily." Changchun's death toll was the second highest in Manchuria, in part due to the lack of a central authority coordinating local responses.[177] A 1920 plague from China killed 27,288 throughout Manchuria, some 3,000 in the various railway towns. Changchun's quarantine office, capable of handling 2,000, was instrumental in its containment – only 29 died locally. A third outbreak came from Inner Mongolia in 1927. Some 1,300 contacted the plague in the Changchun area by 1930, though only 378 died.[178] The capital confronted another outbreak in fall 1940, with 28 victims south of East Plaza in the former railway town.[179]

Cholera was another contagious threat.[180] A summer 1926 outbreak in Shanghai led to international cooperation and compulsory examinations as far away as Changchun, where some Chinese workers were accused of not providing stool samples.[181] The threat returned in October, though not in Changchun.[182] Japanese, and others, in the region also suffered from typhus, scarlet fever, smallpox, and dysentery, the latter an issue especially during the spring thaw. Its incidence in Changchun was four times the norm on the eve of the Manchurian Incident.[183] Lung disease was mounting in the Liaodong Peninsula and all the railway towns, with higher rates among Japanese than Chinese, especially women.[184] The most common issue at Changchun's Mantetsu hospital in 1926 was venereal disease (311), double the next largest groups – eye disease (173) and nose and throat problems (141).[185]

Changchun health officials acted proactively. In addition to having water and sewage systems as well as one of Mantetsu's fifteen hospitals, the railway town possessed one of Mantetsu's five bacteriological laboratories, and travelling clinics served the railway zone at large.[186] Vaccinations of Japanese and Chinese began in 1909, expanding outside the town in 1917.[187] Mantetsu also provided flu shots.[188] Policing the built environment, officials inspected carts and contracted out for garbage and sewage removal beginning in 1907, taking over direct management in 1911. In 1912, the railway town offered two public

Table 4.7
Death rates from infectious diseases among Japanese in Manchuria and Japan (per 10,000), 1925–30

	Manchuria	Japan
Tuberculosis	20.1	19.1
Pneumonia	36.6	29.0
Scarlet fever	2.9	0.04
Measles	2.6	1.9
Diptheria	1.0	0.7

Source: Miura Un'ichi, *Hokenjō kara mita Manshū no jūtaku* (Dairen: Manshū bunka kyōkai, 1935), 6, 7.

restrooms, increasing the number to five in 1916.[189] Water quality inspections began in 1907, and officials sprinkled water on streets to help prevent contagion.[190] Japanese culled wild dogs within the railway town in 1926.[191] Officials could also mobilize the citizenry, such as during a July "fly catching week."[192] Proactive health policies also included education. Medical exams for hospitality industry workers included nutritional and other advice.[193] Visiting specialists discussed hygiene in public lectures, sometimes with reference to Europe and the United States.[194] Noting that Japanese in Manchuria suffered from tuberculosis, dysentery, typhoid fever, and other illnesses, Miura Un'ichi of the Manchuria Medical College, among others, urged adequate lighting, ventilation, insulation, and sanitation. He feared that local statistics for tuberculosis were underreported, as many who contracted it returned to Japan to die. He also noted higher death rates for Japanese in Manchuria for other diseases (Table 4.7).[195] Xinjing later promoted discussions of mass hygiene (*shū eisei*), hosting a "health week" in June 1937 with public lectures.[196]

Changchun Japanese could take measures to address weather, fire, and contagions, but some concerns, such as international issues and developments, were beyond their reach. Given their prominence in the *MNNS*, however, these issues were surely deliberated locally. In addition to covering Chinese and foreign dignitaries passing through Changchun, the paper reported on rival American interests in Manchuria.[197] More immediate was the Soviet peril. Against the backdrop of Japan's withdrawal from Siberia, negotiations over the stillborn Far Eastern Republic took place in Changchun in September 1922.[198] Thereafter, reports of changes in Soviet society under Communist rule as well as the potential for communism's spread through Soviets managing the CER or among White Russians in Kuanchengzi emerged.[199] One article described anti-religious Soviets with portraits of Lenin living alongside Christian refugees in Kuanchengzi.[200] Others focused on strategic issues, such as Soviet rail encroachment on the Amur and in west China.[201] Still others reported movements of officials such as Soviet ambassador to China Lev Karakhan, who had to pass through Changchun.[202] His 1926 recall prompted concerns for a change in Soviet policy, despite the radical change he initially represented.[203]

Chinese challenges were even more immediate. Chinese railway development, such as that via the new Manchurian port at Huludao, periodically challenged Mantetsu's dominance.[204] Chinese authorities also attempted to challenge treaty rights, taxing Japanese merchants and stationing military police in the Changchun railway town.[205] Violence and the threat of it were also present. A confrontation between Chinese and Japanese troops in 1919, labelled the Changchun (or Kuanchengzi) Incident, resulted in eighteen Japanese killed and seventeen wounded, generating outrage in the press in Japan.[206] This followed a 1916 confrontation at Zhengjiatun, 150 kilometres southwest of Changchun. In 1920, the massacre of several hundred Japanese in Nikolayevsk and attacks on Japanese in Hunchun in eastern Jilin surely cast a larger pall.[207]

The warlord regime of Zhang Zuolin often headlined the news. Despite Japan's aid, many saw the regime as destabilizing, provoking Japanese complaints about high taxes and inflation.[208] Zhang's financial need was driven by his campaigns south of the Great Wall, which were also reported. In this context, warlord troop movements could be intimidating. In 1926, some six thousand Japanese troops drilled near Changchun.[209] A week later, some of Zhang's fifteen divisions conducted manoeuvres nearby.[210] An undisclosed number of troops belonging to Heilongjiang warlord Wu Junsheng, a Zhang ally, passed by two weeks later.[211] Perhaps seeking to calm nerves, the *MNNS* reported the arrival of new Japanese units, such as one group of railway guards who were taller than average.[212] The newspaper reported on Kantōgun commander Shirakawa Yoshinori's discussion of troop strength and air defences in Manchuria and north China in 1926, as the Army Ministry extended its area of concern to north China.[213] The Kantōgun intervened to help end a subordinate of Zhang's rebellion in 1925, and the Nationalists' Northern Expedition, launched in 1926, drove Zhang out of Beijing in 1928. The *MNNS* covered the expedition from its invasion of Hunan, including altercations with foreign imperialists.[214] One article reported anti-imperialist sentiment among Chinese even before the Nanjing Incident.[215] Others asserted communist activity in Shanghai before the city's liberation and that Japanese were confronting a possible Soviet communization of China.[216]

Intriguingly, the *MNNS* reported during the Northern Expedition that the United Kingdom was prepared to evacuate Britons from the Yangzi River and that the British were preparing a thousand marines for action – intervention aimed at presumed Soviet support for the Nationalists. Nor was the British government the only one to consider action against the Northern Expedition, as the newspaper discussed some American contingency plans as well.[217] The *MNNS* also reported on Sun Chuanfang's pursuit of provincial independence for Zhejiang in the face of the Northern Expedition.[218] In hindsight, Japanese military intervention in Manchuria in 1931 may not have seemed extraordinary to Japanese in Changchun. It was perhaps also understandable given contemporary events in Germany and Italy discussed in the *MNNS*, including a positive description of Benito Mussolini.[219]

Underscoring international uncertainty were Japanese perceptions of local Chinese. Chinese shopkeepers spoke publicly against carrying Japanese goods in Changchun as early as 1908.[220] Periodic Chinese boycotts of Japanese businesses affected especially restaurants and prostitutes.[221] Japanese concerns were undoubtedly heightened by suspicions of communism among Chinese, such as the communization of East Asia proclaimed by the warlord Feng Yuxiang in 1926.[222] That year saw communist allegations reported in the *MNNS* against a Chinese normal school and labourers in Changchun.[223] Some saw this inclination toward communism as part of a larger wave of anti-Japanese sentiment.[224] On the eve of the Manchurian Incident, a mob of some three thousand Chinese attacked Japanese shops in Qingdao, injuring or killing some sixty Japanese.[225] The Wanbaoshan affair received much coverage that summer, and some feared violence might spread.[226] The intrusion of Chinese soldiers into the railway town and a strike by Chinese vegetable sellers dissatisfied with Japanese police supervision made many Japanese think it unsafe outside the town's borders.[227] A former Chamber of Commerce secretary referred to the era beginning in 1928 poetically as a period of "raging waves."[228]

Manchuria's inherent lawlessness intensified perceived threats of violence. Initially, mounted bandits posed a more immediate threat to Japanese civilians in Changchun than did Chinese or Russian rivals.[229] Bandits were present from the outset – the diplomat Alexander Hosie reported them to be especially prevalent between Changchun and Jilin when he visited in 1896, his group even fighting off an attack.[230] In 1907, the *Yomiuri* reported one Japanese killed in July and a raid by a dozen Russian bandits on a Chinese shop in November, and the *MNNS* reported bandits elsewhere in Jilin Province that month.[231] Another attack along the road to Jilin City in August 1908 was reported in the *MNNS,* which later observed that, in the summer, the thieves were able to hide easily in the tall sorghum.[232] Russians were targets as well – six Chinese robbed two Russian sisters on their horse cart near Kuanchengzi in 1926.[233] Eventually taking to motorized transport, some of the Chinese bandits voiced anti-Japanese sentiments.[234] Bandit raids continued to cause trouble on the eve of the Manchurian Incident, including near Changchun.[235]

Bandits aroused real concerns among Japanese. Kojima Ken'ichi, a graduate of Changchun's commercial school, recalled as a child being warned by Kantōgun soldiers of an impending bandit raid on a railway town southwest of Changchun in 1921. The next day, he saw many corpses laid out in a park. The train in which he commuted to school in Gongzhuling came briefly under rifle fire, and he found bullet holes in the windows of his train car.[236] Like other Manchurian Japanese, Kojima eventually joined the military – Kojima, a cavalry unit. Drilling just before the Manchurian Incident, his unit was deployed the night of 18 September to Changchun where he witnessed fighting. In the wake of the incident, "bandit" and other attacks multiplied, and Kojima could not remain in contact with family given disruptions in communications.[237] Out of necessity, some of Zhang Xueliang's forces turned to banditry after 1931, but Japanese officials used the term *bandit* to describe all opposing Manchukuo, as well as to justify expansion into Rehe. It is perhaps not surprising that a visiting Osaka council member quipped that, if Korea was commonly imagined as a tiger, then Manchuria would be a "mounted bandit."[238]

Despite the elastic definition of *bandit,* such figures were not the only source of violent crime among the Chinese population. Muggings were frequent, and arrests infrequent.[239] An influx of thieves was reported in 1926.[240] In that year, eight Chinese soldiers assaulted a Japanese man outside old Changchun's East Gate; two Chinese with a pistol robbed another in the railway town; a Chinese man armed with a sword tried breaking into a railway town shop; and two Chinese with a getaway vehicle brazenly stole art valued at ¥1,500 on Nihonbashi Dōri on a summer afternoon.[241] A string of assaults in January 1927 worried residents in the old city.[242] That same year,

Chinese bandits brazenly robbed a bank in the old city and a former Russian bank a week later.[243] Graves too were robbed.[244]

Of course, crimes were not committed only by Chinese. In 1926, the *MNNS* reported the suicide of an embezzler, the arrest of a producer of counterfeit morphine, and a suspicious fire and insurance payout. The chair of the Korean association was arrested for embezzlement.[245] Some crimes were committed against Chinese, such as the case of an unscrupulous Japanese official pressuring Chinese to pay more duties to enter the railway town.[246] None of these, however, were violent crimes.

For protection, railway town Japanese looked to local consuls, who, in addition to their diplomatic duties, held judicial and police powers.[247] Consular police provided a paramilitary arm – six officers joined the consulate in Changchun when it opened in 1906, and a Changchun sub-consulate office opened in Nongan in 1916.[248] Broad consular powers, however, rendered administration confusing: the railway towns were at the same time administered by Mantetsu and protected by the Kantōgun. Echoing a popular perception, Changchun and later Shenyang Chamber of Commerce secretary Nozoe Rishō observed that Manchuria's administration had four heads: Mantetsu, the Foreign Ministry, the Kantōgun, and the government-general of the Guandong Peninsula.[249] In 1908, consular police came under the authority of the Guandong Government-General, but that did not end jurisdictional discussions.[250] Consuls like those in Changchun had to walk a "tightrope between the fluctuating but consistent domestic demand for greater Japanese dominance in China and the international pressure to conform to the more limited rules of the treaty system in China."[251] Although some consuls, supported by local Japanese residents' associations, called for a stronger Japanese presence in places like Changchun, in reality consuls were caught between opposing impulses. Consul Tashiro Shigenori's assertive response to the Wanbaoshan affair in 1931, for example, provoked a strong Chinese backlash. Nor could he or his colleagues restrain the Kantōgun. Tashiro could but report clandestine mobilization on the eve of the Manchurian Incident, and then the unprovoked attack on unresisting Chinese troops in Changchun, although he later came to support the Kantōgun.[252]

Some Japanese, such as Yoshida Shigeru, Shenyang consul-general between 1925 and 1928, called for an increased military presence in Manchuria.[253] Japanese civilians forming the Manchuria Youth League in 1928 reinforced this call.[254] Other civilian voices emerged in Dalian, such as the Dalian City Council in 1915 and the Mantetsu Employees Association in

1926, that were critical of the government, the military, and eventually the Youth League, but political instability made them increasingly defensive. Many favouring military action supported the Manchurian Incident as best they could, some later receiving Manchukuo government positions.[255] In Changchun, Japanese demanded a strong military presence in 1922, when a reduction in military personnel sparked scattered protests over fears about increased crime in the city.[256] The British consul in Dalian, however, suggested there was more concern for the economic impact of the loss of troops, especially since Mantetsu similarly protested the withdrawal because, while saving government the expense of stationing troops, it required the company to hire more police.[257] In 1926, some in Changchun formed a patriotic association, the Pure Japan Association (Dai Nihonkoku Suikai), gathering 238 members by the Taishō Emperor's birthday on 31 August.[258]

Mantetsu's first president, Gotō Shinpei, of course, sought to stave off tensions by reaching out to Chinese through "economic and cultural development." Following Gotō, one early *MNNS* article suggested that new structures and systems such as sanitation and education would benefit Chinese.[259] Individual Japanese also made efforts to reach out to Chinese. In 1926, a Sino-Japanese education society in Changchun endeavoured to foster amity.[260] Some went so far as to suggest that the Chinese language be taught in Mantetsu's elementary schools.[261] These efforts, however, were few and unable to overcome their context. Scholars have noted a growing pessimism among Japanese in Manchuria in the late 1920s, chiefly in response to growing concerns about Chinese but also because Mantetsu reduced social services and shifted to a focus on industrial development. As speculations about a military resolution to tension with China grew, Matsusaka saw a "collapse of an imperialist middle ground." Surrounded by large numbers of Chinese, the largely Japanese residents of railway zone cities felt this shift more acutely.[262] Given these realities, along with the financial and emotional investment in places like Changchun, it is understandable why increasing numbers of Japanese civilians might have been willing to support a more extreme solution, and defend it thereafter. In their eyes, the Japanese presence was both lawful and advantageous to Chinese and other neighbours. Noting the lack of Japanese civilian casualties in the Manchurian Incident, Edgar Snow suspected that settlers were warned in advance.[263] The Kantōgun's need for secrecy would have prevented this, of course, but, as the Changchun Boy Scouts activities discussed above suggest, elements of local society could be quickly mobilized as events unfolded.

Japanese in Changchun appear initially to have been more insular than in other railway towns. Physically separated from old Changchun, Japanese did not have to interact with Chinese as much as in other cities. Over time, however, Chinese moved into the railway town, and by the Manchurian Incident the town was more mixed than others.[264] But mixed did not mean integrated: sources offer few examples of the interaction that was evident elsewhere, such as in Korea.[265] After visiting Changchun and other Mantetsu towns in 1926, former prime minister Kiyoura Keigo gave an interview in Dalian's Yamato Hotel. Noting that Japanese outside of Mantetsu regrettably had little interaction with Chinese, Kiyoura urged Japanese in Manchuria to try to better understand Chinese. At the very least, he thought lack of interaction handicapped Manchurian development.[266] The pages of the *MNNS* seem to bear out Kiyoura's concern. Although an editorial as early as 1907 pointed out the necessity for Japanese in Manchuria to learn Chinese, for the most part Chinese appeared in the *MNNS* as either marginalized or threatening, chiefly as brigands, warlords, or communists, or as diseased.[267] More than a few articles used the term *bōkō* (assault or outrage) to describe incidents involving Chinese.[268] While discussions of Japanese are occasionally negative, far more often they are either neutral or infused with the language of progress, using terms such as "development" or "rushing ahead" (*yakushin*). The contrast is clear, and the implication is that the Changchun railway town was a Japanese endeavour supported by some Chinese and challenged by others, and continuing despite them. Japanese took pride in their imperial modernity in Changchun, but at the same time many were nervous about its continuing existence. Although Japanese enclaves represented potential liminal space, Changchun ultimately proved to be more an imperial outpost.

New Capital

While Consul Nishi Haruhiko charitably characterized the 1920s Changchun railway town as appropriate to northern Manchuria, Consul Tashiro Shigenori thought it a "hick town" (*issō yabo na shigai*) in comparison with Tianjin.[269] Clearly, with the establishment of Manchukuo, the new capital faced the challenge of becoming a livelier and more sophisticated city. Woodhead reported no cinemas in 1932, and nightlife only in Japanese restaurants and a couple of Russian cabarets.[270] Xinjing did mount some festivities, but many were state run. Perhaps the largest were the week-long celebrations marking Manchukuo's tenth anniversary in 1942. These were centred on the Nanling Athletic Complex, east of the zoo, though other events were held at the Monument to the War Dead, the Yamato Hotel, and Tokyo's Hibiya Park.[271] Congratulatory articles appeared in the press, one heralding Manchukuo as a "forerunner" of the Greater East Asia Co-Prosperity Sphere.[272]

Beneath the accolades were tensions. Some officials complained Xinjing was expensive and uncomfortable at the outset.[273] A foreign missionary quipped, "Xinjing is well named the new capital – new shops, new banks, new hotels, new parks, new cinemas, new questions, and new taxes!"[274] And while Xinjing beckoned, the capital was not without its issues. A wartime publication ostensibly by a young boy immigrating to Mudanjiang who passed through Xinjing described it as spacious, with tall buildings and children playing. Given that the boy was aware of the role played by the Capital Construction Bureau (CCB), his perspective and tone seem intended to mollify concerns about moving to Manchukuo, implying Japanese uncertainties about the place.[275] As a child immigrant herself, Ikemiyagi Sumiko remembered liking Xinjing's neatly ordered tall buildings and the parades of vehicles. Her father had come to Manchuria alone when accepting a Xinjing appointment in 1937. His wife and seven children followed a year later, perhaps suggesting caution.[276] And, indeed, the city had trouble keeping up with its growing population. Acknowledging residents' dissatisfaction, the government promised more street lighting in 1935.[277] A 1940 publication recognized the importance of improving standards of living, implying the inadequacies. Failing to do so undercut claims to the capital's modernity, and resolving issues like this was implicit in providing progressive, Asian solutions.[278]

Following the establishment of the puppet state, the most pressing issue for Japanese was housing, because along with Puyi came a flood of officials.[279] In 1927, Changchun offered only five hotels.[280] By 1934, the city had thirty-eight hotels providing 595 Japanese-style rooms and 105 "Western" rooms, enough for fourteen hundred people. Demand was reflected in the rise in hotel rates, which jumped from 1.7 yen per tatami per night in 1931 to 3.6 in 1932 and 4.3 in 1933.[281] By 1932, Mantetsu's aging Yamato Hotel, in the opinion of one reporter, "compare[d] unfavorably" with others in its chain, and few rooms had attached bathrooms.[282] Another opined that it was "admirably clean and tidy," though small, and one was "lucky to get a room there" because the alternative for many "homeless officials" was the "Railway Hotel ... consist[ing] of a string of sleepers in a siding."[283] Three years later, a third reported that "for some time there was such a shortage of housing and hotel accommodations that the South Manchuria Railway had a large number of Pullmans on the sidings functioning as temporary hotels."[284] Many Japanese lived in Kuanchengzi.[285] Some had no choice but to resort to "borrowing gloomy Manchurian homes and making temporary but rapid renovations."[286] Such remodelling was only a stopgap. At the same time, the CCB's first five-year plan promised ten thousand new houses by 1937, including a new subdivision near the southern end of Datong Dajie called "Japan Town" (*Yamato mura*). Begun in the fall of 1934, it was home to more than two thousand by August 1935.[287] A foreign observer reported some six thousand new buildings in Xinjing by 1937.[288]

Postwar memoirs often note housing woes. One senior bureaucrat recalled sharing a room in an official dormitory near Datong Park with a colleague for two weeks, then a room rented in the railway town with two others, and finally a house belonging to yet another colleague, who had been dispatched to Jinzhou. This last accommodation being insufficient for his soon-to-arrive family, he approached another colleague who had a lead on another house, only to find that the Kenpeitai desired it. Using his connections, the official managed to secure it nonetheless, though rent took ¥120 of his monthly ¥550, and he soon had to house a colleague as well as pay to return to Japan to fetch his family. The red brick "Western-style" house was 50 *tsubo* (165 m^2), enabling his family to live a "Western-style life."[289] Arriving in 1938, Okano Kanki, a Jianguo University professor and Kantōgun economic adviser, tried after 1945 as a war criminal, found a five-room apartment in a recently completed officers' residence. Although unfurnished, the brick building was in a Japanese style, including a garden and central heating. He had to change residence when he left the Kantōgun's service, moving to a smaller apartment in a busy shopping area in the former railway town. Two years later, he moved his family to a new Japanese-style residence near Xinjing's Nanling district, almost as large as his first and with a garden. There he stayed four years, alongside other professionals. Fuel shortages during the war ultimately meant a four-kilometre walk to work, and the home was "hellishly" cold in the winter. Despite the cold, Okano found the capital more agreeable than Japan.[290]

The influx after the establishment of Manchukuo fundamentally altered local Japanese society. Although some Japanese remained in agriculture and commerce, more were bureaucrats, managers, and engineers – the technicians of empire – reinforcing, perhaps, Earl Kinmonth's observation that *sarariiman* and college graduates were Manchukuo's "chief beneficiaries" (Table 4.8).[291] Chinese and Koreans in the capital too found work in

Table 4.8

Occupational distribution of the populations of Manchukuo and Xinjing by ethnicity, 1940 (percent)

	Chinese		Japanese		Korean		Others		Total	
	M	X	M	X	M	X	M	X	M	X
Agriculture, forestry, husbandry, and fishing	38.1	10.9	7.5	0.3	43.1	5.2	16.1	0.003	37.6	8.2
Industry	2.8	14.2	11.5	7.3	3.0	11.4	9.8	4.2	3.0	12.5
Commerce	3.3	12.6	9.9	11.2	4.1	9.2	5.0	18.4	3.4	12.2
Civil service and professional	2.3	9.5	13.5	19.5	3.9	15.7	9.3	21.7	2.6	12.0
Household service	1.0	2.6	1.8	3.7	0.9	3.5	1.9	2.8	1.0	2.9
Transportation	0.3	0.02	3.7	3.7	0.6	4.1	0.01	2.6	0.4	2.5
Mining	0.6	0.001	4.2	1.1	0.5	0.003	0.003	0.0	0.7	0.004
Other	2.2	7.3	4.6	7.5	2.6	8.1	11.4	17.8	2.3	7.4
Not employed	49.4	40.9	43.3	45.6	41.3	42.6	45.2	32.0	49.0	42.0

Note: Unlike Table 4.5, this table includes those not employed. The figures for Manchukuo do not include the Guandong Peninsula. Many of the "others" involved in husbandry were Mongolians. A study for the end of 1937 indicates similar numbers (excluding figures for the unemployed): 71% of Manchurians (Chinese, Manchus, Mongolians) engaged in commerce, 9% in manufacturing, commerce, or transportation, and less than 5% in government service. For Japanese the figures were, respectively, 3%, 45%, and almost 25%, and for Koreans 68%, 10%, and less than 5%. "Manchuria as a Demographic Frontier," *Population Index* 11, no. 4 (1945): 263.

Source: Manshū teikoku genjū jinkō tōkei (Shinkyō: Manshū teikoku chianbu keimushi, 1940), 8–11.

the bureaucracy in greater numbers, despite being more engaged in agriculture in Manchukuo generally. Comparatively more Chinese and Koreans were also engaged in industry, many as unskilled labourers. At the top, many were simply figureheads, as Japanese exercised authority through the policy of "leading from within," pairing Japanese advisers with non-Japanese leaders. Xinjing's mayor in 1937, for example, was Tōdai graduate Xu Shaoqing, advised by deputy mayor Sekiya Teizō.[292]

Constructing Manchukuo did not alter Japanese priorities of health and education. A second hospital was added in 1936 east of Datong Plaza (including underground facilities in case of air attack), supplemented by a hospital attached to Xinjing Medical University, a separate facility for Chinese located in the heart of old Changchun built in 1941, a recuperative rest area west of South Lake, and other clinics and wards across the city. Japanese publications applauded this infrastructure, although the construction of new hospitals in Harbin, Qiqihar, and Shenyang provoked foreign suspicions that they were tied to military ambitions.[293]

As in Changchun before the incident, the expansion of Xinjing's education infrastructure was assisted by funds donated by the residents' society.[294] With the addition of new elementary schools every year between 1934 and 1940 – two schools each in 1936 and 1940 – by 1942 Xinjing offered seven higher schools and ten elementary schools for Japanese students. There were also two new schools training youth for colonial development as well as a young adult school (*seinen gakkō*).[295] The school system for non-Japanese was less developed. In 1935, Xinjing had only one school solely for Koreans but space was set aside within several Japanese schools for Koreans.[296] Already by 1934 these schools served more than 5,000 Japanese and 630 Korean students. That year nineteen elementary schools served 3,000 Chinese students, including a kindergarten, nine high schools, and the two girls' middle schools built by Chinese before the Manchurian Incident.[297] Former prime minister Zheng Xiaoxu donated funds for a new Chinese school in Nanling in 1935.[298] Few schools appear in Xinjing's Chinese sectors on a 1941 map of the city, indicating not only their relative scarcity but also their lesser size, and perhaps lesser significance for the cartographer.[299] For students other than Japanese, Korean, or Chinese, accommodations were even more limited. Two private institutions catered to Mongolian education, including a lecture hall and a small library. Foreign missionary schools in 1935 included a day care centre, elementary schools, a handicrafts school, a vocational school, a medical college, a girls' high school, and a nursing school.[300]

In education, Xinjing assumed a national role. At the postsecondary level, in 1942 the capital offered two teacher's colleges, a veterinary college, a law school, an engineering college, a medical college, and a foreign student's school, drawing students from across Manchukuo.[301] Planners concentrated many of these east of Datong Dajie and south of the athletic complex at Nanling. At the heart of this area was Datong Academy, a school primarily for Chinese students but that also accepted Koreans and Taiwanese, with a name appropriated from the era in which Puyi ruled as regent.[302] Xinjing's postsecondary centrepiece was Jianguo (National Foundation) University, founded in 1938, south of the National Foundation Shrine. Joining these were more specialized institutions, such as a music school in 1934 and an art museum in 1940. A second library and a national chemical laboratory were planned, but it is uncertain if they were built.[303] Other professional schools by 1942 included schools for the police, the Kenpeitai, and postal employees. Private institutions included a professional school, a commercial school, a technical school, three typing schools, two automotive repair schools, and a school for the blind.[304]

The capital also hosted cultural institutions, such as Manchukuo's central museum (1939) on Datong Dajie near West Park, featuring many items transferred from Shenyang.[305] A Manchuria-Japan Cultural Association oversaw restoration work of Manchukuo's cultural heritage.[306] In order to familiarize Japanese personnel with local customs – as well as teach Japanese traditional means of dealing with Manchuria's cold, arid climate – in 1940 a museum of Manchurian ethnology opened south of South Lake. Separate halls focused on the various construction techniques involved in northern Manchurian, White Russian, Korean, Japanese, and southern Manchurian or Chinese rural houses.[307] In 1942 a Greater East Asia Literary Society met in Xinjing before sending delegates to an empire-wide conference in Tokyo.[308]

Manchukuo's education infrastructure often aimed more to propagandize – if not assimilate – than educate, especially after 1937.[309] This was part of a larger propaganda effort often linked to Xinjing's built environment. Just as Xinjing was described as an "ideal city" or an "ideally modern city," Manchukuo was often touted as an "ideal state" (Ch, *lixiang guojia;* Jp, *risō kokka*), rationally planned and organized, and propaganda often celebrated the "spirit of national foundation (*jian guo*)." Within that larger effort were roles for educators. A 1935 conference promoting proper spiritual training for educators, for example, included a group prayer at the Monument to the War Dead.[310] The outbreak of war accelerated this trend. Observing that education could revitalize the lives of states as well as individuals, Tamura Toshio envisioned the emergence of an explicitly "rising Asia" (*kōA*) style of education, and Manchukuo's becoming an "education state." A Tōdai graduate in economics, Tamura worked as an administrator in Sendai before coming to Manchuria in 1930. Beginning in the Finance Department, he held various positions in the Manchukuo government before moving to Datong Academy in 1938.[311] He later opined that war provided the opportunity to revolutionize society.[312] As part of the Japanese "racial effort" (*minzoku doryōku*) advancing East Asian civilization, the bureaucrat Minagawa Toyoji predicted that Japan's role as leader and harmonizer in Manchukuo would further advances through education.[313]

Symbolizing ethnic harmony, Jianguo University's student body included Japanese, Koreans, Chinese, Mongolians, White Russians, and Chinese from Taiwan, a cross-section that, it was hoped, would constitute the core of Manchukuo's future leaders. The curriculum included military training along with foreign languages and other academic subjects. Vice-chairman Sakuta Shōichi, a former professor at Kyoto University with a Tōdai doctorate in economics and law, sketched Japan's emerging Asian role in "Light of Asia," the lead article of the first issue of the university's journal *Kenkoku* (Ch, *Jianguo*). In it he noted that, having absorbed "light" from across Asia and Europe, Japanese had begun transferring it to the Asian mainland in the guise of Japanese culture, contributing to an Asian renaissance. Having previously absorbed "light" from western Asia in the form of religion, European "light" was now declining and seeking new infusions from Asia, but Japan and Manchukuo would lead resistance against the West.[314]

Many observers emphasized the role of youth in the creation of a new order.[315] With a focus on youth mobilization and youthful "spirit," Xinjing promoted physical exercise, encouraging sports, whether affiliated with school programs or in the wider community. Recreation was a means of "arousing the national spirit raising ethnic harmony."[316] To this end, Xinjing's infrastructure enabled recreation for all. Datong Park included two swimming pools, a sumo arena seating ten thousand, and four clay tennis courts. In winter it offered a skating rink. Four grass tennis courts were situated in Baishan Park and additional courts (of unknown type) could be found in Shuntian and Mudan Parks.[317] The capital also boasted a golf course and horse race track, the latter the subject of discussion since 1927.[318] Manchukuo director-general Takebe Rokuzō, a 1918 graduate of Tōdai Law School, organized recreational baseball, tennis, and skating near the Hall of State.[319] After the war, former Manchurian Electric employees reminisced about playing rugby, baseball, volleyball, and ice hockey as well as boating, playing in brass bands, and acting on stage.[320] A 1941 map of the city shows three new baseball diamonds, one within the complex in Nanling and one nearby.[321] The city's sports infrastructure was sufficiently developed that some thirteen hundred youths participated in an athletic meet in Xinjing in 1940.[322]

Unlike Xinjing's expanding health infrastructure, the capital's growing education and recreation infrastructure had explicit ideological significance. This was also true for tourism. Showing off the new capital, buses conducted tours of Xinjing in both Japanese and Chinese.[323] Xinjing's Japan Tourist Bureau office and its publications listed itineraries of the city's main highlights.[324] Japanese tourism flourished, and some planners discussed building a rail line under the ocean floor from Shimonoseki to Busan to speed transport.[325] Describing a "bus tour of Shinkyō," Kenneth Ruoff notes that the tourism boom, especially around 1940, resulted in "self-administered citizenship training ... as patriotism spurred mass consumerism and consumerism spurred patriotism."[326]

Supporting tourism was Xinjing's growing media industry. Documentary newsreels produced by Man'ei, Mantetsu, and others featured Xinjing, among other subjects.[327] New press and radio outlets also displayed the capital in its best light. Iwanaga Yūkichi, a former railway station chief in Changchun, advised the Kantōgun in establishing the new Manchukuo News Agency (Manshūkoku Tsūshinsha) in 1932, four years before becoming head of Japan's first national press agency distributing official views across the empire, Dōmei Tsūshinsha. With a monopoly on official news in the puppet state, the Manchukuo News Agency served an explicitly propagandist role. Designed by Nakamura Yoshihei and built in 1938, its head office was located at the southern edge of the railway town on Chūō Dōri, closer to the Kantōgun Headquarters than the Manchukuo state offices on Shuntian Dajie.[328] Propaganda was also implicit in Radio Xinjing's service, which began on 10 March 1933 from the Denden building on Datong Plaza.[329] The IJA thereafter "carpeted villages in China and Manchukuo with handbills and leaflets" on many topics.[330] News reporting aimed to portray developments in the puppet state favourably, such as, for example, the 1937 integration of the railway zone into Manchukuo as ending unequal treaty rights and contributing to Manchukuo's development.[331] In reality, integrating Mantetsu's railway towns with their neighbouring urban areas unified municipal authority in all Manchukuo's cities, including the capital, but rationalized administration remained under Japanese control.

For Chinese, growing Japanese authority was disastrous. Edgar Snow thought that, by 1933, any Chinese willing to collaborate had already lost faith in the benefits of Japanese administration, given the increasingly harsh realities of Japanese rule. Most literate Chinese were bitter, and illiterate peasants simply hunkered down to weather the storm.[332] The novelist Mei Niang, raised in Changchun, returned after studying in Kobe between 1936 and 1938 and condemned aspects of Manchukuo in her work.[333]

For Japanese, society in Xinjing expanded rapidly yet, in its essentials, continued in much the same manner as it had before. Given the time needed to construct new infrastructure, the district around Yoshinomachi initially remained Xinjing's main shopping district.[334] Rapid growth meant the expansion of services, and by 1940 Japanese businesses included 256 restaurants, 81 cafes and coffee shops, and 47 stores for Western clothing and tailors.[335] The capital also attracted major department stores, including Churin, Takarayama, and Seiyō.[336] Founded in 1867, Churin (Ch: Qiulin yanghang; Jp: Chūrin yōkō; also spelled Tsurin, Tschurin) was one of Manchuria's few successful Russian merchant endeavours. Expanding with the China Eastern Railway, the chain included general and department stores across the Russian Far East and Manchuria, selling European souvenirs to visiting Japanese.[337] Although some major Japanese department stores opened in Manchuria after Japan acquired rights there, they were few before the Manchurian Incident. Mitsukoshi opened an outlet in Dalian in 1927 and a small branch in Xinjing in 1933. Takashimaya's first overseas outlet was a small store specializing in Western clothing in Xinjing in 1935, with a similar store opening in Shenyang in 1936. Smaller stores opening outlets in the new capital included Chōjia (1933, from Korea), Minakai (1933), and Takarayama (1937), Minakai on Datong Dajie north of Datong Plaza, and Takarayama east of the Guandong Government headquarters on Xinfalu. After the outbreak of war in 1937, major department store chains further increased their overseas presence.[338]

The capital's entertainment infrastructure also expanded. In addition to organized sports, a third theatre opened in 1935; a dance hall, the Monte Carlo – where the owner hung a sign advertising when "Kawashima Yoshiko is now here" – was doing business by 1936; and a new cinema opened its doors in 1944. An outdoor music amphitheatre that could seat fifteen thousand opened in Datong Park in 1938. West Park's zoo moved to a larger facility on the west side of Nanling in 1938, alongside a petting zoo, flower gardens, and a botanical garden. Through the zoo ran streams from South Lake and

Shuntian Park to the Yitong River. A smaller zoo was also built inside Mudan Park.[339] Despite Manchukuo's Pan-Asian orientation, residents had an appetite for Hollywood movies: for example, *Manhattan Melodrama,* starring Clark Gable, played in Xinjing soon after its 1934 release.[340] Entertaining troops, bunraku masters from Osaka toured Manchukuo from summer 1935 to spring 1937, presumably stopping in Xinjing.[341]

Religious institutions flourished. The number of Shinto shrines overseas expanded rapidly following the Manchurian Incident, 32 by 1935 and 110 more by 1940. Including those planned or under construction, there were 332 by war's end in Manchuria, all sanctifying the imperial project.[342] Also active outside Xinjing were Mongolian-speaking Japanese Buddhist priests residing in western monasteries, who presumably spent some time in the capital preparing and reporting assignments.[343] The capital witnessed an expansion of Buddhist institutions, especially secondary complexes south of the railway town, where there appeared two more Nichiren and two Tiandai institutions, a second Shingon temple, and a Rinzai Zen temple. The capital's Yamato Hotel hosted a conference of Japanese Buddhist associations from across Manchuria in August 1934. Attending was Ōmura Keigon, director of the All Japan Young Buddhist Association.[344] The 1940 census noted 195 men and 53 women engaged in religious work in the capital.[345] By 1942, Manchukuo was home to at least eight Buddhist schools, alongside those of Tenrikyō and Konkōkyō.[346] The Daoyuan World Red Swastika Society (Manjikai) sat on the corner of Datong Dajie and Xingren Dalu, but other structures were off main thoroughfares. Between Datong Plaza and the Japanese-inspired buildings housing the Kantōgun Headquarters and Guandong Government offices emerged large structures for Higashi Honganji, a block to the west of Datong Dajie, and Tenrikyō, a block east of that main boulevard. A Tendai temple was built north of Shuntian Park, behind Mangyō headquarters, and a Nishi Honganji temple west of the new palace.[347] Locations of religious institutions in proximity to Manchukuo's key agencies suggest some kind of official support. Indeed, Manjikai had official patronage – including Zhang Jinghui – although it remained independent from the government. Acknowledging shared civilizational views, Manchukuo ideologues reached out to redemptive societies like Manjikai. Originally, the Shenyang branch of an organization founded in Jinan in 1921, Manjikai broke away and moved to its new Xinjing headquarters "in the style of a Chinese temple" in 1934. Manjikai perhaps interested some Japanese, given links with Ōmotokyō, despite official suppression of the latter in 1935.[348]

As Japanese officials were often suspicious of religious institutions, their appearance in Xinjing perhaps reflects the reality that constructing Manchukuo did not end many of the tensions plaguing Japanese in Manchuria. Although Mantetsu gained added responsibilities, the company and its employees, concerned about losing rights and privileges, vainly contested military efforts expanding Manchukuo's purview. In Dalian, in particular, civilians protested against the new order emanating from Xinjing.[349] Nor did establishing Manchukuo remove the threat of violence. The *MNNS* reported growing Soviet air forces in the region in the 1930s, sometimes with reference to poison gas.[350] Xinjing announced air raid drills in 1935 for the next eleven months, focusing on particular issues such as gas or fire for an entire month.[351] The defection to Japan of a commissar from the People's Commisariat for Internal Affairs (NKVD) led to the sudden arrest of Marshal Vasily Blyukher, the long-serving Soviet military head in eastern Siberia.[352] Fighting broke out six weeks later at Zhanggufeng, on the Manchukuo border near where the commissar crossed over.

Banditry persisted and was supplemented by the presence of guerrillas; while the capital was peaceful, missionaries reported "an atmosphere of terror" in city outstations.[353] General Li Du led anti-Japanese resistance in northern Jilin in 1932, which required 7,000 troops to suppress.[354] A foreign observer reported that there were 70,000 bandits across Manchukuo in August 1933, up from Mutō Tomio's estimate of 60,000 in 1930.[355] Four were taken prisoner in the capital's outskirts in 1935.[356] In 1933, Edgar Snow saw "patrol cars and pill-boxes along railways," "grim reminders of the still frequent attacks on trains and settlements."[357] Guerrilla attacks resulted in Kantōgun troops escorting technicians who installed the Japan–Manchukuo telephone cable to Xinjing and "built electrified barbed-wire enclosures around the relay stations."[358]

Xinjing's planning included a consideration for police, but the capital's policing also developed over time.[359] In 1935, regular police replaced the "special mobile police squads" deployed in the capital and Harbin. These were augmented in 1937, when, having made Manchukuo's legal system more like Japan's, Japan relinquished extraterritorial privileges and integrated the Foreign Ministry's consular police with that of the puppet state. The capital's police then came under the direct authority of the prime minister, combined with the military in a new Department of Public Peace, which included "forest" and "coastal" police forces charged with bandit and smuggling suppression.[360] Police supervised the Chinese *baojia* system of local self-defence and could execute bandits on the spot if deemed necessary.[361]

Xinjing's police were headquartered inside the Second Government Building. In 1935, the four stations within and five outside Xinjing included 176 Japanese and 1,521 Manchurian officers, the internal stations being on the southwest and northeast edges of the mercantile district, inside the old city, and in Nanling.[362] At 11.6 percent, there were slightly more Japanese officers in the city than the Manchukuo average of 8.1 percent in 1939. A secret security bureau (Ch, *Baoanju;* Jp, *Hoankyoku*) formed in 1937 dealt with foreign threats out of an office on Wumalu, the east-west road running south of the consulate in the former mercantile district, before moving to the Ministry of Public Security and a compound on the corner of Damalu and Sanmalu in 1945. By 1942, special bureaus in Xinjing and each province oversaw around a million fingerprints to monitor labourers, residential certificates, and census information.[363] Police also ran the large Xinjing Prison. Among those Mantetsu researchers arrested on suspicion of communist links in 1943 by the Kantōgun was one moved to this prison before being released in 1944, having met detained anti-Japanese guerrillas and Korean Christians.[364] Adjacent to the mosque about two hundred metres south of Puyi's residence in the old mercantile district, the jail's crenellated walls and towers resembled a European castle, a motif repeated in the police academy in Nanling, which opened in 1937 and subsequently published its own journal.[365]

Already in 1932 Woodhead noted "a growing antipathy" between Chinese and Japanese and warned that "the efficiency at which the Japanese aim in whatever they undertake is distasteful to the Chinese. They do not desire or appreciate it – however beneficial the ultimate results may be."[366] Yet Japanese governance continued in this manner, bolstered by enhanced authority. Unsurprisingly, Manchukuo officials made "all references to the old state under China ... taboo. The people are not allowed to use the names 'Manchuria,' 'Northeastern Province,' or any name suggestive of these." A Chinese tailor in Xinjing, for example, was forced to change the sign over his shop reading "Northeast Tailor."[367] Officials banned postage stamps and other relics of the previous era, burned Nationalist and anti-Japanese publications, and monitored migrant workers.[368] They could not root out anti-Japanese sentiments, however, even among Xinjing's elite students. Many students reportedly favoured communism, including a son of Prime Minister Zhang Jinghui.[369]

The administration used a range of methods to monitor the population. Officials monitored Chinese via the *baojia* system, and Koreans through the Japanese household registration system. Food rationing cards were assigned based on ethnicity – blue for Japanese, yellow for Koreans, and red for others.[370] Japanese surveillance resulted in many arrests, some reported overseas, including four Mongol officers executed for passing information to the Soviet Union in 1936 and more than two hundred Chinese arrested in Andong in 1937, many of whom were executed.[371] Health policy was double edged – while improving conditions, Japanese simultaneously augmented surveillance and their ability to influence individuals through social welfare initiatives.[372] At the heart of Manchukuo's surveillance system was the Concordia Association. A forerunner of sorts of the Imperial Rule Assistance Association in Japan, this was a mass political party designed to mobilize and monitor the population. Despite Pan-Asianist trappings, it too was a modernist project ensuring popular support for the regime without recourse to foreign practices such as democracy.[373] Significantly, its main office lay one block south of Datong Plaza on Datong Dajie, behind the First Government Building, with a training facility a half dozen blocks further south.[374]

Despite the need for security, Xinjing's actual military presence was small. In addition to a Gendarmerie Training Institute (1936) located in the prison were a Military Ordinance School (1938) and east of the Yitong River a Military Academy (1939). The academy graduated its first class of thirty-four in July 1938.[375] The only military present in the city initially were railway guards. In February 1933, they were joined by the Imperial Guards, a cavalry corps of 1,295, recruited from Manchus, garrisoned north of the new palace site. Joining this unit that March was the Manchukuoan 4th Cavalry Brigade, which had acquitted itself well in the invasion of Rehe and was renamed the Independent Cavalry Corps for Guarding the Capital.[376] In appreciation of the cavalry, the capital celebrated "Love Horses Day" (Ch, *Aimare;* Jp, *Aibahi*) on 3 May 1942.[377]

The thin military presence in Xinjing can be explained partly by the location of an IJA base north of the city, with its own airfield and wireless facility.[378] This base made strategic sense: if war broke out, the Kantōgun anticipated invading the Soviet Union; in that event, Xinjing, along with Shenyang and Harbin, was to serve as a depot. (Significantly, Soviet spy Ozaki Hotsumi found no evidence of preparations in Xinjing for an assault on the USSR in the summer of 1941.[379]) At the start of the war with China, the bases in these cities could supply twenty divisions for three months. Xinjing was also an airbase, home to the 15th Air Brigade (two air reconnaissance companies) and the Second Air Group headquarters, although the latter moved north in 1940.[380] After 1942, Xinjing became home to the Second Air Army – the First served the home islands – one of six at war's end.[381] The base had no radar installation, reflecting Japan's relatively tardy development of such technology.

Ōkura Kinmochi – a former Mantetsu director and later a member of the House of Peers – thought a strong military presence unnecessary. Citing a 1938 statement by prime minister Konoe Fumimaro, in 1940 he observed that Japanese had realized "that the practice of one nation invading the territory of another merely to reap profit for itself was already out of date." More useful was economic development and "establishing cultural centres all over the country ... [which] has made the life of the Manchukuoan people more cheerful and civilized."[382] This attitude was apparent in an issue of the literary Chinese monthly *Qilin,* published in the capital and devoted to the city's transformation from a "small wilderness outpost" to Manchukuo's "number one city." In the first of ten sections, Li Guangyue described Xinjing as having a positive Japanese presence evident in flags and the names of buildings and neighbourhoods. Others portrayed the city as progressive and peaceful, a place where electric trams ran along bustling streets with large department stores and where children sang happily in the street about "building the nation" (*jianguo*). Yoshinomachi was notable for its international atmosphere and Datong Plaza for flowers and eye-catching buildings. Tellingly, however, in this Chinese publication the term "merry-go-round" appears in Japanese *kana.*[383]

With the founding of the puppet state, civilian and military officials formed the All Orchid Club for Japanese and "Manchurians" to relax together.[384] Yet despite the ethnic harmony promised by the administration, these efforts were few and far between. For example, Xinjing's neighbourhoods, to which residents were assigned by government or corporate affiliation, in effect segregated the city, privileging residents according to a racial hierarchy. Japanese officials and bureaucrats travelling arterial roadways in the railway town and capital section would have taken in views of parks and fine buildings housing government and corporate offices, and on non-arterials would have seen blocks of civilian housing assigned by corporations, but, after their construction, few Chinese would have needed to be in these districts. Parallel to Chūō Dōri and Datong Dajie was a roadway running east through the railway town and down Damalu into the old city that served the needs of most Chinese, and many Japanese could live their daily lives without visiting that side of the city.

Although Chinese and Japanese shared Xinjing, they lived in parallel worlds. A French missionary characterized the capital in 1945 as one of extremes:

"Xinjing contains in reality three distinct and separate cities: the new town, a kind of Asian New York, reserved just about exclusively for Japanese and foreigners, the former Mantetsu concession, half-Japanese half-Chinese, and the Chinese city." He described the new town as having broad avenues, large and peaceful parks, government buildings remarkable for their "bold" (*hardi*) and oriental styles, grand hotels and stores, schools, and cinemas. The railway town was active and densely inhabited, with small hotels, restaurants, and stores, but no particular "cachet." The Chinese city "present[ed] a violent contrast" to the new. While Japanese built the new city "with the perfection of the latest urban planning methods" representing the "most advanced modern civilization," Chinese continued to live much as they had for millennia, in houses sometimes built of thatch and cobs on roads impassable to cars.[385] Not much had changed for Chinese – Woodhead thought the roads of the Chinese city "almost impassable" in 1932, in marked contrast to the railway town's "broad well-surfaced streets."[386] Underscoring this sense of inequality was the reality that, while Japanese constituted only 1 percent of Manchukuo's population, they consumed about a third of available household coal.[387] A 1935 survey found that Japanese in Manchuria sent fifteen times more telegrams than Chinese.[388] The disparity in wealth between Chinese and Japanese in Xinjing was also evident in the capital's 1937 absorption of the railway town. Although Xinjing collected 635,871 yuan in taxes in 1937, that tripled to 1,895,642 in 1938 when the railway zone's return to Manchukuo integrated the Japanese population into the city.[389] It is worth noting, moreover, that despite amalgamation, Japanese education infrastructure and shrines remained under the authority of the Japanese embassy after 1937.[390]

Worse for the capital's Chinese residents than failed promises, an oppressive police state, and de facto segregation, in 1936 the nearby village of Mengjiatun – only a few kilometres southwest of the new palace – became home to the IJA's Unit 100. Comprising between six hundred and eight hundred men, this unit was perhaps Manchuria's second most active bacteriological warfare unit after Unit 731. Occupying some twenty square kilometres, the unit commanded a large farm, underground laboratories, and three crematoria. Tight security included an electrified fence. Commanded by Major Wakamatsu Yūjirō, personnel conducted medical experiments on Chinese rounded up by Japanese police in the capital, resulting in "hundreds, if not thousands" of deaths. Not content to study the effects of narcotics, pesticides, plague, anthrax, and other diseases on human subjects in the laboratory, Unit 100 personnel were also active in the field. Like Unit 731 in Harbin, branch units acted throughout Manchuria, and were active in China, Mongolia, and the Soviet Union during the war, attempting to infect civilian populations by airborne and other means. Field experiments apparently took place in and around the capital – bringing to mind a possible connection with Xinjing's 1940 plague outbreak.[391]

Also injurious to Chinese was the drug trade, even in the new capital. Although opium addiction had been evident since the nineteenth century, it was considered worse in Jilin than Fengtian, given the proximity to northern bandits who smuggled the drug.[392] Japan participated in the 1909 International Opium Commission to curb the trade, but it was lucrative. Japan was thought to be a major producer, smuggling much into China via Manchuria.[393] The Manchukuo government agreed to address the drug trade more effectively, construct clinics for opium and other drug addicts – including one in the capital – and launch a ten-year suppression program in 1938. At the same time, Manchukuo encouraged the production and sale of opium as a means of enhancing state revenues and weakening Chinese resistance.[394] The trade was more or less an open secret. The British consul in Dalian, for example, was aware of it, reporting increasing imports landing in that city. Imports averaged around 25,000 pounds annually in 1920–24 but jumped to 85,000 pounds in 1925–29, and then increased again to more than 140,000 pounds in 1929 and almost 165,000 pounds in 1933. In that last year, the Guandong Government-General reported returns of ¥30,087 for an unknown quantity of cocaine, almost triple the figures for 1930 and 1931.[395] Japan was not the only colonial state funding itself through opium sales, but the impacts on individual Chinese, Koreans, and Japanese were often devastating.[396]

Activities like bacteriological experiments and drug trafficking were not featured in the media, but rumours as to their existence surely circulated. Unit 100 security was less strict than Unit 731's, as personnel lived not on base but in the capital.[397] And while Dalian may have been the "epicenter" of the Manchurian drug trade – with at one point the highest rate of narcotics consumption in the world, in part due to the transient nature of Manchuria's population – all railway towns likely served as conduits.[398] The media chose to focus on more positive subjects, even with the outbreak of war. Construction was a common trope, as officials resorted to related language in mobilizing wartime opinion with slogans like "Building a New East Asia" and "Building the Greater East Asia Co-Prosperity Sphere." This practice emerged early – a 13 December 1941 public announcement defined the war's goal as "construct[ing] a new order and prosperity for the Greater East Asia Co-Prosperity Sphere."[399] Manchukuo pledged to support Japan against the United States and the United Kingdom when they declared war on the empire on 8 December 1941.[400] Newspapers like the *MNNS* endeavoured to fan patriotic fires by reporting successes and envisioning a reconstructed Asia, as well as parading front-page photos of troops departing Xinjing and Shenyang for the front.[401] They were aided by officials and private citizens in Japan who had been championing the war effort against China with increasing verve since 1937, an effort also evident in new structures symbolizing the rhetoric of expansion and Japan's imperial mystique. Nationwide celebrations held in Japan in 1940 recognizing the year as the 2,600th since the empire's founding were acknowledged across Manchukuo as well.[402]

Putting a damper on any such positive views, shortages and rationing began even before the start of the Pacific War in 1941. Prosecuting the war in China also meant decreased Japanese investment in Manchuria.[403] This resulted in inflation. Using 1937 as a baseline of 100, prices of staples in the capital averaged 248 in 1941 and 9,650 in August 1945. Prices of clothing were similar: 433 in 1941 and 7,590 in August 1945.[404] This trend was also evident in Japan, where inflation was an issue already in 1936, and consumption in 1939 was said to have fallen a quarter below 1937 levels, perhaps as low as during the economic crisis of 1930–31. By early 1941, consumption fell perhaps another 20 percent. Coal shortages were also apparent in 1938, meaning less fuel for heat and power generation.[405] In the last year of the war, all available labour was co-opted into the war effort: Manchurian wartime labour mobilization included not only Chinese and Koreans but also "those whose businesses had been discontinued as a wartime measure" as well as "air-raid victims and disabled veterans." They were organized into "neighbourhood factory" and "patriotic labour corps" systems imported from Japan.[406] Radio broadcasts periodically warned listeners of saboteurs and "political criminals," while radio reports from Yenan and Shanghai suggested that Manchurian labourers were becoming less cooperative.[407] In this context, any invocations of Xinjing's spiritual mobilization and idealistic visions likely sounded increasingly shrill, the delusive summons of a regime drawing near its extinction.

Manchukuo introduced conscription in 1941, requiring all men to undergo a physical exam upon turning nineteen, though they could volunteer at seventeen. Terms of enlistment were three years. Along with provincial governors, the mayor of Xinjing was empowered to act as a conscription officer.[408] Universal male conscription between the ages of eighteen and forty-five, the so-called *nekosogi dōin* (strip the roots mobilization), began July 1945, with many assembling into units in Xinjing. Radio reports from Xinjing suggested that a quota system had been instituted for the entire country, with the Concordia Association organizing goals for local officials.[409] The wartime emergency enabled the Concordia Association to accelerate its operations, expanding its role in mobilizing society.[410]

The puppet capital did not experience the destruction visited upon most Japanese cities in the final year of the war. American bombing of Manchuria beginning July 1944 was directed against targets south of Xinjing, perhaps giving residents some reason for optimism.[411] Thinking it safer than Japan, the son of Prime Minister Zhang Jinghui even returned to Xinjing from Tokyo in 1943.[412] And while officials in Japan ordered the slaughter of dangerous zoo animals in 1943 and in colonial zoos soon after, because some posed potential threats if freed by bombing, Xinjing's zoo did not poison such animals in its care until August 1945, when confronted with invasion, though feeding them had become more difficult after 1941.[413] The end of the war was not the end of difficulties: Japanese in Manchukuo's capital had more to dread at war's end.

Conclusion

Constructing empire in Changchun and Xinjing occurred in diverse contexts. This said, Japanese living in the railway town and later the capital acquired land and evicted residents, organized administrations and founded companies, planned communities and built structures, and participated in a range of activities that shaped and animated urban environments. Japanese also perceived these spaces diversely – as places of work, worship, recreation, and residence – while considering improvements and confronting challenges. Together, these activities and perceptions fostered particular colonial imaginaries, something Japanese often remember favourably today despite the ignominy of defeat and difficult postwar repatriation. The postwar journal *Manshū to Nihonjin* (*Manchuria and the Japanese*), for example, generally defended the purported goals of Asian liberation and ethnic communitarianism, often citing progressive Japanese intentions in an ominous and unstable world. The inaugural issue even reprinted an idealistic 1941 article by Ishiwara Kanji, one of the architects of the Manchurian Incident, about Asia's resurgence under Japan's leadership.[1] The postwar colonial imaginary, however, also includes events following Japan's surrender. After briefly considering the fate of Changchun Japanese in the immediate postwar years, this chapter assesses attitudes exhibited by Japanese in Changchun.

Roads Home

Changchun and Xinjing were also battlegrounds. The railway town was on the front line, so to speak – adjacent to a Russian and later Soviet town and subject to confrontations with Chinese troops. As a result, on the eve of the Manchurian Incident, the railway town was home to the Second Division's 3rd Infantry Brigade headquarters, the 4th Infantry Regiment, and a unit of railway guards. This meant a theoretical troop strength of more than 3,000, although actual strength was less – at the time, the entire Kantōgun totalled only around 10,400.[2] All troops were mobilized during the Manchurian

Incident. Receiving orders just after midnight on 19 September 1931, Major General Hasebe Shōgo, commanding the 3rd Brigade, dispatched elements of the 4th Regiment to reinforce Shenyang and the remainder to attack the roughly 10,000 Chinese troops in the Changchun area. Operations began just before dawn against 650 Chinese soldiers south of Kuanchengzi and an artillery unit with thirty-six cannon and some 2,350 troops at Nanling, before turning to 320 soldiers in the old city of Changchun. Securing Changchun in a day with only forty-three killed and fifty-two wounded, Changchun's Japanese garrison moved on to Jilin City three days later, and then returned for the drive north.[3] Evidence of the fighting was conspicuous.[4]

When the fighting ended and Manchukuo was established, Xinjing did not become a major military centre, but it did figure in the region's defence. Expecting a Soviet attack in or after fall 1945, the Kantōgun began planning for it in 1944. The plan involved relying on border fortifications, which meant few interior defences, and withdrawing to Manchukuo's southeastern mountains, where terrain favoured defence. Against this strategy when war broke out was General Ushiroku Jun, commander of the Third Area Army assigned to southern Manchuria. Concerned for the million Japanese civilians in Manchukuo's cities, and recognizing little to no accommodations in Tonghua, he insisted on their defence. Ushiroku sought to keep the enemy west of the Mantetsu trunk and north of the Tuman rail line, making Xinjing a defensive anchor – one that would not hold.[5]

By that time, the Kantōgun was a shadow of its former self. Although expanded from sixteen to twenty-four divisions, many formations were of questionable worth. Experienced units had transferred to China or Japan, and there were significant deficiencies in training and equipment.[6] Shifting threats further strained resources. For example, a Guandong Defence Army was established with headquarters in Xinjing in 1941, but it was prepared more for police and security than military operations. To confront the Chinese Communist Eighth Route Army, moreover, it transferred to Shenyang in September 1944 and Liaoyuan in June 1945, becoming the 44th Army. Defending the capital in August 1945 was the 30th Army under Lt. General Iida Shōjirō, recalled from retirement. Thirtieth Army Headquarters, with 610 men, was the last army headquarters established by the Kantōgun. Under it was the 148th Infantry Division, formed at the end of July, its officers coming from Xinjing's 101st Guard Unit Headquarters, which was then deactivated. With a strength of 9,828 – though authorized at 12,000 – the 148th included many local conscripts, including 70 to 80 Koreans, and were billeted in local schools. A lack of rifles and bayonets led to an order for five thousand spears, which never arrived. The 133rd Independent Mixed Brigade, also formed in July, was reassigned to the 30th Army on 12 August, adding 4,898 men. Other units south of Xinjing were ordered to the capital but could not comply. The 39th Division, recently arrived from China with 16,274 men, was missing artillery, ammunition, and vehicles.[7]

Convinced that there was no immediate threat, on 8 August, Kantōgun commander Yamada Otozō flew from Xinjing to Dalian to attend a shrine dedication. The million-man Soviet offensive began that night after midnight, joined by Mongolian People's Republic troops the following day. Xinjing was the target of several planes at 1:30 a.m.[8] The unexpected attack caught the Japanese by surprise. The Kantōgun was in the midst of redeploying, new conscripts were en route to assignments, and border fortifications were incomplete. While Ushiroku ordered Xinjing's defenders to effect a last stand and disrupt enemy supply lines, the Kantōgun relocated its headquarters and Manchukuo's government southeast to Tonghua on 11 August, on the mountainous route to Pyongyang. Some officials took their families with them, military familes having priority over those of Mantetsu personnel.[9] The Kantōgun did not learn of any Japanese consideration of surrender until 14 August, five days after the Soviet declaration of war and four days after the first Japanese surrender note, asking that the emperor be retained.[10]

Xinjing's defence was confused. With municipal officials, soldiers hastily erected defensive works around the city and barricades within, but local commanders disagreed over where to assemble perimeter lines, troops began destroying supplies before confidential documents, and refugees clogged transportation lines, hindering reinforcements. Ordered to prepare counterattacks, defenders were reinforced with a tank regiment, anti-aircraft units, a supply and a survey unit, hospital personnel, a detrained battalion unable to reach its division (the 107th), and an additional 3,000 men conscripted from Xinjing and its vicinity. This brought the capital's strength to over 41,000, though 27,000 men in the 107th and 117th Infantry Divisions were ordered to withdraw to the capital from their positions to the west. Of them only about 5,000 of the 117th were able to reach Xinjing, and not until 15 August.[11] Manchukuo troops, including the capital's Imperial Guards and students from the Manchukuo Officers School, were hastily deployed to Xinjing's southeastern flank on 13 August. Fearing being disarmed by the Kantōgun, they revolted the next day, shooting Japanese officers and fleeing across the Yitong, some reassembling there and fortifying their position with cannon.

A Chinese flag first raised over a bank in old Changchun on 15 August sparked shooting between Manchukuo and Japanese troops, some of the latter fleeing east and surrendering to those on the Yitong. That same day, Chinese students at the Manchukuo Military Academy beat their Japanese principal to death. Fighting continued until 19 August, when 200 Soviet airborne troops landed at the airport, reinforced by tanks the next day.[12]

The Kantōgun command was also in disarray. Although the Japanese emperor ordered a ceasefire on 14 August, Kantōgun commander Yamada countermanded that and fighting continued while he dispatched Deputy Chief of Staff Major General Matsumura Tomokatsu to Tokyo on 15 August for instructions. Matsumura flew back to Xinjing two days later, the day after imperial headquarters ordered all Japanese forces to cease operations, tasked with maintaining order over the estimated six days needed to inform Japanese of capitulation. Also arriving on the 17th was Kantōgun Lt. Colonel Prince Takeda Tsuneyoshi, who, with prior experience in the Kantōgun – including bacteriological weapons research – was to ensure that the imperial order was followed. In the following days, officers were summoned for briefings.[13] Eager to halt Japanese losses and requesting a speedy Soviet occupation of Manchuria, captured Kantōgun chief of staff Hata Shunroku was released by the Soviets to fly to Changchun on 19 August, advising that Japanese forces wait to surrender to Soviet forces rather than Chinese.[14] Representing Kantōgun Headquarters and Japanese forces in the capital, Matsumura and Lt. Colonel Kuwa Masahiko surrendered Xinjing that day, although Soviet-intercepted radiograms broadcast from the city show the Kantōgun ordered its forces to surrender the day before.[15]

Although sporadic fighting continued outside the capital through 30 August, active resistance crumbled quickly with Japan's surrender on 15 August. On 1 September, the Soviet Zabaikal Front headquarters took up residence in Xinjing's Kantōgun offices and the former capital's southern suburbs became a gathering point for surrendering Japanese. There they formed labour battalions for reconstruction work, but many deserted as fears of deportation to the Soviet Union arose. Overseeing these 20,000 to 30,000 men was 148th Division commander Lt. General Suemitsu Motohiro, who established a headquarters in the Man'ei complex on the city's southern side.[16]

Aaron Moore has found that, around the date of Japan's surrender, "servicemen abroad were panicked about their relatives – particularly those trapped in the colonies."[17] They had reason to be, because overseas Japanese were subject to robbery, rape, and revenge. In Xinjing, Chinese and Korean intrusions into Japanese homes after 15 August led Soviet airborne officers, who took the Concordia Association building for their headquarters, to allow about a thousand Japanese to retain rifles for protection. Chinese assaults on Japanese settlers near Xinjing produced casualties, prompting the dispatch of elements of the 148th to protect the settlers. Eventually some 30,000 Soviet troops occupied the city, many also assaulting and raping Japanese.[18] Neither Japanese military police nor Manchukuoan troops policing Chinese sections of Changchun could withstand Red Army pillaging.

In addition to the 664,000 Japanese military personnel in Manchuria at war's end were some 1,550,000 Japanese civilians, almost as many as the 1,574,100 in Korea, Taiwan, and the rest of China.[19] Some 70,000 Japanese fled into northern Korea upon the Soviet invasion, though 30,000 returned, unable to cross into the south.[20] Some Japanese managed to get back to Japan quickly – there have been allegations that the Kantōgun and Mantetsu employees evacuated their families ahead of other Japanese.[21] Unit 731's Ishii Shirō was in Xinjing a few days after the emperor's 15 August speech. After ordering the destruction of facilities and equipment and the evacuation of his top scientists, he flew to Japan from Dalian. Others accompanied equipment and notes to Busan and Japan by rail and sea. Unit 100's Wakamatsu Yūjirō was less fortunate: he was repatriated later, but his presence ensured the destruction of evidence.[22]

Declaring that Manchukuo had merely been a facade for the Japanese Army preparing to attack the USSR, Soviet forces seized men and materials as war booty, including from corporations associated with the Kantōgun.[23] Research materials and library collections were also targeted.[24] Ordered on 23 August to procure 500,000 Japanese for labour service in the Soviet Union, the People's Commissariat for Internal Affairs (NKVD) commandeered civilians as well as soldiers, initially sending them to camps inside the Soviet border established 8 or 9 August. The Soviets ultimately seized more than 600,000 Japanese, as well as 30,599 Chinese, Korean, and other non-Japanese servicemen, though 90 percent of the latter were soon returned home. In 1946, American officials asked that the Japanese be repatriated with remaining civilians, but they were unsuccessful and reported that the Soviets used some Japanese for propaganda and military purposes in Manchuria.[25] In confiscating materials linked to the Japanese war effort, Soviet officials compelled the sale of some institutions using devalued Soviet occupation currency. One was the Qiulin network, by then "the largest wholesale and retail mercantile organization in North Manchuria."[26] Soviet authorities alleged that the Hong Kong and Shanghai Bank had, with Japanese help, unfairly acquired the company in 1937, and that Japanese took it over after the outbreak of the Pacific War in 1941.[27]

To dismantle and transfer physical infrastructure, Soviet officers demanded blueprints and commandeered Japanese and Chinese workers, sometimes Japanese prisoners of war and Soviet troops. When the Soviets were finished, local mobs were permitted to plunder what remained. "In the process," an American report notes, "thousands of buildings and homes were destroyed."[28] Many industries were targeted, including electric power generation and cement manufacture. The Dafengman dam on the Songhua, providing power to Harbin and Changchun, fell quickly into Soviet hands, and Chinese Communists severed transmission lines to Shenyang.[29] Asked by US president Harry Truman to report on Japanese assets in Manchuria, Edwin Pauley visited in summer 1946. He reported the former capital fared poorly:

> At Changchun the Japanese had built an imposing capital for Manchukuo. The government buildings were modern steel and concrete structures. Excellent modern housing was built as homes for the ruling Japanese and their Manchurian puppets. Most of these buildings are now a mass of debris. According to the Chinese the destruction of the government buildings was done by the Soviet troops. They first removed all usable equipment and then since the buildings were comparatively fireproof, fired the rooms one by one. The destruction of the housing was accomplished both by the Soviets and the Chinese mobs. Fighting between the Chinese National forces and Chinese Communists after the Soviet withdrawal resulted in some further damage, but by far the largest destruction occurred during the Soviet occupation.[30]

Pauley found the city's "wrecked condition" to be "appalling" and reported that pumps and other items needed to maintain infrastructure had been removed. He also reported that the Soviet troops in Changchun, among other cities, "were a particularly undisciplined lot. Street robbery, rape and murder were widespread. These 'shock' troops were replaced after the first two weeks by better-disciplined soldiers. Nevertheless looting and attendant disorders continued at a reduced scale. Little distinction was made between the treatment accorded Chinese and Japanese. With few exceptions these conditions prevailed in all areas taken over."[31] Visiting Puyi's residence, the Chinese diplomat Zhang Jia'ao (Chang Kia-ngau) found little – "even all the light bulbs had been removed." Going to the library he found crates for packing books and paintings and retrieved several books from the Ming Dynasty.[32] The improvised nature of Soviet looting is evidenced by a 1954 Central Intelligence Agency (CIA) report noting that much that had been taken was left "rusting on station platforms at the major towns and cities along the Trans-Siberian Railway ... completely exposed to the weather."[33] Although Soviet confiscations received international attention, nothing could prevent them. The only American military presence on the ground in Manchuria at war's end was a six-man mission dropped by parachute 16 August near Shenyang to rescue prisoners of war there and at Xi'an, 125 kilometres south of Changchun, just as Soviet troops arrived, and to establish an intelligence network in the region.[34]

Ominously, the Soviet presence appeared potentially lasting. The Cairo Declaration promised Manchuria's return to China, but negotiations at Yalta – concluded on Japan's Empire Day, 11 February 1945 – assigned the railway and its southern terminus to the USSR. Soviet and Chinese diplomats agreed on 14 August to jointly administer Mantetsu's former main lines as a renamed Chinese Changchun Railway. Headquartered in Changchun, the railway had a Russian manager, a Chinese deputy manager, and "a large number of Mantetsu's technicians." Soviet troops also assumed control of Dalian and Lüshun, where diplomats established jurisdictional autonomy for Soviet citizens, and initially sought joint management of power plants, factories, and eight airports, likely including Changchun's.[35] Zhang Jia'ao despaired, writing:

> It seems that the Soviets are preparing to create in Inner Mongolia, Rehe, and Chahar a special regime that will completely surround the nine northeastern provinces [Manchukuo]. I'm afraid even the Manchurian coastline is in danger of being blockaded. When the Northeast has been entirely surrounded in this way, the jointly managed Chinese Changchun Railroad will be like a dagger piercing our heart. Moreover, with blood having been drained from the entire body, the Northeast is bound to become a sitting duck for the Soviet Union.[36]

The establishment of the People's Republic of China in 1949 eventually checked this influence, as the Soviet Union agreed to relinquish Dalian and Lüshun in 1950 and the Changchun Railway in 1952. Negotiations had proved prickly, but the Korean War extended the presence of Soviet troops through 1955 out of concern about American troops landing on the Liaodong Peninsula.[37]

Although the Soviet Union cooperated with the Chinese Nationalists after Japan's surrender, the Soviet presence in Manchuria ultimately benefited the Chinese Communist Party (CCP) more. The Japanese had effectively suppressed Communist resistance in Manchukuo, even among Koreans, who were often more receptive to anti-Japanese messages, but, with Japan's defeat, the CCP saw an opportunity and ordered troops into Manchuria on 28 August. In the following days, CCP troops cooperated with Soviet forces in taking Shanhaiguan and began fanning across the region.[38] This reignited China's civil war, forcing difficult choices upon not only Chinese but others as well. In the interest of cooperation with the Nationalists, the Soviets asked the CCP to withdraw from cities, prompting the party to recruit Koreans, although some reportedly joined unwillingly.[39] Japanese were similarly conflicted, with many joining CCP forces, not all by choice.[40] Some Japanese aided the Nationalists, supporting Zhang Jia'ao in negotiations with Soviet officials by detailing production figures.[41] Other Japanese troops took to raiding the countryside like bandits.[42] The disposition of Japanese troops was thus a concern for all. American and Nationalist Chinese officials had ordered Japanese forces to surrender to the Nationalists and hold Manchurian cities against the Communists, but Changchun's distance from Nationalist-controlled territory rendered enforcement difficult. Soviet officials allowed the Nationalists into Changchun as early as December 1945, but Nationalist troops marching north did not reach Shenyang until January 1946. A Nationalist detachment of 223 arrived in Changchun on 5 January, but Soviets disarmed some 5,000 men raised locally for the Nationalists that month on the grounds of their former Japanese connections. The Nationalists could do little then but dispatch Madame Chiang to the city from 22 to 25 January to raise morale.[43] Later that spring, Soviet military forces suddenly withdrew from Manchurian cities; they left Changchun on 13 April, rejecting a Nationalist request to delay withdrawing from that city to coincide with the arrival of government reinforcements held back at Sipingjie.[44] Soviet forces also conveniently left behind stores of Japanese arms for Chinese Communists, although an American report claimed also that Soviets armed railway guards and left armed Soviet soldiers in civilian attire in support of CCP forces.[45] Surrounding Changchun then were some 30,000 Communist troops, who used heavy artillery to overcome hastily organized Nationalist forces – chiefly former Manchukuo troops – after three days of fighting in April.[46] The Communists withdrew in May, however, following the arrival of US-supported Nationalist troops from the south. Despite the Communist use of heavy artillery on the city centre, the Nationalist commander made the former Datong Plaza his headquarters, overseeing a force of 4,000, some 3,000 recruited locally.[47] Arriving in Changchun on 30 May, Chiang Kai-shek offered to negotiate with Communist officials, but Lin Biao declined to meet and fighting continued despite a truce.[48] When the war recommenced in earnest in 1948, the Communists retook Changchun after a 150-day siege and more than 100,000 civilian deaths. The 1946 fighting had witnessed defensive works built chiefly around the former Datong Plaza, but in 1948 the entire city became a battleground. Changchun's fall on 18 October 1948 was two days after Jinzhou's, and, with Shenyang's fall on 2 November, there was at last a conclusion to fighting in Manchuria.[49]

Intense fighting occurred in Changchun because it figured prominently in CCP strategy. Having little organizational support in Manchuria, the party shifted to an urban-centred strategy rather than the rural one used in China south of the Great Wall. In addition to assuming that Manchuria's rural Chinese were politically indifferent, the party realized that the bulk of usable materials and potential recruits were to be found in the major cities and along railway lines. Initially the CCP also considered turning Changchun into a capital for a new base area stretching from Mongolia across northern Manchuria.[50] Rather than give up the city in 1946, Mao Zedong suggested to Lin Biao that the party "turn Changchun into Madrid," fighting for every inch.[51] Noting that Changchun lost a third of its buildings and population during the 1948 siege, one author likened the loss of life to that in Hiroshima, given that about the same numbers perished, though Changchun's were chiefly to famine, as the Communists did not permit civilians to leave the city in search of food.[52]

Contributing to tensions, Changchun was also a focal point in the emerging Cold War. In February 1946, a Soviet Army chief of staff in Changchun publicly linked any withdrawal of Soviet troops from Manchuria to American troops withdrawing from China.[53] This was in part a response to an American warship's visiting Dalian in October 1945 and marines landing in Tianjin in the fall, quickly getting into firefights with Chinese Communist troops before leaving the following fall.[54] American general Douglas MacArthur responded by stating that American troops were free to go anywhere enemy troops could be found, including Manchuria.[55] Changchun's significance also led some Americans to advocate establishing a presence there. Leo Sturgeon, American consul-general in Shanghai, recommended in November 1945 "that our principal and perhaps first attention in Manchuria be given to the establishment of a mission or office in Changchun." He also helped confirm Nationalist indications to Richard Butrick, acting chief of the Foreign Service Administration, that "Changchun is to be [the] nerve center [of] Manchuria," prompting Butrick to consider sending Sturgeon or someone similar at the "soonest possible."[56] A consulate subsequently opened in October 1946 under Consul-General O. Edmund Clubb, who remained until October 1947.[57]

Although few Americans reached postwar Manchuria, some asserted the region's significance. Writing in *Foreign Affairs,* the geologist Harry Foster Bain emphasized Manchuria's potential as a grainery and ore source for heavy industry, given "extensive" Japanese surveys. He even complimented Japan's idealistic "young officers [who] began as reformers ... with worthy ideals" but succumbed to more senior militarists.[58] A 1947 CIA report noted that "Manchuria represents the major direction of current Soviet interests," to ensure "control over resources and development of Manchuria, and the maintenance there of a regime sympathetic to the USSR."[59] This perspective endured. A decade later, Francis Jones reported that, even though much Manchurian industry "produced only semi-processed goods for export to Japan ... there were numerous exceptions to this rule" in Changchun, Shenyang, and Dalian, even after Soviet seizures and postwar destruction.[60] Former consul-general Clubb predicted that postwar Manchuria would be "the fulcrum of Communist Power in northeast Asia," while others lamented that the Soviet Union was garnering what Japan had sought in Manchuria.[61] Such concerns were apparent also in American military thinking. Some US strategists recommended engaging enemy forces in Manchuria on the basis of Japanese experiences, opining that "ground forces in South Manchuria should be concentrated along lines running through Shenyang and Xinjing areas" and that "operations in North Manchuria should be mounted along interior lines based upon Harbin, Qiqihar, and Xinjing. To control the South Manchurian heartland is to master the greater part of the whole country."[62] Early American contingency plans against the USSR involved carrier-based sorties to aid in withdrawing allied forces from north China and Korea and, in the 1950s, nuclear-armed American B-29s attacking key Soviet cities from a ring of bases including some in western China, as Manchuria was expected to be quickly overrun by the Soviets.[63] Soviet military deployments contributed to American suspicions. During the Korean War, for example, Soviet troops reportedly prepared to defend Changchun with a nearby garrison and deployed heavy bombers to the city's airfield.[64]

Changchun Japanese were caught amid these events, Stalin himself targeting Changchun for bombing in August 1945.[65] Takasaki Tatsunosuke, successor to Ayukawa Yoshisuke as Mangyō president, heard Xinjing's air raid sirens just after midnight. Ordered to destroy coal mines lest they fall into Soviet hands, he spent the next few days organizing a civilian association with Yoshida Shin, a retired general who formerly commanded the Guandong Defence Army and had recently become Manchuria Telegraph and Telephone president. From their headquarters in the Minakai department store, they unsuccessfully encouraged the commander in charge of the capital to declare it a demilitarized zone. They also recommended not evacuating the capital's residents, in order to first aid Japanese fleeing remoter areas. Beginning on 11 August, they pressed civilians into building defensive works.[66]

Some fled. Ikemiyagi Sumiko sheltered underground when Soviet planes began bombing the city, mistaking them for American B-29s. Bombs left a large hole near the municipal hospital, and rumours circulated that trucks were taking Japanese troops to the train station from nearby Kantōgun barracks. She attempted to evacuate to the suburbs but was dogged by mobs and heavy rain. Returning home, she heard the emperor's speech on the radio accepting the Potsdam Declaration. In the following days, she heard rifle shots to the south when Manchurian troops rebelled and witnessed Japanese troops and colonists straggle into the capital. Although gas and water service stopped, she continued to have electricity.[67] Tani Miyuki's fictional – perhaps loosely autobiographical – *Changchun Tale* provides a glimpse into the bleak nature of life in the city for Japanese residents in the chaos following the surrender. According to the book, only Japanese reported for work the morning of 9 August. Asked to bring his personal effects to the ministry, the protagonist was given a sword and assigned guard duties in addition to burning documents. On 15 August, he heard the emperor's speech and, later that day, was aware of a Soviet plane landing in the field behind the Supreme Court building. Although some Japanese soon opted to evacuate, the protagonist elected to stay. Allowed to remain in the ministry's dormitory, he spent the next eight months finding food, helping Japanese refugees, and confronting typhus. The city's tramways became open-air markets, and he managed to find rice wine for New Year celebrations, hiding cash in his clothes and avoiding Soviet and Chinese soldiers. CCP forces were also present but willing to ignore Japanese for the most part. In the fall, though, they demanded the residents' association provide three hundred blankets. Some Japanese Kenpeitai resided in the dormitory briefly, collaborating with Soviet forces before being deported to Siberia. Tani suggests that the Japanese in Changchun were by this point living communally – as dictated by survival.[68] Compulsory social "levelling" occurred among Japanese in Dalian as well.[69]

The diplomat Zhang Jia'ao confirmed bleak conditions in Changchun when he arrived in October 1945, noting "the city is now empty" and "prices in Changchun are rather low, but there is a shortage of goods." The Soviets had closed banks and the printing bureau and had confiscated puppet currency. As a result, "the market has completely ceased to function."[70] Many Japanese outside the puppet capital nonetheless headed to it. In Yushu, 150 kilometres northeast, Marusugi Sakube was heading out to fish in the river when the sirens began on 9 August. He was able to reach Xinjing only on 10 October and Japan on 8 September 1946.[71] In Qiqihar, Nakamura Tazuko rushed to the station the morning of 9 August to try to send a woman and her children back to the capital – she had gone to meet her husband, recently called for duty. Unable to get to Changchun herself, she remained in Qiqihar until September 1946.[72]

Thousands of Japanese able to evade Soviet troops and Chinese posses aimed for the puppet capital in an attempt to escape to Japan, though many died en route, often in mass or solitary suicide.[73] By May 1946, some 206,000 Japanese crowded into Changchun – almost double the 1940 number – having endured a cold winter. Ikemiyagi Sumiko recalled temperatures of -30°C, although she could still use her *ondul* flooring for heat. Between cold, hunger, and typhus, some 25,000 Japanese died in Changchun that winter, though some were also caught in the fighting between Chinese Communists and Nationalists. Takasaki remembered the CCP soldiers positively, reporting no rapes by them and that they paid for goods rather than stealing. Between the end of the war and 1949, some 27,000 Japanese died in Changchun, almost 16 percent of postwar Japanese fatalities in Manchuria.[74] Nozoe Rishō also reported cold weather, forced labour for Soviet soldiers, and food shortages.[75] Sources typically report the danger of cholera, but the Changchun region also experienced plague, glanders, and anthrax in 1946, 1947, and 1951, perhaps a legacy of Unit 100. Another legacy was an enormous burial pit of victims uncovered by farmers in 1949.[76]

To confront shared challenges, the Japanese residents' association established clinics and other forms of assistance. Soviet troops presented another kind of challenge. Soviet officials required Japanese to wear red armbands and aid in acquiring war booty, warning that any harm done to Soviet personnel would be on pain of death for all Japanese in the city. Not all Japanese complied with the edict, and some accused those who collaborated of treason. Japanese presumably received some form of pay, though, as Chinese donned armbands as well to obtain work. Yet rampant inflation rendered any income of little value – prices for staples and clothing had rocketed from the 1937 baseline of 100 to 36,816 and 40,432, respectively, by the time Nationalist troops arrived in the spring of 1946.[77]

Most Japanese managed to leave Changchun by the end of 1947 – the US vice-consul there reported in January 1948 only around 1,000 Japanese and 1,500 Koreans "at [the] bottom of [the] ladder suffering and destitute."[78] Repatriation proved difficult. Soviet officials ignored requests from Japanese residents, preferring instead to focus on collecting war booty, and, with the sabotaging of rail lines, the Chinese Civil War disrupted transportation and communications. Many Japanese who had evacuated to northern Korea could not proceed further after the arrival of Soviet forces; others stuck in China became pawns in the Chinese Civil War. Ten thousand to twenty thousand (or more) Japanese gathered in Tonghua, where some joined Communist forces. Others joined Nationalists fighting Korean communists in February 1946, leading to reprisals. Citing Japanese figures, Lu Minghui reported five hundred arriving in Tonghua from Changchun, but noted 25 percent larger Chinese estimates for the Japanese total.[79] American and Nationalist officials had little choice but to prioritize repatriating those Japanese who were south of the Great Wall, though fears of more Japanese joining Communist ranks likely prompted evacuation efforts once Nationalist forces reached Changchun. Repatriation remained difficult, even within Nationalist zones. Japanese in Changchun had to make repeated requests to Tokyo for aid, ultimately raising their own funds to effect their return. Altogether, over a million Japanese were repatriated from Manchuria by September 1948, and the process continued into the 1950s.[80] Also fleeing Manchuria were hundreds of thousands of Koreans – potentially as many as one million – whom Chinese commonly identified as Japanese agents, subjecting them to abuse, even in Changchun.[81] Inevitably, the repatriation process missed some Japanese, even in Manchukuo's former capital.[82] Desperate, a group of forty-eight walked from Changchun to Shenyang in June 1948.[83]

Ironically, as Soviet officials refused to allow repatriation via Yingkou and Dalian, the only port available to Japanese was Huludao in southwestern

Manchuria, where the Americans had established a temporary base. In earlier decades, a Dutch firm had begun constructing the port at Huludao on behalf of Zhang Xueliang to challenge Japan's domination of Manchurian trade through Dalian, but Japanese completed it after the Manchurian Incident.[84] Getting to Huludao from places like Changchun in 1946 was challenging. Many arrived sick and died in the port, buried facing Japan near Huludao's Mount Cishan.[85] Transportation was often indirect and crude. After leaving Changchun on an open freight car with a barrel to use as a toilet, Ikemiyagi Sumiko spent a week in Shenyang and then two weeks in Jinzhou before being allowed to board a ship for Japan. A cholera outbreak on board delayed later voyages.[86] Also leaving Changchun in July in an open freight car, the protagonist in *Changchun Tale* travelled directly to Jinzhou but was detained there, also due to a cholera outbreak. Three weeks passed before those in the camp were allowed to proceed to Huludao.[87] It took a month for Toide Takeshi, born in Changchun the year after the Manchurian Incident, his mother, and two younger siblings to reach Japan from Changchun in September and October 1946, and another week to reach their father's birthplace on Shikoku. Despite the ordeal, they were more fortunate than Toide's father, who never arrived home.[88]

Many Japanese were unable to repatriate in 1946 because Chinese authorities detained them, especially technicians deemed vital to war needs.[89] For example, Nationalists declared the father of Endō Homare a technician because he ran a pharmaceutical company in the capital, and later the Eighth Route Army did the same. In addition to watching others leave Changchun, comforting refugees and the dying, seeing to explosive chemicals under successive military occupations, and contending with looters, cholera, and hunger, her family had also to endure the siege. Leaving less than a month before the city's fall in 1948, not all members of her family survived, and some who did suffered flashbacks and survivors' guilt. Navigating the perils of early Communist China and its various campaigns, they spent two years in Yanji, where there was a small Japanese community, and three in Tianjin, before arriving in Japan in 1953 following the Korean ceasefire. Born in Xinjing in 1941, Endō was one of many Japanese who set foot in Japan after the war for the very first time.[90]

Also suffering extended hardship and loss were the more than 600,000 Japanese soldiers and civilians detained in the Soviet Union who endured years of hard labour in coal mines, lumberyards, and fisheries, despite being physically unfit and of low productivity – 26,000 from Xinjing alone.[91] Ten appear to have escaped to Changchun in 1948 and were repatriated.[92] Most eventually returned to Japan in 1956, but were often perceived to have acquired a communist taint, as was Endō Homare. And they were not the only ones stigmatized. Japanese women who conceived in the two months following the surrender would have been ready to give birth the summer of 1946, prompting popular concerns for potentially Soviet- or Chinese-fathered progeny in Japan.[93] Repatriation continued for decades, as others continued to straggle home, including orphans taken in by Chinese.[94]

Imperial Attitudes

Japanese ventured to and shaped colonial outposts for diverse purposes, but together they constructed and occupied spaces that shared characteristics with society in Japan. For Henri Lefebvre, built space is historically coded, betraying underlying economic and social systems. Uniform structures in the era of modern capitalism can represent the "triumph of homogeneity," given that the commodification of space results in "the production of virtually identical 'cells'" where consumers' lifestyles are constrained by social norms. Lefebvre pointed to 1907 as the year when painters, becoming aware of this, revolutionized the representation of space.[95] This was the year Japanese began building in Changchun, and the railway town's planning, architecture, and economy followed Japanese and international practices, generally supporting Lefebvre's argument. Nishizawa Yasuhiko would concur, given his assertion that colonial architecture is properly part of "world architecture," its frontier development linked to practices at home, nearby, and globally. Japan's modern colonial architecture was like improvements in sanitation, electrical power, and the economy – replicating practices elsewhere while adapting to new settings. Moreover, it was another means of enticing the support of foreign peoples by improving lifestyles and assimilating them, a tactic that went back, in the context of Changchun, to Gotō Shinpei, who sought to "carry out the strategy of hegemony under the banner of the kingly way (*ōdō*)."[96] The Japanese inability to genuinely revolutionize the city after 1931 means that Xinjing's planning, architecture, and economy further corroborates Lefebvre, despite Japanese claims of transcendence. The imperial capital remained essentially a capitalist and colonial space – in fact, Manchukuo may have been doomed not only by the limitations noted above but also by those inherent to all authoritarian projects. Although acknowledging the potential for multiple modernities, Charles Taylor observes that, despite capitalist society's issues, "the various forms of fascism and related authoritarianism have failed."[97]

Diplomats and soldiers carved out and defended the Japanese presence in Changchun, but civilians created this space, reported on it, and brought memories of it to Japan after 1945. In addition to being a town and city, Changchun and Xinjing were lived spaces and included residents' activities and perspectives that, like planning, architecture, and economy, reflected patterns elsewhere. Habituating to the built environment, inhabitants walked its streets, imbibing it in pursuit of their daily affairs as they passed buildings and posters or grasped its imagery in currency, stamps, and other paraphernalia (Figure 5.1). Lived space is meaningful, revealing a relationship between space and identity. Dan Shao has shown how Manchurian space – in her case, territory – helped define evolving Manchu identities.[98] Noting that, after the First World War, Japanese increasingly perceived colonial enclaves as "imperial space," Emer O'Dwyer observed that "empires are cultural phenomena that depend upon broad societal consensus," and that Dalian "was made more Japanese through the expansion of civil society."[99] Similarly, the Japanese experience in Changchun and Xinjing represented more than an expanding railway or a military-run fiefdom. Colonial urbanism also involved evolving local identities, created by Japanese through their activities and emerging within the broader framework of a larger imperial identity. Generally modern and patriotic, this identity initially shared the reflexively progressive view of the imperial project held by men such as Nitobe Inazō.[100] Although some endeavoured to shift this identity after 1931 to include Pan-Asianist trappings and augmented state authority, it remained imperial and modern, and repatriates returned with memories of it as such, in addition to the distress of the journey home.

Of course, for those born or raised from youth overseas, "home" was not necessarily Japan; still, linguistic and other realities of life made them Japanese. Louise Young might observe they were part of a "total empire," Jun Uchida might note their contributions to creating a modern Japanese state and empire, and Lori Watt and Mariko Tamanoi might suggest that any alienation they experienced on their return contributed to the formation of postwar Japanese society.[101] Such a cohort is important, because these individuals were often inclined to a more accommodating view of non-Japanese. Japanese in Manchuria, for example, sometimes adopted Chinese pronunciations of certain Chinese characters (*kanji*), such as *ma* for *horse*, as in *maro*

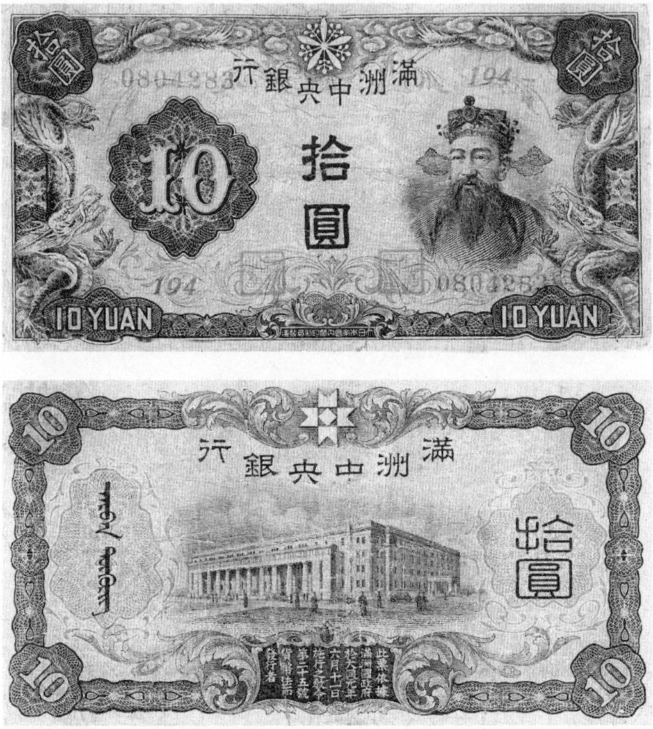

Figure 5.1 Ten-yuan note. Manchukuo currency featured Manchurian locales and state iconography, such as the new central bank on the ten-yuan note. The figure here is perhaps Zhao Gongming, a Daoist prosperity god.

(horse road) or *macho* (horse cart), or even *yancho* (goat cart), using such pronunciations in Japan.[102] One former railway town resident recalled teasing a Russian with the Chinese taunt of "big nose" (*dabizi*).[103] The author of *Changchun Tale* frequently used the Chinese character *gu* (Jp, *ko* [thigh]) to refer to a bureaucratic "section," which is nonsensical in Japanese though acceptable in Chinese. More generally, while the protagonist's dormitory retained vestiges of Japan, such as a small household shrine (*kamidana*), he did not see his life in the capital as simply Japanese. He noted differing Chinese and Japanese names for bureaus and made fun of how poorly a Japanese friend spoke Chinese.[104] Although Japanese generally sought to lead and assimilate, some were perhaps becoming "bicultural."[105]

Some Japanese, including some in the military, believed in Pan-Asianism. Manchukuo's rhetoric came from civilian ideologues such as Tachibana

Shiraki who were genuine Pan-Asianists.[106] Reaching out to help Chinese motivated many Japanese – such as Mantetsu researcher Itō Takeo – to take up work in Manchuria before 1931.[107] Another such figure was Ōuchi Takao, who moved to Changchun in 1921 to enrol in the Changchun Commercial School. After working briefly for Mantetsu, he became a translator of Chinese literature. Working in Xinjing after the Manchurian Incident, he was a believer in racial harmony, despite Chinese friends' scepticism.[108] Etō Toshio and Miyazawa Jirō opened Datong Academy in 1932, which was initially located north of the main rail station on the outskirts of the former Russian railway town but later joined other academic institutions and the police academy in Xinjing's southeastern corner. With a motto of *teishin funan* (volunteer to go where it is difficult), the academy aimed to train Manchukuo's future leaders, not just Japanese, in ideology and practical matters.[109] Andrew Hall found language instructors optimistically working toward uniting the empire through language, even if they were sidelined after 1943.[110] Some in the film industry may also have supported a Pan-Asian vision. Although film was an important propaganda tool, some within the industry – and by extension likely some in the publishing industry – may have accepted Manchukuo's racial harmony as genuine.[111] Even some foreign visitors thought many Japanese were genuine. A British diplomat noted that "whether or not the world wants Japanese in Manchukuo, one must anyhow recognize that the Japanese are an extremely efficient people and are in dead earnest. Many of them honestly believe they have a mission to make this country the paradise of the East."[112]

The pioneer photojournalist Kuwahara Kineo is renowned for his affectionate portrayal of Tokyo. In 1940 – the year 2600 for Japanese – Kuwahara visited Manchuria, joining a Mantetsu photographic crew. His work was featured in a postwar publication, *Manchuria 1940,* a title that echoed other work (e.g., *Tokyo 1937*). Pictures of Xinjing appear amid photos of soybeans, industries, and open spaces. Among the images catching his eye were the open spaces of the new capital and vast supplies of bricks lying in wait. While images like these perhaps typically indicate an expectation of potential, this does not seem to have been Kuwahara's judgment: the caption he provided for a photo of a streetscape said that only in Xinjing could be found "this kind of modern-style, wretched city."[113] Of course, such an observer's postwar stance can be questioned as an attempt to distance himself from militarism and failure, but this sentiment seems consistent with Kuwahara's earlier work. If so, it suggests that not all Japanese found Manchukuo's new capital agreeable. Yet finding views in this vein is challenging. Surrealist painter Suzuki Yasunori's 1936 *Kokuto kensetsu* (*Constructing the Capital*) depicts apparently angry Chinese and primitive tools employed in building Xinjing, but his work also supported the view that Japanese leadership in Manchuria was necessary.[114] Few Japanese were willing to publicly challenge the dominant discourse, especially after the outbreak of war.[115] The flamboyant Kawashima Yoshiko did so, drawing police surveillance and possibly assassination.[116] This reluctance would likely have been more the case for Japanese in Changchun and Xinjing than elsewhere in the region, given the amplified authority of Japanese and Manchukuo officials and the heightened concerns that came with residing among a larger population of non-Japanese. Moreover, Japanese in Xinjing presumably supported wartime security measures as much if not more than their fellow citizens at home.

A tension within the Japanese colonial imaginary regarding relationships with Chinese and others was evident from the outset. Although China had long been a model and source of wealth for Japanese, views changed radically over the late nineteenth and early twentieth centuries.[117] Travel and academic literature conveyed critical views of Chinese, since observations of their conditions often fell short of Japanese expectations.[118] In his 1909 trip to Manchuria, for example, the novelist Natsume Sōseki noted that Chinese were diligent workers, but in a serial newspaper column he observed with distaste that they were often "dirty."[119] A similar tension emerged in Manchukuo. The Kantōgun initially heeded some of the concerns of the more genuine Pan-Asianists, although increasingly ignored them over the 1930s in asserting control. This change drove men such as Komai Tokuzō, a former Mantetsu agricultural expert and first director-general of the Council of State's General Affairs Board, out of Manchukuo's senior administration, to be replaced by Tokyo technocrats such as Hoshino Naoki, who were more interested in augmenting state authority in order to renovate society. Yet Pan-Asianists themselves often held problematic views. Komai, for example, accepted a "semi-imperial" form of government for Manchukuo.[120] Others naively assumed Chinese would happily accept some kind of shared arrangement in Manchuria with Japanese, with Japanese playing leading roles.[121] This perspective was evident in various contexts, including seemingly altruistic endeavours like self-improvement movements for Manchukuoans.[122] Others perceived Chinese more stereotypically. In addition to recalling the Chinese love for melons, for example, after the war Okano Kanki described workers at a Jilin match factory as "using not yet modernized handicraft tools yet working honestly and efficiently, as busy as beavers." After reporting that they engaged in bestiality, he then implicitly, and revealingly, contrasted the workers with a Japanese acquaintance. During the war, this man lost everything he made on the continent, but, due to his "indomitable nature," proved a success in postwar Japan.[123]

Of course, any society contains a range of attitudes, although some observers, such as Yoshimi Yoshiaki, think Manchukuo and Occupied China generally attracted more self-interested carpetbaggers.[124] Yet even such self-serving individuals shared certain attitudes with those favouring Pan-Asianism. In addition to the hopes and fears present in the social imaginary noted above, Japanese in Changchun and Xinjing typically assumed their presence to be legitimate. Accepting it as rightful granted them expectations that their communities would continue and flourish, a shared social world built as "a community of time as well as space."[125] Yet while constructing empire – "incremental imperialism," to Young – meant progress, it also meant living as a minority group in close proximity with others, many of whom were unreceptive to the Japanese presence.[126] Empire was more tangible for those overseas, and emerging challenges to Japanese perceptions and expectations engendered defensiveness and eventual support for radical solutions.

Cities like Changchun were designed by planners and architects, financed by corporate and government officials, but lived in by people, many carrying memories and visions of life overseas when they returned home. These perceptions were multifaceted and evolving, but several themes appear persistent. Japanese society in Changchun was modern, yet retained a strong nativist sentiment. It was capitalist, yet willing to experiment with organizational aspects of that system. It was proud of local achievements, though harboured continuing anxieties with respect to existential threats. And it was imperial, complicit in the expansion of the Japanese empire, aware that Changchun and Xinjing were on its front lines. Postwar Japanese society retains all four of these dimensions, and, while it is more internationalist in outlook, pride in prewar imperial undertakings, as in constructing Changchun and Xinjing, remains evident.

Today, Manchuria represents a kind of intellectual prison for Japanese. Many extol Japanese actions there before 1945, dismissing some of the more extreme measures as aberrant or necessary because of the war. Yet clearly, the Japanese presence in Manchurian towns and cities was generally less altruistic and more uncertain than positive postwar accounts tend to depict. The inaugural issue of *Manshū to Nihonjin,* for example, included an essay by the former Manchukuo bureaucrat Furumi Tadayuki justifying Japanese actions. Reminding readers that Manchukuo was to be an ideal country practising ethnic harmony, Furumi insisted that the young Japanese who went there were passionately committed to creating a new order and that, despite losing the war, Japanese learned much there of use for building postwar Japan. Nor was Furumi alone in this view – quite a few Japanese remained proud of their activities in Manchuria.[127] Hoshino Naoki went so far as to call Manchukuo a "twentieth-century Atlantis."[128] Small wonder that Yamamuro Shin'ichi, in his award-winning 1993 study *Kimera* (*Chimera*), prompted debate in denouncing Manchukuo.[129] Many have simply avoided negative aspects of the Japanese experience – for example, in reviewing Koshizawa Akira's study of planning in Changchun and Xinjing, Nishizawa Yasuhiko noted that Koshizawa did not consider civilian contributions to Japanese imperialism.[130] A generally positive narrative has blinded – and continues to blind – many to the realities of empire building, but a more complete understanding of the cares and concerns of Japanese in places like Changchun might help shift attitudes. Observing that "a city brings together in the same space different ages, offering to our gaze a sedimented history of tastes and cultural forms," Paul Ricoeur suggests that "the city gives itself as both to be seen and to be read." Although individual buildings represent specific narratives, "the city ... gives rise to more complex passions." In part this is because cities can serve as territorial *lieux de mémoire,* subject to contestation.[131] Scholars such as Yamamuro and Nishizawa, among others, show that this contestation is underway.

Epilogue

Corporations like Mantetsu were dismantled during the American occupation of Japan, but did not entirely disappear. Though partially bombed, its Tokyo headquarters was repaired by December 1946 and occupied by American personnel as the Mantetsu Apartments.[132] The building later became an annex for the US Embassy, housing for several decades on its top two floors the US Information Agency. Manchurian infrastructure was likewise repurposed by Chinese. Changchun's long central avenue became Stalin Boulevard, later People's Boulevard. A tall memorial to Changchun's liberation by Soviet forces, erected in 1961, remains the central icon on People's Plaza (formerly Datong Plaza). The bank on People's Plaza reportedly became a joint staff headquarters for Soviet, Chinese, and North Korean officers at the outset of the Korean War before it returned to being a bank.[133] Some prominent Chinese returned to liberated Changchun, such as Li Yuqin – Puyi's fourth wife – who passed away in 2001, and rumours reported Kawashima Yoshiko there, escaping execution.[134] Changchun Film Studio took over the former Man'ei grounds. Many of Xinjing's sports facilities and official buildings remain, several housing government or academic institutions, distinguishing Changchun from the more industrial cities in China's northeast. Although Changchun gained the now enormous Jiefang Automotive Company (First Auto Works) in 1953, occupying some of the former Man'ei and Unit 100 grounds, Manchukuo's *Badabu* (Eight Big Ministry) buildings, as the Manchukuo state buildings are now called in China, have become something of a tourist destination. So is the Jingyuetan Reservoir, currently encompassing two hundred square kilometres of picturesque scenery and skiing. A pre-war Japanese presence lurks within Changchun today.

Although Japan refused to offer reparations, it has provided much developmental aid to China. One project inaugurated after normalizing relations in 1972 was the China–Japan Friendship Purification Plant in Changchun's northeastern suburb of Xinglongshan, east of the Yitong River, built in 1986–88 with loans from the Japan International Cooperation Agency. Providing around 40 percent of the city's water needs, the plant received Japanese aid for upgrading in the early 1990s and 2000s, indicating a long-term commitment on the part of Japan to Chinese aid.[135] East of the southern end of the old Manchukuo government buildings along the east bank of the Yitong can also be found the Sino-Japanese Friendship Hall, another joint project. Opened in August 1998, the hall features a Japanese garden and hosts a variety of events, including receptions of high-level dignitaries.[136] Another instance of cooperation involves the joint construction of a massive new monorail system – the longest monorail network in the world – in Chongqing by Changchun Railway Vehicles – formerly the Changchun Car Company, founded in 1954 in the former Russian settlement – and Hitachi. With support from the Japan Bank for International Cooperation, this network is to help Chongqing serve as a gateway to the opening of western China to development.[137]

Although Chinese and Japanese corporations can cooperate, the governments of Japan and the People's Republic of China commemorate the Manchurian Incident and the Asia-Pacific War contrarily. Japanese politicians have prayed at Yasukuni Shrine and bureaucrats have defended less than critical portrayals of Japan's wartime history in textbooks, but the People's Republic of China has promoted patriotic assertions in various ways, including designating 18 September as National Humiliation Day (*Guochiri*) in 2001, to remember the Manchurian Incident annually.[138] This observance was to help bring China's "century of humiliation," beginning with the Opium Wars, to a close, but it also raises public attention. For Chinese, the Manchurian Incident is typically portrayed as the start of the Anti-Japanese War, paving the way for the establishment of the People's Republic. Yet China displayed a level of restraint during China's 1956 war crime trials. Of the 1,062 Japanese defendants, 969 had been taken prisoner in Manchuria. Yet only 45 high-ranking Manchukuo officials and Japanese generals were convicted. The remainder were pardoned and repatriated immediately; those convicted returned to Japan by 1964. Leniency was intended to help re-establish relations with Japan in a manner supporting those more inclined to assist the People's Republic; indeed, some of the pardoned formed a group urging better relations. Chinese media then supported the state's action by placing the blame for war more generally on militarism and imperialism than on Japanese specifically.[139] This view echoed the judgment of the Tokyo War Crimes Trials and early Cold War historiography absolving Japanese society at large from responsibility in building empire.

In reality, constructing empire meant expanding Japan's developing society as well as its imperial authority. The two proceeded together interdependently, even if motivations were not exactly aligned. Building a modern Manchuria meant both creating a sphere of Japanese dominion on the Asian mainland as well as continuing to build a modern Japan. If some Japanese needed inducement, others leaped at opportunities. The result was a diverse range of activities that mostly defy simple categorizing as essentially "good" or "bad." Coming to terms with the totality of Japanese involvement in Manchuria requires accepting a view embracing the various aspects of this experience.

Postwar Chinese and Japanese views of Manchuria, the war era, and each other naturally continue to shift.[140] Perhaps a more nuanced historical view, embracing the entirety of this varied experience, may one day emerge. This would be useful for more than ensuring friendly diplomatic relations. Murakami Haruki suggests that issues arising from the puppet state continue to trouble contemporary Japan's well-being. Manchuria stalks the Japanese psyche in his novel *The Wind-Up Bird Chronicle*, but he also draws explicit parallels between it and the 1995 sarin gas attack in Tokyo in his first work of non-fiction. While Japan's best and brightest went to Manchuria "full of possibilities," they needed to escape Japan's state structure in order "to find an effective outlet for all their energy." Concluding that "in that sense ... they had pure motives," he finds them similar to Aum Shinrikyō cultists who were "Manchuria-like," suffering from a "lack of broad world vision, and the alienation between language and actions that results from this."[141]

Human beings are storytellers, and we tend to believe the stories we tell ourselves. There are, however, consequences to the particular stories we choose to tell. The stories Japanese have told themselves about constructing empire in Manchuria have ranged over the course of the twentieth century and into the twenty-first from the triumphant to the sorrowful. Both were true, albeit for different facets of that experience. Yet the entire range is necessary to understand the experience. Japanese officials justified their presence in Manchuria with idealistic visions and emotional tugs but would never have succeeded without the active participation of civilians who either shared these goals or pursued related ones of their own. Any burden regarding the guilt of empire in Manchuria has to be broadly shared. Constructing empire involved not only soldiers, bureaucrats, and corporations, but ordinary citizens as well.

Represented to Japanese as an imperial and modern statement, the Japanese railway town at Changchun in actuality also had much for its Japanese inhabitants to be anxious about. The town's context inherently and continuously challenged its modernity and prosperity. Manchukuo's capital, Xinjing, seemingly offered an array of solutions for these existential anxieties yet ultimately failed to solve them, simultaneously making some issues worse and introducing new ones. Anxieties rebounded, eventually compounded by the miseries of invasion and repatriation and complicated by the needs of postwar reconstruction. Although Japanese today are often aware of the outline of this history, there is space yet to fill in for individual Japanese to further deconstruct its empire and legacies. After all, "in every respect, the citizen remains the ultimate arbiter."[142]

Notes

Abbreviations

Journals

CIED	*Chronology of International Events and Documents*
MTN	*Manshū to Nihonjin* (*Manchuria and the Japanese*)
RGAPCI	*Reports of the General Assembly of the Presbyterian Church in Ireland*

Journals Cited as Newspapers

MKZ	*Manshū kenchiku zasshi* (*Journal of Manchurian Architecture*) – published as *Manshū kenchiku kyōkai zasshi* (*Journal of the Manchurian Architecture Association*) 1921–33
TK	*Toshi kōron* (*Urban Review*)

Newspapers

MNNS	*Manshū nichi nichi shinbun* (*Manchuria Daily News*) – published as *Manshū nippō* (*Manchuria Daily*) 1927–35 and *Manshū shinbun* 1944–45
YS	*Yomiuri shinbun* (*Yomiuri News*)

Archives

HIWRP	Hoover Institution on War, Revolution, and Peace
NAS	National Archives of Scotland

Other

CIA	Central Intelligence Agency
FRUS	United States Department of State, *Foreign Relations of the United States*
MFKEZ	*Mantetsu fuzokuchi keiei enkaku zenshi* (*History of the Development and Management of Mantetsu Attached Land*)
SSC	*Shinkyō shigai chizu* (*Street Map of Shinkyō*)
STKH	*Shinkyō toshi kensetsu hōsaku* (*Plans for the Construction of Shinkyō*)

Preface

1 Ian Buruma, *The Wages of Guilt: Memories of War in Germany and Japan* (New York: Farrar, Straus, and Giroux, 1994); Bill Sewell, "Postwar Japan and Manchuria," in *Japan at the Millennium: Joining Past and Future,* ed. David W. Edgington (Vancouver: UBC Press, 2003), 97–119.

2 For example, Sekai bunkasha, ed., *Wasureenu Mantetsu: ima aratani tadoru Chūgoku tōhoku chihō kyōshū no arubamu* (Tokyo: Sekai bunkasha, 1988).

3 Geoff Eley, "What Produces Fascism: Preindustrial Traditions or a Crisis of a Capitalist State," *Politics and Society* 12, no. 1 (1983): 71.

4 William Appleman Williams, *The Tragedy of American Diplomacy,* rev. ed. (New York: Dell, 1962), 9.

5 Caroline Elkins and Susan Pedersen, "Settler Colonialism: A Concept and Its Uses," in *Settler Colonialism in the Twentieth Century: Projects, Practices, Legacies,* ed. Caroline Elkins and Susan Pedersen (New York: Routledge, 2005), 1–20; Jordan Sand, "Subaltern Imperialists: The New Historiography of the Japanese Empire," *Past and Present* 225, no. 1 (2014): 273–88.

6 For example, Robert A. Bickers, *Britain in China: Community, Culture, and Colonialism, 1900–1949* (Manchester: Manchester University Press, 1999).

7 Ibid., 125; Mark R. Peattie, "The Japanese Treaty Port Settlements in China, 1895–1937," in *The Japanese Informal Empire in China, 1895–1937,* ed. Peter Duus, Ramon H. Myers, and Mark R. Peattie. (Princeton, NJ: Princeton University Press, 1989), 170.

8 "Manshū to wa nan datta no ka: toku shū," *Kan* 10 (Summer 2002); Nakami Tatsuo, ed., *Manshū to wa nan datta no ka* (Tokyo: Fujiwara shoten, 2006).

9 Shokuminchi bunka gakkai, Chūgoku tōhoku rinkan jūyonnenshi sōhenshitsu, ed., Tokushū: *Manshūkoku to wa nan datta no ka: NitChū kyōdō kenkyū* (Tokyo: Shōgakukan, 2008); Shokuminchi bunka gakkai, ed., *Kindai Nihon to Manshūkoku* (Tokyo: Fuji shuppan, 2014).

10 Koshizawa Akira, *Manshūkoku no shuto keikaku: Tōkyō no genzai to mirai o tou* (Tokyo: Nihon keizai hyōronsha, 1988); *Harupin no toshi keikaku, 1898–1945* (Tokyo: Sōwasha, 1989); and "Taiwan, Manshū, Chūgoku no toshi keikaku," in *Kindai Nihon to shokuminchi,* vol. 3, ed. Ōe Shinobu et al. (Tokyo: Iwanami shoten, 1993), 183–241.

11 Fujimori Terunobu, *Nihon no kindai kenchiku,* 2 vols. (Tokyo: Iwanami shoten, 1993); Fujimori Terunobu and Wang Tan, eds., *Zenchōsa higashi Ajia kindai no toshi to kenchiku* (Tokyo: Taisei kensetsu, 1996).

12 Nishizawa Yasuhiko, "Manshūkoku no kensetsu jigyō," in *Manshūkoku no kenkyū,* ed. Yamamoto Yūzō (Tokyo: Ryokuin shobō, 1995), 377–460; *Umi o watatta Nihonjin kenchikuka: 20 seiki zenhan no Chūgoku tōhoku chihō ni okeru kenchiku katsudō* (Tokyo: Shōkokusha, 1996); *Manshū toshi monogatari* (Tokyo: Kawade shobō shinsha, 1996); and *Nihon shokuminchi kenchiku ron* (Nagoya: Nagoya daigaku shuppansha, 2008).

13 David D. Buck, "Railway City and National Capital: Two Faces of the Modern in Changchun," in *Remaking the Chinese City: Modernity and National Identity, 1900–1950,* ed. Joseph W. Esherick (Honolulu: University of Hawai'i Press, 1999), 65–89; David Vance Tucker, "Building 'Our Manchukuo': Japanese City Planning, Architecture, and Nation-Building in Occupied Northeast China" (PhD diss., University of Iowa, 1999); William Sewell, "Japanese Imperialism and Civic Construction in Manchuria" (PhD diss., University of British Columbia, 2000); Qinghua Guo, "Changchun: Unfinished Capital Planning of Manzhouguo, 1932–1942," *Urban History* 31, no. 1 (2004): 100–17.

14 Henri Lefebvre, *The Production of Space,* trans. Donald Nicholson-Smith (Malden, MA: Blackwell, 1991), 36–46, 413–15.

15 James J. Orr, *The Victim as Hero: Ideologies of Peace and National Identity in Postwar Japan* (Honolulu: University of Hawai'i Press, 2001), 6–10, 137–42, 156–69.

16 For discussions of Hugh Byas, Andrew Pooley, Edgar Snow, Putnam Weale, and H.G.W. Woodhead, see Peter O'Connor, *The English-Language Press Networks of East Asia, 1918–1945* (Folkestone, UK: Global Oriental, 2010). Weale and Woodhead are also discussed in Bickers, *Britain in China.*

17 Mark Metzler, *Lever of Empire: The International Gold Standard and the Crisis of Liberalism in Prewar Japan* (Berkeley: University of California Press, 2006), 33, 250.

18 Prasenjit Duara, *Sovereignty and Authenticity: Manchukuo and the East Asian Modern* (Lanham, MD: Rowman and Littlefield, 2004), 41. A contrary view is Nishimura Shigeo, *Chūgoku kindai tōhoku chiikishi kenkyū* (Kyoto: Hōritsu bunkasha, 1984).

19 Juha Janhunen, *Manchuria: An Ethnic History* (Helsinki: Finno-Ugrian Society, 1996).
20 Duara, *Sovereignty and Authenticity,* 59–61, 76–79; Suk-jung Han, "The Problem of Sovereignty: Manchukuo, 1932–1937," *positions* 12, no. 2 (2004): 457–78; David Tucker, "Colonial Sovereignty in Manchuria and Manchukuo," in *The State of Sovereignty: Territories, Laws, Populations,* ed. Douglas Howland and Luise White (Bloomington: Indiana University Press, 2009), 75–93; Thomas David DuBois, "Inauthentic Sovereignty: Law and Legal Institutions in Manchukuo," *Journal of Asian Studies* 69, no. 3 (2010): 749–70.
21 See Bill Sewell, "Railway Outpost and Puppet Capital: Urban Expressions of Japanese Imperialism in Changchun, 1905–1945," in *Colonialism and the Modern World: Selected Studies,* ed. Gregory Blue et al. (Armonk, NY: M.E. Sharpe, 2002), 283–98; "Kyū Manshū ni okeru senzen Nihon no machizukuri katsudō," *Nichibunken Foramu* 160 (December 2003); "Manshūkoku kokuto 'Shinkyō' no datsukōchiku," in *Nitchū sensōki Chūgoku no shakai to bunka,* ed. Ezra Vogel and Hirano Ken'ichirō (Keio University Press, 2010), 291–327; "Beans to Banners: The Evolving Architecture of Prewar Changchun," in *Harbin to Hanoi: The Colonial Built Environment in Asia, 1840 to 1940,* ed. Laura Victoir and Victor Zatsepine (Hong Kong: Hong Kong University Press, 2012), 37–57; and "Manufacturing Japan in Manchuria," in *Resilient Japan: Papers Presented at the 24th Annual Conference of the Japan Studies Association of Canada,* ed. Bill Sewell (Halifax: Japan Studies Association of Canada, 2013), Chap. 8, Kindle.

Introduction

1 Imperial Japanese Government Railways, *An Official Guide to Eastern Asia: Trans-Continental Connections between Europe and Asia,* vol. 1, *Manchuria and Chōsen* (Tokyo: Imperial Japanese Government Railways, 1913), 5, 62.
2 A partial list, organized chronologically, includes Okabe Makio, *Manshūkoku* (Tokyo: Sanseido, 1978); Komagome Takeshi, *Shokuminchi teikoku Nihon no bunka tōgō* (Tokyo: Iwanami shoten, 1996); Louise Young, *Japan's Total Empire: Manchuria and the Culture of Wartime Imperialism* (Berkeley: University of California Press, 1998); Yanagisawa Asobu, *Nihonjin no shokuminchi keiken: Dairen Nihonjin shōkōgyōsha no rekishi* (Tokyo: Aoki shoten, 1999); Yoshihisa Tak Matsusaka, *The Making of Japanese Manchuria, 1904–1932* (Cambridge, MA: Harvard University Press, 2003); Tsukase Susumu, *Manshū no Nihonjin* (Tokyo: Yoshikawa, 2004); Nishizawa Yasuhiko, *Nihon shokuminchi kenchiku ron* (Nagoya: Nagoya daigaku shuppansha, 2008); and Emer O'Dwyer, *Significant Soil: Settler Colonialism and Japan's Urban Empire in Manchuria* (Cambridge, MA: Harvard University Press, 2015).
3 Frank W. Iklé, "The Triple Intervention: Japan's Lesson in the Diplomacy of Imperialism," *Monumenta Nipponica* 22, nos. 1/2 (1967): 122–30; Mutsu Munemitsu, *Kenkenroku: A Diplomatic Record of the Sino-Japanese War, 1894–1895* (Tokyo: University of Tokyo Press, 1982).
4 Guandong (Jp, Kantō), "east of the Pass," refers to the region beyond Shanhaiguan, the easternmost gate of the Great Wall, where it meets the sea.
5 Erik Esselstrom, *Crossing Empire's Edge: Foreign Ministry Police and Japanese Expansionism in Northeast Asia* (Honolulu: University of Hawai'i Press, 2009), 50–53, 85–90, 99–108.
6 Alvin D. Coox, "The Kwantung Army Dimension," in *The Japanese Informal Empire in China, 1895–1937,* ed. Peter Duus, Ramon H. Myers, and Mark R. Peattie (Princeton, NJ: Princeton University Press, 1989), 395–428.
7 C. Walter Young, *Japan's Special Position in Manchuria* (Baltimore: Johns Hopkins University Press, 1931), 69–86; Igor R. Saveliev and Yuri S. Pestushko, "Dangerous Rapprochement: Russia and Japan in the First World War, 1914–1916," *Acta Slavica Iaponica* 18 (2001): 19–41.

8 Masuda Hajimu, "Rumors of War: Immigration Disputes and the Social Construction of American-Japanese Relations, 1905–1913," *Diplomatic History* 33, no. 1 (2009): 1–37; Michael H. Hunt, *Frontier Defense and the Open Door: Manchuria in Chinese-American Relations, 1895–1911* (New Haven, CT: Yale University Press, 1973), 108–13; Akira Iriye, *Pacific Estrangement: Japanese and American Expansion, 1897–1911* (Cambridge, MA: Harvard University Press, 1972), 206–27; Mark Metzler, *Lever of Empire: The International Gold Standard and the Crisis of Liberalism in Prewar Japan* (Berkeley: University of California Press, 2006), 58–66, 125–29.

9 Young, *Japan's Special Position,* 193–238; Metzler, *Lever of Empire,* 148.

10 Paul E. Dunscomb, *Japan's Siberian Intervention, 1918–22: "A Great Disobedience against the People"* (Lanham, MD: Lexington Books, 2011); Frederick R. Dickinson, *War and National Reinvention: Japan in the Great War, 1914–1919* (Cambridge, MA: Harvard University Press, 1999), 180–200.

11 Dickinson, *War and National Reinvention,* 159–74, 182–87; Metzler, *Lever of Empire,* 98–109, 124–25.

12 Gavan McCormack, *Chang Tso-lin in Northeast China, 1911–1928: China, Japan, and the Manchurian Idea* (Stanford, CA: Stanford University Press, 1977); Ronald Suleski, *Civil Government in Warlord China: Tradition, Modernization and Manchuria* (New York: Peter Lang, 2002); Kwong Chi Man, "Finance and the Northern Expedition: From the Northeast Asian Perspective, 1925–1928," *Modern Asian Studies* 48, no. 6 (2014): 1695–739.

13 Rana Mitter, *The Manchurian Myth: Nationalism, Resistance, and Collaboration in Modern China* (Berkeley: University of California Press, 2000), 21–37; Nishimura Shigeo, *Chūgoku kindai tōhoku chiikishi kenkyū* (Kyoto: Hōritsu bunkasha, 1984), 205–22.

14 Matsusaka, *Making of Japanese Manchuria,* 363–77; Felix Patrikeeff, *Russian Politics in Exile: The Northeast Asian Balance of Power, 1924–1931* (Oxford: Palgrave Macmillan, 2002).

15 Hoover Institution on War, Revolution, and Peace, XX536, Robert Smith reports, Robert Smith, "The Week in Manchuria. Notes on Local Currencies, finances, etc" (1932), 29; Metzler, *Lever of Empire,* 135–36.

16 Barbara Brooks, *Japan's Imperial Diplomacy: Consuls, Treaty Ports, and War in China, 1895–1938* (Honolulu: University of Hawai'i Press, 2000), 91–92; Mark R. Peattie, *Ishiwara Kanji and Japan's Confrontation with the West* (Princeton, NJ: Princeton University Press, 1975), 115–18.

17 Akira Iriye, "Chang Hsüeh-liang and the Japanese," *Journal of Asian Studies* 20, no. 1 (1960): 33–43.

18 Edgar Snow, *Far Eastern Front* (London: Jarrolds, 1934), 68.

19 Tetsuya Sakai, "The Soviet Factor in Japanese Foreign Policy, 1923–1937," *Acta Slavica Iaponica* 6 (1988): 30–33; Yanagisawa, *Nihonjin no shokuminchi keiken,* 235–37.

20 Chen Benshan, ed., *Riben qinlüe Zhonguo dongbei shi* (Changchun: Jilin daxue chubanshe, 1989), 229–37; Mitter, *Manchurian Myth,* 29, 31, 157, 159–60.

21 Yanagisawa, *Nihonjin no shokuminchi keiken,* 168–72.

22 Suleski, *Civil Government,* 118–24, 212.

23 Arthur de C. Sowerby, "The Exploration of Manchuria," *Geographical Journal* 54, no. 2 (1919): 88–89.

24 Thomas R. Gottschang and Diana Lary, *Swallows and Settlers: The Great Migration from North China to Manchuria* (Ann Arbor: University of Michigan Press, 2000), 38–40, 169; Suleski, *Civil Government,* 91–98.

25 Brooks, *Japan's Imperial Diplomacy,* 114–15; Hyun Ok Park, *Two Dreams in One Bed: Empire, Social Life, and the Origins of the North Korean Revolution in Manchuria* (Durham, NC: Duke University Press, 2005), 94–95, 127–29; Pak Yong-sok, *Manpōzan jiken kenkyū: Nihon teikoku shugi no tairiku shinryaku seisaku no ikkan toshite* (Tokyo: Daiichi

shobō, 1981); Wang Lin and Gao Shuying, eds., *Wanbaoshan shijian* (Jilin: Renmin chubanshe, 1991).

26 South Manchuria Railway, *Second Report on Progress in Manchuria: To 1930* (Dairen: South Manchuria Railway, 1931), 7, 17; Suleski, *Civil Government,* 88–89; Westel W. Willoughby, *The Sino-Japanese Controversy and the League of Nations* (Baltimore: Johns Hopkins University Press, 1935), 395–96.

27 Takehiko Yoshihashi, *Conspiracy at Mukden: The Rise of the Japanese Military* (New Haven, CT: Yale University Press, 1963); Sadako N. Ogata, *Defiance in Manchuria: The Making of Japanese Foreign Policy, 1931–1932* (Berkeley: University of California Press, 1964); Peattie, *Ishiwara Kanji,* 87–133; Alvin D. Coox, *Nomonhan: Japan against Russia, 1939* (Stanford, CA: Stanford University Press, 1985), 1:17–39, 67–68; Richard T. Phillips, "'A Picturesque but Hopeless Resistance': Rehe in 1933," *Modern Asian Studies* 42, no. 4 (2008): 1–18; Snow, *Far Eastern Front,* 248–53. Japanese also seized four counties north of the Great Wall from Hubei Province and parts of two counties from the former province of Chahar. Waller Wynne, Jr., *The Population of Manchuria* (Washington, DC: US Government Printing Office, 1958), 6, 7, 85.

28 Parks Coble, *Facing Japan: Chinese Politics and Japanese Imperialism, 1931–1937* (Cambridge, MA: Harvard University Press, 1991); Youli Sun, *China and the Origins of the Pacific War, 1931–1941* (New York: St. Martin's Press, 1993), 41–62; Marjorie Dryburgh, *North China and Japanese Expansion, 1933–1937: Regional Power and the National Interest* (Richmond, UK: Curzon Press, 2000). Japanese planes may have threatened Beijing and Tianjin to compel the truce. Snow, *Far Eastern Front,* 254–58.

29 Coox, *Nomonhan,* 1:47–48, 58–60, 63–66.

30 Amano Yōichi, *Dabaokuo no matsueitachi: Firipin Nikkei kimin* (Nagoya: Fūbaisha, 1990); Hayase Shinzo, "The Japanese Residents of 'Dabao-kuo'," in *The Philippines under Japan: Occupation Policy and Reaction,* ed. Ikehata Setsuho and Ricardo Trota Jose (Quezon City, PH: Ateneo de Manila University Press, 1999), 247–87; Hatano Sumio, *Taiheiyō sensō to Ajia gaikō* (Tokyo: Tōkyō daigaku shuppansha, 1996), 115–16.

31 Young, *Japan's Total Empire;* Sandra Wilson, *The Manchurian Crisis and Japanese Society, 1931–33* (London: Routledge, 2001); Jürgen Osterhammel, "'Technical Co-Operation' between the League of Nations and China," *Modern Asian Studies* 13, no. 4 (1979): 661–80.

32 Gunther Stein, *Far East in Ferment* (London: Methuen, 1936), 23; Snow, *Far Eastern Front,* 84–85.

33 Bunroku Yoshioka, "Manchoukuo in Co-Prosperity Sphere," *Contemporary Japan* 11, no. 11 (1942): 1584–91.

34 James William Morley, ed., *Japan Erupts: The London Naval Conference and the Manchurian Incident, 1928–32* (New York: Columbia University Press, 1984); Coox, *Nomonhan,* 1: 60–62, 67–73; Dryburgh, *North China and Japanese Expansion;* James Boyd, "In Pursuit of an Obsession: Japan in Inner Mongolia in the 1930s," *Japanese Studies* 22, no. 3 (2002): 289–303; Owen Lattimore, "The Phantom of Mengkukuo," *Pacific Affairs* 10, no. 4 (1937): 420–27; Li Narangoa, "Japanese Geopolitics and the Mongol Lands, 1915–1945," *European Journal of East Asian Studies* 3, no. 1 (2004): 45–67.

35 Coble, *Facing Japan;* Sun, *China and the Origins,* 5–12, 32–39.

36 William C. Kirby, *Germany and Republican China* (Stanford, CA: Stanford University Press, 1984), 234–35; Michele Fatica, "The Beginning and the End of the Idyllic Relations between Mussolini's Italy and Chiang Kai-shek's China (1930–1937)," in *Italy's Encounters with Modern China: Imperial Dreams, Strategic Ambitions,* ed. Maurizio Marinelli and Giovanni Andornino (London: Palgrave Macmillan, 2014), 89–115.

37 El Salvador and the Vatican recognized Manchukuo in 1934, Italy and Spain in 1937, followed by German and Japanese client states after war's outbreak in 1939 and 1941. David Tucker, "Colonial Sovereignty in Manchuria and Manchukuo," in *The State of Sovereignty:*

Territories, Laws, Populations, ed. Douglas Howland and Luise White (Bloomington: Indiana University Press, 2009), 75–93. Some Japanese claimed Soviet recognition in April 1941. *The Manchoukuo Year Book, 1942* (Tokyo: Ajia tōkeisha, 1942), 364.

38 John J. Stephan, *The Russian Far East: A History* (Stanford, CA: Stanford University Press, 1994), 182–87, 190–99, 212–13, 233–35; Coox, *Nomonhan,* 1:74–91; Jonathan Haslam, *The Soviet Union and the Threat from the East* (Pittsburgh: University of Pittsburgh Press, 1992).

39 Coox, *Nomonhan;* Tsujita Fumio, "Kyū Manshū Toragashira yōsai no chōsa hōkoku," *Gunji shigaku* 43, no. 1 (2007): 51–72; George Alexander Lensen, *The Strange Neutrality: Soviet–Japanese Relations during the Second World War, 1941–1945* (Tallahassee, FL: Diplomatic Press, 1972), 21–34.

40 David Tucker, "France, Brossard Mopin, and Manchukuo," in *Harbin to Hanoi: The Colonial Built Environment in Asia, 1840 to 1940,* ed. Laura Victoir and Victor Zatsepine (Hong Kong: Hong Kong University Press, 2012), 61–64; Warren I. Cohen, *America's Response to China: A History of Sino-American Relations,* 5th ed. (New York: Columbia University Press, 2010), 117–23.

41 Robert J.C. Butow, *Tojo and the Coming of the War* (Stanford, CA: Stanford University Press, 1961), 343–44; Miyake Masaki, ed., *Shōwa-shi no gunbu to seiji: Taiheiyō sensō zen'ya* (Tokyo: Daiichi hōki, 1983), 47; James William Morley, ed., *Japan's Road to the Pacific War,* vol. 5, *The Final Confrontation: Japan's Negotiations with the United States, 1941* (New York: Columbia University Press, 1994), 216, 322.

42 British Foreign Office Files for Japan and the Far East, Series 1: Embassy and Consular Archives – Japan (1905–40), 262/1710/635–37, Miles W. Lampson to Austin Chamberlin, 24 April 1928; 262/1710/638–41, Berthold George Tours to Miles W. Lampson, 18 April 1928.

43 262/1708/140, British Foreign Office Files for Japan and the Far East, Series 1: Embassy and Consular Archives – Japan (1905–1940) [Frederick Edgar Wilkinson], "A Review of the Past and Present Policy of Japan in South Manchuria," 21 February 1928.

44 George H. Blakeslee, "Outstanding Facts in the Present Situation in China," *Annals of the American Academy of Political and Social Science* 138 (July 1928): 51.

45 John E. Orchard, "Japanese Expansion in China," *Annals of the American Academy of Political and Social Science* 152 (November 1930): 328–37.

46 Frank R. Eldridge, "Manchuria: The Race for New Resources," *Annals of the American Academy of Political and Social Science* 168 (July 1933): 99, 102.

47 Although Woodhead is unclear about which foreign communities, he does note White Russian approval. H.G.W. Woodhead, *A Visit to Manchukuo* (Shanghai: Mercury Press, 1932), 82–85.

48 Robert A. Bickers, *Britain in China: Community, Culture, and Colonialism, 1900–1949* (Manchester: Manchester University Press, 1999), 150, 227.

49 Zara Steiner, *The Lights That Failed: European International History, 1919–1933* (Oxford: Oxford University Press, 2005), 725.

50 Willoughby, *Sino-Japanese Controversy,* 392; John R. Stewart, "Manchuria as Japan's Economic Life-Line," *Far Eastern Survey* 4, no. 23 (1935): 182–86.

51 Juha Janhunen, *Manchuria: An Ethnic History* (Helsinki: Finno-Ugrian Society, 1996); and David Sneath, "Beyond the Willow Palisade: Manchuria and the History of China's Inner Asian Frontier," *Asian Affairs* 34, no. 1 (2003): 4–11. On growing links, see Nishimura, *Chūgoku kindai tōhoku.*

52 Richard L. Edmonds, "The Willow Palisade," *Annals of the Association of American Geographers* 69, no. 4 (1979): 599–621.

53 Robert H.G. Lee, *The Manchurian Frontier in Ch'ing History* (Cambridge, MA: Harvard University Press, 1970), 66–67 and 138–81; "Manshū denpōkyoku no kaishi," *Yomiuri shinbun* (hereafter *YS*), 28 December 1906, 1.

54 One example is Hattori Noboru, *Manshū* (Tokyo: Seikyōsha, 1913). Later publications specializing in photojournalism reaffirmed this, such as Mantetsu's *Manshū Gurafu* (*Manchuria Graph*). See also Young, *Japan's Total Empire,* 15.
55 Peter Duus, "Japan's Informal Empire in China, 1895–1937: An Overview," in Duus, Myers, and Peattie, *Japanese Informal Empire,* xi–xxix.
56 Ramon H. Myers, "Japanese Imperialism in Manchuria: The South Manchuria Railway Company, 1906–1933," in ibid., *Japanese Informal Empire,* 109n34; South Manchuria Railway, *Second Report on Progress,* 84; M. Royama, "The South Manchuria Railway Zone and the Nature of Its Administration," *Pacific Affairs* 3, no. 11 (1930): 1023.
57 Brooks, *Japan's Imperial Diplomacy,* 118–26; Young, *Japan's Special Position.*
58 Matsusaka, *Making of Japanese Manchuria,* 86–92, though there are many publications on Mantetsu.
59 "Tōkyō no ManMō kinenkan," *Manshū nichi nichi shinbun* (*Manchuria Daily News*) (hereafter *MNNS*), 11 August 1926, 2; "Mantetsu no ManMō kinenkan," *MNNS,* 8 September 1926, 1; "Mantetsu no nijūshūnen iwai," *Ōsaka mainichi shinbun* (*Osaka Daily News*), 18 March 1927. There are many works on the Mantetsu research department – one first-hand account is Takeo Itō, *Life along the South Manchurian Railway: The Memoirs of Ito Takeo,* trans. Joshua Fogel (Armonk, NY: M.E. Sharpe, 1988).
60 "Mantetsu birujingu shinchiku kōji," *Doboku kenchiku kōji kahō* 12, no. 6 (1936): 298–303; Nishizawa Yasuhiko, *Umi o watatta Nihonjin kenchikuka: 20 seiki zenhan no Chūgoku tōhoku chihō ni okeru kenchiku katsudō* (Tokyo: Shōkokusha, 1996), 55, 58.
61 Minami Manshū tetsudō kabushiki kaisha chōsaka, *Minami Manshū ni okeru Nihon no keizaiteki seiryoku* (n.p.: Manshū tetsudō, 1912), 10–12; Matsusaka, *Making of Japanese Manchuria,* 114–39.
62 Norio Tamaki, *Japanese Banking: A History, 1859–1959* (New York: Cambridge University Press, 1995).
63 Bank of Chosen, *Economic History of Manchuria* (Seoul: Bank of Chosen, 1921), 275; Metzler, *Lever of Empire;* 55–58, 105–6; Nishizawa, *Nihon shokuminchi kenchiku,* 131–37, 166–68.
64 South Manchuria Railway, *Second Report on Progress,* 110–12; Manshū tetsudō kabushiki kaisha chihōbu nōmuka, *Manshū zairai nōgyō* (Dairen: Manshū tetsudō chihōbu, 1935), 40.
65 (Manshūkoku) Jitsugyōbu rinji sangyō chōsakyoku, *Manshūkoku juyō shōhin gaikoku bōseki tōkei* (Shinkyō: [Manshūkoku] Jitsugyōbu rinji sangyō chōsakyoku, 1937), 1–9.
66 David Wolff, "Bean There: Toward a Soy-Based History of Northeast Asia," in *Harbin and Manchuria: Place, Space, and Identity,* ed. Thomas Lahusen (Durham, NC: Duke University Press, 2001), 241–52; John R. Stewart, "The Soya Bean and Manchuria," *Far Eastern Survey* 5, no. 21 (1936): 221–26; W. Mark Fruin, *Kikkoman: Company, Clan, and Community* (Cambridge, MA: Harvard University Press, 1983).
67 Mark R. Peattie, "The Japanese Treaty Port Settlements in China, 1895–1937," in *The Japanese Informal Empire,* Duus, Myers, and Peattie, 172.
68 Kamishima Jirō, *Kindai Nihon no seishin kōzō* (Tokyo: Iwanami, 1961).
69 Sandra Wilson, "The Discourse of National Greatness in Japan, 1890–1919," *Japanese Studies* 25, no. 1 (2005): 41, 43–44.
70 Cohen, *America's Response to China,* 55–68; Herbert Croly, *Willard Strait* (New York: Macmillan, 1924), 210; Hunt, *Frontier Defense,* 108–13
71 Brooks, *Japan's Imperial Diplomacy,* 119.
72 A.M. Pooley, ed., *The Secret Memoirs of Count Tadasu Hayashi, G.C.V.O.* (New York: G. P. Putnam's Sons, 1915), 265–68, 301.
73 Toyokichi Iyenaga, "Japan in South Manchuria," in *Japan and Japanese-American Relations,* ed. George H. Blakeslee (New York: G.E. Stechert, 1912), 272–73.

74 Wilson, "Discourse of National Greatness in Japan."
75 Carol Gluck, *Japan's Modern Myths: Ideology in the Late Meiji Period* (Princeton, NJ: Princeton University Press, 1985), 88–90; Donald Keene, "The Sino-Japanese War of 1894–95 and Its Cultural Effects in Japan," in *Tradition and Modernization in Japanese Culture,* ed. Donald H. Shively (Princeton, NJ: Princeton University Press, 1971), 121–75; Mark R. Peattie, "Japanese Attitudes toward Colonialism, 1895–1945," in *The Japanese Colonial Empire, 1895–1945,* ed. Ramon H. Myers and Mark R. Peattie (Princeton, NJ: Princeton University Press, 1984), 80–127; Naoko Shimazu, *Japanese Society at War: Death, Memory and the Russo-Japanese War* (Cambridge: Cambridge University Press, 2009).
76 Shumpei Okamoto, "The Emperor and the Crowd: The Historical Significance of the Hibiya Riot," in *Conflict in Modern Japanese History: The Neglected Tradition,* ed. Tetsuo Najita and J. Victor Koschmann (Princeton. NJ: Princeton University Press, 1982), 258–75.
77 Ian Nish, *Japanese Foreign Policy in the Interwar Period* (Westport, CT: Praeger, 2002), 76–77.
78 One example is Minami Manshū tetsudō kabushiki kaisha sōseishitsu chihōbu zanmuseiri iinkai, *Mantetsu fuzokuchi keiei enkaku zenshi* (Tokyo: Ryūkei shosha, 1977), 1:1. On this "blood debt," see Young, *Japan's Total Empire,* 92–93.
79 Jung-Sun N. Han, "Empire of Comic Visions: Japanese Cartoon Journalism and Its Pictorial Statements on Korea, 1876–1910," *Japanese Studies* 26, no. 3 (2006): 296; Annika A. Culver, *Glorify the Empire: Japanese Avant-Garde Propaganda in Manchukuo* (Vancouver: UBC Press, 2013), 11–33.
80 James Boyd, "'This Stalwart Fellow of Five Lands and Two Seas': The Life of Fukushima Yasumasa," *War and Society* 30, no. 3 (2011): 177–88.
81 Sakurai Tadayoshi, *Nikudan* (Tokyo: Eibun Shinshisha, 1906).
82 Wilson, *Manchurian Crisis,* 30–74; Young, *Japan's Total Empire,* 61–78.
83 Jennifer Robertson, "Japan's First Cyborg? Miss Nippon, Eugenics and Wartime Technologies of Beauty, Body and Blood," *Body and Society* 7, no. 1 (2001): 2–3.
84 Suleski, *Civil Government,* 29–30.
85 Gregory J. Kasza, *The State and the Mass Media in Japan, 1918–1945* (Berkeley: University of California Press, 1988), 57–61, 168–265.
86 Wilson, *Manchurian Crisis,* 68, quoting Gluck, *Japan's Modern Myths,* 9.
87 Akira Iriye, "Kayahara Kazan and Japanese Cosmopolitanism," in *Personality in Japanese History,* ed. Albert M. Craig and Donald H. Shively (Berkeley: University of California Press, 1970), 373–98.
88 Wilson, *Manchurian Crisis.*
89 Young, *Japan's Total Empire,* 8–14.
90 Ibid., 68–78; Barak Kushner, et. al. *The Thought War: Japanese Imperial Propaganda* (Honolulu: University of Hawai'i Press, 2006), 19–21; Culver, *Glorify the Empire;* Anne Wilkes Tucker et al., *The History of Japanese Photography* (New Haven, CT: Yale University Press, 2003), 151, 315–21, 374.
91 Hiromi Mizuno, *Science for the Empire: Scientific Nationalism in Modern Japan* (Stanford, CA: Stanford University Press, 2009); Aaron Stephen Moore, *Constructing East Asia: Technology, Ideology and Empire in Japan's Wartime Era, 1931–1945* (Stanford, CA: Stanford University Press, 2013).
92 Daqing Yang, *Technology of Empire: Telecommunications and Japanese Expansion in Asia, 1883–1945* (Cambridge, MA: Harvard University Press, 2010), 8–10, 400–3; Janis Mimura, *Planning for Empire: Reform Bureaucrats and the Japanese Wartime State* (Ithaca, NY: Cornell University Press, 2011), 3–6.
93 Tucker, "Colonial Sovereignty," 80–83; Itō, *Life along the South Manchurian Railway,* 123–33, 151–53, 156–77, 186–93, 203.
94 Nishizawa, *Nihon shokuminchi kenchiku ron,* 2–5.

95 Andre Schmid, "Colonialism and the 'Korea Problem' in the Historiography of Modern Japan: A Review Article," *Journal of Asian Studies* 59, no. 4 (2000): 951–76.
96 Yoshimi Yoshiaki, *Grassroots Fascism: The War Experience of the Japanese People,* trans. Ethan Mark (New York: Columbia University Press, 2015), 45–46.
97 Han, "Empire of Comic Visions," 301.
98 Oguma Eiji, *Tan'itsu minzoku shinwa no kigen* (Tokyo: Shin'yosha, 1995).
99 Eri Hotta, *Pan-Asianism and Japan's War, 1931–1945* (New York: Palgrave Macmillan, 2007).
100 James L. Huffman, *Creating a Public: People and Press in Meiji Japan* (Honolulu: University of Hawai'i Press, 1997), 380.
101 James Dorsey, "Literary Tropes, Rhetorical Looping, and the Nine Gods of War: 'Fascist Proclivities' Made Real," in *The Culture of Japanese Fascism,* ed. Alan Tansman (Durham, NC: Duke University Press, 2009), 409–31.
102 Charles Taylor, *Modern Social Imaginaries* (Durham, NC: Duke University Press, 2004), 91.
103 D. Eleanor Westney, *Imitation and Innovation: The Transfer of Western Organizational Patterns to Meiji Japan* (Cambridge, MA: Harvard University Press, 1987).
104 Noboru Kawazoe, *Contemporary Japanese Architecture,* trans. David Griffith (Tokyo: Kokusai bunka shinkokai, 1965), 13, 17–19.
105 Gregory Clancey, *Earthquake Nation: The Cultural Politics of Japanese Seismicity, 1868–1930* (Berkeley: University of California Press, 2006); William H. Coaldrake, *Architecture and Authority in Japan* (London: Routledge, 1996), 238.
106 Henri Lefebvre, *The Production of Space,* trans. Donald Nicholson-Smith (Malden, MA: Blackwell, 1991); Anthony Giddens, *The Constitution of Society* (Berkeley: University of California Press, 1984); Manuel Castells, *City, Class, and Power* (New York: St. Martin's Press, 1978).
107 Mariko Asano Tamanoi, *Memory Maps: The State and Manchuria in Postwar Japan* (Honolulu: University of Hawai'i Press, 2009), 49, 151–52.
108 Noriko J. Horiguchi, *Women Adrift: The Literature of Japan's Imperial Body* (Minneapolis: University of Minnesota Press, 2012).
109 Andrew Gordon, *Labor and Imperial Democracy in Prewar Japan* (Berkeley: University of California Press, 1992).
110 Gluck, *Japan's Modern Myths,* 187–89. One relevant example is Jeffrey E. Hanes, *The City as Subject: Seki Hajime and the Reinvention of Modern Osaka* (Berkeley: University of California Press, 2002), 46–52.
111 Taylor, *Modern Social Imaginaries,* 24–25, 182–83.
112 O'Dwyer, *Significant Soil,* 5.
113 Marjorie Dryburgh, "Japan in Tianjin: Settlers, State and the Tensions of Empire before 1937," *Japanese Studies* 27, no. 1 (2007): 19–34; Joshua A. Fogel, "'Shanghai-Japan': The Japanese Residents' Association of Shanghai," *Journal of Asian Studies* 59, no. 4 (2000): 927–50.
114 Jun Uchida, *Brokers of Empire: Japanese Settler Colonialism in Korea, 1876–1945* (Cambridge, MA: Harvard University Press, 2011); Todd A. Henry, *Assimilating Seoul: Japanese Rule and the Politics of Public Space in Colonial Korea, 1910–1945* (Berkley: University of California Press, 2014).
115 Bickers, *Britain in China.*
116 For example, see Leo Ou-fan Lee, *Shanghai Modern: The Flowering of a New Urban Culture in China, 1930–1945* (Cambridge, MA: Harvard University Press, 1999); Di Wang, *Street Culture in Chengdu: Public Space, Urban Commoners, and Local Politics, 1870–1930* (Stanford, CA: Stanford University Press, 2003).
117 Lee, *Manchurian Frontier,* 19–23, 73, 113, 135–37, 161–62; Koshizawa Akira, *Manshūkoku no shuto keikaku: Tōkyō no genzai to mirai o tou* (Tokyo: Nihon keizai hyōronsha, 1988), 32–35; Satō Akira, *Manshū zōen shi* (Tokyo: Nihon zōen shūkei kyōkai, 1985), 71; Dangdai

Zhongguo de Jilin congshu bianjibu, *Dangdai Zhongguo de Jilin,* vol. 2 (Beijing: Dangdai Zhongguo chubanshe, 1991), 340; James Reardon-Anderson, *Reluctant Pioneers: China's Expansion Northward, 1644–1937* (Stanford, CA: Stanford University Press, 2005), 41–43, 50.

118 David D. Buck, "Railway City and National Capital: Two Faces of the Modern in Changchun," in *Remaking the Chinese City: Modernity and National Identity, 1900–1950,* ed. Joseph W. Esherick (Honolulu: University of Hawai'i Press, 1999), 66.

119 H.E.M. James, *The Long White Mountain, or, A Journey in Manchuria* (London: Longmans, Green, 1888), 8, 295, 374, 377–78.

120 Dangdai Zhongguo de Jilin congshu bianjibu, *Dangdai Zhongguo de Jilin,* 2:340; "Jō sōtoku no hokkō," *MNNS,* 20 November 1907, 1.

121 Komine Kazuo, *Manchuria: kigen, shokumin, haken* (Tokyo: Ochanomizu shobō, 1991), 89–91.

122 James Boyd, "Undercover Acolytes: Honganji, the Japanese Army, and Intelligence-Gathering Operations," *Journal of Religious History* 37, no. 2 (2013): 189, 203.

123 Tsukase, *Manshū no Nihonjin,* 7–9.

124 Henry James Whigham, *Manchuria and Korea* (London: Isbister, 1904), 49, 54, 57; "Shina tairiku ni okeru rekkyō no tetsudō," *YS,* 6 February 1903, 1.

125 William Greener, *A Secret Agent in Port Arthur* (London: Archibald Constable, 1905), 36–37.

126 Rosemary Quested, *The Russo-Chinese Bank: A Multi-National Financial Base of Tsarism in China* (Birmingham, UK: University of Birmingham Press, 1977), 30–34.

127 Société des missions étrangères, *Compte-rendu des travaux* (1902), 88.

128 Quested, *Russo-Chinese Bank,* 43.

129 Steven G. Marks, *Road to Power: The Trans-Siberian Railroad and the Colonization of Asian Russia, 1850–1917* (Ithaca, NY: Cornell University Press, 1991), 155–56, 165–66.

130 Société des missions étrangères de Paris, Chine, Mandchourie, 567M, sub-folder 14, *Le R.P. Gaston Lebel, Missionnaire en Mandchourie* (Paris: Flers-de-l'Orne, 1908), 14.

131 Imperial Japanese Government Railways, *Official Guide,* 62.

132 B.L. Putnam Weale, *The Re-Shaping of the Far East,* vol. 2 (London: Macmillan, 1905), 497–99, 509–10.

133 W.H. Birkbeck, "Third Japanese Army Operations from 11 March 1905 to the Conclusion of Hostilities," in *The Russo-Japanese War: Reports from British Officers Attached to the Japanese Forces in the Field,* vol. 2, ed. British General Staff, War Office (London: His Majesty's Stationery Office, 1907), 482.

134 A.L. Haldane, "A Japanese Cavalry Raid against the Russian Lines of Communication in January, February, and March 1905," in ibid., 66–82, 553–56; General Aleksey Kuropatkin, *The Russian Army and the Japanese War: Being Historical and Critical Comments on the Military Policy and Power of Russia and on the Campaign in the Far East,* trans. Captain A.B. Lindsay, ed. Major E.D. Swinton (New York: E.P. Dutton, 1909), 1:232–42, 2:321–22.

135 "Daini no gyōsen," *YS,* 23 March 1905, 5; "Chōshun no chisei," *YS,* 24 March 1905, 5; "Chōshun no hōgyō jinchi," *YS,* 31 March 1905, 5; "Wagagun hokushin no jiki," *YS,* 15 May 1905, 2; "Teki zensen o sutsu?", *YS,* 24 June 1905, 2.

136 "Roosevelt Steps into the Breach," *Globe,* 21 August 1905, 1, 6.

137 "Oyama's Front 15 Miles: Russian Critic Believes Greatest Battle of the War Is to Come," *New York Times,* 5 April 1905, 5; "Fears for Linevitch Even among Russians," *New York Times,* 28 August 1905, 2.

138 "Russia Outwitted in Peace Treaty?" *New York Times,* 12 September 1905.

139 For example, "Chōshun hōmen no shūrai," *YS,* 22 September 1905, 5; "Chōshun kaisha no junbi," *YS,* 2 May 1906, 2.

140 “Minami Manshū tetsudō annai,” *MNNS,* 14 December 1907, 3; “Chōshun tetsudō fuzokuchi no taiyūbō,” *MNNS,* 27 January 1908, 2; “Kanjōshi teishajō mondai,” *YS,* 27 July 1906, 2; “Kanjōshi (Kuwanjōshi) no kyōkai,” *YS,* 15 August 1906, 2; “Kanjōshi kyōkai kyōteian,” *YS,* 16 December 1906, 2; “Kanjōshi mondai no sōten,” *YS,* 7 January 1907, 2; “Kanjōshi mondai ryakuketsu,” *YS,* 14 April 1907, 2; “Chōshun teishajō ichi,” *YS,* 21 June 1907, 2.

141 H. Enselme, *A travers la Mandchourie: Le Chemin de fer de l'est Chinois d'après la mission du Capitaine H. de Bouillane de Lacoste et du Capitaine Enselme* (Paris: J. Rueff, 1904), 114. The presence of rabbits was reported in “Menuki no shōkinyoko ga usagi no kariba datta,” *MNNS,* 6 June 1926, 7. On sharing and transfer see Manshikai, ed., *Manshū kaihatsu yonjūnenshi,* vol. 3 (Tokyo: Manshū kaihatsu yonjūnenshi kankōkai, 1965), 65; and Koshizawa, *Manshūkoku no shuto keikaku,* 46–50.

142 “Chōshun sonota no kaihō,” *YS,* 13 January 1907, 2.

143 Imperial Japanese Government Railways, *Official Guide,* 65–66.

144 Dimensions reported in “Chōshun shōfuchi no kikō,” *YS,* 22 August 1910, 2.

145 Hashiya Hiroshi, *Teikoku Nihon to shokuminchi toshi* (Tokyo: Yoshikawa kōbunkan, 2004), 14–18, 40–45; Koshizawa, *Manshūkoku no shuto keikaku,* 82–86.

146 Sowerby, “The Exploration of Manchuria,” 89.

147 Nishizawa, *Nihon shokuminchi kenchiku ron,* 112–14, 406; Koshizawa, *Manshūkoku no shuto keikaku,* 12–29; Kitaoka Shin'ichi, *Gotō Shinpei: gaiko to bijyon* (Tokyo: Chūō kōronsha, 1988).

148 Bill Sewell, “Reconsidering the Modern in Japanese History: Modernity in the Service of the Prewar Japanese Empire,” *Japan Review* 16 (2004): 213–58.

149 Jeffry A. Frieden, “International Investment and Colonial Control: A New Interpretation,” *International Organization* 48, no. 4 (1994): 559–93.

150 Ogata, *Defiance in Manchuria,* 118–25; Mimura, *Planning for Empire,* 41–69; Yamamuro Shin'ichi, *Manchuria under Japanese Dominion,* trans. Joshua A. Fogel (Philadelphia: University of Pennsylvania Press, 2006), 123–25; Prasenjit Duara, *Sovereignty and Authenticity: Manchukuo and the East Asian Modern* (Lanham, MD: Rowman and Littlefield, 2004); Tucker, “Colonial Sovereignty.”

151 Snow, *Far Eastern Front,* 223–25, 229, 263.

152 Peter Fleming, *One's Company: A Journey to China* (London: Jonathan Cape, 1934), 73–81.

153 Culver, *Glorify the Empire,* 43.

154 Yamamuro, *Manchuria under Japanese Dominion,* 61–81; Lincoln Li, *The China Factor in Modern Japanese Thought: The Case of Tachibana Shiraki, 1881–1945* (Albany: State University of New York Press, 1996).

155 Edmund S.K. Fung, “Anti-Imperialism and the Left Guomindang,” *Modern China* 11, no. 1 (1985): 39–76; Dan Shao, *Remote Homeland, Recovered Borderland: Manchus, Manchoukuo, and Manchuria, 1907–1985* (Honolulu: University of Hawai'i Press, 2011), 136–41.

156 *Kokutai no hongi: Cardinal Principles of the National Entity of Japan,* ed. Robert King Hall, trans. John Owen Gauntlett (Cambridge, MA: Harvard University Press, 1949), 5, 7, 8, 10–11, 30, 39, 59, 63, 75, 105; Suk-jung Han, “The Problem of Sovereignty: Manchukuo, 1932–1937,” *positions* 12, no. 2 (2004): 471–73.

157 Duara, *Sovereignty and Authenticity,* 64–65, 253; Han, “The Problem of Sovereignty,” 469; Thomas David DuBois, “Inauthentic Sovereignty: Law and Legal Institutions in Manchukuo,” *Journal of Asian Studies* 69, no. 3 (2010): 752–53.

158 Yamamuro, *Manchuria under Japanese Dominion,* 97, 110; Robert B. Valliant, “Japanese Involvement in Mongol Independence Movements, 1912–1919,” *Mongolia Society Bulletin* 11, no. 2 (1972): 1–32. Jin published a description of the new state in Jin Bidong, *ManMō no chishiki* (Tokyo: Hibonkaku, 1934).

159 Phyllis Birnbaum, *Manchu Princess, Japanese Spy: The Story of Kawashima Yoshiko, the Cross-Dressing Spy Who Commanded Her Own Army* (New York: Columbia University Press, 2015), 105–10, 219.

160 *Manchoukuo Year Book, 1942,* 122–33.

161 Pu Yi, *From Emperor to Citizen: The Autobiography of Aisin-Gioro Pu Yi,* vol. 2 (Peking: Foreign Languages Press, 1964), 275–76; Paul Kramer, ed., *The Last Manchu: The Autobiography of Henry PuYi, Last Emperor of China* (New York: Pocket, 1987), 177.

162 Snow, *Far Eastern Front,* 277–79.

163 Yamamuro, *Manchuria under Japanese Dominion,* 93–97.

164 Pu Yi, *From Emperor to Citizen,* 2:289–90.

165 Yamamuro, *Manchuria under Japanese Dominion,* 164–5; Mutō Tomio, *Watakushi to Manshukoku* (Tokyo: Bungei shunjū, 1988), 306–24; Kenneth J. Ruoff, *Imperial Japan at Its Zenith: The Wartime Celebration of the Empire's 2,600th Anniversary* (Ithaca, NY: Cornell University Press, 2010).

166 Manshūkoku kokumuin kōhōsho, *Manchoukuo: A Comprehensive Pictorial Presentation* (Tokyo: Asahi shinbunsha, 1942), 11–14.

167 Pu Yi, *From Emperor to Citizen,* Vol. 2, 254–55; Peter Zarrow, *After Empire: The Conceptual Transformation of the Chinese State, 1885–1924* (Stanford, CA: Stanford University Press, 2012), 270–71.

168 Yamamuro, *Manchuria under Japanese Dominion,* 97–115.

169 On this distinction, see David P. Barrett, "Introduction: Occupied China and the Limits of Accommodation," in *Chinese Collaboration with Japan, 1932–1945: The Limits of Accommodation,* ed. David P. Barrett and Larry N. Shyu (Stanford, CA: Stanford University Press, 2001), 8–12.

170 Yamamuro, *Manchuria under Japanese Dominion,* 4–6, Mitter, *Manchurian Myth,* 27–28, 93–102. On Taiwan, see Leo T.S. Ching, *Becoming "Japanese": Colonial Taiwan and the Politics of Identity Formation* (Berkeley: University of California Press, 2001).

171 Snow, *Far Eastern Front,* 268, 271–74.

172 Woodhead, *Visit to Manchukuo,* 2, 36, 86–91.

173 For the Manchus, see Shao, *Remote Homeland,* 101–2, 138, 155–56. The Mongolian response is reported by the missionary-turned-reporter Jean-Cyprien Balet, who favoured Manchukuo, and the Indian civil-servant-turned-Tibetologist Charles Bell: see J.C. Balet, *La Mandchourie, historique, politique, economique, son avenir* (Paris: Payot, 1932), 191–96, and Charles Bell, "The Struggle for Mongolia," *Journal of the Royal Central Asian Society* 24 (1937): 59–63, 66–67. For Korean responses, see Brooks, *Japan's Imperial Diplomacy,* 115; and Park, *Two Dreams in One Bed,* 124–61.

174 Pu Yi, *From Emperor to Citizen,* 2:173–214; Kramer, *Last Manchu,* 115–25; Yamamuro, *Manchuria under Japanese Dominion,* 145–54.

175 Marjorie Dryburgh, "The Fugitive Self: Writing Zheng Xiaoxu, 1882–1938," in *Writing Lives in China, 1600–2010,* ed. Marjorie Dryburgh and Sarah Dauncey (London: Palgrave Macmillan, 2013), 121–28.

176 Yamamuro, *Manchuria under Japanese Dominion,* 103, 110; Mitter, *Manchurian Myth,* 27–28; Rikugunshō chōsahan hen, *Manshūkoku seiritsu no ikisatsu to sono kokka kikō ni tsuite* (Tokyo: Rikugunshō chōsahan, 1932), 5–7; Chō Kinhaku, *Shinkokka daiManshū* (Tokyo: Tōkyō shobō, 1932); Manshūkokushi hensan kankōkai, *Manshūkokushi* (Tokyo: Kokusai zenrin kyōkai, 1973), 1:5, 2:120, 199–201, 212–13.

177 Mitter, *Manchurian Myth,* 78; DuBois, "Inauthentic Sovereignty," 754.

178 Fei Cui and Ren Zhaoxiang, "Zhao Xinbo Ju'e Yichan'an Jiemi," *Longmen zhen* 10 (2013): 84. I am grateful to Yuan Jianda for bringing this to my attention.

Chapter 1: City Planning

1 The railway towns in Shenyang, Liaoyang, and Changchun occupied 11.72, 6.48, and 5.04 km^2 respectively. Minami Manshū tetsudō kabushiki kaisha sōseishitsu chihōbu zanmuseiri iinkai, *Mantetsu fuzokuchi keiei enkaku zenshi* (Tokyo: Ryūkei shosha, 1977) (hereafter *MFKEZ*), 33–34. Chinese Changchun included 2.34 km^2. Shinkyō tokubetsushi shichōkanbō shomuka, *Yakushin kokuto no iyō* (Shinkyō: Shinkyō tokubetsushi kōsho, 1940), 1:28.

2 *MFKEZ* 3:338; Koshizawa Akira, *Manshūkoku no shuto keikaku: Tōkyō no genzai to mirai o tou* (Tokyo: Nihon keizai hyōronsha, 1988), 47–50; "Gotō sōsai no hōppo shisatsu," *Yomiuri shinbun*, 13 July 1907, 1.

3 Koshizawa, *Manshūkoku no shuto keikaku,* 51–53.

4 "Chōshun tokuden," *Manshū nichi nichi shinbun* (hereafter *MNNS*), 26 January 1908, 2; Koshizawa, *Manshūkoku no shuto keikaku,* 51–60; Inoue Nobuō, *Chōshun enkakushi* (Dairen: ManMō bunka kyōkai, 1922), 35–36.

5 Nishizawa Yasuhiko, *Nihon shokuminchi kenchiku ron* (Nagoya: Nagoya daigaku shuppansha, 2008), 232–34.

6 Koshizawa, *Manshūkoku no shuto keikaku,* 53–54.

7 Shinkyō tokubetsushi shichōkanbō shomuka, *Kokuto Shinkyō: Kenkoku jūshūnen kinan* (Shinkyō: Shinkyō tokubetsushi kōsho, 1942), 16.

8 Izumi Renji, *Chōshun jijō* (Chōshun: Chōshun Nihōsha, 1912), 146–52; Koshizawa, *Manshūkoku no shuto keikaku,* 54–57, 62–64.

9 Koshizawa, *Manshūkoku no shuto keikaku,* 57–58.

10 H.G.W. Woodhead, *A Visit to Manchukuo* (Shanghai: Mercury Press, 1932), 37–38.

11 Matsumiya Kichirō, ed., *Shinkyō* (Hōten: Mantetsu tetsudō sōkyoku eigyōkyoku ryōkyokuka, 1937), 4; Satō Akira, *Manshū zōen shi* (Tokyo: Nihon zōen shūkei kyōkai, 1985), 81–82; *Shinkyō shigai chizu* (Tokyo: Kanemitsusha shiryōbu, 1982) (hereafter *SSC*).

12 Koshizawa, *Manshūkoku no shuto keikaku,* 57–68.

13 Matsumiya, *Shinkyō*, 4.

14 "Mantetsu no keiei," *MNNS,* 5 February 1908, 4.

15 "Sakusei jigyō no kaishi," *MNNS,* 13 February 1908, 4. Rapid town growth posed challenges, but a steady water supply was achieved by 1926. "Yoyaku mizu no anshin dekiru: Chōshun no jōsuidō," *MNNS,* 1 July 1926, 4.

16 On zoning in Japan, see André Sorenson, *The Making of Urban Japan: Cities and Planning from Edo to the Twenty-First Century* (London: Routledge, 2002), 108–24.

17 "Chōshun shigai no kenchiku to Mantetsu," *MNNS,* 3 March 1908, 2.

18 "Menuki no shōkinyoko ga usagi no kariba datta," *MNNS,* 6 June 1926, 7.

19 Gaimushō tsūshōkyoku, *Chōshun no jijō* (n.p.: Gaimushō, 1929), 61 and map in front matter; Koshizawa, *Manshūkoku no shuto keikaku,* 72–73, 79, 81; Nishizawa, *Nihon shokuminchi kenchiku ron*, 29, 149–50, 234.

20 "Kitamongai dōrō shūzen," *MNNS,* 9 September 1908, 4.

21 Shinkyō tokubetsushi shichōkanbō shomuka, *Kokuto Shinkyō* (1942), 18; Shinkyō tokubetsushi shichōkanbō shomuka, *Yakushin kokuto no iyō*, 28; David D. Buck, "Railway City and National Capital: Two Faces of the Modern in Chanchun," in *Remaking the Chinese City: Modernity and National Identity, 1900–1950,* ed. Joseph W. Esherick (Honolulu: University of Hawai'i Press, 1999), 78; Koshizawa, *Manshūkoku no shuto keikaku,* 52–56.

22 Inoue, *Chōshun enkakushi,* 8–9; Kantōgun shireibu, ed., *Minami Manshū shuyō toshi keizai jōtai* (n.p.: Kantōgun shireibu, 1924), 2:361.

23 For example, Minami Manshū tetsudō kabushiki kaisha shomubu chōsaka, ed., *Minami Manshū tetsudō kabushiki kaisha dainiji jūnenshi* (Dairen: Minami Manshū tetsudō, 1928).

24 Koshizawa Akira, "Taiwan, Manshū, Chūgoku no toshi keikaku," in *Kindai Nihon to shokuminchi,* vol. 3, ed. Ōe Shinobu et al. (Tokyo: Iwanami shoten, 1993), 200.

25 "Chōshun fuzokuchi," *MNNS,* 5 February 1908, 4.
26 Dazai Matsusaburō, *Manshū gendaishi* (Dairen: Mantetsu, 1925), 11; Yamada Hisetarō, *ManMō toyū zenshi,* (Tokyo: Nikkan Shina jijōsha, 1926), 2:24; Kantōgun shireibu, *Minami Manshū shuyō toshi keizai jōtai,* 2:360.
27 "Yoshinomachi han'eisaku," *MNNS,* 19 August 1926, 4.
28 For example, Hattori Noboru, *Manshū* (Tokyo: Seikyōsha, 1913), 466, 473.
29 Sorenson, *Making of Urban Japan,* 108–9.
30 Toshi kenkyūkai, "Toshi keikaku to hōritsu hitsuyō," *Toshi kōron* (*Urban Review*) (hereafter *TK*) 2, no. 2 (1919): 1.
31 Gotō Shinpei, "Toshi kaizen to toshi kenkyūkai no shimei," *TK* 4, no. 1 (1921): 2–8; Gotō Shinpei, "Toshi no kairyō to shimin no kakugo," *TK* 3, no. 1 (1920): 3.
32 For example, see the pseudonymous Hokuto Oiboshi, "Manshū toshi keikaku gaikan," *TK* 4, no. 11 (1921): 38–40; and (Osaka mayor) Seki Hajime, "Kinsei toshi no hatten to toshi keikaku," *TK* 7, no. 12 (1924): 2–22.
33 Studies of urban development as modernist projects include Koshizawa, *Manshūkoku no shuto keikaku;* Jordan Sand, *House and Home in Modern Japan: Architecture, Domestic Space, and Bourgeois Culture, 1880–1930* (Cambridge, MA: Harvard University Press, 2003); Sorenson, *Making of Urban Japan;* and Gregory Clancey, *Earthquake Nation: The Cultural Politics of Japanese Seismicity, 1868–1930* (Berkeley: University of California Press, 2006).
34 Hozumi Shigetō, "Sekai chūshin toshi sōken no keikaku ni tsuite," *TK* 2, no. 7 (1919): 25–36 and no. 8 (1919): 27–33.
35 Takei Takashirō, "Toshi no kōen keikaku," *TK* 2, no. 11 (1919): 36–42 and no. 12 (1919): 42–48.
36 Shigenaga Hisomu, "Yūen no kinō ni tsuite," *TK* 5, no. 1 (1922): 48–50.
37 Ōta Kenkichi and Kitamura Tokutarō, "Toshi keikaku to kōen," *TK* 6, no. 7 (1923): 24–36. An appraisal of Tokyo parks after the great Kantō earthquake is Ōya Reijō, "Teito fukkō to kōen," *TK* 7, no. 3 (1924): 15–20.
38 Sano Riki, "Daitoshi no kenchikubutsu," *TK* 3, no. 3 (1920): 18–28; and "Toshi kenchiku no kaizen," *TK* 5, no. 9 (1922): 15–31. Both versions of Sano's given name appear in prewar publications, but Riki perhaps more commonly.
39 Anami Tsuneichi, "Toshi keikaku no sekkyokuka," *TK* 5, no. 5 (1922): 33–48.
40 For example, Jeffrey E. Hanes, *The City as Subject: Seki Hajime and the Reinvention of Modern Osaka* (Berkeley: University of California Press, 2002).
41 See, for example, Ōsuga Iwao, "Risō teki toshi," *TK* 18, no. 8 (1934): 41–53 and no. 10 (1934): 37–52.
42 On Le Corbusier, see Robert Fishman, *Urban Utopias in the Twentieth Century: Ebenezer Howard, Frank Lloyd Wright, and Le Corbusier* (New York: Basic Books, 1977), 163–263.
43 Norton Ginsburg, "Ch'ang-ch'un," *Economic Geography* 23, no. 4 (1947): 293.
44 The other success was in communications. Étienne Dennery, "Problèmes d'Extrême-Orient," *Annales de géographie* 46, no. 262 (1937): 346.
45 Until 1937, Harbin was the other special municipality. *The Manchoukuo Year Book 1942* (Tokyo: Ajia tōkeishi, 1942), 150, 342.
46 *Manshū kenchiku zasshi* (*Journal of Manchurian Architecture*) (hereafter *MKZ*) 12, no. 6 (1932). See also Manshū teikoku rinji kokuto kensetsu kyoku, *Kokuto kensetsu ni tsuite* (n.p.: Manshū teikoku rinji kokuto kensetsu kyoku, 1940), 25–30; Koshizawa, *Manshūkoku no shuto keikaku,* 110–11.
47 Nishizawa, *Nihon shokuminchi kenchiku ron,* 58–64.
48 Aiga Kensuke, "Kenkoku zengo no omoidasu," *MKZ* 22, no. 10 (1942): 9.
49 Nishizawa Yasuhiko, "Manshūkoku no kensetsu jigyō," in *Manshūkoku no kenkyū,* ed. Yamamoto Yūzō (Tokyo: Ryokuin shobō, 1995), 408.

50 *Manchoukuo Year Book, 1942*, 959; Koshizawa, *Manshūkoku no shuto keikaku*, 94, 110. The Chinese figurehead was Ruan Zhenduo (Yuan Chen-tse). David Tucker, "Colonial Sovereignty in Manchuria and Manchukuo," in *The State of Sovereignty: Territories, Laws, Populations*, ed. Douglas Howland and Luise White (Bloomington: Indiana University Press, 2009), 82–83.

51 Nishizawa Yasuhiko, *Umi o watatta Nihonjin kenchikuka: 20 seiki zenhan no Chūgoku tōhoku chihō ni okeru kenchiku katsudō* (Tokyo: Shōkokusha, 1996), 106–19.

52 The five to work under Aiga were Oka Ōji (later president of the association), Suzuki Masao (graduated Tokyo Industrial College, 1911), Kariya Tadama (Waseda University, 1914), Mita Nobuske (Tōkyō kōtō kōgyō gakkō fusetsu kyōin yōseijo, 1905), and Osono Tadasuke. Oka Ōji, "Manshū kenkoku jūnen to kenchiku zakkan," *MKZ* 22, no. 10 (1942): 2.

53 Aiga, "Kenkoku zengo no omoidasu," 7.

54 Koshizawa, *Manshūkoku no shuto keikaku*, 152–57; Manshū kaikoshū kankōkai, ed., *Aa Manshū: kuni tsukuri sangyō kaihatsusha no shuki* (Tokyo: Manshū kaikoshū kankōkai, 1965), 57–58, 918.

55 Aiga, "Kenkoku zengo no omoidasu," 5.

56 Ibid., 8.

57 Sano Riki, "Manshū no kokuto kensetsu keikaku," *Toshi mondai* 17, no. 2 (1933): 51.

58 Meetings and representatives in Minami Manshū tetsudō kabushiki kaisha keizai chōsakai, *Shinkyō toshi kensetsu hōsaku* (Dairen: Minami Manshū tetsudō, 1935) (hereafter *STKH*), i–iv; Koshizawa, *Manshūkoku no shuto keikaku*, 93–95, 110–11; Nishizawa, "Manshūkoku no kensetsu jigyō," 410–14.

59 Mantetsu published discussions similar to the *STKH* on these five cities as well as a general guide to planning Manchurian towns: Minami Manshū tetsudō kabushiki kaisha keizai chōsakai, *Manshū toshi kensetsu ippan hōsaku* (Dairen: Minami Manshū tetsudō, 1935).

60 *STKH*, i, 17. See also "Manshūkoku kokuto kensetsu keikaku gaiyō," *MKZ* 13, no. 11 (1933): 34–40.

61 Yūki Seitarō, "Kokuto kensetsu no kaiko to tenbō," *MKZ* 14, no. 2 (1934): 35–37; Yūki Seitarō, "Kokuto daiShinkyō kensetsu to nisan no mondai," *Manshū gijutsu kyōkaishi* 10, no. 58 (1934): 548.

62 Nakano Kinjirō, "Kokuto Shinkyō no kensetsu," *Dōryo no kairyō* 15, no. 12 (1933), 166; J.C. Balet, *La Mandchourie, historique, politique, economique, son avenir* (Paris: Payot, 1932), 97.

63 *STKH*, 6, 10.

64 Ibid., 17, 19, 24.

65 Ibid., 9, 78, 81, 90, 94, 97–99, 117.

66 Ibid., 26. On Xinjing's "ideal" nature, see, for example, *MKZ* 12, no. 6 (1932) and Manshū jijō annaijo, *Shinkyō jijō* (Shinkyō: Manshū jijō annaijo, 1934), 68.

67 Aiga, "Kenkoku zengo no omoidasu," 9.

68 *STKH*, 6, 78, 92, 103.

69 A foreign observer confirmed only five square kilometres were built on in 1937. J.R. S[tewart], "Hsinking – Manchuria's Boom Town," *Far Eastern Survey* 6, no. 6 (1937): 69.

70 Sano, "Manshū no kokuto kensetsu keikaku," 42, 51.

71 *STKH*, 102–9

72 Ibid., 26–27.

73 Yūki, "Kokuto daiShinkyō kensetsu to nisan mondai," 548.

74 Manshūkoku seifu kokumuin kokuto kensetsukyoku, *Kokuto daiShinkyō* (Shinkyō: Manshūkoku seifu kokumuin kokuto kensetsukyoku, 1933), 11.

75 Yūki, "Kokuto kensetsu no kaiko to tenbō," 35.

76 *STKH*, 33–36.

77 Nagami Ken'ichi, "Manshūkoku sandai toshi no kōen sonota," *Kōen ryokuchi* 3, nos. 4/5 (1939): 31.
78 *STKH*, 37.
79 *STKH*, 12–14, 78–85; David Tucker, "France, Brossard Mopin, and Manchukuo," in *Harbin to Hanoi: The Colonial Built Environment in Asia*, ed. Laura Victoir and Victor Zatsepine (Hong Kong: Hong Kong University Press, 2012), 66–68; Kondō Sōkō, "Yūki Seitarōsan o shinobu," in Manshū kaikoshū kankōkai, *Aa Manshū*, 112–13; Koshizawa, *Manshūkoku no shuto keikaku*, 100–8.
80 Nagami, "Manshūkoku sandai toshi no kōen sonota," 31; *STKH*, 97–98; Koshizawa, *Manshūkoku no shuto keikaku*, 100–8.
81 Ibid., 19, 37–43, 87–99; "Manshūkoku kokuto kensetsu keikaku gaiyō," 34–40; Koshizawa, *Manshūkoku no shuto keikaku*, 95–100. Alternative plans for Xinjing can be found in the *STKH bessatsu*.
82 Satō, *Manshū zōen shi*, 199.
83 *STKH*, 19.
84 Or *zentei*, as Gomibuchi and Koshizawa use the term *tei* (Ch, *ting*) for "court." *STKH*, 39; Koshizawa, *Manshūkoku no shuto keikaku*, 166.
85 *SSC*; Manshūkoku kokumuin kōhōsho, *Manchoukuo: A Comprehensive Pictorial Presentation* (Tokyo: Asahi shinbusha, 1942); Nishizawa, "Manshūkoku no kensetsu jigyō," 434–36; Satō, *Manshū zōen shi*, 60–61; Tsuda Yoshiki, "'Manshūkoku' kenkoku chūreibyō to kenkoku shinbyō no kenchiku ni tsuite," *Kanagawa daigaku 21-seiki COE puroguramu kenkyū suishin kaigi* (March 2008), 77; Nakajima Michio, "Shinto Deities That Crossed the Sea: Japan's 'Overseas Shrines,' 1868 to 1945," *Japanese Journal of Religious Studies* 37, no. 1 (2010): 35.
86 On the altar, see Murata Jirō, "Ten o matsuru kenchiku," *MKZ* 14, no. 3 (1934): 3–12; "Zai Shinkyō kōsaijō, Tendan shinchiku kōji gaiyō," *MKZ* 14, no. 3 (1934): 23; and Fueki Hideo, "Gyōkai no konjaku," *MKZ* 22, no. 11 (1942): 37. On Puyi and the temple, see Pu Yi, *From Emperor to Citizen: The Autobiography of Aisin-Gioro Pu Yi*, vol. 2 (Peking: Foreign Languages Press, 1964), 278–79, 300–1; Yamamuro Shin'ichi, *Manchuria under Japanese Dominion*, trans. Joshua A. Fogel (Philadelphia: University of Pennsylvania Press, 2006), 163–65; Nishizawa, "Manshūkoku no kensetsu jigyō," 437; and Tsuda, "'Manshūkoku' kenkoku chūreibyō to kenkoku shinbyō."
87 A discussion of this and other Guandi temples in Manchuria is Murata Jirō, "Kanteibyō kenchikushi no kenkyū," *MKZ* 9, no. 12 (1929): 1–45, and 10, no. 2 (1930): 1–33.
88 Thomas David DuBois, "Manchukuo's Filial Sons: States, Sects and the Adaptation of Graveside Piety," *East Asian History* 36 (December 2008): 10–15.
89 Laurence G. Liu, *Chinese Architecture* (London: Academy Editions, 1989), 35–53, 247–56; Nancy Shatzman Steinhardt, *Chinese Imperial City Planning* (Honolulu: University of Hawai'i Press, 1990); Bo Xinian, "Guanyu Mingdai gongdian tanmiaodeng dajianzhuqun zongti guihua shoufa de chubu tantao," in *Jianzhu lishi yanjiu*, ed. He Yeju (Beijing: Zhongguo jianzhu gongye chubanshe, 1992), 25–48; Zixuan Zhu and Reginald Yin-Wang Kwok, "Beijing: The Expression of National Political Ideology," in *Culture and the City in East Asia*, ed. Won Bae Kim et al. (Oxford: Clarendon Press, 1997), 127–30.
90 Koshizawa, *Manshūkoku no shuto keikaku*, 93–100; Koshizawa, "Taiwan, Manshū, Chūgoku no toshi keikaku," 208; Koshizawa Akira, "Shinkyō to Daitōkō no kensetsu kōsō," *Doboku gakkaishi* 78, no. 8 (1993): 24. A critique of Koshizawa along these lines is Zhang Zhenjia and Yang Jianping, "Watakushitachi kara mita 'Shinkyō to Daitōkō no kensetsu kōsō,'" *Doboku gakkaishi* 79, no. 12 (1994): 53–55.
91 *STKH*, 19, 100.
92 Ibid., 5–14.

93 The *STKH* did include a Mantetsu report on some of the cosmological significances involved in traditional Chinese planning. Ibid., 87–99, 127–30.
94 Nakano, "Kokuto Shinkyō no kensetsu," 166.
95 *STKH*, 19, 37–46.
96 Ibid., 12, 18, 43, 80, Appendix 1; Nakano, "Kokuto Shinkyō no kensetsu," 167.
97 SōA kenchiku renmei, "Manshū kenchiku no tenbō," *Gendai kenchiku* 8 (January 1940): 3.
98 *Shinkyō no gaikyō* (Shinkyō: Shinkyō shōkō kōkai, 1942), 11; *Manchoukuo Year Book, 1942*, 742.
99 *STKH*, 79. An earlier civic centre was in Seoul. Nishizawa, *Nihon shokuminchi kenchiku ron*, 94.
100 Mutō Tomio, *Watakushi to Manshukoku* (Tokyo: Bungei shunjū, 1988), 61.
101 Hōten tetsudōkyoku ryokyakukakari, *Shinkyō* (Hōten: Hōten tetsudōkyoku ryokyakukakari, 1941), 3; Shinkyō tokubetsushi shichōkanbō shomuka, *Kokuto Shinkyō* (1942), 210; *Shinkyō no gaikyō*, 110–11.
102 See the topographical view in Nakazawa Kiyoshi, "Shinkyōto keikaku ni taisuru shoken," *MKZ* 12, no. 6 (1932): 36. Koshizawa discusses the emerging capital street network in *Manshūkoku no shuto keikaku*, 120–33.
103 Sano, "Manshū no kokuto kensetsu keikaku," 43. Changchun rumours reported a secret underground railway between the Bank of Manchukuo and the main railway station.
104 Satō, *Manshū zōen shi*, 43, 94; Nagami, "Manshūkoku sandai toshi no kōen sonota," 32.
105 *STKH*, 66–69.
106 Ibid., 49.
107 Kitakōji Ken and Watanabe Manabu, *Chōshun, Kitsurin* (Tokyo: Kokusho kankōkai, 1982).
108 Hajime Miura, "Hsinking, Capital of Manchoukuo," *Far Eastern Review* 37 (March 1941): 97; Koshizawa, *Manshūkoku no shuto keikaku*, 169–70.
109 *SSC*; Shinkyō shōkō kaigijo, *DaiShinkyō keizai gaikan* (Shinkyō: Shinkyō shōkō kaigijo, 1937), 37–38. Bus routes are in Chōshun Kanjōshikai, ed., *Kanjōshi monogatari* (Tokyo: Chōshun Kanjōshikai, 2006), 6.
110 Shinkyō tokubetsushi shichōkanbō shomuka, *Kokuto Shinkyō* (1942), 106–7; *Shinkyō no gaikyō*, 39–44.
111 Shinkyō tokubetsushi shichōkanbō shomuka, *Kokuto Shinkyō* (1942), 107–8, 175.
112 Satō, *Manshū zōen shi*, 19.
113 *STKH*, 11, 20–21, 61–62, 101.
114 "Midori no rakuen o teikyō," *MNNS*, 9 August 1935, 5.
115 *STKH*, 96; Torita Ryūichi, "Toshi bōkū to kūchi," *TK* 14, no. 8 (1931): 15–20.
116 (Rikugun Taisa) Kuwabara Shirō, "Toshi keikaku to bōhō," *TK* 15, no. 5 (1932): 12–16.
117 Ikeda Kanji, "Aranaru toshi keikaku he (1)," *MKZ* 18, no. 7 (1938): 26; Tōkyōshi kikakubu keikakuka, "Doitsu ni okeru bōkū bōka taisaku," *MKZ* 18, no. 9 (1938): 24–30.
118 A photo and plan is in *MKZ* 21, no. 6 (1941) and Manshū jijō annaijo, *Shinkyō jijō*, 72. See also Koshizawa, *Manshūkoku no shuto keikaku*, 139–44.
119 Manshūkoku seifu kokumuin kokuto kensetsukyoku, *Kokuto daiShinkyō*, 19–21.
120 Shinkyō tokubetsushi shichōkanbō shomuka, *Kokuto Shinkyō* (Shinkyō: Manshū jijō annaijo, 1940), 110; Shinkyō tokubetsushi shichōkanbō shomuka, *Kokuto Shinkyō* (1942), 204–5.
121 Satō Akira, "Shinkyō no kōen," in Manshū kaikoshū kankōkai, *Aa Manshū*, 212–15; Inuzuka Yasuhiro, "Shinkyō dōshokubutsuen kō," *Chiba daigaku daigakuin jinbun shakai kagaku kenkyūka* 18, no. 2 (2009): 15–25.
122 Mayumi Itoh, *Pioneers of Sino-Japanese Relations: Liao and Takasaki* (New York: Palgrave Macmillan, 2012), 140–42.
123 Miura, "Hsinking," 96.

124 Kitakōji and Watanabe, *Chōshun, Kitsurin,* 40.
125 Satō, Akira, Eguchi Hidematsu, and Toyoshima Masayoshi, "Shinkyō tokubetsushi no ryokuchi keikaku ni tsuite," *Kōen rakuchi* 3, nos. 4/5 (1939): 11.
126 Satō, *Manshū zōen shi,* 94–95.
127 Nagami, "Manshūkoku sandai toshi no kōen sonota," 34; *SSC;* Shinkyō tokubetsushi shichōkanbō shomuka, *Kokuto Shinkyō* (1940), 111; Shinkyō tokubetsushi shichōkanbō shomuka, *Kokuto Shinkyō* (1942), 205.
128 Satō Akira, "Shinkyō tokubetsushi no kenkoku jūshūnen kinen jigyō," *Kōen ryokuchi* 17, no. 9 (1942): 27–31.
129 *STKH,* 62–63, noted the following figures, among others, for people per park hectare for comparison: London (1,680), Greater London (1,175), Paris (1,422), Berlin (4,540), New York (1,710), Washington DC (1,193), Chicago (1,521), Boston (519), Philadelphia (645), Tokyo (10,700), Yokohama (3,900), Osaka (36,700), Nagoya (33,200).
130 (Nagoya mayor) Ōiwa Isao, "Toshibi no hatsuyō to biteki kyōyō no kanyō," *TK* 15, no. 1 (1932): 4; Kitamura Tokutarō, "Kōen wa naze hitsuyō to naruka," *TK* 15, no. 2 (1932): 27–37.
131 Nagami, "Manshūkoku sandai toshi no kōen sonota," 32, 34.
132 Satō, *Manshū zōen shi,* 198–99; Nagami, "Manshūkoku sandai toshi no kōen sonota," 25. Oka published more than fifty articles in the *MKZ* on gardens in China and Manchuria.
133 Satō, *Manshū zōen shi,* 74, 77.
134 Shinkyō tokubetsushi shichōkanbō shomuka, *Yakushin kokuto no iyō,* 29.
135 For example, *Shinkyō no gaikyō,* 13.
136 Satō, *Manshū zōen shi,* 81–100.
137 Ogawa Takuma, "Zōenka Orishimo Yoshinobu ni yoru kindai rokuka shisō no tankan to jissen," *Hōsei daigaku daigakuin dezain kōgaku kenkyūka kiyō* 2 (March 2013): 1–8.
138 *Manchoukuo Year Book, 1942,* 942; Numata Soyao, "Manshūkoku toyū keikaku no genjō," in *Dai rokkai zenkoku toshi mondai kaigi: sōkai bunken 4: sōkai yōroku,* ed. Zenkoku toshi mondai kaigi (Tokyo: Zenkoku toshi mondai kaigi, 1939), 224–27.
139 Manshūkoku seifu kokumuin kokuto kensetsukyoku, *Kokuto daiShinkyō,* 7; Shinkyō tokubetsushi shichōkanbō shomuka, *Kokuto Shinkyō* (1942), 203; Shinkyō tokubetsushi shichōkanbō shomuka, *Yakushin kokuto no iyō,* 9.
140 Satō, *Manshū zōen shi,* 77, 79.
141 Manshū jijō annaijo, ed., *Manshūkoku chihōshi* (Shinkyō: Manshūjijō annaijō, 1940), 4; Shinkyō tokubetsushi shichōkanbō shomuka, *Yakushin kokuto no iyō,* 6.
142 Nakano, "Kokuto Shinkyō no kensetsu," 168.
143 Manshū jijō annaijo, *Shinkyō jijō,* 72.
144 "Jōgetsutan chosuichi," *MNNS,* 24 August 1935, 5; Shinkyō tokubetsushi shichōkanbō shomuka, *Yakushin kokuto no iyō,* 7; *Manchoukuo Year Book, 1942,* 742; Koshizawa, *Manshūkoku no shuto keikaku,* 134–39.
145 Kokumuin sōmuchō jōhōsho, *Manshūkoku no gairan* (Shinkyō: Shinkyō kōshō, 1934), 113.
146 Nagami, "Manshūkoku sandai toshi no kōen sonota," 27.
147 "Manshūkoku kokuto kensetsu keikakuhō no kaishō," *Toshi mondai* 28, no. 2 (1939): 116–17.
148 Nagami, "Manshūkoku sandai toshi no kōen sonota," 25; Satō, *Manshū zōen shi,* 199.
149 Makino Masami, "Manshūkoku no kenchiku torishimori gaikyō," *MKZ* 19, no. 1 (1939): 35–36; Ōno Rokuichirō, "Nichi-Man-Shi toshi no bunkateki keizaiteki renkei ni tsuite," in Zenkoku toshi mondai kaigi, *Dai rokkai zenkoku toshi mondai kaigi,* 151–68; Numata, "Manshūkoku toyū keikaku no genjō," 224–27.
150 See, for example, Kenchiku gakkai Shinkyō shibu, "Kokuto kensetsu keikaku ni tsuite," *Kenchiku zasshi* 13, no. 9 (1938): 167–82; Nakano, "Kokuto Shinkyō no kensetsu."

151 Muroi Osamu, "Manshūkoku kokuto kensetsu keikaku no shōkai," *Kenchiku gyōsei* 3, no. 9 (1939): 19.
152 Sano, "Manshū no kokuto kensetsu keikaku," 37; Sano Riki, "Manshū no kokuto kensetsu," *Kenchiku zasshi* 47, no. 575 (1953): 1243.
153 Yūki, "Kokuto daiShinkyō kensetsu to nisan mondai," 548; Yūki, "Kokuto kensetsu no kaiko to tenbō," 35.
154 Shinkyō tokubetsushi shichōkanbō shomuka, *Kokuto Shinkyō* (1942), 201.
155 Japan was not alone in this – see Richard H. Grove, *Ecology, Climate and Empire: Colonialism and Global Environment History, 1400–1940* (Cambridge, UK: White Horse Press, 1997).
156 Shinkyō tokubetsushi shichōkanbō shomuka, *Kokuto Shinkyō* (1942), 93.
157 Shinkyō tokubetsushi shichōkanbō shomuka, *Yakushin kokuto no iyō*, 5–7, 10–11. The term *yakushin* is stronger in Japanese, implying also "breakthrough" or "leap."
158 Ibid., 14–16.
159 Ibid., 6, 10–11.
160 Ibid., 8–11.
161 Ibid., 20–21.
162 Ibid., 22, 30, 23–26.
163 Kishida Hideto, "Manshūkoku kenkoku jūshūnen to sono kenchiku," *MKZ* 22, no. 11 (1942): 2.
164 Malcolm Duncan Kennedy, "The Diaries of Captain Malcolm Duncan Kennedy, 1917–1946," unpublished diary transcripts for 12 December 1933, 25 April 1934, and 28 April 1934, University of Sheffield Library, http://librarysupport.shef.ac.uk/kennedy_diaries.pdf.
165 Estela Duque, "Militarization of the City: Implementing Burnham's 1905 Plan of Manila," *Fabrications: The Journal of the Society of Architectural Historians, Australia and New Zealand* 19, no. 1 (2009): 63–64.

Chapter 2: Imperialist and Imperial Facades

1 Lewis Mumford, *The Culture of Cities* (New York: Harcourt, Brace, 1938), 299, 403.
2 Indicating continental residences were 22 full-time and 268 part-time members in 1910, and 496 full-time and 1,999 part-time members in 1942. Nishizawa Yasuhiko, *Umi o watatta Nihonjin kenchikuka: 20 seiki zenhan no Chūgoku tōhoku chihō ni okeru kenchiku katsudō* (Tokyo: Shōkokusha, 1996), 3–4.
3 Ibid., 5.
4 Ibid., 19–23, 27; Nishizawa Yasuhiko, *Nihon shokuminchi kenchiku ron* (Nagoya: Nagoya daigaku shuppansha, 2008), 45, 48–49, 52. On Okada see ibid., 354–60.
5 Nishizawa, *Umi o watatta nihonjin kenchikuka,* 33–39; Koshizawa Akira, *Manshūkoku no shuto keikaku: Tōkyō no genzai to mirai o tou* (Tokyo: Nihon keizai hyōronsha, 1988), 70–71; Nishizawa Yasuhiko, *Manshū toshi monogatari* (Tokyo: Kawade shobō shinsha, 1996), 103–5; Nishizawa, *Nihon shokuminchi kenchiku ron,* 49–51, 173–77.
6 Matsumuro Shigemitsu, "Manshū daigaku to kenchikuka," *Manshū kenchiku zasshi* (*Journal of Manchurian Architecture*) (hereafter *MKZ*) 1, no. 1 (1921): 2–4; and "Seikatsu kaizen no kenchiku," *MKZ* 1, no. 2 (1921): 2–14.
7 William H. Coaldrake, *Architecture and Authority in Japan* (London: Routledge, 1996), 222–39.
8 George L. Hersey, *High Victorian Gothic: A Study in Associationism* (Baltimore, MD: Johns Hopkins University Press, 1972); Georg Germann, *Gothic Revival in Europe and Britain: Sources, Influences and Ideas,* trans. Gerald Onn (Cambridge, MA: MIT Press, 1972).
9 Mark Crinson, *Empire Building: Orientalism and Victorian Architecture* (London: Routledge, 1996).

10 Dallas Finn, *Meiji Revisited: The Sites of Victorian Japan* (New York: Weatherhill, 1995), 35, 153, 154–55, 163.

11 Fujimori Terunobu, *Nihon no kindai kenchiku* (Tokyo: Iwanami shoten, 1993), 1:91–96; David B. Stewart, *The Making of a Modern Japanese Architecture, 1868 to the Present* (Tokyo: Kodansha, 1987), 23–27; Finn, *Meiji Revisited,* 17.

12 Finn, *Meiji Revisited,* 97–98; Coaldrake, *Architecture and Authority,* 217–18; Fujimori, *Nihon no kindai kenchiku,* 1:169–95; Stewart, *Modern Japanese Architecture,* 35–38; Nishizawa, *Nihon shokuminchi kenchiku ron,* 385.

13 Fujimori, *Nihon no kindai kenchiku,* 1:218–35; Noboru Kawazoe, *Contemporary Japanese Architecture,* trans. David Griffith (Tokyo: Kokusai bunka shinkokai, 1965) 15; Finn, *Meiji Revisited,* 93, 101; Stewart, *Modern Japanese Architecture,* 37–38, 48–55.

14 Fujimori, *Nihon no kindai kenchiku,* 1:249–57; Coaldrake, *Architecture and Authority,* 218–21; Stewart, *Modern Japanese Architecture,* 55–62.

15 Coaldrake, *Architecture and Authority,* 240; Finn, *Meiji Revisited,* 106–11, 174–85.

16 Finn, *Meiji Revisited,* 99–103, 148–50; Fujimori, *Nihon no kindai kenchiku,* 1:236, 242–48.

17 Coaldrake, *Architecture and Authority,* 232, 250; Kawazoe, *Contemporary Japanese Architecture,* 15–17; Jordan Sand, *House and Home in Modern Japan: Architecture, Domestic Space, and Bourgeois Culture, 1880–1930* (Cambridge, MA: Harvard University Press, 2003), 111–14.

18 Stewart, *Modern Japanese Architecture,* 41; Henry D. Smith, "Tokyo as an Idea: An Exploration of Japanese Urban Thought until 1945," *Journal of Japanese Studies* 4, no. 1 (1978): 53–57.

19 Manshikai, ed., *Manshū kaihatsu yonjūnenshi,* vol. 3 (Tokyo: Manshū kaihatsu yonjōnenshi kankōkai, 1965), 300–5.

20 Mantetsu no kenchiku to gijutsujin henshū i'inkai, *Mantetsu no kenchiku to gijutsujin* (Tokyo: Mantetsu kenchikukai, 1976), 60.

21 Nishizawa, *Nihon shokuminchi kenchiku ron,* 149–51.

22 "Chōshuneki no gaichiku," *Manshū nichi nichi shinbun* (*Manchuria Daily News*) (hereafter *MNNS*), 29 October 1926, 4.

23 A postwar publication describes the spires as being in an "English Gothic style" and names two architects other than Ichida. Mantetsu no kenchiku to gijutsujin henshū i'inkai, *Mantetsu no kenchiku to gijutsujin,* 86.

24 Matsumiya Kichirō, ed., *Shinkyō* (Hōten: Mantetsu tetsudō sōkyoku eigyōkyoku ryōkyokuka, 1937), 8.

25 Koshizawa Akira, *Harupin no toshi keikaku, 1898–1945* (Tokyo: Sōwasha, 1989), 86; Nishizawa, *Umi o watatta Nihonjin kenchikuka,* 188–201; Nishizawa, *Manshū toshi monogatari,* 22–26; David Wolff, *To the Harbin Station: The Liberal Alternative in Russian Manchuria, 1898–1914* (Stanford, CA: Stanford University Press, 1999).

26 Muramatsu Shin and Nishizawa Yasuhiko, eds., *Higashi Ajia no kindai kenchiku* (Tokyo: Muramatsu Teijirō sensei taikan kinenkai, 1985), section 6, nos. 21–27.

27 Nishizawa, *Manshū toshi monogatari,* 71.

28 The Yamato Hotel is discussed often. See, for example, ibid., 104; Mantetsu no kenchiku to gijutsujin henshū i'inkai, *Mantetsu no kenchiku to gijutsujin,* 15, 37, 112.

29 Koshizawa, *Manshūkoku no shuto keikaku,* 71–73.

30 Nishizawa, *Umi o watatta Nihonjin kenchikuka,* 66; Nishizawa, *Manshū toshi monogatari,* 105; Nishizawa, *Nihon shokuminchi kenchiku ron,* 265–70, 398.

31 Ono Takeo, "Manshū sesesshon: shiki kenchikuka no tame ni," *MKZ* 1, no. 1 (1921): 26–29.

32 Nishizawa, *Nihon shokuminchi kenchiku ron,* 151, 196.

33 "Reika 36do no kion," *Yomiuri shinbun,* 18 January 1908, 1.

34 *MKZ* 5, no. 6 (1925): 22–23.
35 Manshikai, *Manshū kaihatsu yonjūnenshi,* 3:304; Nishizawa, *Umi o watatta Nihonjin kenchikuka,* 83n57; Nishizawa, *Nihon shokuminchi kenchiku ron,* 153.
36 Nishizawa, *Manshū no toshi monogatari,* 123.
37 "T.N. sei," "Kenchiku oyobi kenchikubutsu ni kansuru minpō no basshō," *MKZ* 5, no. 3 (1925): 69–72.
38 Nishizawa, *Umi o watatta Nihonjin kenchikuka,* 165–70; Nishizawa, *Manshū no toshi monogatari,* 121–23; Nishizawa, *Nihon shokuminchi kenchiku ron,* 75, 124–31, 134–73, 352–60.
39 Henry-Russell Hitchcock and Philip Johnson, *The International Style* (New York: W.W. Norton, 1995).
40 Shimada Fuji, "Kenchiku mudabanashi," *MKZ* 5, no. 2 (1925): 7–12.
41 "H.H. sei," "Shizen oyobi kōsei no biteki chūshin ten," *MKZ* 8, no. 2 (1928): 19–24; 8, no. 4 (1920): 21–40.
42 Photographs in *MKZ* 6, no. 12 (1926): i–v.
43 Photograph, plan, and details in *MKZ* 11, no. 1 (1931): ii–iv, 40.
44 Jonathan M. Reynolds, *Maekawa Kunio and the Emergence of Japanese Modernist Architecture* (Berkeley: University of California Press, 2001), 21–37.
45 Photographs, plans, and details in *MKZ* 12, no. 4 (1932): i–viii, 30.
46 Munekata Shuichi, "Manshū to jūtaku kairyō," *MKZ* 1, no. 1 (1921): 16–25.
47 Matsumuro Shigemitsu, "Seikatsu kaizen to kenchiku," *MKZ* 1, no. 2 (1921): 2–14.
48 "Seikatsu kaizen to seikatsu risō no tettei," *MKZ* 1, no. 7 (1921): 14–22.
49 See, for example, "Kaoku kenchiku no hōshin," *MNNS,* 14 May 1908, 2.
50 Mantetsu no kenchiku to gijutsujin henshū i'inkai, *Mantetsu no kenchiku to gijutsujin,* 114–18.
51 Izumi Renji, *Chōshun jijō* (Chōshun: Chōshun Nihōsha, 1912), 12.
52 "Higashi Honganji shutchōjo naramu," *MNNS,* 30 September 1908, 4.
53 Kondō Isaburō, "Manshū ni okeru saitei ondo zuhyō ni tsuite," *MKZ* 1, no. 7 (1921): 23–25.
54 Onogi Takaharu, "Tōshin tetsudō yori keishōseru Mantetsu shataku," *MKZ* 2, no. 7 (1922): 23–28.
55 Matsumuro Shigemitsu, "Kiro ni tatsu kenchikuka," *MKZ* 2, no. 1 (1922): 10–12, no. 2 (1922): 2–12, no. 3 (1922): 2–17.
56 Tanabe Toshiaki, "Manshū ni okeru jūtaku mondai no kichō," *MKZ* 2, no. 7 (1922): 2–4.
57 "Jūtaku no madori oyobi setsubi no kaizen," *MKZ* 4, no. 4 (1924): 14–22, no. 5 (1924): 15–24, no. 6 (1924): 35–43, and no. 7 (1924): 38–43.
58 Suzuki Masao, "Atarashii ie," *MKZ* 4, no. 3 (1924): 66–70.
59 For example, Matsumuro Shigemitsu, "Shokuminchi wa yoroshiku dokuritsu shitaru bunka o kensetsu subeshi," *MKZ* 4, no. 3 (1924): 6–15.
60 Oka Ōji, "Manshū kenkoku jūnen to kenchiku zakkan," *MKZ* 22, no. 10 (1942): 1–4.
61 Seki Hajime, "Kinsei toshi no hatten to toshi keikaku," *Toshi kōron* (*Urban Review*) (hereafter *TK*) 7, no. 12 (1924): 2–22.
62 Bill Sewell, "Beans to Banners: The Evolving Architecture of Prewar Changchun," in *Harbin to Hanoi: The Colonial Built Environment in Asia, 1840 to 1940* (Hong Kong: Hong Kong University Press, 2012), 37–57.
63 Miki Kiyoshi, "The China Affair and Japanese Thought," *Contemporary Japan* 6, no. 4 (1938): 601.
64 Eri Hotta, *Pan-Asianism and Japan's War, 1931–1945* (New York: Palgrave Macmillan, 2007); Kevin M. Doak, *A History of Nationalism in Modern Japan: Placing the People* (Boston: Brill, 2007), 199–202, 233–50.
65 Oka Ōji, "Kindai kenchiku no hakō o ikaga," *MKZ* 16, no. 8 (1936): 1; *The Manchoukuo Year Book, 1942* (Tokyo: Ajia tōkeisha, 1942), 943.

66 Naitō Tairō, "Yakushin Manshūkoku no bunka to kenchiku," *MKZ* 17, no. 1 (1937): 5.

67 Matsumuro, "Shokuminchi wa yoroshiku dokuritsu shitaru bunka o kensetsu subeshi" and "Shinseikatsu no hyōjun," *MKZ* 4, no. 4 (1924): 2–7.

68 Aoi Rō, "Kaikan shinchiku, sōritsu sanshūnen o shukushite kyōkai no shōrai ni kibōsu," *MKZ* 4, no. 3 (1924): 16–18; Suzuki, "Atarashii ie."

69 Oka Ōji, "Manshū ni okeru shinkō kenchiku ni taibōsu," *MKZ* 13, no. 6 (1933): 1; Nishizawa Yasuhiko, "Manshūkoku no kensetsu jigyō," in *Manshūkoku no kenkyū,* ed. Yamamoto Yūzō (Tokyo: Ryokuin shobō, 1995), 377–460. Of the 131 advisers the *MKZ* listed in 1936, 61 were in Dalian, 25 were in Xinjing, 19 were in Shenyang, 6 were in Harbin, 2 were in Jilin City, and the rest were scattered throughout Manchukuo. "Shōwa 11-nendo hyōgi'in," *MKZ* 16, no. 5 (1936): 55. In 1941, however, only one of the 15 new members lived in Xinjing. "Kaihō," *MKZ* 21, no. 9 (1941): 36.

70 This view that Mantetsu was outdated was the opinion of Tsuchiura Kameki, a company housing specialist in Andong and Jilin City. Nihon kōsaku bunka renmei shusai, "Tairiku kenchiku zadankai," *Gendai kenchiku* 8 (January 1940): 49–50.

71 Fujii Sadamu, "Manshū jūtaku kyōkyū jigyō jūnen no ato," *MKZ* 22, no. 11 (1942): 26.

72 Makino Masami, "Kenkoku jūnen to kenchiku bunka," *MKZ* 22, no. 10 (1942): 16–17.

73 Nishizawa, *Nihon shokuminchi kenchiku ron,* 163.

74 Ishii Tatsurō, "Kokumuin o tateru goro," *MKZ* 22, no. 10 (1942): 35–36.

75 Aiga Kensuke, "Kenkoku zengo no omoidasu," *MKZ* 22, no. 10 (1942): 13.

76 Onogi Takaharu, "Gendai kenchiku zakkan," *MKZ* 10, no. 10 (1930): 7–9.

77 Onogi Takaharu, "Manshūkoku shuto kensetsu ni tsuite," *MKZ* 12, no. 6 (1932): 1–2.

78 Oka Ōji, "Manshūkoku shuto kensetsu ni kansuru toshi keikaku narabi ni kenchiku ni taisuru iken," *MKZ* 12, no. 6 (1932): 12.

79 Yumoto Saburō, "Shinkokuto no kensetsu," *MKZ* 12, no. 6 (1932): 6–7.

80 Onogi, "Manshūkoku shuto kensetsu ni tsuite," 4; Oka, "Manshūkoku shuto kensetsu ni kansuru toshi keikaku narabi ni kenchiku ni taisuru iken," 11–12; Ueki Shigeru, "Manshūkoku shinshuto kensetu keikaku ni tsuite," *MKZ* 12, no. 6 (1932): 17; Nakazawa Kiyoshi, "Shinkyōto keikaku ni taisuru shoken," *MKZ* 12, no. 6 (1932): 34; Kusano Tomio, "Kokuto kensetsu he no jokyoku," *MKZ* 12, no. 7 (1932): 1–11; Tanaka Kuniyaku, "Manshūkoku kenchiku hōki seiteijō no konpon yōken ni tsuite," *MKZ* 12, no. 7 (1932): 12–18.

81 Ueda Kyōsuke, "Chōshun o shuto to suru gigi to shuto no toshi keikaku ni tsuite no kibō," *MKZ* 12, no. 6 (1932): 40; Murata Jirō, "Ketsuron," *MKZ* 12, no. 6 (1932): 21.

82 "Shinkyō sōgen," *MKZ* 12, no. 6 (1932): 59.

83 Oka, "Manshū ni okeru shinkō kenchiku ni taibōsu," 1–3.

84 Aiga, "Kenkoku zengo no omoidasu," 8.

85 Manshūkoku seifu kokumuin kokuto kensetsukyoku, *Kokuto daiShinkyō* (Shinkyō: Manshūkoku seifu kokumuin kokuto kensetsukyoku, 1933), 9.

86 Makino, "Kenkoku jūnen to kenchiku bunka," 17.

87 Jonathan M. Reynolds, "Japan's Imperial Diet Building in the Debate over Construction of a National Identity," in *The Culture of Japanese Fascism,* ed. Alan Tansman (Durham, NC: Duke University Press, 2009), 254–75.

88 Nishizawa, *Nihon shokuminchi kenchiku ron,* 95–103.

89 Muramatsu Teijirō, *Nihon kindai kenchiku no rekishi* (Nihon hōsō, 1977), 169–78; Koshizawa, *Manshūkoku no shuto keikaku,* 182–83, 208–12; Stewart, *Modern Japanese Architecture,* 107–11; Reynolds, *Maekawa Kunio,* 89–101.

90 Nishizawa, *Nihon shokuminchi kenchiku ron,* 383–84.

91 Charles D. Musgrove, *China's Contested Capital: Architecture, Ritual, and Response in Nanjing* (Honolulu: University of Hawai'i Press, 2013).

92 Kim Brandt, "The Beauty of Labor: Imagining Factory Girls in Japan's New Order," in Tansman, *Culture of Japanese Fascism,* 115–37. See also Yuko Kikuchi, "The Myth of

Yanagi's Originality: The Formation of 'Mingei' Theory in Its Social and Historical Context," *Journal of Design History* 7, no. 4 (1994): 247–66; Yuko Kikuchi, "Hybridity and the Oriental Orientalism of 'Mingei' Theory," *Journal of Design History* 10, no. 4 (1997): 343–54; and Kim Brandt, *Kingdom of Beauty: Mingei and the Politics of Folk Art in Imperial Japan* (Durham, NC: Duke University Press, 2007).

93 Gwendolyn Wright, *The Politics of Design in French Colonial Urbanism* (Chicago: University of Chicago Press, 1991).

94 David A. Johnson, "A British Empire for the Twentieth Century: The Inauguration of New Delhi, 1931," *Urban History* 35, no. 3 (2008): 462–84; Thomas R. Metcalf, *An Imperial Vision: Indian Architecture and Britain's Raj* (Berkeley: University of California Press, 1989), 238.

95 Photo and floor plan of the Kitsurin tōyō i'in are in *MKZ* 4, no. 2 (1924).

96 Makino, "Kenkoku jūnen to kenchiku bunka," 21.

97 Koshizawa, *Manshūkoku no shuto keikaku,* 182, 188–89, 200–18.

98 Togari Takeshi, "Shin tairiku kenchiku no juritsu he," *MKZ* 19, no. 11 (1939): 3.

99 Makino, "Kenkoku jūnen to kenchiku bunka," 20–21; Nishizawa, *Nihon shokuminchi kenchiku ron,* 111.

100 Kuroki Morifumi, "The Asianism of the Kōa-kai and the Ajia Kyōkai," in *Pan-Asianism in Modern Japanese History: Colonialism, Regionalism and Borders,* ed. Sven Saaler and J. Victor Koschmann (London: Routledge, 2007), 34–51.

101 *MKZ* 14, no. 8 (1934), *MKZ* 17, no. 1 (1937). Photos and footprints for this and other major structures appear on unnumbered pages.

102 Aiga, "Kenkoku zengo no omoidasu," 12.

103 H. Foster Bain, "Manchuria: A Key Area," *Foreign Affairs* 25, no. 1 (1946): 109.

104 Stewart, *Modern Japanese Architecture,* 110.

105 Nishizawa, *Nihon shokuminchi kenchiku ron,* 392.

106 Laurence G. Liu, *Chinese Architecture* (London: Academy Editions, 1989), 250.

107 *MKZ* 16, no. 8 (1936).

108 Nishizawa, *Nihon shokuminchi kenchiku ron,* 107–8.

109 *MKZ* 18, no. 2 (1938): 49.

110 *MKZ* 19, no. 4 (1939).

111 Makino Masami, "Manshūkoku hōga chōsha sekkei yōkō," *MKZ* 18, no. 6 (1938): 1–23.

112 *MKZ* 19, no. 11 (1939).

113 *MKZ* 14, no. 1 (1934).

114 *MKZ* 16, no. 8 (1936).

115 Chuta Ito, "Characteristics of Chinese Architecture," *Contemporary Japan* 9, no. 1 (1940): 25–37.

116 Nishizawa, *Nihon shokuminchi kenchiku ron,* 113.

117 See also Kishi Toshihiko, *Manshūkoku no bijiuaru mejia* (Tokyo: Yoshikawa kōbunkan, 2010).

118 Fueki Hideo, "Gyōkai no konjyaku," *MKZ* 22, no. 11 (1942): 35–36; Koshizawa, *Manshūkoku no shuto keikaku,* 209.

119 Aiga, "Kenkoku zengo no omoidasu," 12; Yaoi Matasaburō, "Kenkoku shinbyō, kenkoku chūreibyō," *MKZ* 23, no. 1 (1943): 12; sketches appeared in *MKZ* 14, no. 4 (1934); photograph in *MKZ* 14, no. 12 (1934).

120 Manshūkoku tsūshinsha, ed., *Manshūkoku gensei* (1939; Tokyo: Hōwa shuppan, 1986), 22.

121 *MKZ* 7, no. 8 (Aug 1932).

122 Yaoi, "Kenkoku shinbyō, kenkoku chūreibyō," 4–13.

123 *MKZ* 17, no. 11 (1937) and *MKZ* 21, no. 1 (1941). Another photo appeared in *MKZ* 23, no. 1 (1943).

124 "Hōnichi senshōkinen kenzōbutsu sekkei zu'an nyūsen happyō," *MKZ* 17, no. 2 (1937), i–vi, 45–46.

125 "Nanrin Kanjōshi chūkonhi," *MNNS*, 15 August 1935, 5. See also photos and discussion in Mantetsu sōkyoku, *Shinkyō* (Hōten: Mantetsu, 1937), 11–12; Shinkyō shōkō kaigijo, *DaiShinkyō keizai gaikan* (Shinkyō: Shinkyō shōkō kaigijo, 1937), x; and Shinkyō tokubetsushi shichōkanbō shomuka, *Kokuto Shinkyō: Kenkoku jūshūnen kinan* (Shinkyō: Shinkyō tokubetsushi kōsho, 1942), xiii.

126 Akiko Takenaka, "Architecture for Mass-Mobilization: The Chūreitou Memorial Construction Movement, 1939–1945," in Tansman, *Culture of Japanese Fascism*, 235–53.

127 The sketches for the top twenty candidates appeared in *MKZ* 17, no. 7 (1937).

128 "Shinkyō bunkai kenchiku tenrankai kiji," *MKZ* 17, no. 11 (1937), 39–40.

129 Sasakura Kiyoshi, "DaitōA kensetsu hakurankai kenchiku ni tsuite," *MKZ* 22, no. 11 (1942), 45–46.

130 Matsuki Genjirō, "Manshū kenchiku gukan," *MKZ* 19, no. 4 (1939): 32–34.

131 Maeda Matsuoto, "Manshūyuki zakki," *MKZ* 23, no. 1 (1943): 39–40.

132 Nihon kōsaku bunka renmei shusai, "Tairiku kenchiku zadankai," 51, 61. Sakakura and Horiguchi are discussed briefly in Reynolds, *Maekawa Kunio.*

133 Inoue Shōichi, *Senjika Nihon no kenchikuka: āto, kitchu, Japanesuku* (Tokyo: Asahi shinbunsha, 1995).

134 "Manshū kenchiku zadankai," *MKZ* 19, no. 11 (1939): 27–33.

135 SōA kenchiku renmei, "Manshū kenchiku no tenbō," *Gendai kenchiku* 8 (January 1940): 2–21.

136 Makino, "Kenkoku jūnen to kenchiku bunka," 24.

137 Kishida Hideto, "Kenchiku jikan," *MKZ* 19, no. 1 (1939): 4–9. Kishida had second thoughts though. See Nihon kōsaku bunka renmei shusai, "Tairiku kenchiku zadankai," excerpted ibid., 23–24. On the substitution of brick for wood, see Muroi Osamu, "Manshū son shiyō moku kōzō no keisan shiryō," *MKZ* 19, no. 2 (1939): 1–7; and Endō Hajime, "Chūgin kurabu no kōsō (renga ni kiku)," *MKZ* 22, no. 10 (1942): 30–34.

138 *MKZ* 19, no. 11 (1939): 4.

139 "Manshū kenchiku zadankai," *MKZ* 19, no. 11 (1939): 30.

140 Makino, "Kenkoku jūnen to kenchiku bunka," 22.

141 Gerdy Troost, "Shinkō kokka no kenchiku," trans. Muroi Osamu, *MKZ* 22, no. 8 (1942): 27–34. On Troost, see Robert R. Taylor, *The Word in Stone: The Role of Architecture in the National Socialist Ideology* (Berkeley: University of California Press, 1974), 126–27.

142 Ōhira Tsutomu, "Nachizu Doitsu o ichibetsu suru," *TK* 21, no. 8 (1938): 108–13, no. 9 (1938): 55–65, and no. 10 (Oct 1938): 48–71.

143 Barbara Miller Lane, *Architecture and Politics in Germany, 1918–1945* (Cambridge, MA: Harvard University Press, 1968); Alex Scobie, *Hitler's State Architecture: The Impact of Classical Antiquity* (University Park: Pennsylvania State University Press, 1990).

144 John Zukowsky, ed., *The Many Faces of Modern Architecture: Building in Germany between the World Wars* (Munich: Prestel, 1994), 11–12.

145 Oka Ōji, "Aratanaru seiki no nentō," *MKZ* 21, no. 1 (1941): 1.

146 Anthony King, "Rethinking Colonialism: An Epilogue," in *Forms of Dominance: On the Architecture and Urbanism of the Colonial Enterprise*, ed. Nezar AlSayyad (Aldershot, UK: Avebury, 1992), 352–53.

147 Aiga, "Kenkoku zengo no omoidasu," 13.

148 *MKZ* 15, no. 4 (1935); *MKZ* 16, no. 8 (1936); *MKZ* 16, no. 10 (1936).

149 *MKZ* 9, nos. 10 and 11 (1929).

150 *MKZ* 7, no. 8 (1927).

151 J.R. S[tewart], "Hsinking – Manchuria's Boom Town," *Far Eastern Survey* 6, no. 6 (1937): 69. See also John R. Stewart, "Pu-Yi at Last to Have a Palace," *Far Eastern Survey* 7, no. 22 (1938): 264.

152 Kasahara Toshirō, "Manshū kenchiku shokan," *MKZ* 18, no. 10 (1938): 1–3; *Manchoukuo Year Book, 1942*, 930–31.

153 Matsuki, "Manshū kenchiku gukan." Following this article are examples of work by modernists Erich Mendelsohn and Serge Chermayeff.
154 *MKZ* 14, no. 8 (1934); *MKZ* 17, no. 11 (1937); *MKZ* 18, no. 10 (1938).
155 Nishizawa, *Nihon shokuminchi kenchiku ron,* 122, 133–34, 137–42.
156 "Manshū chūō ginkō sōkō honkenchiku o kataru zadankai," *MKZ* 18, no. 10 (1938): 5–14.
157 *MKZ* 14, no. 10 (1934); *MKZ* 15, no. 11 (1935).
158 *MKZ* 15, no. 11 (1935).
159 *MKZ* 19, no. 3 (1939). The Tokyo Maritime Insurance Building was originally one less storey than in Figure 2.16.
160 *MKZ* 17, no. 11 (1937).
161 Mantetsu no kenchiku to gijutsujin henshū i'inkai, *Mantetsu no kenchiku to gijutsujin*, 55.
162 *MKZ* 21, no. 4 (1941). Early sketches appeared in *MKZ* 19, no. 9 (1939).
163 Shinkyō tokubetsushi shichōkanbō shomuka, *Kokuto Shinkyō* (1942), 202.
164 *MKZ* 14, nos. 1, 10, and 11 (1934).
165 Fueki, "Gyōkai no konjyaku," 37.
166 Nishizawa, *Nihon shokuminchi kenchiku ron,* 48; *MKZ* 15, no. 11 (1935); "Shinkyō Kenpeitai," *MNNS,* 13 August 1935, 5; "Sanzen to kagayaku gomonshō," *MNNS,* 17 August 1935, 5.
167 *Shinkyō shigai chizu* (Tokyo: Kanemitsusha shiryōbu, 1982) (hereafter *SSC*); John R. Stewart, "Four Years of Manchoukuo," *Far Eastern Survey* 5, no. 6 (1936): 54.
168 *MKZ* 14, no. 11 (1934); *MKZ* 15, no. 1 (1935).
169 *MKZ* 14, nos. 1 and 9 (1934).
170 *MKZ* 16, no. 6 (1936).
171 Kenchiku gakkai Shinkyō shibu, "Kokuto Shinkyō kensetsu no gaiken," *Kenchiku zasshi* 13, no. 9 (1938): 181.
172 Residences for the bank governor and the general affairs director are in *MKZ* 15, no. 7 (1935) and *MKZ* 16, no. 6 (1936). Photos of new residences for the Kantōgun chief of staff and Mantetsu director are in *MKZ* 14, no. 1 (1934). Other photos are in *MKZ* 19, no. 1 (1939). Onogi Takaharu's private residence was smaller but similar. See *MKZ* 14, no. 12 (1934).
173 David Tucker, "France, Brossard Mopin, and Manchukuo," in *Harbin to Hanoi: The Colonial Built Environment in Asia, 1840–1940,* ed. Laura Victoir and Victor Zatsepine (Hong Kong: Hong Kong University Press), 59–81; *MKZ* 16, no. 7 (1936).
174 *MKZ* 16 no. 6 (1936) and 19, no. 4 (1939).
175 *MKZ* 16, no. 4 (1936).
176 See, for example, the various sketches and plans for the Xinjing Industrial Centre in *MKZ* 19, no. 3 (1939), and for the Manchuria Recreation Centre in *MKZ* 19, no. 9 (1939). On the recreation centres planned in Manchukuo's seven largest cities, see Miyachi Jirō, "Shinkyō tai'ikukan sekkei yōshi," *MKZ* 19, no. 9 (1939): 19–21.
177 *MKZ* 19, no. 10 (1939); *MKZ* 22, no. 12 (1942); *MKZ* 21, no. 5 (1941).
178 See, for example, "Kyō no Manshū jūtaku den," *Gendai kenchiku* 4 (September 1939): 62–63; and Hideshima Tsutomu, "Manshū ni okeru toshi keikaku to shūdan jūkusei," *Jūtaku* 27, Nno. 6, (1942): 174–82. Some private residences mixed Western-style rooms with rooms featuring Japanese tatami: *MKZ* 16, no. 4 (1936). An exhibition of residential designs in Manchukuo was held on 2–6 June 1939 at the Xinjing Takarayama department store. "Manshū jūtaku ni kansuru tenrankai," *MKZ* 19, no. 6 (1939): 41–45.
179 Nishizawa, *Nihon shokuminchi kenchiku ron,* 166–67. On "culture houses," see Sand, *House and Home in Modern Japan.*
180 Fujii, "Manshū jūtaku kyōkyū jigyō jūnen no ato," 33–34.
181 Zheng Bingwen (Jp, Tei Heibun), "Mankei jūtaku no dōkō ni tsuite," *MKZ* 22, no. 10 (1942): 25–29.
182 Fujii, "Manshū jūtaku kyōkyū jigyō jūnen no ato," 24–26.

183 Oka, "Manshū kenkoku jūnen to kenchiku zakkan," 2.

184 On Chinese residential construction, see Fukuoka Shōichirō, "Manshū ni okeru jūtaku no madoiriguchi narabi ni shōtenjō no kairyō ni tsuite," *MKZ* 6, no. 8 (1926); Fukuoka Shōichirō, "Shina naichi ni okeru kenchiku no gaikyō," *MKZ* 6, no. 7 (1926); Kishima Katsumi, ed., *Shina jūtaku shi* (Dairen: Mantetsu, 1932); Ōizumi Kazu, "Manshū saisō no kokoromi ni yoru jūtaku shiken kaoku ni tsuite," *MKZ* 7, no. 9 (1927): 1–26; Ōizumi Kazu, "Kita Shina jūtaku no bekkan," *MKZ* 10, no. 1 (1930): 19–29. On Russian construction, see Ōizumi Kazu, "Kanchi ni okeru Rojin jūtaku," *MKZ* 8, nos. 6–8 (1928); "Kindai Manshū kenchiku shi ni kansuru zadankai," *MKZ* 16, no. 2 (1936): 3–21;Yazaki Takayoshi, "KitaMan toshi jūtaku shian ni tsuite," *MKZ* 19, no. 5 (1939): 1–16.

185 The November 1928 issue of the *MKZ* (8, no. 11) focused on electric appliances and other amenities in homes. See Kuriyama Tōji (of the South Manchurian Electric Corporation), "Jūtaku to denki setsubi"; Warashina Asayoshi, "Jūtaku no danbō setsubi"; Ōizumi Kazu, "Jūtaku to kanki"; and Ōizumi Kazu, "Jūtaku to pechika." See also Nagatake Shinji, "Attakai ie," *MKZ* 9, nos. 1 and 2 (1929), as well as Warashina Asayoshi, "Jūtakuyō danbō onsuikan no hainetsu no riyō no ichirei," *MKZ* 9, no. 2 (1929): 21–23.

186 Fujii, "Manshū jūtaku kyōkyū jigyō jūnen no ato," 21–34.

187 Ibid., 21–22.

188 Fujii does not elaborate on what was meant by the term *Manchurian* in this context, except to say that this fourth complex looked "somehow more lavish." Fujii, "Manshū jūtaku kyōkyū jigyō jūnen no ato," 22.

189 *MKZ* 15, no. 7 (1935).

190 Photos and floor plans for dormitories for employees of the central bank, Denden, and other corporations, as well as for military and government personnel, appear in *MKZ* 15, no. 7 (1935) and 16, no. 3 (1936).

191 *SSC.*

192 Fujii, "Manshū jūtaku kyōkyū jigyō jūnen no ato," 24–33.

193 Yūki Seitarō, "Kokuto kensetsu no kaiko to tenbō," *MKZ* 14, no. 2 (1934): 36.

194 Makino, "Kenkoku jūnen to kenchiku bunka," 16.

195 Fuse Tadashi, Washio Kenzō, and Takabayashi Toshiaki, " Kenbutsu kiso shūi no jiban tōketsusen ni tsuite," *MKZ* 21, no. 10 (1941).

196 Fujii, "Manshū jūtaku kyōkyū jigyō jūnen no ato," 21–34.

197 Yamazaki Tadao, "Shojūtaku no kōsei," *MKZ* 15, no. 4 (1935): 3–9.

198 Hamada Yoshio and Yamazaki Tadao, "Manshū kenkō jūkyo no kōsei," *MKZ* 18, no. 3 (1938): 21–28, no. 4 (1938): 10–15, and no. 5 (1938): 15–18.

199 Shōbara Shin'ichi, "'Kokumin jūtaku (Nikkei tekiō sumai) sekkei kenshō boshū' shinsa kōki," *MKZ* 24, no. 1 (1944): 2–3; Tabei Taisuke, "Kokumin jūtaku sekkei shokan," *MKZ* 24, no. 1 (1944): 3–5; Kōri Kikuo, "Tatami nashi jūtaku kara saishōkan jūtaku he," *MKZ* 24, no. 1 (1944): 9–10; Takahara Kazuhide, "Mantaku no jūtaku ni tsuite," *MKZ* 24, no. 2 (Feb 1944): 5–10. On "national housing," see Gregory Clancey, "Designing a Home for the *Yamato Minzoku*: Race, Housing and Modernity in Wartime Japan," *Asian Studies Review* 29 (2005): 123–41.

200 Oka, "Aratanaru seiki no nentō," 1.

201 Koinuma Heishirō, "Jūtaku mondai ni tsuite," *MKZ* 22, no. 9 (1942): 19–20.

202 Hoshino Shōichi, "Gisō to kenchiku," *MKZ* 18, no. 8 (1938): 14–17; Tōkyō shiyakusho, "Bōkū toshi keikaku yori mitaru bōgo shisetsu gaiyō," *MKZ* 19, no. 2 (1939): 31–36 and no. 3 (1939): 32–43; Itō Hajime, "Bakudan no iryoku bunseki," *MKZ* 23, no. 12 (1943); Itō Hajime, "Kūshū kiken ritsu," *MKZ* 24, no. 1 (1944); Hamada Yoshio and Yamazaki Tadao, "Jūkyo chōyō to bōkū taiō gijutsu," *MKZ* 24, no. 2 (1944): 1–5.

203 Kuwabara Eiji, "Kagaku gijutsu shintaisei ni tsuite," *MKZ* 22, no. 1 (1942): 3–20; Manshūkoku kyōwakai, "Kagaku gijutsu rengō bukai kessei yōkō setsumei sho," *MKZ* 22, no. 1 (1942):

21–27; Yakushijin Ken'ichi, "Kokumin jūtaku ronkō," *MKZ* 22, no. 5 (1942): 1–10; Yakushijin Ken'ichi, "Jūtaku dangi," *MKZ* 22, no. 8 (1942): 35; Washio Kenzō, "Kenchiku kagaku kyōgikai setchi o kibōsu," *MKZ* 21, no. 1 (1941): 2–4.

204 Kokumuin kenchiku kyoku, "Kenchikubutsu senji kikaku settei kansuru kaisetsu," *MKZ* 24, no. 5 (1944): 29–32.

205 Hideshima Tsutomu, "Shintoyū keikakuhō ni tsuite," *MKZ* 23, no. 5 (1943): 3–21. Excerpts of the new law are in "Shintoyū keikakuhō oyobi dōshikō kisoku," *MKZ* 23, no. 5 (1943): 24–46.

206 Makino Masami, "Kōtoku jūichi nen Manshū kenchikukai no kaiko," *MKZ* 25, no. 1 (1945): 23–24.

207 See *MKZ* 24, no. 2 (1944).

208 Ikeda Kanji, "Manshū kenchiku to hōjin eisei no ikkō sasshi," *MKZ* 15, no. 1 (1935): 27.

209 Photos and a floor plan are in *MKZ* 22, no. 12 (1942).

210 Clarence Aasen, *Architecture of Siam: A Cultural History Interpretation* (Kuala Lumpur: Oxford University Press, 1998), 242–43.

211 Manshikai, *Manshū kaihatsu yonjūnenshi,* 3:293.

212 S[tewart], "Hsinking," 69.

213 Stewart, "Pu-Yi at Last to Have a Palace," 264. The description of the style was apparently from a Japanese publication. For the author, starting construction on the palace was significant also because it meant that Puyi was staying in Manchuria and not moving to Beijing.

214 Manshūkokushi hensan kankōkai, *Manshūkokushi* (Tokyo: Kokusai zeurin kyōkai, 1973), 1:758.

215 Pu Yi, *From Emperor to Citizen: The Autobiography of Aisin-Gioro Pu Yi* (Peking: Foreign Languages Press, 1964), 2:255. A description and photos are in *MKZ* 14, no. 3 (1934).

Chapter 3: Economic Development

1 Jean-Baptiste Du Halde, *Description géographique, historique, chronologique, politique, et physique de l'empire de la Chine et de la Tartarie chinoise* ... (The Hague: H. Scheurleer, 1736).

2 H.E.M. James, *The Long White Mountain, or A Journey in Manchuria* (London: Longmans, Green, 1888), 374.

3 Ibid., 293.

4 Robert H.G. Lee, *The Manchurian Frontier in Ch'ing History* (Cambridge, MA: Harvard University Press, 1970), 5–6.

5 Arthur de C. Sowerby, "The Exploration of Manchuria," *Geographical Journal* 54, no. 2 (1919): 79.

6 Du Halde, *Description géographique,* 6.

7 Franklin Hiram King, *Farmers of Forty Centuries, or, Permanent Agriculture in China, Korea and Japan* (1911; London: Cape, 1939), 159.

8 Arthur Judson Brown, *New Forces in Old China: An Inevitable Awakening,* 2nd ed. (New York: Fleming H. Revell, 1907), 123.

9 B.L. Putnam Weale, *Manchu and Muscovite: Being Letters from Manchuria Written during the Autumn of 1903* (London: Macmillan, 1904), 425–26; Lee, *Manchurian Frontier,* 64–66.

10 Alexander Williamson, *Journeys in North China, Manchuria, and Eastern Mongolia; with Some Account of Corea* (London: Smith, Elder, 1870), 2:67.

11 Man-houng Lin, "China's 'Dual Economy' in International Trade Relations, 1842–1949," in *Japan, China, and the Growth of the Asian International Economy, 1850–1949,* ed. Kaoru Sugihara (New York: Oxford University Press, 2005), 182; John R. Stewart, "The Soya Bean and Manchuria," *Far Eastern Survey* 5, no. 21 (1936): 222.

12 Kwong Chi Man, "Finance and the Northern Expedition: From the Northeast Asian Perspective, 1925–1928," *Modern Asian Studies* 48, no. 6 (2014): 1699.
13 Stewart, "Soya Bean," 222–23; David Wolff, "Bean There: Toward a Soy-Based History of Northeast Asia," in *Harbin and Manchuria: Place, Space, and Identity,* ed. Thomas Lahusen (Durham, NC: Duke University Press, 2001), 246.
14 James Reardon-Anderson, *Reluctant Pioneers: China's Expansion Northward, 1644–1937* (Stanford, CA: Stanford University Press, 2005), 186.
15 King, *Farmers of Forty Centuries,* 357–58; Imperial Maritime Customs of China, *The Soya Bean of Manchuria* (Shanghai: Statistical Department of the Inspectorate General of Customs, 1911), 6.
16 Hanchao Lu, "Arrested Development: Cotton and Cotton Markets in Shanghai, 1350–1853," *Modern China* 18, no. 4 (1992): 468–99.
17 Lin, "China's 'Dual Economy'," 188.
18 Weale, *Manchu and Muscovite,* 429.
19 Historical Section, Foreign Office, *Manchuria* (London: His Majesty's Stationery Office, 1920), 48.
20 Palladius, "An Expedition through Manchuria from Pekin to Blagovestchensk in 1870," trans. E. Delmar Morgan, *Journal of the Royal Geographic Society of London* 42 (1872): 169.
21 Man-houng Lin, "Interpretive Trends in Taiwan's Scholarship on Chinese Business History, 1600 to the Present," *Chinese Studies in History* 31, no. 3–4 (1998): 65–94.
22 Reardon-Anderson, *Reluctant Pioneers;* Thomas R. Gottschang and Diana Lary, *Swallows and Settlers: The Great Migration from North China to Manchuria* (Ann Arbor: University of Michigan Press, 2000).
23 Henry James Whigham, *Manchuria and Korea* (London: Isbister, 1904), 53.
24 Williamson, *Journeys in North China,* 2:198.
25 *Reports of the General Assembly of the Presbyterian Church in Ireland* (September? 1883): 290.
26 H.E.M. James, "A Journey in Manchuria," *Proceedings of the Royal Geographical Society and Monthly Record of Geography* 9, no. 9 (1887): 562. Elsewhere James called Kuanchengzi "the greatest place of commerce in northern Manchuria" with "the largest emporium in the north." James, *Long White Mountain,* 370–71, 374.
27 Alexander Hosie, *Manchuria: Its People, Resources and Recent History* (New York: C. Scribner's, 1904), 22, 148, 189.
28 Société des missions étrangères, *Compte-rendu des travaux* (1899), 79.
29 Imperial Japanese Government Railways, *An Official Guide to Eastern Asia: Trans-Continental Connections between Europe and Asia,* vol. 1, *Manchuria and Chōsen* (Tokyo: Imperial Japanese Government Railways, 1913), 66.
30 Weale, *Manchu and Muscovite,* 439, 443–45.
31 B.L. Putnam Weale, *The Fight for the Republic of China* (London: Hurst and Blackett, 1918), 17.
32 "Les Russes en Asie," *Annales de géographie* 10, no. 49 (1901): 89.
33 W.V. Lloyd, "Notes on the Russian Harbours of the Coast of Manchuria," *Journal of the Royal Geographical Society of London* 37 (1867): 218n.
34 Whigham, *Manchuria and Korea,* 46, 51–52.
35 B.S. Zhigalov, "KVZhD v Dal'nyvostochnoy Politikye Rossii, 1906–1914," *Vestnik Tomskovo Gosudarstvennovo Universiteta* 1, no. 2 (2008): 37.
36 Mantetsukai, *Mantetsu yonjūnen shi* (Tokyo: Yoshikawa kōbunkan, 2007), 520, 523; "NichiRo tetsudō renraku kaishi," *Yomiuri shinbun* (hereafter *YS*), 21 February 1909, 1.
37 "Chōshun no Rokoku shōnin," *Manshū nichi nichi shinbun* (*Manchuria Daily News*) (hereafter *MNNS*), 13 February 1908, 2.
38 Inoue Nobuō, *Chōshun enkakushi* (Dairen: ManMō bunka kyōkai, 1922), 18.

39 For example, "Manshū no sangyō," *YS,* 5 April 1905, 2; "Chōshunfu," *YS,* 16 April 1905, 2; "Chōshun Kitsurin aida no chiri to bussan," *YS,* 19 September 1905, 4.

40 Imperial Japanese Government Railways, *Official Guide,* 63–66.

41 Minami Manshū tetsudō kabushiki kaisha shomubu chōsaka, ed., *Minami Manshū tetsudō kabushiki kaisha dainiji jūnenshi* (Dairen: Minami Manshū tetsudō, 1928), 192.

42 Minami Manshū tetsudō kabushiki kaisha sōmubu chōsaka, *Manshū Shinagawa tetsudō ensen chihō ni okeru daizu no demawari zōka jijō oyobi sono taiōsaku* (Dairen: Minami Manshū tetsudō, 1931), 71–72.

43 "TōShin Mantetsu renraku," *MNNS,* 12 November 1907, 2; "ChōKan tetsudō kaitsū," *MNNS,* 26 November 1907, 2; "Mantetsu no renraku jitchi," *MNNS,* 10 July 1908, 2; "Rokoku no tōshin kōro," *MNNS,* 12 November 1907, 2.

44 Historical Section, Foreign Office, *Manchuria,* 59.

45 David Wolff, "Open Jaw: A Harbin-centered View of the Siberian-Manchurian Intervention, 1917–1922," *Russian History* (Pittsburgh) 36 (2009): 339–59; Minami Manshū tetsudō kabushiki kaisha sōmubu chōsaka, *Manshū Shinagawa tetsudō,* 1–2, 4.

46 Tsukase Susumu, *Manshū no Nihonjin* (Tokyo: Yoshikawa, 2004), 159.

47 "Chōshun Dairen aida ni," *MNNS,* 24 August 1926, 2.

48 "ChōHa aida no ōrai," *MNNS,* 11 September 1926, 3.

49 Exports from Dalian to Japan dwarfed all others, including those to the United Kingdom (10%), China (7.8%), Germany (6.3%), the United States (3%), Norway (1.5%), Italy (1.4%), Holland (1.3%), Denmark (0.8%), France (0.5%), and Sweden (0.5%). J.C. Balet, *La Mandchourie: historique, politique, economique, son avenir* (Paris: Payot, 1932), 136–37.

50 Out of a total of ¥2,063,842,000, the breakdown was: Japan ¥1,510,754,000, the USSR ¥465,015,000, the United Kingdom ¥39,590,000, the United States ¥26,400,000, France ¥21,086,000, Sweden ¥850,000, and Denmark ¥157,000. Soviet, British, and French investments were primarily in railways, though Soviet figures included mining and forestry operations. Senta Manzō, *Shin Manshū he no rihyō* (Tokyo: Senshinsa, 1932), 112–13, apparently citing Sada Kōjirō, *ManMō ni okeru Nihon tōshin gaku: ManMō ni okeru sekai kakkoku no tōshin gaku* (Dairen: Mantetsu, 1929).

51 John R. Stewart, "Foreign Investments in Manchuria," *Far Eastern Survey* 4, no. 11 (1935): 82.

52 South Manchuria Railway, *Second Report on Progress in Manchuria: To 1930* (Dairen: South Manchuria Railway, 1931), 125–26.

53 Inoue, *Chōshun enkakushi,* 29–30, 41–42.

54 "Denwa mōshikomi kensū," *MNNS,* 13 February 1908, 4; Historical Section, Foreign Office, *Manchuria,* 38.

55 Bank of Chosen, *Economic History of Manchuria* (Seoul: Bank of Chosen, 1921), 277.

56 Tōa keizai chosakyoku, *The Manchuria Year Book, 1931* (Tokyo: Tōa keizai chosakyoku, 1931), 50–51, 171.

57 "Chōshunfu nōgyō jōkyō," *MNNS,* 19 August 1908, 4.

58 Kuroda Kashirō, *Manshū kiyō* (n.p.: Mantetsu, 1910), 1:44–45, 75–76; 2:108–12.

59 Inoue, *Chōshun enkakushi,* 113.

60 "Mame no fusaku," *YS,* 12 November 1907, 1; Izumi Renji, *Chōshun jijō* (Chōshun: Chōshun Nihōsha, 1912), 252–81.

61 Manshū tetsudō kabushiki kaisha chihōbu nōmuka, *Manshū zairai nōgyō* (Dairen: Manshū tetsudō chihōbu, 1935), 9–10.

62 William Shurtleff and Akiko Aoyagi, comp., *History of Soybeans and Soyfoods in Canada (1831–2010): Extensively Annotated Bibliography and Sourcebook* (Lafayette, CA: Soyinfo Center, 2010), 90.

63 Yu Ye and Xiuqi Fang, "Land Use Change in Northeast China in the Twentieth Century: A Note on Source, Methods and Patterns," *Journal of Historical Geography* 35, no. 2

(2009):325. The "golden age" of soy production in southern Manchuria was between 1908 and 1915. James Kai-sing Kung and Nan Li, "Commercialization as Exogenous Shocks: The Effect of the Soybean Trade on Migration in Manchurian Villages, 1895–1934," *Explorations in Economic History* 48 (2011): 580.

64 Yu Ye and Xiuqi Fang, "Spatial Pattern of Land Cover Changes across Northeast China over the Past 300 Years," *Journal of Historical Geography* 37 (2011): 414–16.

65 King, *Farmers of Forty Centuries*, 357–58.

66 Manshū jijō annaijo, *Shinkyō jijō* (Shinkyō: Manshū jijō annaijo, 1934), 59–65.

67 K. Asakawa, "Japan in Manchuria – II," *Yale Review* 17 (November 1908): 274; Takashima Masaaki, "NichiRo senkōki 'Manshū' (Chūgoku tōhokubu) ni okeru Nikkei jiba ginkō no bunseki," in *Hiroshima keizai daigaku sōritsu yonjūshūnen kinen ronbunshū* (Hiroshima: Hiroshima keizai daigaku, 2007), 37.

68 Minami Manshū tetsudō shomubu chōsaka, *Manshū ni okeru suisanbutsu no jukyū* (Dairen: Minami Manshū tetsudō shomubu chōsaka, 1929), 293.

69 "Chōshuneki no chikashitsu shisetsu," *MNNS*, 1 February 1927, 4.

70 This nickname is in many sources. One on development especially after the First World War is *Shinkyō no gaikyō* (Shinkyō: Shinkyō shōkō kōkai, 1942), 1. Another source suggests the term originated in Changchun's being Mantetsu's northernmost collection point. Manshū jijō annaijo, *Shinkyō jijō*, 47.

71 "Chōshun mo shinkoku no hashiri," *MNNS*, 9 October 1926, 8.

72 Manshū jijō annaijo, *Shinkyō jijō*, 35–36. See also Minami Manshū tetsudō kabushiki kaisha rinji keizai chōsa i'inkai, *Manshū daizu hinshitsu tōkyū satei ni kansuru chōsa* (Dairen: Minami Manshū tetsudō, 1929).

73 Izumi, *Chōshun jijō*, 219–21; Manshū jijō annaijo, *Shinkyō jijō*, 40.

74 Tōa keizai chosakyoku, *Manchuria Year Book, 1931* 174–75.

75 "Kōryō no hanashi," *MNNS*, 29 November 1907, 3; Manshū jijō annaijo, *Shinkyō jijō*, 35.

76 Inoue, *Chōshun enkakushi*, 111.

77 Minami Manshū tetsudō shomubu chōsaka, ed., *Manshū awa ni kansuru chōsa* (Dairen: Minami Manshū tetsudō shomubu chōsaka, 1925), 62–63, 91–111.

78 Minami Manshū tetsudō kabushiki kaisha keizai chōsakai, *Manshū ni okeru ama jijō* (Dairen: Minami Manshū tetsudō keizai chōsakai, 1935); Manshū tetsudō kabushiki kaisha chihōbu nōmuka, *Manshū zairai nōgyō;* Maeda Seiichi, *Manshūkoku to tensai tōgyō* (Tokyo: Maeda Seiichi, 1932).

79 *The Manchoukuo Year Book, 1942* (Tokyo: Ajia tōkeisha, 1942), 531–34.

80 Manshū jijō annaijo, *Shinkyō jijō*, 37; Minami Manshū tetsudō kabushiki kaisha, *Manshū ni okeru jūshi no seisanryō ni tsuite* (Shinkyō: Shinkyō shisha chōsashitsu, 1940); Manshūkoku sangyōbu, *Nikuchiku jukyū ni kansuru chōsa hōkokusho* (Shinkyō: Manshūkoku sangyōbu daijin kanbō shiryōka, 1938), 112–13.

81 "Manshū keizaikai tenbō," *MNNS*, 14 December 1936.

82 Minami Manshū tetsudō shomubu chōsaka, *Manshū ni okeru suisanbutsu no jukyū*, 293–95, 303–5.

83 Kuroda, *Manshū kiyō*, 2:123–38.

84 "Shōchu no hanashi," *MNNS*, 11 December 1907, 3.

85 Shinkyō shōkō kaigijo, *DaiShinkyō keizai gaikan* (Shinkyō: Shinkyō shōkō kaigijo, 1937), 139; Minami Manshū tetsudō kabushiki kaisha chōsaka, *Minami Manshū ni okeru Nihon no keizaiteki seiryoku* (n.p.: Manshū tetsudō, 1912), 36.

86 Manshū jijō annaijo, *Shinkyō jijō*, 46.

87 "ManMō ni okeru honpō seiryoku no gaiyō," in *Gendaishi shiryō 11: zoku: Manshū jihen*, ed. Kobayashi Tatsuo, Shimada Toshihiko, and Inaba Masao (Tokyo: Misuzu shobō, 1965), 155–98.

88 Manshū jijō annaijo, *Shinkyō jijō*, 37.

89 Minami Manshū tetsudō kabushiki kaisha sōmubu chōsaka, *Manshū no sen'i kōgyō* (Dairen: Minami Manshū tetsudō, 1931), 55.
90 In addition to Nishizawa, see Yanagisawa Asobu, "ZaiMan Nihonjin," in *Manshūkoku to wa nan datta no ka: NitChū kyōdō kenkyū*, ed. Shokuminchi bunka gakkai, Chūgoku tōhoku rinkan jūyonnenshi sōhenshitsu (Tokyo: Shōgakukan, 2008), 223–26.
91 Manshū jijō annaijo, *Shinkyō jijō*, 44; Minami Manshū tetsudō kabushiki kaisha shomubu chōsaka, ed., *Manshū ni okeru garasu kōgyō* (Dairen: Minami Manshū tetsudō shomubu chōsaka, 1923), 47–49, 209–10; Minami Manshū tetsudō kabushiki kaisha rinji keizai chōsa i'inkai, ed., *Manshū shuyō toshi no mokuzai jukyū jōkyō* (Dairen: Minami Manshū tetsudō, 1930), 274–76.
92 Kuroda, *Manshū kiyō*, 2:132; *Shinkyō no gaikyō*, 1; Minami Manshū tetsudō kabushiki kaisha rinji keizai chōsa i'inkai, *Manshū shuyō toshi no mokuzai jukyū jōkyō*, 244–76.
93 Manshū jijō an'naisho, *Shinkyō jijō*, 38.
94 Ibid., 40–41, 47, 50.
95 Ibid., 38.
96 Minami Manshū tetsudō kabushiki kaisha shomubu chōsaka, ed., *Manshū ni okeru bōsekigyō* (Dairen: Minami Manshū tetsudō, 1923), 186.
97 Minami Manshū tetsudō kabushiki kaisha sōseishitsu chihōbu zanmuseiri iinkai, *Mantetsu fuzokuchi keiei enkaku zenshi* (Tokyo: Ryūkei shosha, 1977) (hereafter *MFKEZ*), 3:508; Manshū jijō annaijo, *Shinkyō jijō*, 38.
98 Izumi, *Chōshun jijō*, 282–86; "Manshū menka no shōrai," *MNNS*, 3 April 1926, 8.
99 Minami Manshū tetsudō kabushiki kaisha shomubu chōsaka, *Manshū no meriyasu kōgyō* (Dairen: Minami Manshū tetsudō, 1929), 73–76. Changchun's 37 cotton factories in 1925 followed Dalian's 320, Andong's 66, and Shenyang's 50. The survey included both light and heavy manufacturing, and noted 702 factories in all. "Manshū shokōgyō no jōtai," *MNNS*, 19 December 1926, 8.
100 Minami Manshū tetsudō kabushiki kaisha sōmubu chōsaka, *Manshū no sen'i kōgyō*, 33–35.
101 Manshū jijō annaijo, *Shinkyō jijō*, 37–38.
102 Ibid., 59.
103 As some publications noted. Chōshun chōsain, *Chōshun ni okeru Kashō shiba narabi hanbai soshiki chōsa* (n.p., 1926); Izumi, *Chōshun jijō*, 95–104, 160–76, 181–214, 219–33.
104 Ishida Takehiko, "Chūgoku tōhoku ni okeru ryōsan no dōkō: Manshū jihen mae ni okeru," *Hokkaidō daigaku keizaigaku kenkyū* 24, no. 1 (1974): 148.
105 Manshū jijō annaijo, *Shinkyō jijō*, 40–41.
106 Ibid., 40, 42.
107 Kuroda, *Manshū kiyō* 2:138, 144–49; Izumi, *Chōshun jijō*, 95–104, 160–76, 181–214, 219–33.
108 Bao Xi, *Xinjingshi shanghui* (Xinjing[?]: Huibian, 1934), 3.
109 Ōgaki Tsurutada, *Shuto Shinkyō no keizaiteki hatten saku* (Dairen: Manshū bunka kyōkai, 1933). A 1934 discussion of measures is Manshū jijō annaijo, *Shinkyō jijō*, 57–59.
110 Haruo Iguchi, *Unfinished Business: Ayukawa Yoshisuke and U.S.–Japan Relations, 1937–1953* (Cambridge, MA: Harvard University Press, 2003); Janis Mimura, *Planning for Empire: Reform Bureaucrats and the Japanese Wartime State* (Ithaca, NY: Cornell University Press, 2011).
111 Stewart, "Foreign Investments in Manchuria," 84–85.
112 Manshū jijō annaijo, *Shinkyō jijō*, 42, 48, 51, 59–60.
113 John R. Stewart, "Four Years of Manchoukuo," *Far Eastern Survey* 5, no. 6 (1936): 54–55; Bitō Masayoshi, ed., *Yakushin tojō no daiShinkyō* (Shinkyō: Shinkyō shōkō kaigijo, 1936), 32–33.

114 Stewart, "Foreign Investments in Manchuria," 82–83. Noting that Manchukuo's contributions were "minute," Stewart suggested that "to use a slang expression, the Japanese Government and the S.M.R. [South Manchuria Railway] have been 'holding the bag' financially for the new state," ibid., 56.

115 Baron Kimmochi Ohkura, "Japan and Manchoukuo's Industrial Development," *Contemporary Japan* 9, no. 7 (1940): 852; Edwin W. Pauley, *Report on Japanese Assets in Manchuria to the President of the United States* (Washington, DC: US Government Printing Office, July 1946), 5.

116 Minami Manshū tetsudō kabushiki kaisha chihōbu, *Chihō keiei tōkei nenpō* (Dairen: Minami Manshū tetsudō chihōbu, 1938), 328–53.

117 Nishizawa Yasuhiko, "'Manshūkoku' no kensetsu jigyō," in *Manshūkoku no kenkyū*, ed. Yamamoto Yūzō (Tokyo: Ryokuin shobō, 1995), 423.

118 See works such as Mantetsu keikakubu gyōmuka, *Manshū shuyō kaisha teikanshū* (Dairen: Manshū keizai kenkyūkai, 1934).

119 See, for example, the 1944 listing of the members of the Manchuria Association of Mining and Industry in Manshū kōkō gijitsu'in kyōkai, *Manshū kōkō nenkan Kōtoku jūichi nenpan* (Shinkyō: TōA bunka toshokan kabushiki kaisha, 1944), 303–469.

120 Manshūkoku tsūshinsha, *Manshū kaitaku nenkan* (Shinkyō: Manshūkoku tsūshinsha, 1942); Louise Young, *Japan's Total Empire: Manchuria and the Culture of Wartime Imperialism* (Berkeley: University of California Press, 1998), 356–58; *Shinkyō shigai chizu* (Tokyo: Kanemitsusha shiryōbu, 1982).

121 Manshikai, ed., *Manshū kaihatsu yonjūnenshi* (Tokyo: Manshū kaihatsu yonjūnenshi kankōkai, 1965), 3:300–15.

122 Areas of operation were not listed for 18 firms, 11 of which were headquartered in the capital. Of the 108 firms, 45 were headquartered in Dalian, 26 in Xinjing, 19 in Shenyang, 4 each in Yingkou and Andong, 2 each in Fushun and Harbin, and 1 each in Jilin City, Anshan, Tieling, and Lüshun. Two were in other cities. The Jilin firm is listed as operating only in Xinjing. Shimizu gumi Manshū shiten, *Nenkan* (n.p.: Shimizu gumi Manshū shiten, 1936), 53–61.

123 Nihon keizai shi kenkyūjo, ed., *Onoda semento hyakunen shi* (Tokyo: Onoda semento kabushiki kaisha, 1981), 345–48, 359–66, 391–98; Shimizu gumi Manshū shiten, *Nenkan*, 140–43. On Onoda and Japan's colonial cement industry see Nishizawa Yasuhiko, *Nihon shokuminchi kenchiku ron* (Nagoya: Nagoya daigaku shuppansha, 2008), 288–99.

124 Shimizu kensetsu hyakugojūnen shi hensan i'inkai, *Shimizu kensetsu hyakugojūnen shi* (Tokyo: Shimizu kensetsu kabushiki kaisha, 1953), 136, 147.

125 Nishimura Kiichi, "Manshū hitotoku," *Toshi kōron* (hereafter *TK*) 18, no. 12 (1935): 82; Shimizu gumi Manshū shiten, *Nenkan*, 39, 43–44.

126 Shimizu kensetsu hyakugojūnen shi hensan i'inkai, *Shimizu kensetsu hyakugojūnen shi*, 112–13, 121, 124–25, 147–48.

127 Nishizawa, "'Manshūkoku' no kensetsu jigyō," 381–38.

128 Manshū jijō annaijo, *Shinkyō jijō*, 38, 43, 45; Shimizu gumi Manshū shiten, *Nenkan*, 153–61, 166, 180–81, 240–46; Koshizawa Akira, *Manshūkoku no shuto keikaku: Tōkyō no genzai to mirai o tou* (Tokyo: Nihon keizai hyōronsha, 1988), 113–14.

129 See Linda Clarke, *Building Capitalism: Historical Change and the Labour Process in the Production of the Built Environment* (London: Routledge, 1992).

130 Shinkyō shōkō kaigijo, *DaiShinkyō keizai gaikan*, 123.

131 Manshū keizai jijō annaijo, *Kokuto Shinkyō keizai jijō* (Dairen: Manshū bunka kyōkai, 1933), 53–54.

132 Manshū jijō annaijo, *Shinkyō jijō*, 42.

133 *Manchoukuo Year Book, 1942*, 529–30.

134 Ibid., 45; Hoshino Tatsuo, ed., *Manshū shuyō toshi shōkō benran* (Dairen: Minami Manshū tetsudō chihōbu shōkōka, 1935), 70–71.
135 Yokohama shōkin ginkō chōsaka, *Manshū mengyō no gaikan* (n.p.: Yokohama shōkin ginkō, 1941), 9.
136 John R. Stewart, "Mukden Population Reaches Million Mark," *Far Eastern Survey* 9, no. 7 (1940): 84.
137 Shinkyō shōkō kaigijo, *DaiShinkyō keizai gaikan,* 139, 158–60.
138 Manshūkoku jitsugyōbu rinji sangyō chōsakyoku, *Komugiko narabi ni seiko kōgyō ni kansuru chōsasho* (Shinkyō: Manshūkoku tosho kabushiki kaisha, 1937), 72.
139 Manshū jijō annaijo, *Shinkyō jijō,* 45–47.
140 *MFKEZ* 3:509, 513–14.
141 Shinkyō shōkō kaigijo, *DaiShinkyō keizai gaikan,* 139; Manshū keizai jijō annaijo, *Kokuto Shinkyō keizai jijō,* 2, 38–40.
142 *Shinkyō no gaikyō,* 48–66.
143 *Manchoukuo Year Book, 1942,* 224.
144 Shinkyō shōkō kaigijo, *DaiShinkyō keizai gaikan,* 37–38, 203–18, 230–32, 246–47; Manshū keizai jijō annaijo, *Kokuto Shinkyō keizai jijō,* 2, 24–25; Yoneda Masabumi, "Shinkyō Kitsurin kokudō kōji hōkoku," *Doboku gakkaishi* 21, no. 11 (1935): 1611–26.
145 For example, see Manshū jijō annaijo, *Shinkyō jijō,* 32, 47.
146 Manshū keizai jijō annaijo, *Kokuto Shinkyō keizai jijō,* 2.
147 Minami Manshū tetsudō kabushiki kaisha keizai chōsakai, ed., *Manshū tsūshin jigyō hōsaku* (Dairen: Minami Manshū tetsudō keizai chōsakai, 1936), 73–77.
148 Denden is referred to as MTT in Daqing Yang, *Technology of Empire: Telecommunications and Japanese Expansion in Asia, 1883–1945* (Cambridge, MA: Harvard University Press, 2010), 97–98. Receivers' images and technical information are available at the Japan Radio Museum, http://www.japanradiomuseum.jp/.
149 *Manchoukuo Year Book, 1942,* 743; Yang, *Technology of Empire,* 160–69, 194.
150 "Imon hikōki ga yōka ni kuru," *MNNS,* 5 December 1926, 4.
151 Bitō, *Yakushin tojō no daiShinkyō,* 11–14.
152 "Dairen Ōsaka aida no yūbin hikō osoren," *MNNS,* 16 July 1926, 2; "NichiMan renraku hikō wa ashita hiraika," *MNNS,* 10 September 1926, 2; "Nihon kōkū hikōki kiHan," *MNNS,* 21 September 1926, 2; *Manchuria Year Book, 1931,* 161. A sixty-three-hour flight from Paris to Beijing was celebrated in "Pari kara Pekin he," *MNNS,* 29 June 1926, 2.
153 Yang, *Technology of Empire,* 163.
154 Manshū keizai jijō annaijo, *Kokuto Shinkyō keizai jijō,* 24–25; Shinkyō shōkō kaigijo, *DaiShinkyō keizai gaikan,* 44–48; "Japanese Aroused by Weakness of Civil Aviation," *Far Eastern Survey* 4, no. 8 (1935): 62–63.
155 H.G.W. Woodhead, *A Visit to Manchukuo* (Shanghai: Mercury Press, 1932), 3.
156 Carl Hans Pollog, "Le trafic mondial aérien au cours de l'année 1933–1934," *Revue aéronautique international* 5 (1935): 288.
157 Carl Hans Pollog, "Le trafic mondial aérien au cours de l'année 1934–1935," *Revue aéronautique international* 6 (1936): 388, 393.
158 Russell E. Hall, "Expanding Airways in the Far East," *Far Eastern Survey* 6, no. 9 (1937): 97.
159 "Yon, go jikan de todoku Dairen-Shinkyō no sokutatsubin," *MNNS,* 23 June 1937, 2.
160 Nihon kōkū yusō kabushiki kaisha, *Nihon kōkū yusō kabushiki kaisha jūnenshi* (Tokyo: Nihon kōkū yusō kabushiki kaisha, 1938), 24, 33.
161 *Manchoukuo Year Book, 1942,* 584.
162 Hall, "Expanding Airways in the Far East"; Dorothy Borg, "Japanese Establish Airlines in China," *Far Eastern Survey* 8, no. 11 (1939): 132–33.

163 Hiki Hisao, "Chūgoku 'seihoku rūto kūro' no kaihatsu," pts. 1–3, *Manshū to Nihonjin* (hereafter *MTN)* 6 (December 1978): 21–25, 7 (November 1979): 25–32, and 8 (October 1981): 28–37.
164 Grayson Kirk, "Wings over the Pacific," *Foreign Affairs* 20, no. 2 (1942): 293–302.
165 Philip S. Jowett, *Rays of the Rising Sun: Armed Forces of Japan's Asian Allies, 1931–1945,* vol. 1, *China and Manchukuo* (Solihull, UK: Helion, 2004), 90–91, 106, 109.
166 Balet, *Mandchourie,* 181–82.
167 *Manchoukuo Year Book, 1942,* 244.
168 Bitō, *Yakushin jotō no daiShinkyō,* 62–64.
169 *Manchuria Year Book, 1931,* 235–44. A branch of the Bank of Manchukuo opened in 1926. "Chūō ginkō no setsuritsu," *MNNS,* 9 July 1926, 8.
170 These were the Ifa and Xinjing Banks, with reserves similar to those in Yitong. *Manchoukuo Year Book, 1942,* 248.
171 "Manshū kōgyō ginko setsuritsu," *YS,* 11 June 1936, 3.
172 Shinkyō tokubetsushi shichōkanbō shomuka, *Kokuto Shinkyō* (Shinkyō: Manshū jijō annaijo, 1940), 109; Hōten tetsudōkyoku ryokyakukakari, *Shinkyō* (Hōten: Hōten tetsudōkyoku ryokyakukakari, 1941), 5. On Man'ei, see Hu Chang and Gu Quan, *Manying: Guoce dianying mianmian guan* (Beijing: Zhonghua shuju chubanshe, 1990); Yamaguchi Takeshi, *Maboroshi no kinema Man'ei: Amakasu Masahiko to katsudō gunzō* (Tokyo: Heibonsha, 1989); and Michael Baskett, *The Attractive Empire: Transnational Film Culture in Imperial Japan* (Honolulu: University of Hawai'i Press, 2008).
173 Among many works on Yamaguchi is Baskett, *Attractive Empire,* 77–84.
174 Ibid., 115–20.
175 John P. Fox, *Germany and the Far Eastern Crisis, 1931–1938* (Oxford: Clarendon Press, 1982), 146–74; *Manchoukuo Year Book, 1942,* 367–70, 373, 918, 924, 955; William C. Kirby, *Germany and Republican China* (Stanford, CA: Stanford University Press, 1984), 140–44, 243–44.
176 Stewart, "Foreign Investments in Manchuria," 84.
177 Ibid., 85.
178 Izumi, *Chōshun jijō,* 233–36; Minami Manshū tetsudō kabushiki kaisha chōsaka, *Minami Manshū ni okeru Nihon no keizaiteki seiryoku,* 35–36; Historical Section, Foreign Office, *Manchuria,* 58; Minami Manshū tetsudō kabushiki kaisha keizai chōsakai, ed., *Manshū kayakurui tōsei hōsaku: Manshū matchi kōgyō hōsaku* (n.p.: Minami Manshū tetsudō keizai chōsakai, 1935), 36–37; *MFKEZ* 3:516; Manshū jijō annaijo, *Shinkyō jijō,* 39; *Manchoukuo Year Book, 1942,* 236, 542–43.
179 Stewart, "Foreign Investments in Manchuria," 81, 83–85.
180 "Hankanhanmin no Manshū sekiyu kaisha sōritsu," *Ōsaka mainichi shinbun,* 31 October 1934; *Manchoukuo Year Book, 1942,* 237.
181 Roy H. Akagi, "The Future of American Trade with Manchukuo," *Annals of the American Academy of Political and Social Science* 211 (September 1940): 138–43.
182 Stewart, "Foreign Investments in Manchuria," 84; John R. Stewart, "The War and Western Interests in North China," *Far Eastern Survey* 7, no. (1938): 232.
183 Hachirō Arita, "The Greater East Asian Sphere of Common Prosperity," *Contemporary Japan* 10, no. 1 (1941): 9–15.
184 Takeo Sekiguchi, "The Wartime Role of Manchoukuo," *Contemporary Japan* 13, no. 2 (1944): 176.
185 Ibid., 178–81, 184.
186 Okano Kanki, "Manshūkoku jidai no zuisō," *MTN* 10 (February 1988): 62.
187 Lin, "Interpretive Trends in Taiwan's Scholarship," 86–87.

188 Margaret S. Culver, "Manchuria: Japan's Supply Base," *Far Eastern Survey* 14, no. 12 (1945): 161–62.

189 Mayumi Itoh, *Pioneers of Sino-Japanese Relations: Liao and Takasaki* (New York: Palgrave Macmillan, 2012), 27–28; Iguchi, *Unfinished Business.*

190 Culver, "Manchuria," 162.

191 Washio Kenzō, "Zuisō: Hōten, Shinkyō ni tsukawashite," *Manshū kenchiku zasshi* 19, no. 2 (1939): 25–29.

Chapter 4: Colonial Society

1 Christopher M. Isett, *State, Peasant, and Merchant in Qing Manchuria, 1644–1862* (Stanford, CA: Stanford University Press, 2007), 310–11.

2 Kang Chao, "Demographic Development in Manchuria, 1924–1941," *Bulletin of the Institute of Modern History* 10 (1981): 352, 354, 370; Thomas R. Gottschang and Diana Lary, *Swallows and Settlers: The Great Migration from North China to Manchuria* (Ann Arbor: University of Michigan Press, 2000); Robert H.G. Lee, *The Manchurian Frontier in Ch'ing History* (Cambridge, MA: Harvard University Press, 1970); James Reardon-Anderson, *Reluctant Pioneers: China's Expansion Northward, 1644–1937* (Stanford, CA: Stanford University Press, 2005); Ronald Suleski, *Civil Government in Warlord China: Tradition, Modernization, and Manchuria* (New York: Peter Lang, 2002).

3 Tim Wright, "Growth of the Modern Chinese Coal Industry: An Analysis of Supply and Demand, 1896–1936," *Modern China* 7, no. 3 (1981): 324–27; Minami Manshū tetsudō kabushiki kaisha shomubu chōsaka, *Manshū kōgyō rōdō jijō* (Dairen: Minami Manshū tetsudō shomubu chōsaka, 1925); Minami Manshū tetsudō kabushiki kaisha keizai chōsakai, *Manshū rōdō tōsei hōsaku* (Dairen: Minami Manshū tetsudō keizai chōsakai, 1935); David Tucker, "Labor Policy and the Construction Industry in Manchukuo: Systems of Recruitment, Management, and Control," and Ju Zhifen, "Northern Chinese Laborers and Manchukuo," both in *Asian Labor in the Wartime Japanese Empire: Unknown Histories,* ed. Paul H. Kratoska (Armonk, NY: M.E. Sharpe, 2005), 25–57 and 61–78.

4 Hoover Institution on War, Revolution and Peace (hereafter HIWRP), Julean Herbert Arnold papers, box 10: China/Labor Conditions. US Commercial Attaché, "China Labor and Industrial Conditions," n.d., 1, 9.

5 Manshū jijō annaijo, *Shinkyō jijō* (Shinkyō: Manshū jijō annaijo, 1934), 43.

6 Gottschang and Lary, *Swallows and Settlers;* James Kai-sing Kung and Nan Li, "Commercialization as Exogenous Shocks: The Effect of the Soybean Trade on Migration in Manchurian Villages, 1895–1934," *Explorations in Economic History* 48 (2011): 569.

7 One woman's views are in Ida Pruitt, *A Daughter of Han: The Autobiography of a Chinese Working Woman. From the Story Told Her by Nin Lao T'ai-t'ai* (Stanford, CA: Stanford University Press, 1967), 7, 39, 43, 130–33, 166.

8 "Manshū kara no gaikoku yūbin," *Manshū nichi nichi shinbun* (*Manchuria Daily News*) (hereafter *MNNS*), 23 June 1926, 2; "Manchoukuo Bank Reports Handling $480,000,000 in Remittances to Foreign Countries," *Toronto Daily Star* 2 April 1935, 15.

9 Edwin G. Beal, Jr., "The 1940 Census of Manchuria," *Far Eastern Quarterly* 4, no. 3 (1945): 243–62.

10 Chao, "Demographic Development in Manchuria," 355, 362, 372; Frank Leeming, "Reconstructing Late Ch'ing Fengt'ien," *Modern Asian Studies* 4, no. 4 (1970): 309n9.

11 Gaimushō tsūshōkyoku, *Chōshun no jijō* (n.p.: Gaimushō 1929), 59.

12 Manshūkoku seifu kokumuin kokuto kensetsukyoku, *Kokuto daiShinkyō* (Shinkyō: Manshūkoku seifu kokuto kensetsukyoku, 1933), 5, 6, 12; Tōa keizai chosakyoku, *The Manchuria Year Book, 1931* (Tokyo: Tōa keizai chosakyoku, 1931), 7.

13 Chao, "Demographic Development in Manchuria," 375.

14 Manshikai, ed., *Manshū kaihatsu yonjūnenshi*, vol. 1 (Tokyo: Manshū kaihatsu yonjūnenshi kankōkai, 1964), 31–32; and Louise Young, *Japan's Total Empire: Manchuria and the Culture of Wartime Imperialism* (Berkeley: University of California Press, 1998), 44–45.

15 *Teikoku tōkei-nenkan, 1938* (*Statistical Yearbook of the Japanese Empire*), in E.B. Schumpeter, ed., *The Industrialization of Japan and Manchukuo* (London: Routledge, 2000), 78.

16 John J. Stephan, "Hijacked by Utopia: American Nikkei in Manchuria," *Amerasia Journal* 23, no. 3 (1997): 1–42; Jonathan Dresner, "International Labour Migrants' Return to Meiji-era Yamaguchi and Hiroshima: Economic and Social Effects," *International Migration* (Geneva) 46, no. 3 (2008): 65–94; and Joseph Barber, Jr., *Hawaii: Restless Rampart* (Indianapolis: Bobbs-Merrill, 1941), 148–55.

17 Minami Manshū tetsudō kabushiki kaisha chōsaka, *Minami Manshū ni okeru Nihon no keizaiteki seiryoku* (n.p.: Manshū tetsudō, 1912), 31–34.

18 HIWRP XX536, Robert Smith reports. Robert Smith, "The Japan-Manchukuo Economic Conference of Business Interests at Dairen," 229.

19 Noriko J. Horiguchi, *Women Adrift: The Literature of Japan's Imperial Body* (Minneapolis: University of Minnesota Press, 2012), 72.

20 Benkan zaijing jizhe quanti dongyuan, "Da Xinjingshi de dongtai," *Qilin* 2, no. 6 (1942): 105; Waller Wynne, Jr., *The Population of Manchuria* (Washington, DC: US Government Printing Office, 1958), 28, 29. The latter notes an enumerated, as opposed to a registered, 1940 population of 555,000. I am grateful to Norman Smith for bringing the former to my attention.

21 Nakano Kinjirō, "Kokuto Shinkyō no kensetsu," *Dōryo no kairyō* 15, no. 12 (1933): 166.

22 *The Manchoukuo Year Book, 1942* (Tokyo: Ajia tōkeisha, 1942), 118–20.

23 Hashiya Hiroshi, *Teikoku Nihon to shokuminchi toshi* (Tokyo: Yoshikawa kōbunkan, 2004), 67.

24 Chao, "Demographic Development in Manchuria"; Kōjima Reikichi, "The Population of the Prefectures and Cities of Japan in Most Recent Times," trans. Edwin G. Beal, Jr., *Far Eastern Quarterly* 3, no. 4 (1944): 358–59.

25 Chao, "Demographic Development in Manchuria"; Kōjima, "Population of the Prefectures and Cities of Japan."

26 John R. Stewart, "Mukden Population Reaches Million Mark," *Far Eastern Survey* 9, no. 7 (1940): 84; Hashiya, *Teikoku Nihon to shokuminchi toshi*, 52, 61–65, 74.

27 Kōjima, "Population of the Prefectures and Cities of Japan," 358–59.

28 Japanese in Dalian numbered 8,248 in 1906 (43.7%), 50,778 in 1920 (34.8%), 88,793 in 1929 (34.3%), 134,329 in 1935 (37.0%), and 192,558 in 1942 (23.3%). Kō En, "Soshakuchi mejia Dairen shinbun to Manshū hakkei," *Jyaanaru obu gurobaru mejia stajiizu* 4 (2009): 22.

29 A figure of 227,420 included Taiwanese. John R. Stewart, "Four Years of Manchoukuo," *Far Eastern Survey* 5, no. 6 (1936): 54; Catherine Porter, "Korea and Formosa as Colonies of Japan," *Far Eastern Survey* 5, no. 9 (1936): 88.

30 *Manshū teikoku genjū jinkō tōkei* (Shinkyō: Manshū teikoku chianbu keimushi, 1940), 8–9. Chao indicates 3.3% Koreans and 2.3% Japanese in "Demographic Development in Manchuria," 374.

31 Wynne, *Population of Manchuria*, 21.

32 *Shinkyō shigai chizu* (Tokyo: Kanemitsusha shiryōbu, 1982) (hereafter *SSC*).

33 Cemil Aydin, *The Politics of Anti-Westernism in Asia: Visions of World Order in Pan-Islamic and Pan-Asian Thought* (New York: Columbia University Press, 2007), 166–84; Li Narangoa, "Educating Mongols and Making 'Citizens' of Manchukuo," *Inner Asia* 3, no. 2 (2001): 101–26.

34 *Manchoukuo Year Book, 1942,* 120, 122.

35 John R. Stewart, "Manchoukuo Announces a Mongol Program," *Far Eastern Survey* 9, no. 5 (1940): 58–60.

36 Henning Haslund-Christensen, "In the Mongol Encampments, 1937," *Journal of the Royal Central Asian Society* 25, no. 2 (1938): 180, 190.

37 H.E.M. James, *Long White Mountain or, A Journey in Manchuria* (London: Longmans, Green, 1888), 377–78; Manshū jijō annaijo, *Shinkyō jijō,* 17–19.

38 Tajima Daisuke, "'Manshūkoku' ni okeru Kaimin bochi sen'i mondai," *Ritsumeikan bungaku* 619 (2010): 552–59.

39 "Chōshun fuzokuchi no hōnin ichiman ni tassu," *MNNS,* 28 February 1926, 3; "Taiwan Manshū Nanshin sankaku kōrō kettei," *MMNS,* 2 March 1926, 1; "Fuzokuchi no hōnin kyūsen yomyō," *MNNS,* 25 August 1926, 4. The last reports eleven present in 1925: seven men and four women.

40 Shinkyō tokubetsushi shichōkanbō shomuka, *Yakushin kokuto no iyō* (Shinkyō: Shinkyō tokubetsushi kōsho, 1940), 12–13.

41 Xu Xueji, "Zai Manzhouguo de Taiwanren gaodengguan: yi Datong xueyuan de biyesheng weili," *Taiwanshi yanjiu* 19, no. 3 (2012): 95–150. See also Xu Xueji, ed., *Rizhishiqi zai Manzhou de Taiwanren* (Taibei: Zhongyang yanjiuyuan jindaishi yanjiusuo, 2004); and Lin Man-houng, "Nihon no kaigunryoku to kyōkyō no chūtai: 1930 nendai no Taiwan Manshū aida bōeki o chūshin," in *Shōwa Ajia shugi no jitsuzō: teikoku Nihon to Taiwan, "Nan'yō," "Minami Shina,"* ed. Matsuura Masataka (Kyoto: Minerva, 2007), 344–71.

42 H. Enselme, *A travers la Mandchourie: Le Chemin de fer de l'est Chinois d'après la mission du Capitaine H. de Bouillane de Lacoste et du Capitaine Enselme* (Paris: J. Rueff, 1904), 112–16.

43 B.S. Zhigalov, "KVZhD v Dal'nyvostochnoy Politikye Rossii, 1906–1914," *Vestnik Tomskovo Gosudarstvennovo Universiteta* 1, no. 2 (2008): 30.

44 "Kajin to gaikokujin no sū," *MNNS,* 19 May 1926, 3; Minami Manshū tetsudō, *Chōshun chihō an'nai: Shiheigai, Kōshurei, Chōshun, Kitsurin* (n.p.: Minami Manshū tetsudō, 1927); H.G.W. Woodhead, *A Visit to Manchukuo* (Shanghai: Mercury Press, 1932), 2.

45 Serge Cipko, "Ukrainians in Manchuria, China: A Concise Historical Survey," *Past Imperfect* 1 (1992): 160, 162, 163.

46 Minami Manshū tetsudō kabushiki kaisha shomubu chōsaka, ed., *Minami Manshū tetsudō kabushiki kaisha dainiji jūnenshi* (Dairen: Minami Manshū tetsudō, 1928), 427.

47 James, *Long White Mountain,* 379, 472.

48 Ibid., 204, 378; *Missionary Herald of the Presbyterian Church in Ireland* (May 1876): 91–92; F.W.S. O'Neill, *The Call of the East: Sketches from the History of the Irish Mission to Manchuria, 1869–1919* (London: James Clarke, 1919), 11, 119.

49 Société des missions étrangères de Paris, Chine, Mandchourie, 564/678, "Mandchourie Septentrionale, Province du Ghirin"; *Compte-rendu des travaux* (1898), 9; and Gérard Moussay and Brigitte Appavou, *Répertoire des membres de la sociéte des missions étrangères* (Paris: Archives des Missions Étrangères, 2004), 268.

50 Presbyterian Historical Society, Andrew Weir, "Notes on the History of the Irish Presbyterian Mission in Changchun" (1931?), 5, 7; Société des missions étrangères, *Compte-rendu des travaux* (1923), 51.

51 *Reports of the General Assembly of the Presbyterian Church in Ireland* (hereafter *RGAPCI*) (1901) and (1921). The figure of 1,605 in 1918 is in O'Neill, *Call of the East,* 124.

52 Société des missions étrangères, *Compte-rendu des travaux* (1904), 72; Société des missions étrangères de Paris, Chine, Mandchourie, 567 M/48, "Compte rendu du travaux des Missionaires de la Mandchourie Septentrionale Durant l'exercise 1912–1913," 13.

53 British Foreign Office Files for Japan and the Far East, Series 1: Embassy and Consular Archives – Japan (1905–40) 262, 1504, 335–7, "Aide-Memoire," British Embassy, Tokyo, 1 May 1919; Presbyterian Historical Society, Weir, "Notes," 4; O'Neill, *Call of the East,* 122.

54 Listed as 18 Britons, 4 Americans, 16 French, 1 Swede, 12 Czechoslovakians, and 1 other. *Manchuria Year Book, 1931,* 117, 170.

55 Across Manchukuo there were 7,239 Soviets, 1,322 Poles, 393 Britons, 333 Germans, 322 French, 185 Americans, 30 Italians, and 1,842 others in 1937. *Manchoukuo Year Book, 1942,* 121–22, 741.

56 Missionary work is listed as "other" in Table 4.5.

57 Four foreigners were listed as teachers, 5 as medical doctors, 71 as having religious work, 104 as having official work, and 196 as being engaged in commerce. *Manshū teikoku genjū jinkō tōkei* (1940), 9, 11.

58 *RGAPCI* (June 1933): 19.

59 J.H. Proctor, "The Response of Scottish Missionaries to Political Conditions in Manchuria, 1872–1950," *Mission Studies* 16, no. 2 (1999): 58.

60 *RGAPCI* (June 1935): 14; Léon Lannay, "Hsinking: Capitale du Manchoukouo," *Echos Missionnaires* 17 (April 1945): 118.

61 Pedro Iacobelli, "The Vatican's Shift of Its Missionary Policy in the Twentieth Century: The Mission of the Augustinian Fathers of the Assumption in Manchuria," *Asian Cultural Studies* 36 (2010): 91–104.

62 A. Hamish Ion, *The Cross and the Rising Sun,* vol. 2, *British Protestant Missionary Movement in Japan, Korea, and Taiwan, 1865–1945* (Waterloo, ON: Wilfrid Laurier University Press, 1993), 223–24.

63 National Archives of Scotland (hereafter NAS), ACC 7548 23 B, Stewart to Boyd, Kydd, Stockman, Brown, 22 April 1941.

64 NAS, ACC 7548 24 B, "Manchuria Mission Conference," 21 August 1942.

65 Many letters in the NAS report this. See, for example, NAS, ACC 7548 22 B, Grieve to Brown, 28 June 28, 1941. See also Proctor, "Response of Scottish Missionaries," 59–60; A. Hamish Ion, *The Cross and the Rising Sun,* vol. 1, *The Canadian Protestant Missionary Movement in the Japanese Empire, 1872–1931* (Waterloo, ON: Wilfrid Laurier University Press, 1990), 225–29, 233; A. Hamish Ion, *The Cross in the Dark Valley: The Canadian Protestant Missionary Movement in the Japanese Empire, 1931–1945* (Waterloo, ON: Wilfrid Laurier University Press, 1999), 160–62, 223–34.

66 NAS, ACC 7548 23 B, "Copy of Statement Enclosed in Letter Sent by Rev. A. F. Fulton, Irish Presbyterian Missionary in Manchuria, of Date 20th February, 1941."

67 Charles Bell, "The Struggle for Mongolia," *Journal of the Royal Central Asian Society* 24 (1937): 57.

68 United States Department of State, *Foreign Relations of the United States, Diplomatic Papers, 1941,* vol. 5, *The Far East* (Washington, DC: US Government Printing Office, 1956), documents 482, 985, 987, 1009, 1010.

69 NAS, ACC 7548 23 B, "Religious Organisations in Japan" and "Reform Plans for the Christian Church"; NAS, ACC 7548 23 B, Campbell to Brown, 18 June 1941; Mark R. Mullins, "Ideology and Utopianism in Wartime Japan: An Essay on the Subversiveness of Christian Eschatology," *Japanese Journal of Religious Studies* 21, nos. 2–3 (1994): 261–80.

70 Ion, *Cross in the Dark Valley,* 81–112. Missionary protests are in NAS, ACC 7548 23 B, "Religious Organisations in Japan."

71 NAS, ACC 7548 25 B, "National Christian Council of China, Overseas Newsletter, Oct. 1945."

72 NAS, ACC 7548 25 B, Brown to McMinn, 3 September 1945; T.M. Barker, "War: From Behind Closed Doors" (pamphlet, n.p., n.d.). I am grateful to Dr. John Dunlop for bringing this pamphlet to my attention.

73 Tsukase Susumu, "NichiRo sensō mae ni okeru zaiMan Nihonjin no katsudō," *Nagano daigaku kiyō* 22, no. 4 (2001): 139, 147.

74 Kurahashi Masano, *Kita no karayukisan* (Tokyo: Kyōei shobō, 1989), 149; Bill Mihalopoulos, "Modernization as Creative Problem Making: Political Action, Personal Conduct and Japanese Overseas Prostitutes," *Economy and Society* 27, no. 1 (1998): 50–73.

75 "Jinkō," *MNNS,* 11 March 1908, 4.

76 Tsukase Susumu, *Manshū no Nihonjin* (Tokyo: Yoshikawa, 2004), 15–20.

77 For every 1,000, 22 soldiers and 144 sailors were afflicted. Average rates for the ten countries surveyed were 61.81 and 76.4 per 1,000. "Karyūbyō o taiji shitaka," *MNNS,* 15 October 1926, 7, and 16 October 1926, 7.

78 Fujime Yuki, "The Licensed Prostitution System and the Prostitution Abolition Movement in Modern Japan," *positions* 5, no. 1 (1997): 135–70; Sidney Xu Lu, "Good Women for Empire: Educating Overseas Female Emigrants in Imperial Japan, 1900–45," *Journal of Global History* 8, no. 3 (2013): 440–49; Kurahashi, *Kita no karayukisan,* 165–67.

79 Ignoring the "miscellaneous" and unemployed categories. "Kunai hōjin shokugyō betsu," *MNNS,* 18 March 1908, 4.

80 The three largest groups were from Kumamoto (155), Nagasaki (137), and Fukuoka (76). "Zairyūmin fukenbetsu," *MNNS,* 1 April 1908, 4.

81 "Shinmingai zairyūmin shokugyōbetsu," *MNNS,* 25 June 1908, 4.

82 "Chōshun shin shigai," *MNNS,* 5 February 1907, 4.

83 Tsukase, *Manshū no Nihonjin,* 35–36; "Wato Shōkō," *Zaisei keizai* 3, no. 11 (1919): 43–44.

84 "Nijūnen ijō ijūsha," *MNNS,* 31 July 1926, 4.

85 Tsukase, *Manshū no Nihonjin,* 31, 51–55, 171–72.

86 For example, see Dresner, "International Labour Migrants' Return," 86.

87 A 1926 report, for example, showed the ten most represented prefectures were Kagoshima (644), Fukuoka (556), Kumamoto (555), Nagano (494), Saga (487), Yamaguchi (434), Hiroshima (413), Tokyo (351), Osaka (252), and Aichi (252). "Chōshun fuzokuchi no hōnin ichiman ni tassu," *MNNS,* 28 February 1926, 3.

88 "Manshū kara naichi he: nisenman en," *MNNS,* 1 June 1926, 2.

89 A smaller third peak occurred in 1934–35. Chao, "Demographic Development in Manchuria," 360; Gottschang and Lary, *Swallows and Settlers,* 38–41.

90 For example, Arango argues that "migration is too diverse and multifaceted to be explained by a single theory." Joaquin Arango, "Explaining Migration: A Critical View," *International Social Science Journal* 52, no. 165 (2000): 283.

91 Yanagisawa Asobu, "'Manshū jihen' o meguru shakai keizai shi kenkyū no shodōkō," *Rekishi hyōron* 377 (September 1981): 50–59; Yanagisawa Asobu, "'Manshū' shōkō imin no gutai zō: NichiRo sengo no Manshū tokō jijō," *Rekishi hyōron* 513 (January 1991): 42–53; Yanagisawa Asobu, *Nihonjin no shokuminchi keiken: Dairen Nihonjin shōkōgyōsha no rekishi* (Tokyo: Aoki shoten, 1999), 23–70.

92 *Manchoukuo Year Book, 1942,* 947.

93 Tsukase, *Manshū no Nihonjin,* 36, 165–88; Woodhead, *Visit to Manchukuo,* 37, 83.

94 Earl H. Kinmonth, "The Impact of Military Procurements on the Old Middle Classes in Japan, 1931–1941," *Japan Forum* 4, no. 2 (1992): 247–65; Earl H. Kinmonth, "The Mouse That Roared: Saitō Takao, Conservative Critic of Japan's 'Holy War' in China," *Journal of Japanese Studies* 25, no. 2 (1999): 352–55.

95 Matsuura Rō, *Shinkyō kyoryūminkai shi* (Shinkyō: Shinkyō kyoryūminkai, 1936), 12–18. Shibata was appointed in November 1906. "Chōshun ryōjikan," *Yomiuri shinbun* (hereafter *YS*), 16 November 1906, 2. Other consuls in Gaimushō tsūshōkyoku, *Chōshun no jijō,* 2.

96 "Shinkyō iryūminkai no sainyūde yosan kōsei," *MNNS,* 11 August 1935, 5.
97 Nishizawa Yasuhiko, *Nihon shokuminchi kenchiku ron* (Nagoya: Nagoya daigaku shuppansha, 2008), 189, 220–22.
98 "Chōshun sakkon no shokōji," *MNNS,* 16 September 1908, 4; *RGAPCI* (June 1914): 35.
99 Manshū keizai jijō annaijo, *Kokuto Shinkyō keizai jijō* (Dairen: Manshū bunka kyōkai, 1933), 18.
100 The English clinic may have been in the mercantile district. Manshū jijō annaijo, *Shinkyō jijō,* 19–20; Inoue Nobuō, *Chōshun enkakushi* (Dairen: ManMō bunka kyōkai, 1922), 75–76.
101 "Chōshun tokuden," *MNNS,* 9 May 1908, 2; "Shogakkō no kōenkai to kenkyūkai," *MNNS,* 7 February 1926, 3; "Shimauchisei kifuki," *MNNS,* 18 April 1926, 3.
102 "Chōshun no shōgakko," *MNNS,* 26 February 1908, 4.
103 Minami Manshū tetsudō kabushiki kaisha chihōbu chihōka, *Kyōiku shisetsu yōran* (Dairen: Minami Manshū tetsudō, 1916), 30–1, 47–50. See also Gaimushō tsūshōkyoku, *Chōshun no jijō,* 35.
104 Minami Manshū tetsudō kabushiki kaisha chihōbu chihōka, *Kyōiku shisetsu yōran,* 13–14; Shimada Michihiro, *Manshū kyōiku shi* (Dairen: Bunkyōsha, 1935), 361–63, 382–83, 394–95, 403–4; Inoue, *Chōshun enkakushi,* 62–63; Minami Manshū tetsudō, *Chōshun chihō an'nai.*
105 Shimada, *Manshū kyōiku shi,* 533–43; Inoue, *Chōshun enkakushi,* 60–64.
106 Inoue, *Chōshun enkakushi,* 62–63.
107 "Rinkan toshokan," *MNNS,* 9 June 1926, 4; Minami Manshū tetsudō kabushiki kaisha, *Chōshun jijō* (Dairen: Minami Manshū tetsudō Chōshun chihō jimusho, 1932), 37; Jilinsheng difangzhi bianzuan weiyuanhui, *Jilin shengzhi,* vol. 39, *Wenhua yishuzhi/shehui wenhua* (Changchun: Jilin renmin chubanshe, 1992), 130.
108 "ZenMan toshokan shūkan," *MNNS,* 2 November 1926, 2.
109 Nakajima Michio, "Shinto Deities That Crossed the Sea: Japan's 'Overseas Shrines,' 1868 to 1945," *Japanese Journal of Religious Studies* 37, no. 1 (2010): 29.
110 Gaimushō tsūshōkyoku, *Chōshun no jijō,* 29–31.
111 Manshū jijō annaijo, *Shinkyō jijō,* 17–19; Minami Manshū tetsudō kabushiki kaisha, *Chōshun jijō,* 39–41.
112 Manshū keizai jijō annaijo, *Kokuto Shinkyō keizai jijō,* 16, 19.
113 "Kokusōhi," *MNNS,* 28 May 1926, 3.
114 Elizabeth R. VanderVen, *A School in Every Village: Educational Reform in a Northeast China County, 1904–31* (Vancouver: UBC Press, 2012), 20–37.
115 Inoue, *Chōshun enkakushi,* 63; Gaimushō tsūshōkyoku, *Chōshun no jijō,* 32–33.
116 Ury Eppstein, "Musical Means to Political Ends – Japanese School Songs in Manchuria: Songs before the Establishment of Manchukuo," in *Kyoto Conference on Japanese Studies 1994,* vol. 3 (Kyoto: International Research Center for Japanese Studies, 1996), 209–27.
117 Marjorie Dryburgh, "Japan in Tianjin: Settlers, State and the Tensions of Empire before 1937," *Japanese Studies* 27, no. 1 (2007): 19–34; Joshua A. Fogel, "'Shanghai-Japan': The Japanese Residents' Association of Shanghai," *Journal of Asian Studies* 59, no. 4 (2000): 927–50; Joshua A. Fogel, "Integrating into Chinese Society: A Comparison of the Japanese Communities of Shanghai and Harbin," in *Japan's Competing Modernities: Issues in Culture and Democracy, 1900–1930,* ed. Sharon Minichiello (Honolulu: University of Hawai'i Press, 1998), 45–69.
118 For example, "Chōshun sakkon no shokōji," *MNNS,* 16 September 1908, 4; "Chōshun ni okeru gonenkan no jigyō," *MNNS,* 19 December 1926, 4; "Mantetsu no shikōshinhōkei," *MNNS,* 9 January 1927, 2.
119 "Ōryokukō ni mō ippon ōtekkyō ga kakerareru," *MNNS,* 6 June 1926, 1; "Daireneki shinchiku mitorito," *MNNS,* 10 September 1926, 1.

120 Manshūkoku kokumuin kōhōsho, *Manchoukuo: A Comprehensive Pictorial Presentation* (Tokyo: Asahi shinbusha, 1942), iii–iv.
121 For example, "Yōyaku santō shindai no riyūsha zōka," *MNNS*, 18 April 1926, 3.
122 "Suponji riigu sen: haku o arasou jūichi gumi," *MNNS*, 24 September 1926, 4; "Chōshun yakyū riigusen futatabi ekiyūgun yūshō," *MNNS*, 3 Octtober 1926, 3; "Kōshi isshin no Chōshun yakyūkai," *MNNS*, 11 April 1926, 3; "Shinjin'yō natta zen Chōshun," *MNNS*, 16 April 1926, 3.
123 "Sentetsu yakyūdan," *MNNS*, 24 June 1926, 3; "Sentetsu tai zenChōshun shikiai," *MNNS*, 4 July 1926, 3.
124 Kouchiyama Tsunetaka, *Sono toki: sen'in wa dōsuru* (Tokyo: Bungeisha, 2006), 210–16.
125 *SSC*.
126 "Chōshun taiiku kyōkai shusai," *MNNS*, 4 September 1926, 3; "Rikujō kyōki taikai no junbi ni torikakaru," *MNNS*, 12 September 1926, 4; "Dai ikkai zen Chōshun rikujō kyōki," *MNNS*, 7 October 1926, 3; "Dai ichi shogakkō shūki undōkai," *MNNS*, 22 September 1926, 4; "Kōjōkō undōkai," *MNNS*, 27 September 1926, 4; "Rikujō daiundōkai, *MNNS*, 30 September 1926, 4; "Daiikkai zen Chōshun rikujō kyōki taikai," *MNNS*, 7 October 1926, 3.
127 "Dainikai zen Chōshun dangai jūdō sōhasen," *MNNS*, 27 October 1926, 4.
128 See also Tainaka Chizuru, "'Gaichi' no sumō," *Mejiro daigaku jinbungaku kenkyū* 7 (2011): 117–35.
129 "Chōshun kendōgun no sekihai no ato," *MNNS*, 9 September 1926, 4.
130 "Chōshun kōjō no kōto aki," *MNNS*, 3 July 1926, 3.
131 Shinkyō tokubetsushi shichōkanbō shomuka, *Kokuto Shinkyō: Kenkoku jūshūnen kinan* (Shinkyō: Shinkyō tokubetsushi kōsho, 1942), 174. On hunting, see "Ryōryūkai seri ryōkai," *Manshū Nippō*, 28 August 1931, 5.
132 "Pinpon taikai," *MNNS*, 4 November 1926, 4; "Dōkyū senshū raiChō," *MNNS*, 29 April 1926, 3.
133 "Chōshun jidōsha kyōsō," *Manshū Nippō*, 10 June 1931, 4.
134 "Kokage suzushii zekkō no shōkaike," *MNNS*, 2 June 1926, 3.
135 "Uotsuri ga dekiru," *MNNS*, 6 April 1926, 3; "Nishi kōen no chōgyo," *Manshū Nippō*, 24 August 1931, 4; "Kōen bōto saikai," *MNNS*, 18 July 1926, 3; "Nishi kōenchi no taibōto fukkatsu," *MNNS*, 23 July 1926, 4; "Shūki shageki taikai," *MNNS*, 22 September 1926, 4; "Sukātokai junbi ni torikakeru," *MNNS*, 5 October 1926, 4; "Nishikōen kōrisuberiba," *MNNS*, 23 November 1926, 4. One Japanese in Changchun competed in speedskating: "Kōrisuberi senshūgentaikai," *MNNS*, 28 December 1926, 4.
136 *SSC*.
137 "Chōshun tokuden," *MNNS*, 2 May 1908, 2; "Chōshun tokuden," *MNNS*, 19 November 1907, 2.
138 "Kan'in no miya," *MNNS*, 22 September 1926, 1; "Kiyourasei ikkō," *MNNS*, 1 October 1926, 4; Inoue Masaaki, Sakaguchi Jirō, and Tokutomi Ichirō, eds., *Hakushaku Kiyoura Keigo den*, vol. 2 (Tokyo: Hakushaku Kiyoura Keigo den kankōkai, 1935), 347.
139 "Chōshun nikki," *MNNS*, 8 July 1908, 4.
140 For example, "Chōshun kankei no tetsudōbu no ichidō," *MNNS*, 15 April 1926, 4; "Kanamaru Ishiwara Ōbi sansei okubetsuen," *MNNS*, 20 April 1926, 3.
141 "Chōshun tokuden," *MNNS*, 1 April 1908, 2.
142 "Saikin no shūyōdan," *MNNS*, 15 April 1926, 4; "Chōshun fujin chawakai," *MNNS*, 22 July 1908, 2.
143 "Manshū igakukai no setsuritsu keikaku," *MNNS*, 20 July 1908, 2.
144 "Chinretsu sōshoku kyōgikai," *MNNS*, 9 June 1926, 4.
145 "Nōryōen chikaku kaien," *MNNS*, 9 June 1926, 4; "Hoteru no dansu," *Manshū Nippō*, 30 August 1931, 5.

146 "Kaigun kinenhi to zaigō gunjin bunkai," *MNNS,* 28 May 1926, 3.

147 "Manshū zaigō gunjin sōkai," *MNNS,* 16 June 1926, 2.

148 "Seinen giyūdan kōgun," *MNNS,* 20 April 1926, 3; Shigeo Fujimoto, "Trans-Pacific Boy Scout Movement in the Early Twentieth Century: The Case of the Boy Scout Movement in Osaka, Japan," *Australasian Journal of American Studies* 7, no. 2 (2008): 29–43.

149 "Ishii Baku ga Manshū he kuru," *MNNS,* 9 February 1926, 7; "Ishii Baku no buyō shikai," *MNNS,* 13 March 1926, 4.

150 "Chōshun hajimete no seiyō ongaku taikai," *MNNS,* 8 April 1926, 4; "Chōshun Sazanamikai," *MNNS,* 6 July 1926, 3.

151 Minami Manshū tetsudō kabushiki kaisha, *Chōshun jijō,* 44–45.

152 Minami Manshū tetsudō kabushiki kaisha sōseishitsu chihōbu zanmuseiri iinkai, *Mantetsu fuzokuchi keiei enkaku zenshi* (hereafter MFKEZ) (Tokyo: Ryūkei shosha, 1977), 3:473–76; Manshū keizai jijō annaijo, *Kokuto Shinkyō keizai jijō,* 18–19.

153 "Ajia no hikari," *MNNS,* 18 July 1926, 3; "Yōga tenrankai," *MNNS,* 15 July 1926, 4; "Ōgonkyō jidai," *MNNS,* 30 October 1926, 4.

154 "Manshū rekishi no eigaka," *MNNS,* 24 October 1926, 2.

155 "Chōshun ryōriten an'nai," *MNNS,* 8 July 1908, 4.

156 "Chōshun denwa kaitsū kōku," *MNNS,* 7 October 1908, 4.

157 "Manshū no sake to tobako," *MNNS,* 12 November 1907, 2.

158 Yanagisawa Asobu, "ZaiMan Nihonjin," in *Manshūkoku to wa nan datta no ka: NitChū kyōdō kenkyū,* ed. Shokuminchi bunka gakkai, Chūgoku tōhoku rinkan jūyonnenshi sōhenshitsu (Tokyo: Shōgakukan, 2008), 222.

159 *MNNS,* 6 June 1927, 1.

160 "Yoshinomachigawa o gaichiku," *MNNS,* 5 August 1926, 3; "Nishimura yōkō ga ittō," *MNNS,* 7 October 1926, 3.

161 "Chōshun seishihi," *MNNS,* 22 September 1926, 4.

162 "Kenkokusai," *MNNS,* 7 February 1926, 3; "Chōshun jinja shunkikōreisai," *MNNS,* 23 March 1926, 4; "Chōshun no akimatsuri," *MNNS,* 5 September 1926, 4.

163 "Chōshun no tenchōsetsu," *YS,* 4 November 1907, 2.

164 "Sono hi o machi koregeru kodomo," *MNNS,* 2 May 1926, 2. This article refers to a Dalian kindergarten, but it is reasonable to assume similar activities occurred in Changchun. "Dai ni kai Chōshun shōgyō gakkō sotsugyō shiki," *MNNS,* 27 February 1926, 3.

165 Possibly formed in 1921, as the month and year appear inadvertently switched. "Seinenkai kaisan," *MNNS,* 23 November 1926, 4; "Seinenkai kaisan o ketsugi," *MNNS,* 25 November 1926, 4.

166 "Jitsu ni urarakana tenchō no kashin," *MNNS,* 3 November 1926, 4; "Gonōheiyukigan," *MNNS,* 23 November 1926, 4; "Chōshun no goheiyukiganshiki," *MNNS,* 16 December 1926, 2; "Goheiyukigan," *MNNS,* 18 December 1926, 4; "Tōkamatsuri yōhaishiki," *MNNS,* 6 January 1927, 4; "Gotaisōgitōjitsu," *MNNS,* 29 January 1927, 4.

167 Emer O'Dwyer, *Significant Soil: Settler Colonialism and Japan's Urban Empire in Manchuria* (Cambridge, MA: Harvard University Press, 2015), 36–39.

168 "Chōshun no bōu," *MNNS,* 1 July 1908, 2, and 7 July 1908, 4; "Mantetsu higai dokuhō," *MNNS,* 24 August 1908, 2; "Ōame haizen Chōshun o chūshin ni," *MNNS,* 22 June 1926, 1.

169 "Shinkyō wa kokusho," *MNNS,* 12 August 1935, 2.

170 "Jidōsha mo toerenu jūsū nenrai no ōyuki," *MNNS,* 26 February 1926, 3.

171 "Kitahō Manshū no seikatsu," *MNNS,* 19 February 1908, 4; Mutō, "Waga kaisō (1)," *Manshu to Nihonjin* (hereafter *MTN*) 1 (August 1975): 50.

172 "Shinamachi no kaji," *MNNS,* 10 November 1926, 4; "Chōshunjōnai daika," *MNNS,* 13 January 1927, 4.

173 "Okunai de tabiki," *MNNS,* 24 November 1926, 4.

174 "Chōshun no kasei songai," *MNNS,* 7 May 1926, 3.
175 Minami Manshū tetsudō kabushiki kaisha shomubu chōsaka, *Minami Manshū tetsudō kabushiki kaisha dainiji jūnenshi,* 1145–48.
176 Ruth Rogaski, *Hygienic Modernity: Meanings of Health and Disease in Treaty-Port China* (Berkeley: University of California Press, 2004).
177 "Harrowing Scenes in Stricken China," *Globe,* 7 February 1911, 7; William C. Summers, *The Great Manchurian Plague of 1910–11: The Geopolitics of an Epidemic Disease* (New Haven, CT: Yale University Press, 2012), 54–79, 116–29.
178 "Manshūri ni senpesto," *MNNS,* 8 September 1926, 3; "Haipesuto wa sudeni uchi Mōko ni shinyū shitaka," *MNNS,* 18 December 1926, 2; *MFKEZ,* 3:448–52; South Manchuria Railway, *Second Report on Progress in Manchuria: To 1930* (Dairen: South Manchuria Railway, 1931), 170–76; *Second Report on Progress in Manchuria,* 224–26.
179 Matsumura Takao, "Shinkyō, Nōan pesuto ryūkō (1940-nen) to 731 butai," *Mita gakkai zasshi* 95, no. 3 (2003): 121–49, and no. 4 (2003): 13–34, 96.
180 Inoue, *Chōshun enkakushi,* 72; "Giji chibusu," *MNNS,* 16 October 1926, 4; "Mata chibusu," *MNNS,* 28 October 1926, 4; "Chibusu ni chūi," *MNNS,* 4 November 1926, 4; Shinkyō tokubetsushi shichōkanbō shomuka, *Kokuto Shinkyō* (1942), 177–78.
181 "ZenManshū ni watarite bōeki ni tsutomu," *MNNS,* 25 July 1926, 3; "Manshū o ekibyō kara sukū: eiken gokagetsu no jigyō," *MNNS,* 28 July 1926, 1; "Hashi no koeki to Chōshun no bōeki junbi," *MNNS,* 12 August 1926, 3; "Sankoku kyōdo bōeki," *MNNS,* 12 August 1926, 2; "NichiShiRō no bōeki renraku," *MNNS,* 15 August 1926, 3; "Chōshun no kenben: kūryoku kihi shite," *MNNS,* 26 August 1926, 2.
182 "Korera tsue ni Chōshun o okasazu," *MNNS,* 16 October 1926, 4.
183 "Densenbyō taitō," *Manshū Nippō,* 10 April 1931, 4.
184 "Obitadashii Manshū no haikansha," *MNNS,* 3 December 1926, 3.
185 "Chōshun byōin chūsha gentai," *MNNS,* 11 March 1926, 4.
186 *Fourth Report on Progress in Manchuria to 1934* (Dairen: South Manchuria Railway, 1934), 164–66.
187 *MFKEZ,* 3:447.
188 "Mantetsu eiseika de ryūkan no yobō," *MNNS,* 12 January 1927, 2.
189 *MFKEZ,* 3:437–8, 444.
190 Ibid., 3:443, 445.
191 "Chōshun no yakengari," *MNNS,* 15 February 1926, 3.
192 "Haetori dē," *MNNS,* 31 July 1926, 4.
193 "Sekkyakugyōsha kenkō shindan jitchi," *MNNS,* 8 May 1926, 3.
194 For example, "Toshi eisei" and "Kōgakutō ni mo eiseifu to no yōkyū," *MNNS,* 5 February 1926, 2; "Chōshun no eisei kaigi," *MNNS,* 13 July 1926, 3.
195 Miura Un'ichi, *Manshū no jūtaku to eisei* (Tokyo: Eisei kōgyō kyōkai, [1934?]); Miura Un'ichi, *Hokenjō kara mita Manshū no jūtaku* (Dairen: Manshū bunka kyōkai, 1935); Jordan Sand, *House and Home in Modern Japan: Architecture, Domestic Space, and Bourgeois Culture, 1880–1930* (Cambridge, MA: Harvard University Press, 2003), 141–48.
196 "Shinkyō eisei fukyū shūkan," *MNNS,* 18 June 1937, 3.
197 On foreign dignitaries, see "Chōshun tokuden," *MNNS,* 11 December 1907, 2; "Chōshun tokuden," *MNNS,* 13 March 1908, 2; and "Chin chinjushi kansō," *MMNS,* 16 May 1926, 3. On American interests, see "Manshū kaihō to Beikoku," *MNNS,* 10 July 1908, 2.
198 Harold Scott Quigley, "The Far Eastern Republic: A Product of Intervention," *American Journal of International Law* 18, no. 1 (1924): 89–91.
199 "Kyōsantō no suiun," *MNNS,* 17 October 1926, 8; "Sekka no inbō," *MNNS,* 23 December 1926, 4; "Shirokei Rojin o yūgū suru uramen," *MNNS,* 6 November 1926, 4.
200 "Sekihaku Rojin no mezurashi taishō," *MNNS,* 7 May 1926, 3.
201 "Rōnō Rōkoku no tetsudō keikaku," *MNNS,* 17 November 1926, 2.

202 "Kyokutō seisaku no tenkan de," *MNNS,* 18 February 1926, 1.

203 "Sobieto seifu no kyokutō seisaku ippen," *MNNS,* 8 September 1926, 2.

204 Yoshihisa Tak Matsusaka, *The Making of Japanese Manchuria, 1904–1932* (Cambridge, MA: Harvard University Press, 2003), 312–27, 363–77.

205 "Ryōji no kōgi o kabau tomo omowanu: Shinagawa no jōyaku jūrin," *MNNS,* 31 August 1926, 5; "Jōnai ni okeru Nishō kumiai," *MNNS,* 7 September 1926, 3; "Matamata zeien kyokuin," *MNNS,* 23 December 1926, 4; "Kurihara ryōji no kōshō," *MNNS,* 24 December 1926, 4. On police, see "Kokusai senro o ayuku suru: Shinahei no ōbō," *MNNS,* 27 June 1926, 1.

206 Matsumiya Kanju, "Kanjōshi [Kuanchengzi] jiken," *Ōsaka mainichi shinbun* (*Osaka Daily News*), 29–30 July 1919.

207 Gavan McCormack, *Chang Tso-lin in Northeast China, 1911–1928: China, Japan, and the Manchurian Idea* (Stanford, CA: Stanford University Press, 1977), 38–43; Paul E. Dunscomb, *Japan's Siberian Intervention, 1918–22: "A Great Disobedience against the People"* (Lanham, MD: Lexington Books, 2011), 115–26.

208 "Futō kazei mondai," *MNNS,* 5 November 1926, 4.

209 "Chōshun ni shukuhaku heishi," *MNNS,* 23 September 1926, 4; "Kidō enshū ni saishi: Guntaigawa no kibō," *MNNS,* 5 October 5, 1926, 4; "Ryōdan taikō enshū," *MNNS,* 8 October 8, 1926, 1, 4; "Dōdōtaru hokugun no hikyū," *MNNS,* 9 October 1926, 4; "Chōshun o seiryaku shite daienshū owaru," *MNNS,* 12 October 1926, 2.

210 "Kitsurin jūgo shidan kidō enshū," *MNNS,* 15 October 1926, 4.

211 "Go tokugun," *MNNS,* 31 October 1926, 4.

212 "Ōotoko sorohino," *MNNS,* 17 April 1926, 4.

213 "Manshū no heibi ni jūbun no ryōkai wo," *MNNS,* 13 June 1926, 1; "Rikugunshō de kenkyūchū no ManSen oyobi kita Shina," *MNNS,* 24 July 1926, 1.

214 "Kantō hokupatsu," *MNNS,* 24 August 1926, 2; "Hōten no shōrai to Shō Kaiseki no jitsuryoku," *MNNS,* 6 September 1926, 1; "Eikoku to nangun: Eikoku no kutsū," *MNNS,* 10 September 1926, 1.

215 "Shina no hanteikokushugiteki fūchō," *MNNS,* 7 December 1926, 2.

216 "Nihon o hijō ni osoreteiru," *MNNS,* 25 January 1927, 2; "Roshia no tōhō seisaku to Shina," *MNNS,* 17 December 1926, 2.

217 "Hikiage junbi no naimei itaru," *MNNS,* 12 January 1927, 2; "Chōkō ni kiki semaru Eikoku no sensen tsutaeraru," *MNNS,* 13 January 1927, 1; "Eikoku guntai zokuzoku to," *MNNS,* 24 January 24, 1927, 2; "Shina ni shutsudōsuru Eiguntai," *MNNS,* 25 January 1927, 2.

218 "Sekkō no dokuritsu wa hōkyō anmin," *MNNS,* 30 October 1926, 2; "Sekkō no dokuritsu undō to Kokumintō," *MNNS,* 31 October 1926, 2; 3 November 1926, 2; 4 November 1926, 2.

219 "Heishatsu saishō no ichinichi," *MNNS,* 12 January 1927, 3, and 13 January 1927, 3.

220 "Shinjin no haiNichi ensetsu," *MNNS,* 29 June 1908, 2.

221 Kurahashi, *Kita no karayukisan,* 206–7.

222 For example, "Tōyō sekka no honbu o Urajio ni utsusu keikaku," *MNNS,* 26 November 1926, 2.

223 "Chōshun daini shihangakkō no akaka," *MNNS,* 29 October 1926, 4; "Sekka no ma no te ga Chōshun made nobitekite," *MNNS,* 5 December 1926, 2.

224 "Nihonjin no seimei zaisan jūbun hokan seyo," *Manshū Nippō,* 27 August 1931, 1.

225 "Shinajin yaku sanzenmyō totsujo hōjin o shūgeki," *Manshū Nippō,* 20 August 1931, 1.

226 "Kokuryūkō demo Shina nōmin Sennō no suita suirō hakai," *Manshū Nippō,* 7 July 1931, 1.

227 Tashiro Shigenori, *Omoizuru mama* (Tokyo: Tashiro Shigenori, 1935), 93–96.

228 Nozoe Rishō, "Watakushi no taiken shita nijūhachi nenkan no Manshū," *MTN: Tokubetsu go* 1 (1976): 123–27.

229 Tsukase, *Manshū no Nihonjin*, 87–93.
230 Alexander Hosie, *Manchuria: Its People, Resources and Recent History* (New York: C. Scribner's, 1904), 23–26, 169.
231 "Bazoku Nihonjin o kiru," *YS*, 3 July 1907, 1; "Rokoku bazoku no bōkō," *YS*, 4 December 1907, 1; "Kitsurin no bazoku shōgetsu," *MNNS*, 7 November 1907, 2.
232 "KitsuChō gaidō no bazoku," *MNNS*, 24 August 1908, 2; "Bazokudan no kinkyō," *MNNS*, 20 August 1926, 4.
233 "Ronin shimai bazoku ni au," *MNNS*, 18 December 1926, 4.
234 "Jidōsha bazoku jiken," *MNNS*, 6 July 1926, 3.
235 "Higai hinpin," *Manshū Nippō*, 24 August 1931, 4; "Fuzokuchi ni bazokutan ōkō suru," *Manshū Nippō*, 30 August 1931, 2; "Hizokudan shikiri ni shutsubotsu," *MNNS*, 9 September 1926, 4; "Nanhenkō to Kōten to gappeishita daibazokudan," *MNNS*, 24 November 1926, 4.
236 This raid reportedly occurred at Dunjiatian, but there are no stations by that name, the initial Kanji is likely misprinted and should be the similar *"guo."* Kojima Ken'ichi, "Zokuzoku: Manshū Nisei sanjūnen no tenbyō no jiron," *MTN* 10 (February 1988): 203–4. See also Kojima Ken'ichi, "Manshū Nisei sanjūnen no tenbyō no jiron," *MTN* 8 (October 1981): 68–84.
237 Kojima, "Zokuzoku," 204–7.
238 Young, *Japan's Total Empire*, 142–45; "Chōsen to ieba tora, Manshū to ieba bazoku," *MNNS*, 17 May 1926, 3.
239 An example from a village just south of Changchun is in "Daiton ni gōtō," *MNNS*, 17 April 1926, 4. An arrested Chinese man accused of multiple muggings is in "Gōtō hannin tsukamaru," *MNNS*, 30 November 1926, 4.
240 "Matamoya Mantetsu fuzokuchi de Shinajin kyōzoku no chōryō," *MNNS*, 28 July 1926, 1; "Keibi mondai ni tsuite," *MNNS*, 6 August 1926, 1. The first article highlights a Liaoyang incident but suggests the problem existed in all railway towns.
241 "Hōnin o ōdashita: Shinahei no rōzeki," *MNNS*, 8 October 1926, 4; "Pisutoru kyōtō," *MNNS*, 13 October 1926, 4; "Shinatō o tsutsuke," *MNNS*, 28 October 1926, 4; "Hakuka gōtō araware," *MNNS*, 9 June 1926, 4.
242 "Chōshun no genkai," *MNNS*, 15 January 1927, 4.
243 "Ki ga kuru," *MNNS*, 6 January 1927, 4; "Mangin iri bazoku," *MNNS*, 9 January 1927, 3; "Dōshō ginkō o osou," *MNNS*, 11 January 1927, 2.
244 "Kan no naka kara," *MNNS*, 20 January 1927, 4.
245 "Kaitai hannin no matsuro," *MNNS*, 16 May 1926, 3; "Ōjikakena gizō mohi seizō," *MNNS*, 1 June 1926, 4; "Manshū sekiyū kaika to hokenkin gigoku," *MNNS*, 20 June 1926, 4; "Chōshun Chōsenjinkaichō kōkin niman'en wo," *MNNS*, 1 October 1926, 4.
246 "Inkazeihyō ushiuri," *MNNS*, 5 May 1926, 3.
247 Barbara Brooks, *Japan's Imperial Diplomacy: Consuls, Treaty Ports, and War in China, 1895–1938* (Honolulu: University of Hawai'i Press, 2000), 83–105.
248 Erik Esselstrom, *Crossing Empire's Edge: Foreign Ministry Police and Japanese Expansionism in Northeast Asia* (Honolulu: University of Hawai'i Press, 2009), 45–46, 48, 172n39.
249 Nozoe, "Watakushi no taiken shita nijūhachi nenkan no Manshū," 117–19. Between 1919 and 1932, civilians headed the Guandong Government-General.
250 Esselstrom, *Crossing Empire's Edge*, 48–49.
251 Brooks, *Japan's Imperial Diplomacy*, 79.
252 Ibid., 114–15, 144–45, 240n130.
253 John W. Dower, *Empire and Aftermath: Yoshida Shigeru and the Japanese Experience, 1878–1954* (Cambridge, MA: Harvard University Press, 1979), 64–65, 69–77.
254 Yamamuro Shin'ichi, *Manchuria under Japanese Dominion*, trans. Joshua A. Fogel (Philadelphia: University of Pennsylvania Press, 2006), 61–67; Seki Hiroharu, "The Manchurian

Incident, 1931," in *Japan Erupts: The London Naval Conference and the Manchurian Incident, 1928–32,* ed. James William Morley (New York: Columbia University Press, 1984), 139–42, 153, 157, 171–72, 180–84, 213–15; Ronald Suleski, "Northeast China under Japanese Control: The Role of the Manchurian Youth Corps, 1934–1945," *Modern China* 7, no. 3 (1981): 351–77.

255 Kasagi Yoshiaki, "Manshū kenkoku ni tsuite," *MTN* 10 (February 1988): 161; O'Dwyer, *Significant Soil,* 220–41, 278–301; Mark R. Peattie, *Ishiwara Kanji and Japan's Confrontation with the West* (Princeton, NJ: Princeton University Press, 1975), 90–91. Kasagi was a former Mantetsu researcher. An example of an aggressive response to Zhang's "anti-Japanese" policies is Yamaguchi Shigeji and Mikuni Ichirō, "Taidan: 'Minzoku kyōwa' to 'Manshū kenkoku'," *MTN* 9 (January 1987): 57–59. After serving in the war, Mikuni was a popular figure on Japanese radio and television.

256 *Chōshun jitsugyō shinbun (Changchun Business News)* 15 August 1922, 1.

257 British Foreign Office Files for Japan and the Far East, Series 1: Embassy and Consular Archives – Japan (1905–40) 262/1564/84, E.L.S. Gordon(?), 16 October 1922; 262/1564/204–5, E.L.S. Gordon to Charles Eliot, 16 August 1922; 262/1564/211–12, E.L.S. Gordon to Charles Eliot, 7 August 1922.

258 "Dai Nihonkoku suikai: Chōshun honbu to yakuin," *MNNS,* 7 September 1926, 3; "Chōshun kokusuikai dai ikkai no kanjikai," *MNNS,* 23 September 1926, 4; "Kokusuikai Shibu kaiki hōtaishiki," *MNNS,* 2 November 1926, 4.

259 Nishizawa, *Nihon shokuminchi kenchiku ron,* 406; "Fuzokuchi to Shinjin," *MNNS,* 30 January 1908, 1.

260 "ChūNichi kyōikukai renkankai daiikkai sōkai," *MNNS,* 11 July 1926, 3.

261 Ozawa Yasunosuke, "Manshū no shogakkō ni Shinago o kasuru," *MNNS,* 25 December 1926, 7, and 28 December 1926, 7.

262 Matsusaka, *Making of Japanese Manchuria,* 354–63; O'Dwyer, *Significant Soil,* 206, 242–74, 317–18; Tsukase, *Manshū no Nihonjin,* 167–70.

263 Edgar Snow, *Far Eastern Front* (London: Jarrolds, 1934), 22.

264 Tsukase, *Manshū no Nihonjin,* 35–36, 57, 61–63, 175–76.

265 Jun Uchida, *Brokers of Empire: Japanese Settler Colonialism in Korea, 1876–1945* (Cambridge, MA: Harvard University Press, 2011).

266 "Toku ni zaiMan Hōnin wa Shinajin o rikai seyo," *MNNS,* 8 October 1926, 2. This concern was also evident in Masaaki, Jirō, and Ichirō, *Hakushaku Kiyoura Keigo den,* 2:345–46.

267 "Shinago no hitsuyō," *MNNS,* 30 November 1907, 1.

268 "Matamata zeien kyokuin," *MNNS,* 23 December 1926, 4; "Gunjin goro," *MNNS,* 23 December 1926, 4.

269 Nishi Haruhiko, *Kaisō no Nihon gaikō* (Tokyo: Iwanami shinsho, 1965), 15; Tashiro, *Omoizuru mama,* 72.

270 Woodhead, *Visit to Manchukuo,* 37.

271 Photos and diagrams of fields and buildings appear in *Manshū kenchiku zasshi (Journal of Manchurian Architecture)* (hereafter *MKZ*) 22, no. 10 (1942). Photographs of events are in *MNNS,* 2 March 1942, 3. An "ad balloon" bore a congratulatory message in the sky, as reported in "Kokuto no honsha keishuku adobarun," *MNNS,* 3 March 1942, 3.

272 "Sekai no kasetsu: Kenkoku kore ni jūshūnen," *MNNS,* 1 March 1942, 1; "Kenkoku jūshūnen: yakushin no seki o kaerimiru," *MNNS,* 28 February 1942, 2.

273 Woodhead, *Visit to Manchukuo,* 3, 37.

274 *RGAPCI* (June 1938): 28.

275 Tahata Shūichirō, *Boku no Manshū ryokōki* (Tokyo: Jidōtosho shuppansha, 1943), 91–116.

276 Ikemiyagi Sumiko, "Shinkyō: shūsen zengo no watakushi no omidasu," in *Heiwa no ishizue: rōku taiken shuki; kaigai hikiagesha ga katari tsugu rōku 7,* ed. Heiwa kinen jigyō tokubetsu kikin (Tokyo: Heiwa kinen jigyō tokubetsu kikin, 1997), 244–45, http://www.heiwakinen.jp/library/shiryokan/hikiage07.html.
277 "Usukuragari kokuto no yoru ni," *MNNS,* 16 August 1935, 5.
278 Shinkyō tokubetsushi shichōkanbō shomuka, *Yakushin kokuto no iyō,* 23–26, 30–31.
279 Nozoe, "Watakushi no taiken shita nijūhachi nenkan no Manshū," 116.
280 Minami Manshū tetsudō, *Chōshun chihō an'nai.*
281 Rates in Shenyang rose in the same time frame from 1.6 to 1.74 to 2.5 yen, while in Dalian they remained stable at 1.4 but rose to 1.59 in 1933. Manshū jijō annaijo, *Shinkyō jijō,* 65.
282 Woodhead, *Visit to Manchukuo,* 2.
283 Peter Fleming, *One's Company: A Journey to China* (London: Jonathan Cape, 1934), 73.
284 J.R. S[tewart], "Hsinking – Manchuria's Boom Town," *Far Eastern Survey* 6, no. 6 (1937) 69.
285 Chōshun Kanjōshikai, ed., *Kanjōshi monogatari* (Tokyo: Chōsun Kanjōshikai, 2006), 60–61.
286 Ikeda Kanji, "Manshū kenchiku to hōjin eisei no ikkō sasshi," *MKZ* 15, no. 1 (1935): 27.
287 "Shinkyō no kenchiku kaoku wa myōgonen made ni ichiman to," *MNNS,* 9 August 1935, 2; "Shinkyō saitan no jūtakugai danketsu," *MNNS,* 17 August 1935, 5.
288 S[tewart], "Hsinking," 69.
289 Mutō, "Waga kaisō (1)," 51–53.
290 Okano Kanki, "Manshūkoku jidai no zuisō," *MTN* 10 (February 1988): 60–63, 64.
291 Earl H. Kinmonth, *The Self-Made Man in Meiji Japanese Thought: From Samurai to Salary Man* (Berkeley: University of California Press, 1981), 298–89, 307–8, 346. See also Kinmonth, "The Mouse That Roared," 353–57; and Nishizawa Yasuhiko, "'Manshūkoku' no kensetsu jigyō," in *Manshūkoku no kenkyū,* ed. Yamamoto Yūzō (Tokyo: Ryokuin shobō, 1995), 383-88.
292 "Manshūkoku shuyō jinji kettei," *MNNS,* 12 July 1937, 1.
293 *Shinkyō no gaikyō* (Shinkyō: Shinkyō shōkō kōkai, 1942), 31–35; Shinkyō tokubetsushi shichōkanbō shomuka, *Kokuto Shinkyō* (1942), 168–73, 179–89; "Japanese, Soviet Rush War Plans: Tension Grows," *Toronto Daily Star,* 27 August 1934, 1.
294 "Atarashii chisetsu kōryo," *MNNS,* 15 August 1935, 5.
295 Shinkyō tokubetsushi shichōkanbō shomuka, *Kokuto Shinkyō* (Shinkyō: Manshū jijō annaijo, 1940), 216–22.
296 Shimada, *Manshū kyōiku shi,* 415–31, 464.
297 Manshū jijō annaijo, *Shinkyō jijō,* 16–17; Shimada, *Manshū kyōiku shi,* 761–72.
298 "Tei zensōri no kikin de Shinkyō ni Mannin chūgakkō," *MNNS,* 24 August 1935, 3.
299 *SSC.*
300 Shimada, *Manshū kyōiku shi,* 551–53, 786–87; *Shinkyō no gaikyō,* 28–29.
301 Shinkyō tokubetsushi shichōkanbō shomuka, *Kokuto Shinkyō* (1940), 216–22.
302 Manshū keizai jijō annaijo, *Kokuto Shinkyō keizai jijō,* 16; Manshūkokushi hensan kankōkai, *Manshūkokushi,* (Tokyo: Kokusai zenrin kyōkai, 1973), 2:249–56.
303 Ibid., 226–29; *Shinkyō no gaikyō,* 36.
304 *Shinkyō no gaikyō,* 28–30.
305 Jilinsheng difangzhi bianzuan weiyuanhui, *Jilin shengzhi,* 39:234, 237.
306 Shinkyō tokubetsushi shichōkanbō shomuka, *Kokuto Shinkyō* (1942), 230.
307 Jilinsheng difangzhi bianzuan weiyuanhui, *Jilin shengzhi,* 39:234.
308 "Dai nikai wa Shinkyō de kaisai," *MNNS,* 4 November 1942.
309 Jie Xueshi, *Wei Manzhouguo shi,* rev. ed. (Beijing: Renmin chubansi, 1995), 356–75, 575–601; Sun Jiying, "Tōhoku rinkanki no Chōshun de no shokuminchi doreika kyōiku," in *Kindai Nihon to Manshūkoku,* ed. Shokuminchi bunka gakkai (Tokyo: Fuji shuppan, 2014), 92–109.

310 Shinkyō tokubetsushi kōsho, *Shinkyō shisei gaiyō* (Shinkyō: Shinkyō tokubetsushi kōsho, 1934), 5; *Shinkyō no gaikyō*, 2; "Kyōiku seishin sakkō taikai," *MNNS*, 26 August 1935, 2.

311 Tamura Toshio, "Kyōiku kokka ron," in *Ronsō*, ed. Daitō gakuin, vol. 3 (Shinkyō: Manshū gyōsei gakkai, 1940), 162–64, 181–84, 187–90, 265–70, 280.

312 Tamura Toshio, *Manshūkoku, rinen to jittai* (Shinkyō: Manshūteikoku kyōikukai, 1941).

313 Minagawa Toyoji, *Manshūkoku no kyōiku* (Shinkyō: Ōsakaya goshoten, 1939), 1–8.

314 Sakuta Shōichi, "Ajia no hikari," *Kenkoku* 1, no. 1 (August 1940): 2–5; Bill Sewell and Norio Ota, "Sakuta Shōichi, 'The Light of Asia'," in *Translating the Japanese Occupation of China*, ed. Jonathan Henshaw, Craig Smith, and Norman Smith (Vancouver: UBC Press: forthcoming).

315 See, for example, Lt. Mihashi Wataru, "Ōdō kokka kensetsu o miru," in *Manshū sangyō kensetsu gakuto kenkyūtan hōsoku*, vol. 5 (Tokyo: Manshū sangyō kensetsu gakuto kenkyūdan shiseikai honbu, 1934), 149–51.

316 Shinkyō tokubetsushi shichōkanbō shomuka, *Kokuto Shinkyō* (1942), 173–74.

317 Manshū teikoku rinji kokuto kensetsu kyoku, *Kokuto kensetsu ni tsuite* (n.p.: Manshū teikoku rinji kokuto kensetsu kyoku, 1940), 46; Shinkyō tokubetsushi shichōkanbō shomuka, *Kokuto Shinkyō* (1940), 107–10; Shinkyō tokubetsushi shichōkanbō shomuka, *Kokuto Shinkyō* (1942), 107, 199–209.

318 "Chōshun ni keibajō," *MNNS*, 21 January 1927, 4; "Chōshun keibakai to Kantōgun no shimonan," *MNNS*, 22 January 1927, 4.

319 Okuda Takashi, "Takebe sōmuchōkan no omidasu," in *Aa Manshū: kuni tsukuri sangyō kaihatsusha no shuki*, ed. Manshū kaikoshū kankōkai (Tokyo: Manshū kaikoshū kankōkai, 1965), 108–11; *Manchoukuo Year Book, 1942*, 949–50.

320 Manshū dengyō gaishi hen i'inkai, *Omoidasu no Manshū dengyō*, vol. 2, "*Supōtsu – bunka*" (Tokyo: Manshū dengyō kai, 1977).

321 *SSC*.

322 Manshūkoku kokumuin kōhōsho, *Manchoukuo*, 13–14.

323 Shinkyō tokubetsushi shichōkanbō shomuka, *Kokuto Shinkyō* (1942), 106–7; *Shinkyō no gaikyō*, 39–43.

324 *MKZ* 12, no. 4 (1932); *Shinkyō no gaikyō*, 106–16; Matsumiya Kichirō, ed., *Shinkyō* (Hōten: Mantetsu tetsudō sōkyoku eigyōkyoku ryōkyokuka, 1937).

325 Barak Kushner, *The Thought War: Japanese Imperial Propaganda* (Honolulu: University of Hawai'i Press, 2006), 44–46; Kenneth Ruoff, "Japanese Tourism to Mukden, Nanjing, and Qufu, 1938–1943," *Japan Review* 27 (2014): 171–200.

326 Kenneth J. Ruoff, *Imperial Japan at Its Zenith: The Wartime Celebration of the Empire's 2,600th Anniversary* (Ithaca, NY: Cornell University Press, 2010), 137–46.

327 Mark Nornes, *Japanese Documentary Film: The Meiji Era through Hiroshima* (Minneapolis: University of Minnesota Press, 2003).

328 Tomoko Akami, "Projecting a Fiction of the Nation State to the World: The Manzhouguo News Agency in Japanese-Occupied Northeast China, 1932–1945," in *Entangled Histories: The Transcultural Past of Northeast China*, ed. Dan Ben-Canaan, Frank Grüner, and Ines Prodöhl (New York: Springer, 2014), 205–34; *SSC*.

329 *Manchoukuo Year Book, 1942*, 743; Daqing Yang, *Technology of Empire: Telecommunications and Japanese Expansion in Asia, 1883–1945* (Cambridge, MA: Harvard University Press, 2010), 96–8; Sun Bang, ed., *Wei Man wenhua* (Jilin: Renmin chubanshe, 1993), 259–62, 271–74.

330 Kushner, *Thought War*, 122–27.

331 For example, "Manshūkoku no hatten no tame jigai hōken o teppai suru," *MNNS*, 10 August 1935, 1.

332 Snow, *Far Eastern Front*, 268, 271–74.

333 Norman Smith, *Resisting Manchukuo: Chinese Women Writers and the Japanese Occupation* (Vancouver: UBC Press, 2007), 112–13, 122–23, 125. An overview of Chinese conditions in Manchukuo is Jie, *Wei Manzhouguo shi.*
334 Manshū jijō annaijo, *Shinkyō jijō,* 68.
335 Yanagisawa, "ZaiMan Nihonjin," 222–23.
336 Li Zhenquan, Li Chenggu, and Zhou Jianwu, "Shilun Changchunshi shangye diyu jiegou," *Dili kexue* 9, no. 2 (1989): 134.
337 Mikhail Iosifovich Sladkovskii, *History of Economic Relations between Russia and China* (Jerusalem: Israel Program for Scientific Translations, 1966), 123n55; Felix Patrikeeff, *Russian Politics in Exile: The Northeast Asian Balance of Power, 1924–1931* (Oxford: Palgrave Macmillan, 2002), 200n88; Akiko Yosano, *Travels in Manchuria and Mongolia: A Feminist Poet from Japan,* trans. Joshua A. Fogel (New York: Columbia University Press, 2001), 7, 93, 95.
338 Kawabata Motoh, "Senzen-senchūki ni okeru hyakkaten no kaigai shinshutsu to sono yōin," *Keieigaku ronshū* 49, no. 1 (2009): 1–22.
339 Minami Manshū tetsudō kabushiki kaisha, *Chōshun jijō,* 44–45; Phyllis Birnbaum, *Manchu Princess, Japanese Spy: The Story of Kawashima Yoshiko, the Cross-Dressing Spy Who Commanded Her Own Army* (New York: Columbia University Press, 2015), 158. Pictures of the Monte Carlo are in *MKZ* 16, no. 7 (1936).
340 "Otoko no sekai," *MNNS,* 8 August 1935, 5.
341 Darren-Jon Ashmore, "Kiritake Masako's Maiden's Bunraku," *Electronic Journal of Contemporary Japanese Studies* 5, no. 1 (2005): 3, http://www.japanesestudies.org.uk/articles/2005/Ashmore.html.
342 Nakajima, "Shinto Deities That Crossed the Sea," 29, 35.
343 Haslund-Christensen, "Mongol Encampments," 191.
344 Kiba Akeshi, "Gi Manshūkou shuto Shinkyō no Nihon bukyō ni yoru Manshū bukyō soshikika no mosaku," *Ōtani gakuhō* 81, no. 4 (2002): 1–11.
345 *Manshū teikoku genjū jinkō tōkei* (1940), 8–11.
346 *Shinkyō no gaikyō,* 36–37.
347 *SSC.*
348 Prasenjit Duara, *Sovereignty and Authenticity: Manchukuo and the East Asian Modern* (Lanham, MD: Rowman and Littlefield, 2004), 103–20; Thomas DuBois, "The Salvation of Religion? Public Charity and New Religions of the Early Chinese Republic," in *Charities in the Non-Western World: The Development and Regulation of Indigenous and Islamic Charities,* ed. Rajeswary Ampalavanar Brown and Justin Pierce (New York: Routledge, 2013), 126–31.
349 O'Dwyer, *Significant Soil,* 314–52.
350 "Kūshū! no keihō itari," *MNNS,* 21 June 1937, 2; "Dokugasusen no chishiki," *MNNS,* 21 June 1937, 5; "Kagaku heihin no hanashi," *MNNS,* 26 June 1937, 3, and 27 June 1937, 3. A map of the Amur River border was on the front page of *MNNS,* 28 June 1937.
351 "Bōkū no kyōiku kunren," *MNNS,* 14 August 1935, 5.
352 "Buryuhheru gensui Mosukuwa de hitojichi no kei," *MNNS,* 19 June 1937, 1.
353 *RGAPCI* (June 1933): 19.
354 Makuuchi Mitsuo, *Manshūkoku keisatsu gaishi* (Tokyo: San'ichi seibō, 1996), 132–35.
355 HIWRP, XX536, Robert Smith reports, Robert Smith, "The Japan-Manchukuo Economic Conference of Business Interests at Dairen," 233; Mutō Tomio, *Watakushi to Manshukoku* (Tokyo: Bungeishunjū, 1988), 159.
356 "Kokuto kōgai ni hishū," *MNNS,* 4 July 1931, 5.
357 Snow, *Far Eastern Front,* 268.
358 Yang, *Technology of Empire,* 168.

359 Minami Manshū tetsudō kabushiki kaisha keizai chōsakai, *Shinkyō toshi kensetsu hōsaku* (Dairen: Minami Manshū tetsudō, 1935), 1, 38, 69, 74–75, 96.

360 *Manchoukuo Year Book, 1942,* 342–45; "Manshūkoku bōeihō," *MKZ* 18, no. 9 (1938): 21–23; Thomas David DuBois, "Inauthentic Sovereignty: Law and Legal Institutions in Manchukuo," *Journal of Asian Studies* 69, no. 3 (2010): 764; Minseibu keisatsushi, *Manshūkoku keisatsu gaiyō* (Hōten: Minseibu keisatsushi, 1935), 63–80.

361 Mutō, *Watakushi to Manshukoku,* 157–75.

362 Minseibu keisatsushi, *Manshūkoku keisatsu gaiyō,* 329–76; *SSC.*

363 Makuuchi, *Manshūkoku keisatsu gaishi,* 51–63, 181–92, 226–27; *Manchoukuo Year Book, 1942,* 345–46.

364 Takeo Itō, *Life along the South Manchurian Railway: The Memoirs of Ito Takeo,* trans. Joshua Fogel (Armonk, NY: M.E. Sharpe, 1988), 191, 199–203.

365 *SSC;* Makuuchi, *Manshūkoku keisatsu gaishi,* 40–51, 254, photo insert.

366 Woodhead, *Visit to Manchukuo,* 88.

367 Bell, "Struggle for Mongolia," 55.

368 Suk-jung Han, "The Problem of Sovereignty: Manchukuo, 1932–1937," *positions* 12, no. 2 (2004): 468–69.

369 Yamamuro, *Manchuria under Japanese Dominion,* 213–14; Ronald Suleski, "Manchukuo and Beyond: The Life and Times of Zhang Mengshi," *International Journal of Asian Studies* 14, no. 1 (2017): 77–97.

370 *Manchoukuo Year Book, 1942,* 347–48; Jaeeun Kim, "The Colonial State, Migration, and Diasporic Nationhood in Korea," *Comparative Studies in Society and History* 56, no. 1 (2014): 54–55; Endō Masataka, *Kindai Nihon no shokuminchi tōchi ni okeru kokuseki to koseki: Manshū, Chōsen, Taiwan* (Tokyo: Akashi shoten, 2010).

371 "Japan to Execute Mongol Officials," *Toronto Daily Star,* 21 April 1936, 5; "Execute 4 Mongol Officials," *Toronto Daily Star,* 24 April 1936, 1; "Japs Suppress Plot to Overthrow Puppet State of Manchukuo," *Globe and Mail* (Toronto) 30 March 1937, 15. See also Tsukase Susumu, "The Penetration of Manzhouguo Rule in Manchuria," in *China at War: Regions of China, 1937–45,* ed. Stephen R. MacKinnon, Diana Lary, and Ezra F. Vogel (Stanford, CA: Stanford University Press, 2007), 110–47.

372 Rana Mitter, *The Manchurian Myth: Nationalism, Resistance, and Collaboration in Modern China* (Berkeley: University of California Press, 2000), 121–24.

373 Manshū teikoku kyōwakai, ed., *Manshū teikoku kyōwakai soshiki enkakushi* (Tokyo: Funi shuppan, 1982); Hirano Ken'ichiro, "State Forging and Nation-Destroying: The Case of the Concordia Association of Manchukuo," *East Asian Cultural Studies* 25, nos. 1–4 (1986): 37–57; Duara, *Sovereignty and Authenticity,* 73–76; Young, *Japan's Total Empire,* 287–91.

374 *SSC.*

375 *Manchoukuo Year Book, 1942,* 338; Philip S. Jowett, *Rays of the Rising Sun: Armed Forces of Japan's Asian Allies, 1931–1945,* vol. 1, *China and Manchukuo* (Solihull, UK: Helion, 2004), 13.

376 Jowett, *Rays of the Rising Sun,* 8, 25, 31; Sano Riki, "Manshū no kokuto kensetsu keikaku," *Toshi mondai* 17, no. 2 (1933):44.

377 Tian Shicong, "Dajie xiangbi guanshide xiaocao shuichuande qing," *Qilin* 2, no. 6 (1942): 107; O'Dwyer, *Significant Soil,* 312–13.

378 Nakano, "Kokuto Shinkyō no kensetsu," 167.

379 Chalmers A. Johnson, *An Instance of Treason: Ozaki Hotsumi and the Sorge Spy Ring* (Stanford, CA: Stanford University Press, 1990), 137–39.

380 Military History Section, Headquarters, Army Forces Far East, *Japanese Special Study on Manchuria,* vol. 1, *Japanese Operational Planning against the U.S.S.R.* (Office of the Chief of Military History, Department of the Army, 1955), 20, 28, 42, 62, 75, 82, 90.

381 David M. Glantz, *The Soviet Strategic Offensive in Manchuria, 1945: "August Storm"* (London: Frank Cass, 2003), 79.

382 Baron Kimmochi Ohkura, "Japan and Manchoukuo's Industrial Development," *Contemporary Japan* 9, no. 7 (1940): 850, 851.

383 Benkan zaijing jizhe quanti dongyuan, "Da Xinjingshi de dongtai," 104–15.

384 Toya Torao, "Manshū no mutsumi," in Manshū kaikoshū kankōkai, *Aa Manshū,* 60–64.

385 Lannay, "Hsinking," 117–18. Lannay's description resembles Franklin Hiram King, *Farmers of Forty Centuries, or, Permanent Agriculture in China, Korea and Japan* (1911; London: Cape, 1939), 157, 161–62.

386 Woodhead, *Visit to Manchukuo,* 88.

387 Wright, "Growth of the Modern Chinese Coal Industry," 341.

388 Yang, *Technology of Empire,* 263.

389 Shinkyō tokubetsushi shichōkanbō shomuka, *Yakushin kokuto no iyō,* 17–21.

390 David Tucker, "Colonial Sovereignty in Manchuria and Manchukuo," in *The State of Sovereignty: Territories, Laws, Populations,* ed. Douglas Howland and Luise White (Bloomington: Indiana University Press, 2009), 81.

391 Takasugi Shingo, *731 butai kinsen no ishi o oe: Ima mo tsutzuku kyōfu no jintai jikken* (Tokyo: Tokuma shoten, 1982), 180–96; Sheldon H. Harris, *Factories of Death: Japanese Biological Warfare, 1932–1945, and the American Cover-Up,* rev. ed. (London: Routledge, 2002), 113–34.

392 Yamada Hisetarō, *ManMō toyū zenshi* (Tokyo: Nikkan Shina jijōsha, 1926), 1:318–19.

393 "The International Opium Commission," *British Medical Journal,* no. 1 (1910):94.

394 *Shinkyō no gaikyō,* 31–35; Shinkyō tokubetsushi shichōkanbō shomuka, *Kokuto Shinkyō* (1942), 168–73, 179–89; Okada Yoshimasa, Tatai Yoshio, and Takahashi Masae, eds., *Ahen mondai* (Tokyo: Misuzu shobō, 1986); John M. Jennings, *The Opium Empire: Japanese Imperialism and Drug Trafficking in Asia, 1895–1945* (Westport, CT: Praeger, 1997); Manshū jijō annaijo, *Manshū teikoku gaikan,* 130–31.

395 British Foreign Office Files for Japan and the Far East, Series 1: Embassy and Consular Archives – Japan (1905–40), 262/1889/4–14, Reginald McPherson Austin to Paul Dalrymple Butler, 22 March 1934.

396 Norman Smith, *Intoxicating Manchuria: Alcohol, Opium, and Culture in China's Northeast* (Vancouver: UBC Press, 2012); Miriam Kingsberg, *Moral Nation: Modern Japan and Narcotics in Global History* (Berkeley: University of California Press, 2014).

397 Harris, *Factories of Death,* 117, 118–21.

398 Kingsberg, *Moral Nation,* 29, 44, 117.

399 Eri Hotta, *Pan-Asianism and Japan's War, 1931–1945* (New York: Palgrave Macmillan, 2007), 185.

400 Texts of declarations are in *Manchoukuo Year Book, 1942,* 370–72.

401 For example, "DaitōA kagayaku kaisen daisenka," *MNNS,* 9 March 1942, 4; "Jutujin gakuto hobu tōtō junbi," *MNNS,* 4 November 1943, 1.

402 Kushner, *Thought War,* 119–31; Walter Edwards, "Forging Tradition for a Holy War: The Hakko Ichiu Tower in Miyazaki and Japanese Wartime Ideology," *Journal of Japanese Studies* 29, no. 2 (2003): 289–324; Ruoff, *Imperial Japan at Its Zenith,* 59–60.

403 John R. Stewart, "Severe Retrenchment in Manchoukuo," *Far Eastern Survey* 9, no. 22 (1940): 261–63.

404 Manshūkokushi hensan kankōkai, *Manshūkokushi,* 1:805.

405 M[irriam] S. F[arley], "Japanese Alarmed by Rising Cost of Living," *Far Eastern Survey* 6, no. 6 (1937): 65–66; Kurt Bloch, "Japanese War Economy," *Annals of the American Academy of Political and Social Science* 215 (May 1941): 17–23.

406 Margaret S. Culver, "Manchuria: Japan's Supply Base," *Far Eastern Survey* 14, no. 12 (1945): 161–63.
407 Ibid., 163.
408 *Manchoukuo Year Book, 1942,* 337, 348–49, 351.
409 Culver, "Manchuria," 161.
410 Manshūkokushi hensan kankōkai, *Manshūkokushi,* 1:748–52.
411 Ibid., 754.
412 Suleski, "Manchukuo and Beyond," 85.
413 Mayumi Itoh, *Pioneers of Sino-Japanese Relations: Liao and Takasaki* (New York: Palgrave Macmillan, 2012), 142.

Conclusion

1 Ishiwara Kanji, "TōA renmei to kōA undō," *Manshū to Nihonjin* (hereafter *MTN*) 1 (August 1975): 6–12 (originally in *TōA renmei* 3, no. 7 [1941]: 38–47).
2 Alvin D. Coox, "The Kwantung Army Dimension," in *The Japanese Informal Empire in China, 1895–1937,* ed. Peter Duus et al. (Princeton, NJ: Princeton University Press, 1989), 397.
3 Alvin D. Coox, *Nomonhan: Japan against Russia, 1939* (Stanford: Stanford University Press, 1985), 1:26–27, 32, 34, 37; Minami Manshū tetsudō kabushiki kaisha, *Chōshun jijō* (Dairen: Minami Manshū tetsudō Chōshun chihō jimusho, 1932), 169–72; Manshūkokushi hensan kankōkai, *Manshūkokushi* (Tokyo: Kokusai zenrin kyōkai, 1973), 1:107; Military History Section, Headquarters, Army Forces Far East, *Japanese Special Study on Manchuria,* vol. 2, *Imperial Japanese Army in Manchuria, 1894–1945* (Office of the Chief of Military History, Department of the Army, 1959), 67, 70.
4 Aiga Kensuke, "Kenkoku zengo no omidasu," *Manshū kenchiku zasshi (Journal of Manchurian Architecture)* 22, no. 10 (1942): 5–7.
5 Coox, *Nomonhan,* 2:1068–70; David M. Glantz, *The Soviet Strategic Offensive in Manchuria, 1945: "August Storm"* (London: Frank Cass, 2003), 68–69, 84–89, 189, 193–94; Military History Section, Headquarters, Army Forces Far East, *Japanese Special Study on Manchuria: Japanese Operational Planning against the U.S.S.R.* (Office of the Chief of Military History, Department of the Army, 1955), 1:168–75; Military History Section, US Army Forces Far East, *Record of Operations against Soviet Russia on Northern and Western Fronts of Manchuria and in Northern Korea (August 1945)* (Office of the Chief of Military History, Department of the Army, 1950), 1–6.
6 Coox, *Nomonhan,* 2:1059–66; Glantz, *Soviet Strategic Offensive,* 83, 89, 355–56.
7 Glantz, *Soviet Strategic Offensive,* 68–72, 189, 193; Military History Section, *Record of Operations,* 6, 32–35, 103–8, 266–67.
8 Coox, *Nomonhan,* 2:1067.
9 Glantz, *Soviet Strategic Offensive,* 68–69; Military History Section, *Record of Operations,* 13, 16, 76; Mayumi Itoh, *Japanese War Orphans in Manchuria: Forgotten Victims of World War II* (New York: Palgrave Macmillan, 2010), 24.
10 Daqing Yang, *Technology of Empire: Telecommunications and Japanese Expansion in Asia, 1883–1945* (Cambridge, MA: Harvard University Press, 2010), 355.
11 Manshūkokushi hensan kankōkai, *Manshūkokushi,* 1:755–58, 765–66; Glantz, *Soviet Strategic Offensive,* 68, 80; Military History Section, *Record of Operations,* 11–15, 36–43, 104, 137–40, 266–67; Military History Section, *Japanese Special Study on Manchuria,* 2:39–41, 46, 57–58, 85–96.
12 Coox, *Nomonhan,* 2:1072–3; Glantz, *Soviet Strategic Offensive,* 213; Military History Section, *Record of Operations,* 15–17, 42–43; Wang Wenfeng, "GiManshūkokugun no kaimetsu," in *Kindai Nihon to Manshūkoku,* ed. Shokuminchi bunka gakkai (Tokyo: Fuji

shuppan, 2014), 265–67; Ronald Suleski, "Manchukuo and Beyond: The Life and Times of Zhang Mengshi," *International Journal of Asian Studies* 14, no. 1 (2017): 86.

13 Glantz, *Soviet Strategic Offensive,* 208–9, 252; Coox, *Nomonhan,* 2:1070–72; Sheldon H. Harris, *Factories of Death: Japanese Biological Warfare, 1932–1945, and the American Cover-Up,* rev. ed. (London: Routledge, 2002), 142–43.

14 Glantz, *Soviet Strategic Offensive,* 409.

15 Military History Section, *Record of Operations,* 16–17; Elena Bondarenko, "Exploitation of Japanese POW Labour in the U.S.S.R.," *Far Eastern Affairs* 1 (1995): 73.

16 Ibid., 14–17, 30–31, 43–46.

17 Aaron William Moore, *Writing War: Soldiers Record the Japanese Empire* (Cambridge, MA: Harvard University Press, 2013), 248.

18 Manshūkokushi hensan kankōkai, *Manshūkokushi,* 2:774–76.

19 Lori Watt, *When Empire Comes Home: Repatriation and Reintegration in Postwar Japan* (Cambridge, MA: Harvard University Press, 2009), 39.

20 Mizuno Naoki, "Stories from Beyond the Grave: Investigating Japanese Burial Grounds in North Korea," trans. Mark Caprio, *Asia-Pacific Journal* 12, no. 9 (2014), http://apjjf.org/2014/12/9/Mizuno-Naoki/4085/article.html.

21 One allegation of trains leaving Xinjing for Pyongyang is in Handō Kazutoshi, *Soren ga Manshū ni shinkō shita natsu* (Tokyo: Bungei shunjū, 1999), 204–10. See also Itoh, *Japanese War Orphans in Manchuria,* 23–25.

22 Harris, *Factories of Death,* 244–47.

23 John J. Stephan, *The Russian Far East: A History* (Stanford, CA: Stanford University Press, 1994), 244–49; Donald G. Gillin and Ramon H. Myers, eds., *Last Chance in Manchuria: The Diary of Chang Kia-ngau* (Stanford, CA: Stanford University Press, 1989), 151–74.

24 Takeo Itō, *Life along the South Manchurian Railway: The Memoirs of Ito Takeo,* trans. Joshua Fogel (Armonk, NY: M.E. Sharpe, 1988), 209.

25 Bondarenko, "Exploitation of Japanese," 75–84; Yokote Shinji, "Soviet Repatriation Policy, U.S. Occupation Authorities, and Japan's Entry into the Cold War," *Journal of Cold War Studies* 15, no. 2 (2013): 32, 41–43; United States Department of State, *Foreign Relations of the United States, Diplomatic Papers, 1948,* vol. 7, *The Far East: China* (Washington, DC: US Government Printing Office, 1973) (hereafter *FRUS, 1948*), documents 8, 40, 71.

26 F.C. Jones, "The Role of Manchuria in Communist Strategy," *World Today* 6, no. 5 (1950): 196–205; Felix Patrikeeff, *Russian Politics in Exile: The Northeast Asian Balance of Power, 1924–1931* (Oxford: Palgrave Macmillan, 2002), 97, 120, 186n108.

27 Mikhail Iosifovich Sladkovskii, *History of Economic Relations between Russia and China* (Jerusalem: Israel Program for Scientific Translations, 1966), 226–27n33.

28 Edwin W. Pauley, *Report on Japanese Assets in Manchuria to the President of the United States* (Washington, DC: US Government Printing Office, July 1946), 23–26.

29 Ibid., 26–27.

30 Ibid., 29.

31 Ibid., ix, 7, 9, 23.

32 Gillin and Myers, *Last Chance in Manchuria,* 195.

33 Central Intelligence Agency (hereafter CIA), "Soviet Policy on Reparations from Manchuria and East Germany," 9 June 1954, https://www.cia.gov/library/readingroom/document/cia-rdp80-00810a004300390006-6.

34 Jonathan Blackshear Chavanne, "Collision in Manchuria: Rescue, Intelligence, and the Cold War in Asia, August–September 1945," *Intelligence and National Security* 32, no. 1 (2017): 26–36.

35 Gillin and Myers, *Last Chance in Manchuria,* 168; Dieter Heinzig, *The Soviet Union and Communist China, 1945–1950: The Arduous Road to the Alliance* (Armonk, NY: M.E.

Sharpe, 2004), 58–69; Rowena Ward, "Delaying Repatriation: Japanese Technicians in Early Postwar China," *Japan Forum* 23, no. 4 (2011): 477.

36 Gillin and Myers, *Last Chance in Manchuria,* 72.

37 Heinzig, *Soviet Union and Communist China,* 319–35, 351–56; Francis C. Jones, "Recent Developments in Manchuria," *Journal of the Royal Central Asian Society* 44, no. 2 (1957): 119. See also Zhihua Shen, *Mao, Stalin, and the Korean War: Trilateral Communist Relations in the 1950s,* trans. Neil Silver (New York: Routledge, 2012), 101–4; Zhang Shenfa, "Return of the Chinese Changchun Railway to China by the U.S.S.R.," in *Manchurian Railways and the Opening of China: An International History,* ed. Bruce A. Elleman and Stephen Kotkin (Armonk, NY: M.E. Sharpe, 2010), 171–94; Paul Wingrove, "Mao in Moscow, 1949–50: Some New Archival Evidence," *Journal of Communist Studies and Transition Policies* 11, no. 4 (1995): 309–34.

38 Chong-sik Lee, *Revolutionary Struggle in Manchuria: Chinese Communism and Soviet Interest, 1922–1945* (Berkeley: University of California Press, 1983); Harold Miles Tanner, *The Battle for Manchuria and the Fate of China: Siping, 1946* (Bloomington: Indiana University Press, 2003), 28–47.

39 Kim Sang Won, "The Chinese Civil War and Sino-North Korea Relations, 1945–50," *Seoul Journal of Korean Studies* 27, no. 1 (2014): 93–94; Jones, "Recent Developments in Manchuria," 117.

40 Barak Kushner, *The Thought War: Japanese Imperial Propaganda* (Honolulu: University of Hawai'i Press, 2006), 117–18, 131–38; Donald Gillin and Charles Etter, "Staying On: Japanese Soldiers and Civilians in China, 1945–1949," *Journal of Asian Studies* 42, no. 3 (1983): 497–518; Mayumi Itoh, *Pioneers of Sino-Japanese Relations: Liao and Takasaki* (New York: Palgrave Macmillan, 2012), 56–58, 61; Daqing Yang, "Resurrecting the Empire? Japanese Technicians in Postwar China," in *Japanese Empire in East Asia and Its Postwar Legacies,* ed. Harald Fuess (Munich: Iudicium, 1998), 185–205; Ward, "Delaying Repatriation."

41 Gillin and Myers, *Last Chance in Manchuria,* 161, 171, 207.

42 Steven I. Levine, *Anvil of Victory: The Communist Revolution in Manchuria, 1945–1948* (New York: Columbia University Press, 1987), 139–41; Adam Cathcart and Patricia Nash, "War Criminals and the Road to Sino-Japanese Normalization: Zhou Enlai and the Shenyang Trials, 1954–1956," *Twentieth Century China* 34, no. 2 (2009): 104–5.

43 Levine, *Anvil of Victory,* 38; Gillin and Myers, *Last Chance in Manchuria,* 159–60, 186, 194, 205–7, 214–18.

44 Tanner, *Battle for Manchuria,* 123; *Chronology of International Events and Documents* (hereafter *CIED*) 2, no. 7 (1946): 196.

45 *FRUS, 1948,* document 71.

46 *CIED* 2, no. 8 (1946): 226–27; "Chinese Reds Drive into Changchun," *Globe and Mail;* 17 April 1946, 1 (Toronto). "Chinese Reds Gain Ground in Changchun," *Globe and Mail,* 18 April 1946, 1.

47 *CIED* 2, no. 10 (1946): 272.

48 *CIED* 2, no. 11 (1946): 314; *CIED* 2, no. 14 (1946): 408.

49 Tanner, *Battle for Manchuria,* 206; Frank Dikötter, *The Tragedy of Liberation: A History of the Chinese Revolution, 1945–1957* (New York: Bloomsbury, 2013), 14–22; Odd Arne Westad, *Decisive Encounters: The Chinese Civil War, 1946–1950* (Stanford, CA: Stanford University Press, 2003), 190, 195–99.

50 Tanner, *Battle for Manchuria,* 52–55, 123–24.

51 Shen, *Mao, Stalin, and the Korean War,* 62.

52 Zhang Zhenglong, *Xuebai xiehong: guogong Dongbei dazhuezhan lishi zhenxiang* (Hong Kong: Dadi chubanshe, 1991), 467–70. This was originally published by the People's

Liberation Army but later banned and then republished in Hong Kong. In English, see Dikötter, *Tragedy of Liberation,* 3–22; and Levine, *Anvil of Victory,* 123–24, 133–34.

53 *CIED* 2, no. 5 (1946): 123.

54 Gillin and Myers, *Last Chance in Manchuria,* 97; Levine, *Anvil of Victory,* 37–41.

55 *CIED* 2, no. 6 (1946): 177.

56 United States Department of State, *Foreign Relations of the United States, Diplomatic Papers, 1945,* vol. 7, *The Far East: China* (Washington, DC: United States Government Printing Office, 1969), documents 1129, 1132.

57 O. Edmund Clubb, *The Witness and I* (New York: Columbia University Press, 1974), 70–74.

58 H. Foster Bain, "Manchuria: A Key Area," *Foreign Affairs* 25, no. 1 (1946): 109–11.

59 CIA, "Implementation of Soviet Objectives in China," 15 September 1947, https://www.cia.gov/library/readingroom/document/cia-rdp78-01617a003000080001-9.

60 Jones, "Recent Developments in Manchuria," 119.

61 O. Edmund Clubb, "Manchuria: Communist Keystone," *Military Review* 37, no. 8 (1957): 7; Percy L. Greaves, Jr., "Marshall Comes on Stage: The Real Infamy of Pearl Harbor," *Journal of Historical Review* 4, no. 4 (1983): 425–36.

62 Military History Section, Headquarters, Army Forces Far East, *Japanese Special Study on Manchuria,* vol. 3, pt. 1, *Strategic Study of Manchuria: Military Topography and Geography* (Office of the Chief of Military History, Department of the Army, 1955), 24.

63 Michael A. Palmer, *Origins of the Maritime Strategy: The Development of American Naval Strategy, 1945–1955* (Washington, DC: Naval Historical Center, 1988), 21–23, 95–99; Steven T. Ross, *American War Plans, 1945–50* (New York: Garland, 1988), 16–17, 29, 64.

64 CIA, "1. Arrival of Soviet Troops, Manchuria 2. Ban on Gasoline and Diesel Oil Shipments, Manchuria," 14 December 1950, https://www.cia.gov/library/readingroom/document/cia-rdp82-00457r006500550004-3; CIA, "Arrival of Soviet Heavy Bombers, Manchuria," 18 April 1951, https://www.cia.gov/library/readingroom/document/cia-rdp82-00457r007500410002-9.

65 Glantz, *Soviet Strategic Offensive,* 386.

66 Itoh, *Pioneers of Sino-Japanese Relations,* 30; Manshūkokushi hensan kankōkai, *Manshūkokushi,* 1:765–66, 768–72, 799–803.

67 Ikemiyagi Sumiko, "Shinkyō: shūsen zengo no watakushi no omidasu," in *Heiwa no ishizue: rōku taiken shuki; kaigai hikiagesha ga katari tsugu rōku 7,* ed. Heiwa kinen jigyō tokubetsu kikin (Tokyo: Heiwa kinen jigyō tokubetsu kikin, 1997), 248–53, http://www.heinakinen.jp/library/shinryokan/hikiage07.html.

68 Tani Miyuki, *Chōshun Monogatari* (Fukutamachi, Shizuoka: Mittani Yukio, 1989), 52–112.

69 Yanagisawa Asobu, *Nihonjin no shokuminchi keiken: Dairen Nihonjin shōkōgyōsha no rekishi* (Tokyo: Aoki shoten, 1999), 303–11.

70 Zhang left Changchun on 2 February 1946. Gillin and Myers, *Last Chance in Manchuria,* 73, 76.

71 Marusugi Sakube, "RyūMan nikki," in *Aa Manshū: kuni tsukuri sangyō kaihatsusha no shuki* ed. Manshū kaikoshū kankōkai (Tokyo: Manshū kaikoshū kankōkai, 1965), 831–36.

72 Nakamura Tazuko, "Daini no tatakai," ibid., 822–24.

73 Itoh, *Japanese War Orphans in Manchuria;* Yeeshan Chan, *Abandoned Japanese in Postwar Manchuria: The Lives of War Orphans and Wives in Two Countries* (New York: Routledge, 2010).

74 Ikemiyagi, "Shinkyō," 255; Manshūkokushi hensan kankōkai, *Manshūkokushi,* 2:785–6; Itoh, *Pioneers of Sino-Japanese Relations,* 51–57.

75 Nozoe Rishō, "Watakushi no taiken shita nijūhachi nenkan no Manshū," *MTN: Tokubetsu go* 1 (1976): 140–41.
76 Harris, *Factories of Death*, 117, 132–33.
77 Itoh, *Pioneers of Sino-Japanese Relations*, 51–56; Manshūkokushi hensan kankōkai, *Manshūkokushi*, 2:799–807.
78 *FRUS, 1948*, document 13.
79 Lu Minghui, *Tonghua "2-3" shijian* (Beijing: Shijie zhishi chubanshe, 2006), 27–28.
80 Liaoningsheng Huludaoshi zhengfu shinwen bangongshi Liaoningsheng shehui kexueyuan, ed., *Huludao baiwan Riqiao daqianfan* (Beijing: Wuzhou chuanbo chubanshe, 2005); Manshūkokushi hensan kankōkai, *Manshūkokushi*, 2:811–15; Itoh, *Pioneers of Sino-Japanese Relations*, 53–54; Watt, *When Empire Comes Home*, 50–52, 59–61.
81 Michael Kim, "The Lost Memories of Empire and the Korean Return from Manchuria, 1945–1950: Conceptualizing Manchuria in Modern Korean History," *Seoul Journal of Korean Studies* 23, no. 2 (2010): 207–12; Jones, "Recent Developments in Manchuria," 117.
82 Watt, *When Empire Comes Home*, 105–8, 167–89; Mariko Asano Tamanoi, *Memory Maps: The State and Manchuria in Postwar Japan* (Honolulu: University of Hawai'i Press, 2009), 91–139.
83 *FRUS, 1948*, document 249.
84 Liaoningsheng Huludaoshi zhengfu shinwen bangongshi Liaoningsheng shehui kexueyuan, *Huludao baiwan Riqiao daqianfan*, 2, 4; *The Manchoukuo Year Book, 1942* (Tokyo: Ajia tōkeisha, 1942), 581–82.
85 Nakatsuka Kazumoto, "Kenkoku daigaku Odaka fukusōchō to shūsen," *MTN* 6 (December 1978): 181–94; Kurokawa Kazuo, "Korodō bōekihan," *MTN* 4 (December 1976): 157–62.
86 Ikemiyagi, "Shinkyō," 256.
87 Tani, *Chōshun Monogatari*, 113–18.
88 Toide Takeshi, "Ichū gakusei no Manshū kara no hikiage nikki," *MTN* 3 (1978): 153–68.
89 Anecdotal evidence in Itoh, *Pioneers of Sino-Japanese Relations*, 59–63; Yang, "Resurrecting the Empire," 195–96. One study suggests the number of forcibly detained was small – see Gillin and Etter, "Staying On," 505, 509–11, 513.
90 She later estimated Changchun's total death toll in 1948 to be 300,000. An English translation of an abbreviated version of her experience is Endō Homare, *Japanese Girl at the Siege of Changchun: How I Survived China's Wartime Atrocity*, trans. Michael Brase (Berkeley, CA: Stone Bridge Press, 2016).
91 Bondarenko, "Exploitation of Japanese," 77–84; Manshūkokushi hensan kankōkai, *Manshūkokushi*, 1:818–24, 828–29.
92 CIA, "Political Information: Japanese Repatriation from Manchuria and North China," 4 August 1948, https://www.cia.gov/library/readingroom/document/cia-rdp82-00457r001700510006-5.
93 Watt, *When Empire Comes Home*, 98–102, 111–37.
94 Tamanoi, *Memory Maps*, 84–114; Itoh, *Japanese War Orphans in Manchuria;* Chan, *Abandoned Japanese in Postwar Manchuria.*
95 Henri Lefebvre, *The Production of Space*, trans. Donald Nicholson-Smith (Malden, MA: Blackwell, 1991), 301, 337–38.
96 Nishizawa Yasuhiko, *Nihon shokuminchi kenchiku ron* (Nagoya: Nagoya daigaku shuppansha, 2008), 402–3, 406–8.
97 Charles Taylor, *Modern Social Imaginaries* (Durham, NC: Duke University Press, 2004), 1–2, 82, 180–82, 195–96.
98 Dan Shao, *Remote Homeland, Recovered Borderland: Manchus, Manchoukuo, and Manchuria, 1907–1985* (Honolulu: University of Hawai'i Press, 2011), 3–6.

99 Emer O'Dwyer, *Significant Soil: Settler Colonialism and Japan's Urban Empire in Manchuria* (Cambridge, MA: Harvard University Press, 2015), 13–15, 159, 352.

100 Alexis Dudden, *Japan's Colonization of Korea: Discourse and Power* (Honolulu: University of Hawai'i Press, 2005), 133–43.

101 Louise Young, *Japan's Total Empire: Manchuria and the Culture of Wartime Imperialism* (Berkeley: University of California Press, 1998); Jun Uchida, *Brokers of Empire: Japanese Settler Colonialism in Korea, 1876–1945* (Cambridge, MA: Harvard University Press, 2011); Watt, *When Empire Comes Home,* 10–11; Tamanoi, *Memory Maps.*

102 Mutō, "Waga kaisō (1)," *MTN* 1 (August 1975): 37; Nakatsuka Kazumoto, "Kenkoku daigaku Odaka fukusōchō to shūsen," *MTN* 6 (December 1978): 184; Okano Kanki, "Manshūkoku jidai no zuisō," *MTN* 10 (February 1988): 62.

103 Fujise Takayuki, "Kanjōshi wa ekizochikku Roshiajin machi de atta," in *Kanjōshi monogatari,* ed. Chōshun Kanjōshikai (Tokyo: Chōshun Kanjōshikai, 2006), 71.

104 Tani, *Chōshun Monogatari,* 10, 25, 30.

105 Among others, see the exchange between Philip C.C. Huang, "Biculturality in Modern China and in Chinese Studies," *Modern China* 26, no. 1 (2000): 3–31, and Prasenjit Duara, "Response to Philip Huang's 'Biculturality in Modern China and in Chines Studies,'" *Modern China* 26, no. 1 (2000): 32–37.

106 Prasenjit Duara, *Sovereignty and Authenticity: Manchukuo and the East Asian Modern* (Lanham, MD: Rowman and Littlefield, 2004), 61–65; Eri Hotta, *Pan-Asianism and Japan's War, 1931–1945* (New York: Palgrave Macmillan, 2007), 5–6, 12–13; Lincoln Li, *The China Factor in Modern Japanese Thought: The Case of Tachibana Shiraki, 1881–1945* (Albany: State University of New York Press, 1996); Mark R. Peattie, *Ishiwara Kanji and Japan's Confrontation with the West* (Princeton, NJ: Princeton University Press, 1975), 169–80; Yamamuro Shin'ichi, *Manchuria under Japanese Dominion,* trans. Joshua A. Fogel (Philadelphia: University of Pennsylvania Press, 2006), 61–81; Lincoln Young, *Japan's Total Empire,* 268–82.

107 Itō, *Life along the South Manchurian Railway,* xvii, 29–31, 33–34, 216–26.

108 Okada Hideki, "The Realities of Racial Harmony: The Case of the Translator Ōuchi Takao," *Acta Asiatica* 72 (March 1997): 61–80.

109 Miyazawa Jirō, "Teishin funan," in Manshū kaikoshū kankōkai, *Aa Manshū,* 71–74.

110 Andrew Hall, "The Word Is Mightier Than the Throne: Bucking Colonial Education Trends in Manchukuo," *Journal of Asian Studies* 68, no. 3 (2009): 895–925.

111 Chikako Nagayama, "The Flux of Domesticity and the Exotic in a Wartime Melodrama," *Signs* 34, no. 2 (2009): 369–95.

112 See, for example, Charles Bell, "The Struggle for Mongolia," *Journal of the Royal Central Asian Society* 24 (1937): 55.

113 Kuwahara Kineo, *Manshū Shōwa jūgonen* (Shōbunsha, 1975), 213.

114 Annika A. Culver, *Glorify the Empire: Japanese Avant-Garde Propaganda in Manchukuo* (Vancouver: UBC Press, 2013), 70–72.

115 Julean Arnold reported a pamphlet written by the chairman of the Japanese Chamber of Commerce in Shanghai urging an end to strong-arm tactics in China, but he expected little change given the military situation in North China in March 1937. Hoover Institution on War, Revolution, and Peace, Julean Herbert Arnold papers, box 2, Arnold, "A Japanese Bull in a China Shop," undated manuscript, 37–38.

116 Phyllis Birnbaum, *Manchu Princess, Japanese Spy: The Story of Kawashima Yoshiko, the Cross-Dressing Spy Who Commanded Her Own Army* (New York: Columbia University Press, 2015), 155–56, 167–69, 184–88, 192, 196, 200.

117 Stefan Tanaka, *Japan's Orient: Rendering Pasts into History* (Berkeley: University of California Press, 1993).

118 Joshua A. Fogel, *Politics and Sinology: The Case of Naitō Konan (1866–1934)* (Cambridge, MA: Harvard University Press, 1984); Joshua A. Fogel, *The Literature of Travel in the Japanese Rediscovery of China, 1862–1945* (Stanford, CA: Stanford University Press, 1996).

119 Inger Sigrun Brodey and Sammy I. Tsunematsu, eds., *Rediscovering Natsume Soseki: With the First English Translation of Travels in Manchuria and Korea* (Folkestone, UK: Global Oriental, 2000), 25, 38–39, 66, 125.

120 Yamamuro, *Manchuria under Japanese Dominion*, 105.

121 Li, *The China Factor;* Young, *Japan's Total Empire;* Hotta, *Pan-Asianism*.

122 Yabe Senkichi, "Manshū jidai no omidasu: tamashii ni ikiru hitobito," *MTN* 3 (January 1976): 23–24.

123 Okano, "Manshūkoku jidai no zuisō," 62–64.

124 Yoshimi Yoshiaki, *Grassroots Fascism: The War Experience of the Japanese People*, trans. Ethan Mark (New York: Columbia University Press, 2015), 110–14.

125 Paul Ricoeur, *Memory, History, Forgetting* (Chicago: Chicago University Press, 2004), 130.

126 Young, *Japan's Total Empire*, 427–30.

127 Furumi Tadayuki, "Kantō ni yosete," *MTN* 1 (August 1975): 2–4. Like Furumi, several were former war criminals. Furumi is also discussed in Yamamuro, *Manchuria under Japanese Dominion*. One editorial was more cautious, suggesting the journal endeavoured to situate Manchurian reminiscences within a context of an evolving China. Fujikawa Yūji, "Kantōgen," *MTN* 8 (October 1981): 1.

128 Hoshino Naoki, "Nijū seiki no Atoranthisu," in Manshū kaikoshū kankōkai, *Aa Manshū*, 66–67. See also Bill Sewell, "Postwar Japan and Manchuria," in *Japan at the Millennium: Joining Past and Future*, ed. David W. Edgington (Vancouver: UBC Press, 2003), 97–119.

129 Published in English as Yamamuro, *Manchuria under Japanese Domination*.

130 Nishizawa Yasuhiko, "Shohyō: *Manshūkoku no shuto keikaku*," *Ajia keizai* 38, no. 8 (1989): 109–13.

131 Ricoeur, *Memory, History, Forgetting*, 150–51, 404–11.

132 Lawrence S. Ritchie and Cooper Davis, "Parasitological Findings and Epidemiological Aspects of Epidemic Amebiasis Occurring in Occupants of the Mantetsu Apartment Building, Tokyo, Japan," *American Journal of Tropical Medicine and Hygiene*, s1-28, no. 6 (1948): 804.

133 "Soviet-China Military Headquarters Are Set Up," *Globe and Mail* (Toronto), 14 December 1950, 17.

134 "Li Yuqin: Chinese Emperor's Widow, 73," *New York Times*, 28 April 2001; Birnbaum, *Manchu Princess*, 3.

135 The Chinese name differs slightly: China–Japan People's Friendship Waterworks. Quansheng Zhao, "Japan's Aid Diplomacy with China," in *Japan's Foreign Aid: Power and Policy in a New Era*, ed. Bruce M. Koppel and Robert M. Orr (Boulder, CO: Westview Press, 1993), 168; Han Jinrong et al., "Changchun ZhongRi renming youhao shuichan jingshui jishu de weishengxue diaocha yu pingjie," *Zhongguo weisheng gongchengxue zazhi* 1, no. 1 (1992): 22–24. The 1990–91 upgrades are noted in Lim Hua Sing, "Japan's Official Development Assistance to China, Indonesia, and Singapore," in *APEC and Development Co-operation*, ed. Mohamed Ariff (Singapore: Institute of Southeast Asian Studies, 1998), 72–73. The JICA and Nihon Suidō websites indicate expansions in 2001–2 and after.

136 Fukuhara Masao, "Chūgoku Chōshunshi ni okeru Nihon teian sakutei to sono igi," *Geijutsu: Ōsaka geijutsu daigaku kiyō 22* (1999): 154–64. Its English name is the Changchun International Conference Centre.

137 David S.G. Goodman, *China's Campaign to "Open the West": National, Provincial, and Local Perspectives* (Cambridge: Cambridge University Press, 2004).

138 William A. Callahan, "History, Identity, and Security: Producing and Consuming Nationalism in China," *Critical Asian Studies* 38, no. 2 (2006): 179–208.

139 Jing Chen, "The Trial of Japanese War Criminals in China: The Paradoxy of Leniency," *China Information* 23, no. 3 (2009): 447–72; Cathcart and Nash, "War Criminals," 89–111.

140 See, for example, Peter Hays Gries, "China's 'New Thinking' on Japan," *China Quarterly* 184 (December 2005): 831–50; Parks M. Coble, "China's 'New Remembering' of the Anti-Japanese War of Resistance, 1937–1945," *China Quarterly* 190 (June 2007): 394–410; Sewell, "Postwar Japan and Manchuria."

141 Haruki Murakami, *The Wind-Up Bird Chronicle* (New York: Vintage, 1998) and *Underground* (New York: Vintage, 2001), 361–62.

142 Ricoeur, *Memory, History, Forgetting*, 333.

Bibliography

Archives

British Foreign Office Files for Japan and the Far East, London, UK (FO 262)
Hoover Institution on War, Revolution, and Peace, Stanford, CA
National Archives of Scotland, Edinburgh, UK
Presbyterian Historical Society, Belfast, Northern Ireland, UK
Société des missions étrangères de Paris, France

Newspapers

Chōshun jitsugyō shinbun (*Changchun Business News*)
Globe and Mail (Toronto) – published as the (*Globe*) before 1936
Manshū nichi nichi shinbun (*Manchuria Daily News*) – published as *Manshū Nippō* (*Manchuria Daily*), 1927–35 and *Manshū Shinbun*, 1944–45
Ōsaka mainichi shinbun (*Osaka Daily News*)
Toronto Daily Star
Yomiuri shinbun (*Yomiuri News*)

Books and Articles

Aasen, Clarence. *Architecture of Siam: A Cultural History Interpretation* (Kuala Lumpur: Oxford University Press, 1998).

Akagi, Roy H. "The Future of American Trade with Manchukuo." *Annals of the American Academy of Political and Social Science* 211 (September 1940): 138–43. https://doi.org/10.1177/000271624021100120.

Akami, Tomoko. "Projecting a Fiction of the Nation State to the World: The Manzhouguo News Agency in Japanese-Occupied Northeast China, 1932–1945." In *Entangled Histories: The Transcultural Past of Northeast China*, edited by Dan Ben-Canaan, Frank Grüner, and Ines Prodöhl, 205–34. New York: Springer, 2014. https://doi.org/10.1007/978-3-319-02048-8_13.

Amano Yōichi. *Dabaokuo no matsueitachi: Firipin Nikkei kimin.* Nagoya: Fūbaisha, 1990.

Arango, Joaquin. "Explaining Migration: A Critical View." *International Social Science Journal* 52, no. 165 (2000): 283–96. https://doi.org/10.1111/1468-2451.00259.

Arita, Hachirō. "The Greater East Asian Sphere of Common Prosperity." *Contemporary Japan* 10, no. 1 (1941): 9–15.

Asakawa, K. "Japan in Manchuria – II." *Yale Review* 17 (November 1908): 268–302.

Ashmore, Darren-Jon. "Kiritake Masako's Maiden's Bunraku." *Electronic Journal of Contemporary Japanese Studies* 5, no. 1 (2005). http://www.japanesestudies.org.uk/articles/2005/Ashmore.html.

Aydin, Cemil. *The Politics of Anti-Westernism in Asia: Visions of World Order in Pan-Islamic and Pan-Asian Thought.* New York: Columbia University Press, 2007. https://doi.org/10.7312/aydi13778.

Bain, H. Foster. "Manchuria: A Key Area." *Foreign Affairs* 25, no. 1 (1946): 106–17. https://doi.org/10.2307/20030023.

Balet, J.C. *La Mandchourie: historique, politique, economique, son avenir.* Paris: Payot, 1932.

Bank of Chosen. *Economic History of Manchuria.* Seoul: Bank of Chosen, 1921.

Bao Xi. *Xinjingshi shanghui.* Xinjing(?): Huibian, 1934.

Barber, Joseph, Jr. *Hawaii: Restless Rampart.* New York: Bobbs-Merrill, 1941.

Barker, T.M. "War: From Behind Closed Doors." Pamphlet. N.p., n.d.

Barrett, David P. "Introduction: Occupied China and the Limits of Accommodation." In *Chinese Collaboration with Japan, 1932–1945: The Limits of Accommodation,* edited by David P. Barrett and Larry N. Shyu, 1–17. Stanford, CA: Stanford University Press, 2001.

Baskett, Michael. *The Attractive Empire: Transnational Film Culture in Imperial Japan.* Honolulu: University of Hawai'i Press, 2008. https://doi.org/10.21313/hawaii/9780824831639.001.0001.

Beal, Edwin G., Jr. "The 1940 Census of Manchuria." *Far Eastern Quarterly* 4, no. 3 (1945): 243–62. https://doi.org/10.2307/2049515.

Bell, Charles. "The Struggle for Mongolia." *Journal of the Royal Central Asian Society* 24 (1937): 46–72. https://doi.org/10.108%3068373708730779.

Benkan zaijing jizhe quanti dongyuan. "Da Xinjingshi de dongtai." *Qilin* 2, no. 6 (1942): 104–15.

Bickers, Robert. *Britain in China: Community, Culture, and Colonialism, 1900–1949.* Manchester: Manchester University Press, 1999.

Birnbaum, Phyllis. *Manchu Princess, Japanese Spy: The Story of Kawashima Yoshiko, the Cross-Dressing Spy Who Commanded Her Own Army.* New York: Columbia University Press, 2015.

Bitō Masayoshi, ed. *Yakushin tojō no daiShinkyō.* Shinkyō: Shinkyō shōkō kaigijo, 1936.

Blakeslee, George H. "Outstanding Facts in the Present Situation in China." *Annals of the American Academy of Political and Social Science* 138 (July 1928): 49–53. https://doi.org/10.1177/000271622813800108.

Bloch, Kurt. "Japanese War Economy." *Annals of the American Academy of Political and Social Science* 215 (May 1941): 17–23. https://doi.org/10.1177/000271624121500103.

Bo Xinian. "Guanyu Mingdai gongdian tanmiaodeng dajianzhuqun zongti guihua shoufa de chubu tantao." In *Jianzhu lishi yanjiu,* edited by He Yeju, 25–48. Beijing: Zhongguo jianzhu gongye chubanshe, 1992.

Bondarenko, Elena. "Exploitation of Japanese POW Labour in the U.S.S.R." *Far Eastern Affairs* 1 (1995): 72–85.

Borg, Dorothy. "Japanese Establish Airlines in China." *Far Eastern Survey* 8, no. 11 (1939): 132–33. https://doi.org/10.2307/3022388.

Boyd, James. "In Pursuit of an Obsession: Japan in Inner Mongolia in the 1930s." *Japanese Studies* 22, no. 3 (2002): 289–303. https://doi.org/10.1080/1037139022000036977.

–. "'This Stalwart Fellow of Five Lands and Two Seas': The Life of Fukushima Yasumasa." *War and Society* 30, no. 3 (2011): 177–88. https://doi.org/10.1179/204243411X13123630864589.

–. "Undercover Acolytes: Honganji, the Japanese Army, and Intelligence-Gathering Operations." *Journal of Religious History* 37, no. 2 (2013): 185–205. https://doi.org/10.1111/1467-9809.12027.

Brandt, Kim. "The Beauty of Labor: Imagining Factory Girls in Japan's New Order." In Tansman, *The Culture of Japanese Fascism,* 115–37.

–. *Kingdom of Beauty: Mingei and the Politics of Folk Art in Imperial Japan.* Durham, NC: Duke University Press, 2007. https://doi.org/10.1215/9780822389545.

British General Staff. War Office. *The Russo-Japanese War: Reports from British Officers Attached to the Japanese Forces in the Field.* 3 vols. London: His Majesty's Stationery Office, 1907.

Brodey, Inger Sigrun, and Sammy I. Tsunematsu, eds. *Rediscovering Natsume Soseki: With the First English Translation of Travels in Manchuria and Korea.* Folkestone, UK: Global Oriental, 2000.

Brooks, Barbara. *Japan's Imperial Diplomacy: Consuls, Treaty Ports, and War in China, 1895–1938.* Honolulu: University of Hawai'i Press, 2000.

Brown, Arthur Judson. *New Forces in Old China: An Inevitable Awakening.* 2nd ed. New York: Fleming H. Revell, 1907.

Buck, David D. "Railway City and National Capital: Two Faces of the Modern in Changchun." In *Remaking the Chinese City: Modernity and National Identity, 1900–1950,* edited by Joseph W. Esherick, 65–89. Honolulu: University of Hawai'i Press, 1999.

Bunkyōbu gakumushi sōmuka. *Manshūkoku gakuji yōran.* Hōten: Bunkyōbu gakumushi sōmuka, 1936.

Buruma, Ian. *Inventing Japan, 1853–1964.* New York: Modern Library, 2004.

–. *The Wages of Guilt: Memories of War in Germany and Japan.* New York: Farrar, Straus, and Giroux, 1994.

Butow, Robert J.C. *Tojo and the Coming of the War.* Stanford, CA: Stanford University Press, 1961.

Callahan, William A. "History, Identity, and Security: Producing and Consuming Nationalism in China." *Critical Asian Studies* 38, no. 2 (2006): 179–208. https://doi.org/10.1080/14672710600671087.

Castells, Manuel. *City, Class, and Power.* New York: St. Martin's Press, 1978.

Cathcart, Adam, and Patricia Nash. "War Criminals and the Road to Sino-Japanese Normalization: Zhou Enlai and the Shenyang Trials, 1954–1956." *Twentieth-Century China* 34, no. 2 (2009): 89–111. https://doi.org/10.1179/tcc.2009.34.2.89.

Chan, Yeeshan. *Abandoned Japanese in Postwar Manchuria: The Lives of War Orphans and Wives in Two Countries.* New York: Routledge, 2010.

Changchunshi nanguanqu difang shizhi bianzuan weiyuanhui. *Changchunshi Kuancheng quzhi.* Changchun: Jilin wenshi chubanshe, 1993.

Chao, Kang. "Demographic Development in Manchuria, 1924–1941." *Bulletin of the Institute of Modern History* 10 (1981): 351–75.

Chavanne, Jonathan Blackshear. "Collision in Manchuria: Rescue, Intelligence, and the Cold War in Asia, August–September 1945." *Intelligence and National Security* 32, no. 1 (2017): 26–36.

Chen Benshan, ed. *Riben qinlüe Zhonguo dongbei shi.* Changchun: Jilin daxue chubanshe, 1989.

Chen, Jing. "The Trial of Japanese War Criminals in China: The Paradoxy of Leniency." *China Information* 23, no. 3 (2009): 447–72. https://doi.org/10.1177/0920203X09345189.

Ching, Leo T.S. *Becoming "Japanese": Colonial Taiwan and the Politics of Identity Formation.* Berkeley: University of California Press, 2001.

Chō Kinhaku. *Shinkokka daiManshū.* Tokyo: Tōkyō shobo, 1932.

Chōshun chōsain. *Chōshun ni okeru Kashō shiba narabi hanbai soshiki chōsa.* N.p., 1926.

Chōshun Kanjōshikai, ed. *Kanjōshi monogatari.* Chōshun Kanjōshikai, 2006.

Cipko, Serge. "Ukrainians in Manchuria, China: A Concise Historical Survey." *Past Imperfect* 1 (1992): 155–73.

Clancey, Gregory K. "Designing a Home for the *Yamato Minzoku*: Race, Housing and Modernity in Wartime Japan." *Asian Studies Review* 29, no. 2 (2005): 123–41. https://doi.org/10.1080/10357820500221139.

–. *Earthquake Nation: The Cultural Politics of Japanese Seismicity, 1868–1930.* Berkeley: University of California Press, 2006. https://doi.org/10.1525/california/9780520246072.001.0001.

Clarke, Linda. *Building Capitalism: Historical Change and the Labour Process in the Production of the Built Environment.* London: Routledge, 1992.

Clubb, O. Edmund. "Manchuria: Communist Keystone." *Military Review* 37, no. 8 (1957): 3–9.

–. *The Witness and I.* New York: Columbia University Press, 1974.

Coaldrake, William H. *Architecture and Authority in Japan.* London: Routledge, 1996.

Coble, Parks M. "China's 'New Remembering' of the Anti-Japanese War of Resistance, 1937–1945." *China Quarterly* 190 (June 2007): 394–410. https://doi.org/10.1017/S0305741007001257.

–. *Facing Japan: Chinese Politics and Japanese Imperialism, 1931–1937.* Cambridge, MA: Harvard University Press, 1991. https://doi.org/10.2307/j.ctt1tg5j88.

Cohen, Warren I. *America's Response to China: A History of Sino-American Relations.* 5th ed. New York: Columbia University Press, 2010.

Coox, Alvin D. "The Kwantung Army Dimension." In Duus, Myers, and Peattier, *Japanese Informal Empire,* 395–428.

–. *Nomonhan: Japan against Russia, 1939.* 2 vols. Stanford, CA: Stanford University Press, 1985.

Crinson, Mark. *Empire Building: Orientalism and Victorian Architecture.* London: Routledge, 1996.

Croly, Herbert. *Willard Strait.* New York: Macmillan, 1924.

Culver, Annika A. *Glorify the Empire: Japanese Avant-Garde Propaganda in Manchukuo.* Vancouver: UBC Press, 2013.

Culver, Margaret S. "Manchuria: Japan's Supply Base." *Far Eastern Survey* 14, no. 12 (1945): 160–63. https://doi.org/10.2307/3022806.

Dangdai Zhongguo de Jilin congshu bianjibu. *Dangdai Zhongguo de Jilin.* 2 vols. Beijing: Dangdai Zhongguo chubanshe, 1991.

Dennery, Étienne. "Problèmes d'Extrême-Orient." *Annales de géographie* 46, no. 262 (1937): 337–68. https://doi.org/10.3406/geo.1937.12049.

Dickinson, Frederick R. *War and National Reinvention: Japan in the Great War, 1914–1919.* Cambridge, MA: Harvard University Press, 1999.

Dikötter, Frank. *The Tragedy of Liberation: A History of the Chinese Revolution, 1945–1957.* New York: Bloomsbury, 2013.

Doak, Kevin M. *A History of Nationalism in Modern Japan: Placing the People.* Boston: Brill, 2007.

Dorsey, James. "Literary Tropes, Rhetorical Looping, and the Nine Gods of War: 'Fascist Proclivities' Made Real." In Tansman, *The Culture of Japanese Fascism,* 409–31.

Dower, John W. *Empire and Aftermath: Yoshida Shigeru and the Japanese Experience, 1878–1954.* Cambridge, MA: Harvard University Press, 1979.

Dresner, Jonathan. "International Labour Migrants' Return to Meiji-era Yamaguchi and Hiroshima: Economic and Social Effects." *International Migration* (Geneva) 46, no. 3 (2008): 65–94. https://doi.org/10.1111/j.1468-2435.2008.00462.x.

Dryburgh, Marjorie. "The Fugitive Self: Writing Zheng Xiaoxu, 1882–1938." In *Writing Lives in China, 1600–2010,* edited by Marjorie Dryburgh and Sarah Dauncey, 110–32. London: Palgrave Macmillan, 2013.

–. "Japan in Tianjin: Settlers, State and the Tensions of Empire before 1937." *Japanese Studies* 27, no. 1 (2007): 19–34. https://doi.org/10.1080/10371390701268620.

–. *North China and Japanese Expansion, 1933–1937: Regional Power and the National Interest.* Richmond, UK: Curzon Press, 2000.

Du Halde, Jean-Baptiste. *Description géographique, historique, chronologique, politique, et physique de l'empire de la Chine et de la Tartarie chinoise, enrichie des cartes générales et particulieres de ces pays, de la carte générale et des cartes particulieres du Thibet, & de la Corée; & ornée d'un grand nombre de fi gures & de vignettes gravées en tailledouce.* The Hague: H. Scheurleer, 1736.

Duara, Prasenjit. "Response to Philip Huang's 'Biculturality in Modern China and in Chinese Studies.'" *Modern China* 26, no. 1 (2000): 32–37. https://doi.org/10.1177/009770040002600102.

–. *Sovereignty and Authenticity: Manchukuo and the East Asian Modern.* Lanham, MD: Rowman and Littlefield, 2004.

DuBois, Thomas. "The Salvation of Religion? Public Charity and New Religions of the Early Chinese Republic." In *Charities in the Non-Western World: The Development and Regulation of Indigenous and Islamic Charities,* edited by Rajeswary Ampalavanar Brown and Justin Pierce, 115–46. New York: Routledge, 2013.

DuBois, Thomas David. "Inauthentic Sovereignty: Law and Legal Institutions in Manchukuo." *Journal of Asian Studies* 69, no. 3 (2010): 749–70. https://doi.org/10.1017/S002191181000152X.

–. "Manchukuo's Filial Sons: States, Sects and the Adaptation of Graveside Piety." *East Asian History* 36 (December 2008): 3–27.

Dudden, Alexis. *Japan's Colonization of Korea: Discourse and Power.* Honolulu: University of Hawai'i Press, 2005.

Dujmovic, Nicholas. "Extraordinary Fidelity: Two CIA Prisoners in China, 1952–73." *Studies in Intelligence* 50, no. 4 (2006): 21–36.

Dunscomb, Paul E. *Japan's Siberian Intervention, 1918–22: "A Great Disobedience against the People."* Lanham, MD: Lexington Books, 2011.

Duque, Estela. "Militarization of the City: Implementing Burnham's 1905 Plan of Manila." *Fabrications: The Journal of the Society of Architectural Historians, Australia and New Zealand* 19, no. 1 (2009): 48–67. https://doi.org/10.1080/10331867.2009.10539645.

Duus, Peter. "Japan's Informal Empire in China, 1895–1937: An Overview." In Duus, Myers, and Peattie, *Japanese Informal Empire,* xi–xxix.

Duus, Peter, Ramon H. Myers, and Mark R. Peattie, eds. *The Japanese Informal Empire in China, 1895–1937,* Princeton, NJ: Princeton University Press, 1989.

Edmonds, Richard L. "The Willow Palisade." *Annals of the Association of American Geographers* 69, no. 4 (1979): 599–621. https://doi.org/10.1111/j.1467-8306.1979.tb01285.x.

Edwards, Walter. "Forging Tradition for a Holy War: The Hakko Ichiu Tower in Miyazaki and Japanese Wartime Ideology." *Journal of Japanese Studies* 29, no. 2 (2003): 289–324.

Eldridge, Frank R. "Manchuria: The Race for New Resources." *Annals of the American Academy of Political and Social Science* 168 (July 1933): 95–103. https://doi.org/10.1177/000271623316800113.

Eley, Geoff. "What Produces Fascism: Preindustrial Traditions or a Crisis of a Capitalist State." *Politics and Society* 12, no. 1 (1983): 53–82. https://doi.org/10.1177/003232928301200102.

Elkins, Caroline, and Susan Pedersen. "Settler Colonialism: A Concept and Its Uses." In *Settler Colonialism in the Twentieth Century: Projects, Practices, Legacies,* edited by Caroline Elkins and Susan Pedersen, 1–20. New York: Routledge, 2005.

Elleman, Bruce A., and Stephen Kotkin, eds. *Manchurian Railways and the Opening of China: An International History.* Armonk, NY: M.E. Sharpe, 2010.

Endō, Homare. *Japanese Girl at the Siege of Changchun: How I Survived China's Wartime Atrocity.* Translated by Michael Brase. Berkeley, CA: Stone Bridge Press, 2016.

Endō Masataka. *Kindai Nihon no shokuminchi tōchi ni okeru kokuseki to koseki: Manshū, Chōsen, Taiwan.* Tokyo: Akashi shoten, 2010.

Enselme, H. *A travers la Mandchourie: Le Chemin de fer de l'est Chinois d'après la mission du Capitaine H. de Bouillane de Lacoste et du Capitaine Enselme.* Paris: J. Rueff, 1904.

Eppstein, Ury. "Musical Means to Political Ends: Japanese School Songs in Manchuria – Songs before the Establishment of Manchukuo." In *Kyoto Conference on Japanese Studies, 1994,* vol. 3, 209–27. Kyoto: International Research Center for Japanese Studies, 1996.

Esselstrom, Erik. *Crossing Empire's Edge: Foreign Ministry Police and Japanese Expansionism in Northeast Asia.* Honolulu: University of Hawai'i Press, 2009.

F[arley], M[irriam] S. "Japanese Alarmed by Rising Cost of Living." *Far Eastern Survey* 6, no. 6 (1937): 65–66. https://doi.org/10.2307/3022570.

Fatica, Michele. "The Beginning and the End of the Idyllic Relations between Mussolini's Italy and Chiang Kai-shek's China (1930–1937)." In *Italy's Encounters with Modern China: Imperial Dreams, Strategic Ambitions,* edited by Maurizio Marinelli and Giovanni Andornino, 89–115. London: Palgrave Macmillan, 2014.

Fei Cui, and Ren Zhaoxiang. "Zhao Xinbo Ju'e Yichan'an Jiemi." *Longmen zhen* 10 (2013): 84.

Finn, Dallas. *Meiji Revisited: The Sites of Victorian Japan.* New York: Weatherhill, 1995.

Fishman, Robert. *Urban Utopias in the Twentieth Century: Ebenezer Howard, Frank Lloyd Wright, and Le Corbusier.* New York: Basic Books, 1977.

Fleming, Peter. *One's Company: A Journey to China.* London: Jonathan Cape, 1934.

Fogel, Joshua A. "Integrating into Chinese Society: A Comparison of the Japanese Communities of Shanghai and Harbin." In *Japan's Competing Modernities: Issues in Culture and Democracy, 1900–1930,* edited by Sharon Minichiello, 45–69. Honolulu: University of Hawai'i Press, 1998.

–. *The Literature of Travel in the Japanese Rediscovery of China, 1862–1945.* Stanford, CA: Stanford University Press, 1996.

–. *Politics and Sinology: The Case of Naitō Konan (1866–1934).* Cambridge, MA: Harvard University Press, 1984.

–. "'Shanghai-Japan': The Japanese Residents' Association of Shanghai." *Journal of Asian Studies* 59, no. 4 (2000): 927–50. https://doi.org/10.2307/2659217.

Fox, John P. *Germany and the Far Eastern Crisis, 1931–1938.* Oxford: Clarendon Press, 1982.

Frieden, Jeffry A. "International Investment and Colonial Control: A New Interpretation." *International Organization* 48, no. 4 (1994): 559–93.

Fruin, W. Mark. *Kikkoman: Company, Clan, and Community.* Cambridge, MA: Harvard University Press, 1983.

Fujime, Yuki. "The Licensed Prostitution System and the Prostitution Abolition Movement in Modern Japan." *positions* 5, no. 1 (1997): 135–70. https://doi.org/10.1215/10679847-5-1-135.

Fujimori Terunobu. *Nihon no kindai kenchiku.* 2 vols. Tokyo: Iwanami shoten, 1993.

Fujimori Terunobu, and Wang Tan, eds. *Zenchōsa higashi Ajia kindai no toshi to kenchiku.* Tokyo: Taisei kensetsu, 1996.

Fujimoto, Shigeo. "Trans-Pacific Boy Scout Movement in the Early Twentieth Century: The Case of the Boy Scout Movement in Osaka, Japan." *Australasian Journal of American Studies* 7, no. 2 (2008): 29–43.

Fujise Takayuki. "Kanjōshi wa ekizochikku Roshiajin machi de atta." In Chōshun Kanjōshikai, *Kanjōshi monogatari,* 71.

Fukuhara Masao. "Chūgoku Chōshunshi ni okeru Nihon teian sakutei to sono igi." *Geijutsu: Ōsaka geijutsu daigaku kiyō* 22 (1999): 154–64.

Fung, Edmund S.K. "Anti-Imperialism and the Left Guomindang." *Modern China* 11, no. 1 (1985): 39–76.

Gaimushō tsūshōkyoku. *Chōshun no jijō.* N.p.: Gaimushō, 1929.

Germann, Georg. *Gothic Revival in Europe and Britain: Sources, Influences and Ideas.* Translated by Gerald Onn. Cambridge, MA: MIT Press, 1972.

Giddens, Anthony. *The Constitution of Society.* Berkeley: University of California Press, 1984.

Gillin, Donald, and Charles Etter. "Staying On: Japanese Soldiers and Civilians in China, 1945–1949." *Journal of Asian Studies* 42, no. 3 (1983): 497–518. https://doi.org/10.2307/2055515.

Gillin, Donald G., and Ramon H. Myers, eds. *Last Chance in Manchuria: The Diary of Chang Kia-ngau.* Stanford, CA: Stanford University Press, 1989.

Ginsburg, Norton. "Ch'ang-ch'un." *Economic Geography* 23, no. 4 (1947): 290–307. https://doi.org/10.2307/141787.

Glantz, David M. *The Soviet Strategic Offensive in Manchuria, 1945: "August Storm."* London: Frank Cass, 2003. https://doi.org/10.4324/9780203496244.

Gluck, Carol. *Japan's Modern Myths: Ideology in the Late Meiji Period.* Princeton, NJ: Princeton University Press, 1985.

Goodman, David S.G. *China's Campaign to "Open the West": National, Provincial, and Local Perspectives.* Cambridge: Cambridge University Press, 2004.

Gordon, Andrew. *Labor and Imperial Democracy in Prewar Japan.* Berkeley: University of California Press, 1992.

Gottschang, Thomas R., and Diana Lary. *Swallows and Settlers: The Great Migration from North China to Manchuria.* Ann Arbor: University of Michigan Press, 2000. https://doi.org/10.3998/mpub.22808.

Greaves, Percy L., Jr. "Marshall Comes on Stage: The Real Infamy of Pearl Harbor." *Journal of Historical Review* 4, no. 4 (1983): 425–36.

Greener, William. *A Secret Agent in Port Arthur.* London: Archibald Constable, 1905.

Gries, Peter Hays. "China's 'New Thinking' on Japan." *China Quarterly* 184, no. 1 (2005): 831–50. https://doi.org/10.1017/S0305741005000524.

Grove, Richard H. *Ecology, Climate and Empire: Colonialism and Global Environment History, 1400–1940.* Cambridge, UK: White Horse Press, 1997.

Guo, Qinghua. "Changchun: Unfinished Capital Planning of Manzhouguo, 1932–1942." *Urban History* 31, no. 1 (2004): 100–17. https://doi.org/10.1017/S0963926804001804.

Hall, Andrew. "The Word Is Mightier Than the Throne: Bucking Colonial Education Trends in Manchukuo." *Journal of Asian Studies* 68, no. 3 (2009): 895–925. https://doi.org/10.1017/S002191180999009X.

Hall, Russell E. "Expanding Airways in the Far East." *Far Eastern Survey* 6, no. 9 (1937): 95–101. https://doi.org/10.2307/3022280.

Han, Jung-sun N. "Empire of Comic Visions: Japanese Cartoon Journalism and Its Pictorial Statements on Korea, 1876–1910." *Japanese Studies* 26, no. 3 (2006): 283–302. https://doi.org/10.1080/10371390600986637.

Han, Suk-jung. "The Problem of Sovereignty: Manchukuo, 1932–1937." *positions* 12, no. 2 (2004): 457–78. https://doi.org/10.1215/10679847-12-2-457.

Han Jinrong et al. "Changchun ZhongRi renming youhao shuichan jingshui jishu de weishengxue diaocha yu pingjie." *Zhongguo weisheng gongchengxue zazhi* 1, no. 1 (1992): 22–24.

Handō Kazutoshi. *Soren ga Manshū ni shinkō shita natsu.* Tokyo: Bungei shunjū, 1999.

Hanes, Jeffrey E. *The City as Subject: Seki Hajime and the Reinvention of Modern Osaka.* Berkeley: University of California Press, 2002.

Harris, Sheldon H. *Factories of Death: Japanese Biological Warfare, 1932–1945, and the American Cover-Up.* Rev. ed. London: Routledge, 2002.

Hashiya Hiroshi. *Teikoku Nihon to shokuminchi toshi.* Tokyo: Yoshikawa kōbunkan, 2004.

Haslam, Jonathan. *The Soviet Union and the Threat from the East.* Pittsburgh: University of Pittsburgh Press, 1992.

Haslund-Christensen, Henning. "In the Mongol Encampments, 1937." *Journal of the Royal Central Asian Society* 25, no. 2 (1938): 175–92. https://doi.org/10.108%3068373808730849.

Hatano Sumio. *Taiheiyō sensō to Ajia gaikō.* Tokyo: Tōkyō daigaku shuppansha, 1996.

Hattori Noboru. *Manshū.* Tokyo: Seikyōsha, 1913.

Hayase Shinzo. "The Japanese Residents of 'Dabao-kuo'." In *The Philippines under Japan: Occupation Policy and Reaction,* edited by Ikehata Setsuho and Ricardo Trota Jose, 247–87. Quezon City, PH: Ateneo de Manila University Press, 1999.

Heinzig, Dieter. *The Soviet Union and Communist China, 1945–1950: The Arduous Road to the Alliance.* Armonk, NY: M.E. Sharpe, 2004.

Henry, Todd A. *Assimilating Seoul: Japanese Rule and the Politics of Public Space in Colonial Korea, 1910–1945.* Berkeley: University of California Press, 2014. https://doi.org/10.1525/california/9780520276550.001.0001.

Hersey, George L. *High Victorian Gothic: A Study in Associationism.* Baltimore, MD: Johns Hopkins University Press, 1972.

Hideshima Tsutomu. "Manshū ni okeru toshi keikaku to shūdan jūkusei." *Jūtaku* 27, no. 6 (1942): 174–82.

Hirano, Ken'ichiro. "State Forging and Nation-Destroying: The Case of the Concordia Association of Manchukuo." *East Asian Cultural Studies* 25, nos. 1–4 (1986): 37–57.

Historical Section, Foreign Office. *Manchuria.* London: His Majesty's Stationery Office, 1920.

Hitchcock, Henry-Russell, and Philip Johnson. *The International Style.* New York: W.W. Norton, 1995.

Horiguchi, Noriko J. *Women Adrift: The Literature of Japan's Imperial Body.* Minneapolis: University of Minnesota Press, 2012.

Hoshino Tatsuo, ed., *Manshū shuyō toshi shōkō benran.* Dairen: Minami Manshū tetsudō chihōbu shōkōka, 1935.

Hosie, Alexander. *Manchuria: Its People, Resources and Recent History.* New York: C. Scribner's, 1904.

Hōten tetsudō kyoku ryokaku gakari. *Shinkyō.* Hōten: Man Hōten tetsudō kyoku ryokyaku kakari, 1941.

Hotta, Eri. *Pan-Asianism and Japan's War, 1931–1945.* New York: Palgrave Macmillan, 2007.

Hu Chang and Gu Quan. *Manying: Guoce dianying mianmian guan.* Beijing: Zhonghua shuju chubanshe, 1990.

Huang, Philip C.C. "Biculturality in Modern China and in Chinese Studies." *Modern China* 26, no. 1 (2000): 3–31. https://doi.org/10.1177/009770040002600101.

Huffman, James. *Creating a Public: People and Press in Meiji Japan.* Honolulu: University of Hawai'i Press, 1997.

Hunt, Michael H. *Frontier Defense and the Open Door: Manchuria in Chinese-American Relations, 1895–1911.* New Haven, CT: Yale University Press, 1973.

Iacobelli, Pedro. "The Vatican's Shift of Its Missionary Policy in the Twentieth Century: The Mission of the Augustinian Fathers of the Assumption in Manchuria." *Asian Cultural Studies* 36 (2010): 91–104.

Iguchi, Haruo. *Unfinished Business: Ayukawa Yoshisuke and U.S.–Japan Relations, 1937–1953.* Cambridge, MA: Harvard University Press, 2003.

Ikemiyagi Sumiko. "Shinkyō: shūsen zengo no watakushi no omidasu." In *Heiwa no ishizue: rōku taiken shuki; kaigai hikiagesha ga katari tsugu rōku 7,* edited by Heiwa kinen jigyō tokubetsu kikin, 244–58. Tokyo: Heiwa kinen jigyō tokubetsu kikin, 1997. http://www.heiwakinen.jp/library/shiryokan/hikiage07.html.

Iklé, Frank W. "The Triple Intervention. Japan's Lesson in the Diplomacy of Imperialism." *Monumenta Nipponica* 22, nos. 1/2 (1967): 122–30. https://doi.org/10.2307/2383226.

Imperial Japanese Government Railways. *An Official Guide to Eastern Asia: Trans-Continental Connections between Europe and Asia*. Vol. 1, *Manchuria and Chōsen*. Tokyo: Imperial Japanese Government Railways, 1913.

Imperial Maritime Customs of China. *The Soya Bean of Manchuria*. Shanghai: Statistical Department of the Inspectorate General of Customs, 1911.

Inoue Masaaki, Sakaguchi Jirō, and Tokutomi Ichirō, eds. *Hakushaku Kiyoura Keigo den*. Vol. 2. Tokyo: Hakushaku Kiyoura Keigo den kankōkai, 1935.

Inoue Nobuō. *Chōshun enkakushi*. Dairen: ManMō bunka kyōkai, 1922.

Inoue Shōichi. *Senjika Nihon no kenchikuka: āto, kitchu, Japanesuku*. Tokyo: Asahi shinbunsha, 1995.

"The International Opium Commission." *British Medical Journal* 1910, no. 1, 93–97. https://doi.org/10.1136/bmj.1.2558.93.

Inuzuka Yasuhiro. "Shinkyō dōshokubutsuen kō." *Chiba daigaku daigakuin jinbun shakai kagaku kenkyūka* 18, no. 2 (2009): 15–25.

Ion, A. Hamish. *The Cross and the Rising Sun*. Vol. 2, *The British Protestant Missionary Movement in Japan, Korea, and Taiwan, 1865–1945*. Waterloo, ON: Wilfrid Laurier University Press, 1993.

–. *The Cross and the Rising Sun*. Vol. 1, *The Canadian Protestant Missionary Movement in the Japanese Empire, 1872–1931*. Waterloo, ON: Wilfrid Laurier University Press, 1990.

–. *The Cross in the Dark Valley: The Canadian Protestant Missionary Movement in the Japanese Empire, 1931–1945*. Waterloo, ON: Wilfrid Laurier University Press, 1999.

Iriye, Akira. "Chang Hsüeh-liang and the Japanese." *Journal of Asian Studies* 20, no. 1 (1960): 33–43. https://doi.org/10.2307/2050070.

–. "Kayahara Kazan and Japanese Cosmopolitanism." In *Personality in Japanese History*, edited by Albert M. Craig and Donald H. Shively, 373–98. Berkeley: University of California Press, 1970.

–. *Pacific Estrangement: Japanese and American Expansion, 1897–1911*. Cambridge, MA: Harvard University Press, 1972.

Isett, Christopher M. *State, Peasant, and Merchant in Qing Manchuria, 1644–1862*. Stanford, CA: Stanford University Press, 2007.

Ishida Takehiko. "Chūgoku tōhoku ni okeru ryōsan no dōkō: Manshū jihen mae ni okeru." *Hokkaidō daigaku keizaigaku kenkyū* 24, no. 1 (1974): 141–94.

Ito, Chuta. "Characteristics of Chinese Architecture." *Contemporary Japan* 9, no. 1 (1940): 25–37.

Itō, Takeo. *Life along the South Manchurian Railway: The Memoirs of Ito Takeo*. Translated by Joshua Fogel. Armonk, NY: M.E. Sharpe, 1988.

Itoh, Mayumi. *Japanese War Orphans in Manchuria: Forgotten Victims of World War II*. New York: Palgrave Macmillan, 2010.

–. *Pioneers of Sino-Japanese Relations: Liao and Takasaki*. New York: Palgrave Macmillan, 2012.

Iyenaga, Toyokichi. "Japan in South Manchuria." In *Japan and Japanese-American Relations*, edited by George H. Blakeslee, 249–74. New York: G.E. Stechert, 1912.

Izumi Renji. *Chōshun jijō*. Chōshun: Chōshun Nihōsha, 1912.

James, H.E.M. "A Journey in Manchuria." *Proceedings of the Royal Geographical Society and Monthly Record of Geography* 9, no. 9 (1887): 531–67. https://doi.org/10.2307/1801414.

–. *The Long White Mountain, or, A Journey in Manchuria*. London: Longmans, Green, 1888.

Janhunen, Juha. *Manchuria: An Ethnic History*. Helsinki: Finno-Ugrian Society, 1996.

"Japanese Aroused by Weakness of Civil Aviation." *Far Eastern Survey* 4, no. 8 (1935): 62–63. https://doi.org/10.2307/3021498.

Jennings, John M. *The Opium Empire: Japanese Imperialism and Drug Trafficking in Asia, 1895–1945*. Westport, CT: Praeger, 1997.

Jie Xueshi. *Wei Manzhouguo shi*. Rev. ed. Beijing: Renmin chubansi, 1995.

Jilinsheng difangzhi bianzuan weiyuanhui. *Jilin shengzhi*. Vol. 39, *Wenhua yishuzhi/shehui wenhua*. Changchun: Jilin renmin chubanshe, 1992.

Jin Bidong. *ManMō no chishiki*. Tokyo: Hibonkaku, 1934.

Johnson, Chalmers A. *An Instance of Treason: Ozaki Hotsumi and the Sorge Spy Ring*. Stanford, CA: Stanford University Press, 1990.

Johnson, David A. "A British Empire for the Twentieth Century: The Inauguration of New Delhi, 1931." *Urban History* 35, no. 3 (2008): 462–84.

Jones, F.C. "The Role of Manchuria in Communist Strategy." *World Today* 6, no. 5 (1950): 196–205.

Jones, Francis C. "Recent Developments in Manchuria." *Journal of the Royal Central Asian Society* 44, no. 2 (1957): 116–23. https://doi.org/10.108%3068375708731601.

Jowett, Philip S. *Rays of the Rising Sun: Armed Forces of Japan's Asian Allies, 1931–1945*. Vol. 1. *China and Manchukuo*. Solihull, UK: Helion, 2004.

Ju Zhifen. "Northern Chinese Laborers and Manchukuo." In *Asian Labor in the Wartime Japanese Empire: Unknown Histories*, edited by Paul H. Kratoska, 61–78. Armonk, NY: M.E. Sharpe, 2005.

Kamishima Jirō. *Kindai Nihon no seishin kōzō*. Tokyo: Iwanami, 1961.

Kantōgun shireibu, ed. *Minami Manshū shuyō toshi keizai jōtai*. 2 vols. N.p.: Kantōgun shireibu, 1924.

Kasza, Gregory J. *The State and the Mass Media in Japan, 1918–1945*. Berkeley: University of California Press, 1988.

Kawabata Motoh. "Senzen-senchūki ni okeru hyakkaten no kaigai shinshutsu to sono yōin." *Keieigaku ronshū* 49, no. 1 (2009): 1–22.

Kawabata Sadao. "Denryoku fuzoku no fu'an to sono taisaku." *Manshū dengyō kabushiki kaisha chōsa shiryō* 2, no. 2 (1940): 63–74.

Kawazoe, Noboru. *Contemporary Japanese Architecture*. Translated by David Griffith. Tokyo: Kokusai bunka shinkokai, 1965.

Keene, Donald. "The Sino-Japanese War of 1894–95 and Its Cultural Effects in Japan." In *Tradition and Modernization in Japanese Culture*, edited by Donald H. Shively, 121–75. Princeton, NJ: Princeton University Press, 1971.

Kenchiku gakkai Shinkyō shibu. "Kokuto kensetsu keikaku ni tsuite." *Kenchiku zasshi* 13, no. 9 (1938): 167–82.

Kennedy, Malcolm Duncan. "The Diaries of Captain Malcolm Duncan Kennedy, 1917–1946." Unpublished diary transcripts. University of Sheffield Library. http://librarysupport.shef.ac.uk/kennedy_diaries.pdf.

Kiba Akeshi. "Gi Manshūkou shuto Shinkyō no Nihon bukyō ni yoru Manshū bukyō soshikika no mosaku." *Ōtani gakuhō* 81, no. 4 (2002): 1–11.

Kikuchi, Yuko. "Hybridity and the Oriental Orientalism of 'Mingei' Theory." *Journal of Design History* 10, no. 4 (1997): 343–54. https://doi.org/10.1093/jdh/10.4.343.

–. "The Myth of Yanagi's Originality: The Formation of 'Mingei' Theory in Its Social and Historical Context." *Journal of Design History* 7, no. 4 (1994): 247–66. https://doi.org/10.1093/jdh/7.4.247.

Kim, Jaeeun. "The Colonial State, Migration, and Diasporic Nationhood in Korea." *Comparative Studies in Society and History* 56, no. 1 (2014): 34–66. https://doi.org/10.1017/S0010417513000613.

Kim, Michael. "The Lost Memories of Empire and the Korean Return from Manchuria, 1945–1950: Conceptualizing Manchuria in Modern Korean History." *Seoul Journal of Korean Studies* 23, no. 2 (2010): 207–12.

King, Anthony. "Rethinking Colonialism: An Epilogue." In *Forms of Dominance: On the Architecture and Urbanism of the Colonial Enterprise,* edited by Nezar AlSayyad, 339–55. Aldershot, UK: Avebury, 1992.

King, Franklin Hiram. *Farmers of Forty Centuries, or, Permanent Agriculture in China, Korea and Japan.* London: Cape, 1939. First published 1911.

Kingsberg, Miriam. *Moral Nation: Modern Japan and Narcotics in Global History.* Berkeley: University of California Press, 2014.

Kinmonth, Earl H. "The Impact of Military Procurements on the Old Middle Classes in Japan, 1931–1941." *Japan Forum* 4, no. 2 (1992): 247–65. https://doi.org/10.108%9555809208721460.

–. "The Mouse That Roared: Saitō Takao, Conservative Critic of Japan's 'Holy War' in China." *Journal of Japanese Studies* 25, no. 2 (1999): 331–60. https://doi.org/10.2307/133315.

–. *The Self-Made Man in Meiji Japanese Thought: From Samurai to Salary Man.* Berkeley: University of California Press, 1981.

Kirby, William C. *Germany and Republican China.* Stanford, CA: Stanford University Press, 1984.

Kirk, Grayson. "Wings over the Pacific." *Foreign Affairs* 20, no. 2 (1942): 293–302. https://doi.org/10.2307/20029151.

Kishi Toshihiko. *Manshūkoku no bijiuaru mejia.* Tokyo: Yoshikawa kōbunkan, 2010.

Kishima Katsumi, ed. *Shina jūtaku shi.* Dairen: Mantetsu, 1932.

Kitakōji Ken and Watanabe Manabu. *Chōshun, Kitsurin.* Tokyo: Kokusho kankōkai, 1982.

Kitaoka Shin'ichi. *Gotō Shinpei: gaiko to bijyon.* Tokyo: Chūō kōronsha, 1988.

Kiyoshi, Miki. "The China Affair and Japanese Thought." *Contemporary Japan* 6, no. 4 (1938): 601–10.

Kō En. "Soshakuchi mejia Dairen shinbun to Manshū hakkei." *Jyaanaru obu gurobaru mejia stajiizu* 4 (2009): 21–33.

Kobayashi Tatsuo, Shimada Toshihiko, and Inaba Masao, eds. *Gendaishi shiryō 11: zoku: Manshū jihen.* Tokyo: Misuzu shobō, 1965.

Kōjima, Reikichi. "The Population of the Prefectures and Cities of Japan in Most Recent Times." Translated by Edwin G. Beal, Jr. *Far Eastern Quarterly* 3, no. 4 (1944): 313–61. https://doi.org/10.2307/2049031.

Kokumuin sōmuchō jōhōsho. *Manshūkoku no gairan.* Shinkyō: Shinkyō kōshō, 1934.

Kokumuin sōmuchō tōkeisho. *Manshū teikoku genjū kokō tōkei.* Shinkyō: Kokumuin sōmuchō, 1936.

Kokutai no hongi: Cardinal Principles of the National Entity of Japan. Edited by Robert King Hall. Translated by John Owen Gauntlett. Cambridge, MA: Harvard University Press, 1949.

Komagome Takeshi. *Shokuminchi teikoku Nihon no bunka tōgō.* Tokyo: Iwanami shoten, 1996.

Komine Kazuo. *Manchuria: kigen, shokumin, haken.* Tokyo: Ochanomizu shobō, 1991.

Koshizawa Akira. *Harupin no toshi keikaku, 1898–1945.* Tokyo: Sōwasha, 1989.

–. *Manshūkoku no shuto keikaku: Tōkyō no genzai to mirai o tou.* Tokyo: Nihon keizai hyōronsha, 1988.

–. "Shinkyō to Daitōkō no kensetsu kōsō." *Doboku gakkaishi* 78, no. 8 (1993): 22–25.

–. "Taiwan, Manshū, Chūgoku no toshi keikaku." In *Kindai Nihon to shokuminchi*. Vol. 3., edited by Ōe Shinobu, Asada Kyōji, Mitani Taichirō, Gotō Ken'ichi, Kobayashi Hideo, Takasaki Sōji, Wakabayashi Masatake, and Kawamura Minato, 183–241. Tokyo: Iwanami shoten, 1993.

Kouchiyama Tsunetaka. *Sono toki: sen'in wa dōsuru*. Tokyo: Bungeisha, 2006.

Kramer, Paul, ed. *The Last Manchu: The Autobiography of Henry PuYi, Last Emperor of China*. New York: Pocket, 1987.

Kratoska, Paul H., ed. *Asian Labor in the Wartime Japanese Empire: Unknown Histories*. Armonk, NY: M.E. Sharpe, 2005.

Kung, James Kai-sing, and Nan Li. "Commercialization as Exogenous Shocks: The Effect of the Soybean Trade on Migration in Manchurian Villages, 1895–1934." *Explorations in Economic History* 48, no. 4 (2011): 568–89. https://doi.org/10.1016/j.eeh.2011.07.002.

Kurahashi Masano. *Kita no karayukisan*. Tokyo: Kyōei shobō, 1989.

Kuroda Kashirō. *Manshū kiyō*. 2 vols. N.p.: Mantetsu, 1910.

Kuropatkin, Aleksey. *The Russian Army and the Japanese War: Being Historical and Critical Comments on the Military Policy and Power of Russia and on the Campaign in the Far East*. Translated by Captain A.B. Lindsay, edited by Major E.D. Swinton. 2 vols. New York: E.P. Dutton, 1909.

Kushner, Barak. *The Thought War: Japanese Imperial Propaganda*. Honolulu: University of Hawai'i Press, 2006.

Kuwahara Kineo. *Manshū Shōwa jūgonen*. Tokyo: Shōbunsha, 1975.

Kwong, Chi Man. "Finance and the Northern Expedition: From the Northeast Asian Perspective, 1925–1928." *Modern Asian Studies* 48, no. 6 (2014): 1695–739. https://doi.org/10.1017/S0026749X13000139.

"Kyō no Manshū jūtaku den." *Gendai kenchiku* 4 (September 1939): 62–63.

Lane, Barbara Miller. *Architecture and Politics in Germany, 1918–1945*. Cambridge, MA: Harvard University Press, 1968.

Lannay, Léon. "Hsinking: Capitale du Manchoukouo." *Echos Missionnaires* 17 (April 1945): 117–19.

Lattimore, Owen. "The Phantom of Mengkukuo." *Pacific Affairs* 10, no. 4 (1937): 420–27. https://doi.org/10.2307/2750626.

Lee, Chong-sik. *Revolutionary Struggle in Manchuria: Chinese Communism and Soviet Interest, 1922–1945*. Berkeley: University of California Press, 1983.

Lee, Leo Ou-fan. *Shanghai Modern: The Flowering of a New Urban Culture in China, 1930–1945*. Cambridge, MA: Harvard University Press, 1999.

Lee, Robert H.G. *The Manchurian Frontier in Ch'ing History*. Cambridge, MA: Harvard University Press, 1970. https://doi.org/10.4159/harvard.9780674430709.

Leeming, Frank. "Reconstructing Late Ch'ing Fengt'ien." *Modern Asian Studies* 4, no. 4 (1970): 305–24. https://doi.org/10.1017/S0026749X00011999.

Lefebvre, Henri. *The Production of Space*. Translated by Donald Nicholson-Smith. Malden, MA: Blackwell, 1991.

Lensen, George Alexander. *The Strange Neutrality: Soviet–Japanese Relations during the Second World War, 1941–1945*. Tallahassee, FL: Diplomatic Press, 1972.

"Les Russes en Asie." *Annales de géographie* 10, no. 49 (1901): 89. https://doi.org/10.3406/geo.1901.4837.

Levine, Steven I. *Anvil of Victory: The Communist Revolution in Manchuria, 1945–1948*. New York: Columbia University Press, 1987.

Li, Lincoln. *The China Factor in Modern Japanese Thought: The Case of Tachibana Shiraki, 1881–1945*. Albany: State University of New York Press, 1996.

Li Zhenquan, Li Chenggu, and Zhou Jianwu. "Shilun Changchunshi shangye diyu jiegou." *Dili Kexue* 9, no. 2 (1989): 133–41.

Liaoningsheng Huludaoshi zhengfu shinwen bangongshi Liaoningsheng shehui kexueyuan, ed. *Huludao baiwan Riqiao daqianfan.* Beijing: Wuzhou chuanbo chubanshe, 2005.

Lim Hua Sing. "Japan's Official Development Assistance to China, Indonesia, and Singapore." In *APEC and Development Co-operation,* edited by Mohamed Ariff, 48–89. Singapore: Institute of Southeast Asian Studies, 1998.

Lin, Man-houng. "China's 'Dual Economy' in International Trade Relations, 1842–1949." In *Japan, China, and the Growth of the Asian International Economy, 1850–1949,* edited by Kaoru Sugihara, 179–97. New York: Oxford University Press, 2005.

–. "Interpretive Trends in Taiwan's Scholarship on Chinese Business History: 1600 to the Present." *Chinese Studies in History* 31, no. 3–4 (1998): 65–94. https://doi.org/10.2753/CSH0009-463331030465.

–. "Nihon no kaigunryoku to kyōkyō no chūtai: 1930 nendai no Taiwan Manshū aida bōeki o chūshin." In *Shōwa Ajia shugi no jitsuzō: teikoku Nihon to Taiwan, "Nan'yō," "Minami Shina,"* edited by Matsuura Masataka, 344–71. Kyoto: Minerva, 2007.

Liu, Laurence G. *Chinese Architecture.* London: Academy Editions, 1989.

Lloyd, W.V. "Notes on the Russian Harbours of the Coast of Manchuria." *Journal of the Royal Geographical Society of London* 37 (1867): 212–31. https://doi.org/10.2307/1798527.

Lu, Hanchao. "Arrested Development: Cotton and Cotton Markets in Shanghai, 1350–1853." *Modern China* 18, no. 4 (1992): 468–99. https://doi.org/10.1177/009770049201800404.

Lu, Sidney Xu. "Good Women for Empire: Educating Overseas Female Emigrants in Imperial Japan, 1900–45." *Journal of Global History* 8, no. 3 (2013): 436–60. https://doi.org/10.1017/S1740022813000363.

Lu Minghui. *Tonghua "2-3" shijian* Beijing: Shijie zhishi chubanshe, 2006.

Maeda Seiichi. *Manshūkoku to tensai tōgyō.* Tokyo: Maeda Seiichi, 1932.

Makuuchi Mitsuo. *Manshūkoku keisatsu gaishi.* Tokyo: San'ichi seibō, 1996.

The Manchoukuo Year Book, 1942. Ajia tōkeisha, 1942.

"Manchuria as a Demographic Frontier." *Population Index* 11, no. 4 (1945): 260–74.

Manshikai, ed. *Manshū kaihatsu yonjūnenshi.* 3 vols. Tokyo: Manshū kaihatsu yonjūnenshi kankōkai, 1964–65.

Manshū dengyō gaishi hen i'inkai. *Omoidasu no Manshū dengyō.* Vol. 2, "*Supōtsu–bunka.*" Tokyo: Manshū dengyō kai, 1977.

Manshū jijō annaijo. *Kitsurin jijō.* Shinkyō: Manshū jijō annaijo, 1941.

–. *Manshū kōsan gaiyō.* Shinkyō: Manshū jijō annaijo, 1940.

–, ed. *Manshūkoku chihōshi.* Shinkyō: Manshū jijō annaijo, 1940.

–. *Shinkyō jijō.* Shinkyō: Manshū jijō annaijo, 1934.

Manshū kaikoshū kankōkai, ed. *Aa Manshū: kuni tsukuri sangyō kaihatsusha no shuki.* Tokyo: Manshū kaikoshū kankōkai, 1965.

Manshū keizai jijō annaijo. *Kokuto Shinkyō keizai jijō.* Dairen: Manshū bunka kyōkai, 1933.

Manshū kōkō gijitsu'in kyōkai. *Manshū kōkō nenkan Kōtoku jūichi nenpan.* Shinkyō: TōA bunka toshokan kabushiki kaisha, 1944.

Manshū teikoku chishitsu chōsajo. *Chishitsu chōsajo sanjūichi nen shi.* Shinkyō: Manshū teikoku chishitsu chōsajo, 1940.

Manshū teikoku genjū jinkō tōkei. Shinkyō: Manshū teikoku chianbu keimushi, 1940.

Manshū teikoku genjū jinkō tōkei: Kōtoku shichinen jūgatsu tsuitachi genzai. Shinkyō: Kokumuin sōmuchō tōkeisho, Kokumuin Chianbu keimushi, 1942.

Manshū teikoku genjū kokō tōkei. Shinkyō: Chianbu keimushi, 1939.

Manshū teikoku kyōwakai, ed. *Manshū teikoku kyōwakai soshiki enkakushi.* Tokyo: Funi shuppan, 1982.

Manshū teikoku minseibu kyōikushi. *Manshū teikoku gakuji yōran.* Shinkyō: Manshū teikoku minseibu kyōikushi, 1940.

Manshū teikoku rinji kokuto kensetsu kyoku. *Kokuto kensetsu ni tsuite.* N.p.: Manshū teikoku rinji kokuto kensetsu kyoku, 1940.

Manshū tetsudō kabushiki kaisha chihōbu nōmuka. *Manshū zairai nōgyō.* Dairen: Manshū tetsudō chihōbu, 1935.

Manshūkoku jitsugyōbu rinji sangyō chōsakyoku. *Komugiko narabi ni seiko kōgyō ni kansuru chōsasho.* Shinkyō: Manshūkoku tosho kabushiki kaisha, 1937.

–. *Manshūkoku juyō shōhin gaikoku bōseki tōkei.* Shinkyō: (Manshūkoku) Jitsugyōbu rinji sangyō chōsakyoku, 1937.

Manshūkoku kōgyō kantoku. *Manshūkoku kōku.* Shinkyō: Manshū kōgyō kyōkai, 1939.

Manshūkoku kokumuin kōhōsho. *Manchoukuo: A Comprehensive Pictorial Presentation.* Tokyo: Asahi shinbunsha, 1942.

"Manshūkoku kokuto kensetsu keikakuhō no kaishō." *Toshi mondai* 28, no. 2 (1939): 116–17.

Manshūkoku sangyōbu. *Nikuchiku jukyū ni kansuru chōsa hōkokusho.* Shinkyō: Manshūkoku sangyōbu daijin kanbō shiryōka, 1938.

Manshūkoku seifu kokumuin kokuto kensetsukyoku. *Kokuto daiShinkyō.* Shinkyō: Manshūkoku seifu kokuto kensetsukyoku, 1933.

Manshūkoku tsūshinsha, ed. *Manshūkoku gensei.* Tokyo: Hōwa shuppan, 1986.

–. *Manshū kaitaku nenkan.* Shinkyō: Manshūkoku tsūshinsha, 1942.

Manshūkokushi hensan kankōkai. *Manshūkokushi.* 2 vols. Tokyo: Kokusai zenrin kyōkai, 1973.

"Mantetsu birujingu shinchiku kōji." *Doboku kenchiku kōji kahō* 12, no. 6 (1936): 298–303.

Mantetsu keikakubu gyōmuka. *Manshū shuyō kaisha teikanshū.* Dairen: Manshū keizai kenkyūkai, 1934.

Mantetsu no kenchiku to gijutsujin henshū i'inkai. *Mantetsu no kenchiku to gijutsujin.* Tokyo: Mantetsu kenchikukai, 1976.

Mantetsu sōkyoku. *Shinkyō.* Hōten: Mantetsu, 1937.

–. *Minami Manshū ni okeru sekitangyō.* Dairen: Mantetsu, 1930.

Mantetsukai. *Mantetsu yonjūnen shi.* Tokyo: Yoshikawa kōbunkan, 2007.

Marks, Steven G. *Road to Power: The Trans-Siberian Railroad and the Colonization of Asian Russia, 1850–1917.* Ithaca, NY: Cornell University Press, 1991.

Masuda Hajimu. "Rumors of War: Immigration Disputes and the Social Construction of American-Japanese Relations, 1905–1913." *Diplomatic History* 33, no. 1 (2009): 1–37. https://doi.org/10.1111/j.1467-7709.2008.00745.x.

Matsumiya Kichirō, ed. *Shinkyō.* Hōten: Mantetsu tetsudō sōkyoku eigyōkyoku ryōkyokuka, 1937.

Matsumura Takao. "Shinkyō, Nōan pesuto ryūkō (1940-nen) to 731 butai." *Mita gakkai zasshi* 95, no. 4 (2003): 13–34 and 96, no. 3 (2003): 121–49.

Matsusaburō Dazai. *Manshū gendaishi.* Dairen: Mantetsu, 1925.

Matsusaka, Yoshihisa Tak. *The Making of Japanese Manchuria, 1904–1932.* Cambridge, MA: Harvard University Press, 2003. https://doi.org/10.2307/j.ctt1tfjc1r.

Matsuura Rō. *Shinkyō kyoryūminkai shi.* Shinkyō: Shinkyō kyoryūminkai, 1936.

McCormack, Gavan. *Chang Tso-lin in Northeast China, 1911–1928: China, Japan, and the Manchurian Idea.* Stanford, CA: Stanford University Press, 1977.

Metcalf, Thomas R. *An Imperial Vision: Indian Architecture and Britain's Raj.* Berkeley: University of California Press, 1989.

Metzler, Mark. *Lever of Empire: The International Gold Standard and the Crisis of Liberalism in Prewar Japan*. Berkeley: University of California Press, 2006.

Mihalopoulos, Bill. "Modernization as Creative Problem Making: Political Action, Personal Conduct and Japanese Overseas Prostitutes." *Economy and Society* 27, no. 1 (1998): 50–73. https://doi.org/10.108%3085149800000003.

Mihashi Wataru, Lt. "Ōdō kokka kensetsu o miru." In *Manshū sangyō kensetsu gakuto kenkyūdan hōkoku*, vol. 5, 149–51. Tokyo: Manshū sangyō kensetsu gakuto kenkyūdan shiseikai honbu, 1934.

Military History Section, Headquarters, Army Forces Far East. *Japanese Special Study on Manchuria*. Vol. 1, *Japanese Operational Planning against the U.S.S.R.* Office of the Chief of Military History, Department of the Army, 1955.

–. *Japanese Special Study on Manchuria*. Vol. 2, *Imperial Japanese Army in Manchuria, 1894–1945*. Office of the Chief of Military History, Department of the Army, 1959.

–. *Japanese Special Study on Manchuria*, Vol, 3, Part 1, *Strategic Study of Manchuria: Military Topography and Geography*. Office of the Chief of Military History, Department of the Army, 1955.

Military History Section, US Army Forces Far East. *Record of Operations against Soviet Russia on Northern and Western Fronts of Manchuria, and in Northern Korea (August 1945)*. Office of the Chief of Military History, Department of the Army, 1950. http://www.ibiblio.org/hyperwar/Japan/Monos/pdfs/JM-155/JM-155.pdf.

Mimura, Janis. *Planning for Empire: Reform Bureaucrats and the Japanese Wartime State*. Ithaca, NY: Cornell University Press, 2011.

Minagawa Toyoji. *Manshūkoku no kyōiku*. Shinkyō: Ōsakaya goshoten, 1939.

Minami Manshū tetsudō. *Chōshun chihō an'nai: Shiheigai, Kōshurei, Chōshun, Kitsurin*. N.p.: Minami Manshū tetsudō, 1927.

Minami Manshū tetsudō kabushiki kaisha. *Chōshun jijō*. Dairen: Minami Manshū tetsudō Chōshun chihō jimusho, 1932.

–. *Manshū ni okeru jūshi no seisanryō ni tsuite*. Shinkyō: Shinkyō shisha chōsashitsu, 1940.

Minami Manshū tetsudō kabushiki kaisha chihōbu. *Chihō keiei tōkei nenpō*. Dairen: Minami Manshū tetsudō chihōbu, 1938.

Minami Manshū tetsudō kabushiki kaisha chihōbu chihōka. *Kyōiku shisetsu yōran*. Dairen: Minami Manshū tetsudō, 1916.

Minami Manshū tetusdō kabushiki kaisha chōsaka. *Minami Manshū ni okeru Nihon no keizaiteki seiryoku*. N.p.: Manshū tetsudō, 1912.

Minami Manshū tetsudō kabushiki kaisha keizai chōsakai. *Manshū kayakurui tōsei hōsaku: Manshū matchi kōgyō hōsaku*. N.p.: Minami Manshū tetsudō keizai chōsakai, 1935.

–, ed. *Manshū ni okeru ama jijō*. Dairen: Minami Manshū tetsudō keizai chōsakai, 1935.

–, ed. *Manshū rōdō tōsei hōsaku*. Dairen: Minami Manshū tetsudō keizai chōsakai, 1935.

–, ed. *Manshū toshi kensetsu ippan hōsaku*. Dairen: Minami Manshū tetsudō, 1935.

Minami Manshū tetsudō kabushiki kaisha keizai chōsakai, ed. *Manshū tsūshin jigyō hōsaku*. Dairen: Minami Manshū tetsudō keizai chōsakai, 1936.

–, ed. *Shinkyō toshi kensetsu hōsaku*. Dairen: Minami Manshū tetsudō, 1935.

Minami Manshū tetsudō kabushiki kaisha rinji keizai chōsa i'inkai. *Manshū daizu hinshitsu tōkyū satei ni kansuru chōsa*. Dairen: Minami Manshū tetsudō, 1929.

–, ed. *Manshū shuyō toshi no mokuzai jukyū jōkyō*. Dairen: Minami Manshū tetsudō, 1930.

Minami Manshū tetsudō kabushiki kaisha shomubu chōsaka, ed. *Manshū ni okeru bōsekigyō*. Dairen: Minami Manshū tetsudō shomubu chōsaka, 1923.

–. *Manshū kōgyō rōdō jijō*. Dairen: Minami Manshū tetsudō shomubu chōsaka, 1925.

–. *Manshū ni okeru garasu kōgyō*. Dairen: Minami Manshū tetsudō shomubu chōsaka, 1923.

–. *Manshū no meriyasu kōgyō*. Dairen: Minami Manshū tetsudō, 1929.

–. *Minami Manshū tetsudō kabushiki kaisha dainiji jūnenshi.* Dairen: Minami Manshū tetsudō, 1928.

Minami Manshū tetsudō kabushiki kaisha sōmubu chōsakai. *Manshū no sen'i kōgyō.* Dairen: Minami Manshū tetsudō, 1931.

–. *Manshū Shinagawa tetsudō ensen chihō ni okeru daizu no demawari zōka jijō oyobi sono taiōsaku.* Dairen: Minami Manshū tetsudō, 1931.

Minami Manshū tetsudō kabushiki kaisha sōsaishitsu kōhōka, ed. *Minami Manshū tetsudō kabushiki kaisha sanjūnen ryakushi.* Dairen: Minami Manshū tetsudō, 1937.

Minami Manshū tetsudō kabushiki kaisha sōseishitsu chihōbu zanmuseiri iinkai. *Mantetsu fuzokuchi keiei enkaku zenshi.* 3 vols. Tokyo: Ryūkei shosha, 1977.

Minami Manshū tetsudō shomubu chōsaka, ed. *Manshū awa ni kansuru chōsa.* Dairen: Minami Manshū tetsudō shomubu chōsaka, 1925.

–. *Manshū ni okeru suisanbutsu no jukyū.* Dairen: Minami Manshū tetsudō shomubu chōsaka, 1929.

Minseibu keisatsushi. *Manshūkoku keisatsu gaiyō.* Hōten: Minseibu keisatsushi, 1935.

Mitter, Rana. *The Manchurian Myth: Nationalism, Resistance, and Collaboration in Modern China.* Berkeley: University of California Press, 2000.

Miura, Hajime. "Hsinking, Capital of Manchoukuo." *Far Eastern Review* 37 (March 1941): 95–102.

Miura Un'ichi. *Hokenjō kara mita Manshū no jūtaku.* Dairen: Manshū bunka kyōkai, 1935.

–. *Manshū no jūtaku to eisei.* Tokyo: Eisei kōgyō kyōkai, [1934?].

Miyake Masaki, ed. *Shōwa-shi no gunbu to seiji: Taiheiyō sensō zen'ya.* Tokyo: Daiichi hōki, 1983.

Mizuno, Hiromi. *Science for the Empire: Scientific Nationalism in Modern Japan.* Stanford, CA: Stanford University Press, 2009.

Mizuno Naoki. "Stories from Beyond the Grave: Investigating Japanese Burial Grounds in North Korea." Translated by Mark Caprio. *Asia-Pacific Journal* 12, no. 9 (2014). https://apjjf.org/2014/12/19/Mizuno-Naoki/4085/article.html.

Moore, Aaron Stephen. *Constructing East Asia: Technology, Ideology and Empire in Japan's Wartime Era, 1931–1945.* Stanford, CA: Stanford University Press, 2013.

Moore, Aaron William. *Writing War: Soldiers Record the Japanese Empire.* Cambridge, MA: Harvard University Press, 2013.

Morifumi, Kuroki. "The Asianism of the Kōa-kai and the Ajia Kyōkai." In *Pan-Asianism in Modern Japanese History: Colonialism, Regionalism and Borders,* edited by Sven Saaler and J. Victor Koschmann, 34–51. London: Routledge, 2007.

Morley, James William, ed. *The Final Confrontation: Japan's Negotiations with the United States, 1941.* Vol. 5, *Japan's Road to the Pacific War.* New York: Columbia University Press, 1994.

–. *Japan Erupts: The London Naval Conference and the Manchurian Incident, 1928–32.* New York: Columbia University Press, 1984.

Moussay, Gérard, and Brigitte Appavou. *Répertoire des membres de la sociéte des missions étrangères.* Paris: Archives des Missions Étrangères, 2004.

Mullins, Mark R. "Ideology and Utopianism in Wartime Japan: An Essay on the Subversiveness of Christian Eschatology." *Japanese Journal of Religious Studies* 21, nos. 2–3 (1994): 261–80.

Mumford, Lewis. *The Culture of Cities.* New York: Harcourt, Brace, 1938.

Murakami, Haruki. *Underground.* New York: Vintage, 2001.

–. *The Wind-Up Bird Chronicle.* New York: Vintage, 1998.

Muramatsu Shin and Nishizawa Yasuhiko, eds. *Higashi Ajia no kindai kenchiku.* Tokyo: Muramatsu Teijirō sensei taikan kinenkai, 1985.

Muramatsu Teijirō. *Nihon kindai kenchiku no rekishi.* Tokyo: Nihon hōsō, 1977.

Muroi Osamu. "Manshūkoku kokuto kensetsu keikaku no shōkai." *Kenchiku gyōsei* 3, no. 9 (1939): 19–25.

Musgrove, Charles D. *China's Contested Capital: Architecture, Ritual, and Response in Nanjing.* Honolulu: University of Hawai'i Press, 2013.

Mutō Tomio. *Watakushi to Manshukoku.* Tokyo: Bungeishunjū, 1988.

Mutsu Munemitsu. *Kenkenroku: A Diplomatic Record of the Sino-Japanese War, 1894–1895.* Tokyo: University of Tokyo Press, 1982.

Myers, Ramon H. "Japanese Imperialism in Manchuria: The South Manchuria Railway Company, 1906–1933." In *Japanese Informal Empire,* Duus, Myers, and Peattie, 101–32.

Nagami Ken'ichi. "Manshūkoku sandai toshi no kōen sonota." *Kōen ryokuchi* 3, nos. 4/5 (1939): 25–35.

Nagayama, Chikako. "The Flux of Domesticity and the Exotic in a Wartime Melodrama." *Signs* (Chicago, IL) 34, no. 2 (2009): 369–95. https://doi.org/10.1086/591249.

Nakajima Michio. "Shinto Deities That Crossed the Sea: Japan's 'Overseas Shrines,' 1868 to 1945." *Japanese Journal of Religious Studies* 37, no. 1 (2010): 21–46.

Nakano Kinjirō. "Kokuto Shinkyō no kensetsu." *Dōro no kairyō* 15, no. 12 (1933): 165–74.

Narangoa, Li. "Educating Mongols and Making 'Citizens' of Manchukuo." *Inner Asia* 3, no. 2 (2001): 101–26. https://doi.org/10.1163/146481701793647651.

–. "Japanese Geopolitics and the Mongol Lands, 1915–1945." *European Journal of East Asian Studies* 3, no. 1 (2004): 45–67. https://doi.org/10.1163/1570061033004712.

Nihon keizai shi kenkyūjo, ed. *Onoda semento hyakunen shi.* Tokyo: Onoda semento kabushiki kaisha, 1981.

Nihon kōkū yusō kabushiki kaisha, ed. *Nihon kōkū yusō kabushiki kaisha jūnenshi.* Tokyo: Nihon kōkū yusō, 1938.

Nihon kōsaku bunka renmei shusai. "Tairiku kenchiku zadankai." *Gendai kenchiku* 8 (January 1940): 49–61.

Nish, Ian. *Japanese Foreign Policy in the Interwar Period.* Westport, CT: Praeger, 2002.

Nishi Haruhiko. *Kaisō no Nihon gaikō.* Tokyo: Iwanami shinsho, 1965.

Nishimura Shigeo. *Chūgoku kindai tōhoku chiikishi kenkyū.* Kyoto: Hōritsu bunkasha, 1984.

Nishizawa Yasuhiko. *Manshū toshi monogatari.* Tokyo: Kawade shobō shinsha, 1996.

–. "Manshūkoku no kensetsu jigyō." In *Manshūkoku no kenkyū,* edited by Yamamoto Yūzō, 377–460. Tokyo: Ryokuin shobō, 1995.

–. *Nihon shokuminchi kenchiku ron.* Nagoya: Nagoya daigaku shuppansha, 2008.

–. "Shohyō: *Manshūkoku no shuto keikaku.*" *Ajia keizai* 38, no. 8 (1989): 109–13.

–. *Umi o watatta Nihonjin kenchikuka: 20 seiki zenhan no Chūgoku tōhoku chihō ni okeru kenchiku katsudō.* Tokyo: Shōkokusha, 1996.

Nornes, Mark. *Japanese Documentary Film: The Meiji Era through Hiroshima.* Minneapolis: University of Minnesota Press, 2003.

Numata Soyao. "Manshūkoku toyū keikaku no genjō." In Zenkoku toshi mondai kaigi, *Dai rokkai zenkoku toshi mondai kaigi sōkai: sōkai bunken 4: sōkai yōroku,* 224–27.

O'Connor, Peter. *The English-Language Press Networks of East Asia, 1918–1945.* Folkestone, UK: Global Oriental, 2010.

O'Dwyer, Emer. *Significant Soil: Settler Colonialism and Japan's Urban Empire in Manchuria.* Cambridge, MA: Harvard University Press, 2015.

Ōgaki Tsurutada. *Shuto Shinkyō no keizaiteki hatten saku.* Dairen: Manshū bunka kyōkai, 1933.

Ogata, Sadako N. *Defiance in Manchuria: The Making of Japanese Foreign Policy, 1931–1932.* Berkeley: University of California Press, 1964.

Ogawa Takuma. "Zōenka Orishimo Yoshinobu ni yoru kindai rokuka shisō no tankan to jissen." *Hōsei daigaku daigakuin dezain kōgaku kenkyūka kiyō* 2 (March 2013): 1–8.

Oguma Eiji. *Tan'itsu minzoku shinwa no kigen.* Tokyo: Shin'yosha, 1995.

Ohkura, Baron Kimmochi. "Japan and Manchoukuo's Industrial Development." *Contemporary Japan* 9, no. 7 (1940): 848–55.

Okabe Makio. *Manshūkoku.* Tokyo: Sanseido, 1978.

Okada Hideki. "The Realities of Racial Harmony: The Case of the Translator Ōuchi Takao." *Acta Asiatica* 72 (March 1997): 61–80.

Okada Yoshimasa, Tatai Yoshio, and Takahashi Masae, eds. *Ahen mondai.* Tokyo: Misuzu shobō, 1986.

Okamoto, Shumpei. "The Emperor and the Crowd: The Historical Significance of the Hibiya Riot." In *Conflict in Modern Japanese History: The Neglected Tradition,* edited by Tetsuo Najita and J. Victor Koschmann, 258–75. Princeton, NJ: Princeton University Press, 1982.

O'Neill, F.W.S. *The Call of the East: Sketches from the History of the Irish Mission to Manchuria, 1869–1919.* London: James Clarke, 1919.

Ōno Rokuichirō, "Nichi-Man-Shi toshi no bunkateki keizaiteki renkei ni tsuite." In Zenkoku toshi mondai kaigi, *Dai rokkai zenkoku toshi mondai kaigi sōkai: sōkai bunken 4: sōkai yōroku,* 151–68.

Orchard, John E. "Japanese Expansion in China." *Annals of the American Academy of Political and Social Science* 152 (November 1930): 328–37. https://doi.org/10.1177/000271623015200136.

Orr, James J. *The Victim as Hero: Ideologies of Peace and National Identity in Postwar Japan.* Honolulu: University of Hawai'i Press, 2001.

Osterhammel, Jürgen. "'Technical Co-Operation' between the League of Nations and China." *Modern Asian Studies* 13, no. 4 (1979): 661–80. https://doi.org/10.1017/S0026749X00008507.

Pak Yong-sok. *Manpōzan jiken kenkyū: Nihon teikoku shugi no tairiku shinryaku seisaku no ikkan toshite.* Tokyo: Daiichi shobo, 1981.

Palladius. "An Expedition through Manchuria from Pekin to Blagovestchensk in 1870." Translated by E. Delmar Morgan. *Journal of the Royal Geographic Society of London* 42 (1872): 142–80. https://doi.org/10.2307/1798594.

Palmer, Michael A. *Origins of the Maritime Strategy: The Development of American Naval Strategy, 1945–1955.* Washington, DC: Naval Historical Center, 1988.

Park, Hyun Ok. *Two Dreams in One Bed: Empire, Social Life, and the Origins of the North Korean Revolution in Manchuria.* Durham, NC: Duke University Press, 2005.

Patrikeeff, Felix. *Russian Politics in Exile: The Northeast Asian Balance of Power, 1924–1931.* Oxford: Palgrave Macmillan, 2002.

Pauley, Edwin W. *Report on Japanese Assets in Manchuria to the President of the United States.* Washington, DC: US Government Printing Office, July 1946.

Peattie, Mark R. *Ishiwara Kanji and Japan's Confrontation with the West.* Princeton, NJ: Princeton University Press, 1975.

–. "Japanese Attitudes toward Colonialism, 1895–1945." In *The Japanese Colonial Empire, 1895–1945,* edited by Ramon H. Myers and Mark R. Peattie, 80–127. Princeton, NJ: Princeton University Press, 1984.

–. "The Japanese Treaty Port Settlements in China, 1895–1937." In Duus, Myers, and Peattie, *Japanese Informal Empire,* 166–209.

Phillips, Richard T. "'A Picturesque but Hopeless Resistance': Rehe in 1933." *Modern Asian Studies* 42, no. 4 (2008): 1–18. https://doi.org/10.1017/S0026749X06002708.

Pollog, Carl Hans. "Le trafic mondial aérien au cours de l'année 1933–1934." *Revue aéronautique international* 5 (1935): 283–305.

–. "Le trafic mondial aérien au cours de l'année 1934–1935." *Revue aéronautique international* 6 (1936): 385–97.

Pooley, A.M., ed. *The Secret Memoirs of Count Tadasu Hayashi, G.C.V.O.* New York: G.P. Putnam's Sons, 1915.

Porter, Catherine. "Korea and Formosa as Colonies of Japan." *Far Eastern Survey* 5, no. 9 (1936): 81–88. https://doi.org/10.2307/3021667.

Proctor, J.H. "The Response of Scottish Missionaries to Political Conditions in Manchuria, 1872–1950." *Mission Studies* 16, no. 2 (1999): 47–70.

Pruitt, Ida. *A Daughter of Han: The Autobiography of a Chinese Working Woman. From the Story Told Her by Nin Lao T'ai-t'ai.* Stanford, CA: Stanford University Press, 1967.

Pu Yi. *From Emperor to Citizen: The Autobiography of Aisin-Gioro Pu Yi.* 2 vols. Peking: Foreign Languages Press, 1964.

Quested, Rosemary. *The Russo-Chinese Bank: A Multi-National Financial Base of Tsarism in China.* Birmingham, UK: University of Birmingham Press, 1977.

Quigley, Harold Scott. "The Far Eastern Republic: A Product of Intervention." *American Journal of International Law* 18, no. 1 (1924): 82–92. https://doi.org/10.2307/2189223.

Reardon-Anderson, James. *Reluctant Pioneers: China's Expansion Northward, 1644–1937.* Stanford, CA: Stanford University Press, 2005.

Reynolds, E. Bruce, ed. *Japan in the Fascist Era.* Basingstoke, UK: Palgrave Macmillan, 2004.

Reynolds, Jonathan M. *Maekawa Kunio and the Emergence of Japanese Modernist Architecture.* Berkeley: University of California Press, 2001.

–. "Japan's Imperial Diet Building in the Debate over Construction of a National Identity." In Tansman, *Culture of Japanese Fascism,* 254–75.

Ricoeur, Paul. *Memory, History, Forgetting.* Chicago: Chicago University Press, 2004.

Rikugunshō chōsahan hen. *Manshūkoku seiritsu no ikisatsu to sono kokka kikō ni tsuite.* Tokyo: Rikugunshō chōsahan, 1932.

Ritchie, Lawrence S., and Cooper Davis. "Parasitological Findings and Epidemiological Aspects of Epidemic Amebiasis Occurring in Occupants of the Mantetsu Apartment Building, Tokyo, Japan." *American Journal of Tropical Medicine and Hygiene* s1-28, no. 6 (1948): 803–16. https://doi.org/10.4269/ajtmh.1948.s1-28.803.

Robertson, Jennifer. "Japan's First Cyborg? Miss Nippon, Eugenics and Wartime Technologies of Beauty, Body and Blood." https://doi.org/10.1177/1357034X01007001001.

Rogaski, Ruth. *Hygienic Modernity: Meanings of Health and Disease in Treaty-Port China.* Berkeley: University of California Press, 2004.

Ross, Steven T. *American War Plans, 1945–50.* New York: Garland, 1988.

Royama, M. "The South Manchuria Railway Zone and the Nature of Its Administration." *Pacific Affairs* 3, no. 11 (1930): 1018–34. https://doi.org/10.2307/2750074.

Ruoff, Kenneth. "Japanese Tourism to Mukden, Nanjing, and Qufu, 1938–1943." *Japan Review* 27 (2014): 171–200.

Ruoff, Kenneth J. *Imperial Japan at Its Zenith: The Wartime Celebration of the Empire's 2,600th Anniversary.* Ithaca, NY: Cornell University Press, 2010.

Sakai, Tetsuya. "The Soviet Factor in Japanese Foreign Policy, 1923–1937." *Acta Slavica Iaponica* 6 (1988): 27–40.

Sakurai Tadayoshi. *Nikudan.* Tokyo: Eibun Shinshisha, 1906.

Sakuta Shōichi. "Ajia no hikari." *Kenkoku* 1, no. 1, August 1940, 2–5.

Sand, Jordan. *House and Home in Modern Japan: Architecture, Domestic Space, and Bourgeois Culture, 1880–1930.* Cambridge, MA: Harvard University Press, 2003.

–. "Subaltern Imperialists: The New Historiography of the Japanese Empire." *Past and Present* 225, no. 1 (2014): 273–88. https://doi.org/10.1093/pastj/gtu014.

Sano Riki. "Manshū no kokuto kensetsu." *Kenchiku zasshi* 47, no. 575 (1933): 1243–58.

–. "Manshū no kokuto kensetsu keikaku." *Toshi mondai* 17, no. 2 (1933): 38–39.

Satō Akira. *Manshū zōen shi.* Tokyo: Nihon zōen shūkei kyōkai, 1985.

–. "Shinkyō tokubetsushi no kenkoku jūshūnen kinen jigyō." *Kōen ryokuchi* 17, no. 9 (1942): 27–31.

Satō Akira, Eguchi Hidematsu, and Toyoshima Masayoshi. "Shinkyō tokubetsushi no rokuchi keikaku ni tsuite." *Kōen ryokuchi* 3, no. 4–5 (1939): 7–11.

Saveliev, Igor R., and Yuri S. Pestushko. "Dangerous Rapprochement: Russia and Japan in the First World War, 1914–1916." *Acta Slavica Iaponica* 18 (2001): 19–41.

Schmid, Andre. "Colonialism and the 'Korea Problem' in the Historiography of Modern Japan: A Review Article." *Journal of Asian Studies* 59, no. 4 (2000): 951–76. https://doi.org/10.2307/2659218.

Schumpeter, E.B., ed. *The Industrialization of Japan and Manchukuo.* London: Routledge, 2000.

Scobie, Alex. *Hitler's State Architecture: The Impact of Classical Antiquity.* University Park: Pennsylvania State University Press, 1990.

Sekai bunkasha, ed. *Wasureenu Mantetsu: ima aratani tadoru Chūgoku tōhoku chihō kyōshū no arubamu.* Tokyo: Sekai bunkasha, 1988.

Seki Hiroharu. "The Manchurian Incident, 1931." In Morley, *Japan Erupts,* 139–230.

Sekiguchi, Takeo. "The Wartime Role of Manchoukuo." *Contemporary Japan* 13, no. 2 (1944): 176–84.

Senta Manzō. *Shin Manshū e no rihyō.* Tokyo: Senshinsha, 1932.

Sewell, Bill. "Beans to Banners: The Evolving Architecture of Prewar Changchun." In *Harbin to Hanoi: The Colonial Built Environment in Asia, 1840 to 1940,* edited by Laura Victoir and Victor Zatsepine, 37–57. Hong Kong: Hong Kong University Press, 2012.

–. "Japanese Imperialism and Civic Construction in Manchuria." PhD diss., University of British Columbia, 2000.

–. "Postwar Japan and Manchuria." In *Japan at the Millennium: Joining Past and Future,* edited by David W. Edgington, 97–119. Vancouver: UBC Press, 2003.

–. "Reconsidering the Modern in Japanese History: Modernity in the Service of the Prewar Japanese Empire." *Japan Review* 16 (2004): 213–58.

Sewell, Bill, and Norio Ota. "Sakuta Shōichi, 'The Light of Asia.'" In Henshaw, Smith, and Smith, *Translating the Japanese Occupation of China.*

Shao, Dan. *Remote Homeland, Recovered Borderland: Manchus, Manchoukuo, and Manchuria, 1907–1985.* Honolulu: University of Hawai'i Press, 2011.

Shaw, Henry I., Jr. "The United States Marines in North China." Washington, DC: Historical Branch, G-3 Division, 1960.

Shen, Zhihua. *Mao, Stalin, and the Korean War: Trilateral Communist Relations in the 1950s.* Translated by Neil Silver. New York: Routledge, 2012.

Shimada Michihiro. *Manshū kyōiku shi.* Dairen: Bunkyōsha, 1935.

Shimazu, Naoko. *Japanese Society at War: Death, Memory and the Russo-Japanese War.* Cambridge: Cambridge University Press, 2009.

Shimizu gumi Manshū shiten. *Nenkan.* N.p.: Shimizu gumi Manshū shiten, 1936.

Shimizu kensetsu hyakugojūnen shi hensan i'inkai, ed. *Shimizu kensetsu hyakugojūnen shi.* Tokyo: Shimizu kensetsu, 1953.

Shinkyō no gaikyō. Shinkyō: Shinkyō shōkō kōkai, 1942.

Shinkyō shigai chizu. Tokyo: Kanemitsusha shiryōbu, 1982.

Shinkyō shōkō kaigijo. *DaiShinkyō keizai gaikan.* Shinkyō: Shinkyō shōkō kaigijo, 1937.

Shinkyō tokubetsushi kōsho. *Shinkyō shisei gaiyō.* Shinkyō: Shinkyō tokubetsushi kōsho, 1934.

Shinkyō tokubetsushi shichōkanbō shomuka. *Yakushin kokuto no iyō.* Shinkyō: Shinkyō tokubetsushi kōsho, 1940.

–. *Kokuto Shinkyō.* Shinkyō: Manshū jijō annaijo, 1940.

–. *Kokuto Shinkyō: Kenkoku jūshūnen kinan.* Shinkyō: Shinkyō tokubetsushi kōsho, 1942.

Shokuminchi bunka gakkai, Chūgoku tōhoku rinkan jūyonnenshi sōhenshitsu, ed. *Manshūkoku to wa nan datta no ka: NitChū kyōdō kenkyū.* Tokyo: Shōgakukan, 2008.

Shokuminchi bunka kakkai, ed. *Kindai Nihon to Manshūkoku.* Tokyo: Fuji shuppan, 2014.

Shurtleff, William, and Akiko Aoyagi, comp. *History of Soybeans and Soyfoods in Canada (1831–2010): Extensively Annotated Bibliography and Sourcebook.* Lafayette, CA: Soyinfo Center, 2010.

Sing, Lim Hua. "Japan's Official Development Assistance to China, Indonesia, and Singapore." In *APEC and Development Co-operation,* edited by Mohamed Ariff, 48–89. Singapore: Institute of Southeast Asian Studies, 1998.

Sladkovskii, Mikhail Iosifovich. *History of Economic Relations between Russia and China.* Jerusalem: Israel Program for Scientific Translations, 1966.

Smith, Henry D. "Tokyo as an Idea: An Exploration of Japanese Urban Thought until 1945." *Journal of Japanese Studies* 4, no. 1 (1978): 45–80. https://doi.org/10.2307/132072.

Smith, Norman. *Intoxicating Manchuria: Alcohol, Opium, and Culture in China's Northeast.* Vancouver: UBC Press, 2012.

–. *Resisting Manchukuo: Chinese Women Writers and the Japanese Occupation.* Vancouver: UBC Press, 2007.

Sneath, David. "Beyond the Willow Palisade: Manchuria and the History of China's Inner Asian Frontier." *Asian Affairs* 34, no. 1 (2003): 3–11. https://doi.org/10.108%306837032000054289.

Snow, Edgar. *Far Eastern Front.* London: Jarrolds, 1934.

SōA kenchiku renmei. "Manshū kenchiku no tenbō." *Gendai kenchiku* 8 (January 1940): 2–21.

Sorenson, André. *The Making of Urban Japan: Cities and Planning from Edo to the Twenty-First Century.* London: Routledge, 2002.

South Manchuria Railway. *Second Report on Progress in Manchuria: To 1930.* Dairen: South Manchuria Railway, 1931.

–. *Third Réport on Progress in Manchuria,* 1907–32. Dairen: South Manchuria Railway, 1932.

–. *Fourth Report on Progress in Manchuria to 1934.* Dairen: South Manchuria Railway, 1934.

–. *Fifth Report on Progress in Manchuria to 1936.* Tokyo: Herald Press, 1936.

–. *Sixth Report on Progress in Manchuria to 1939.* Tokyo: Herald Press, 1939.

Sowerby, Arthur de C. "The Exploration of Manchuria." *Geographical Journal* 54, no. 2 (1919): 73–89. https://doi.org/10.2307/1779709.

Stein, Gunther. *Far East in Ferment.* London: Methuen, 1936.

Steiner, Zara. *The Lights That Failed: European International History, 1919–1933.* Oxford: Oxford University Press, 2005.

Steinhardt, Nancy Shatzman. *Chinese Imperial City Planning.* Honolulu: University of Hawai'i Press, 1990.

Stephan, John J. "Hijacked by Utopia: American Nikkei in Manchuria." *Amerasia Journal* 23, no. 3 (1997): 1–42. https://doi.org/10.17953/amer.23.3.v85519832j5304um.

–. *The Russian Far East: A History.* Stanford, CA: Stanford University Press, 1994.

Stewart, David B. *The Making of a Modern Japanese Architecture: 1868 to the Present.* Tokyo: Kodansha, 1987.

Stewart, John R. "Foreign Investments in Manchuria." *Far Eastern Survey* 4, no. 11 (1935): 81–85. https://doi.org/10.2307/3023027.

–. "Four Years of Manchoukuo." *Far Eastern Survey* 5, no. 6 (1936): 51–58. https://doi.org/10.2307/3022669.

–. "Manchoukuo Announces a Mongol Program." *Far Eastern Survey* 9, no. 5 (1940): 58–60. https://doi.org/10.2307/3022294.

–. "Manchuria as Japan's Economic Life-Line." *Far Eastern Survey* 4, no. 23 (1935): 182–86. https://doi.org/10.2307/3022242.
–. "Mukden Population Reaches Million Mark." *Far Eastern Survey* 9, no. 7 (1940): 84.
–. "Pu-Yi at Last to Have a Palace." *Far Eastern Survey* 7, no. 22 (1938): 264.
–. "The Soya Bean and Manchuria," *Far Eastern Survey* 5, no. 21 (1936): 221–26.
–. "Severe Retrenchment in Manchukuo." *Far Eastern Survey* 9, no. 22 (1940): 261–63.
–. "The War and Western Interests in North China." *Far Eastern Survey* 7, no. 20 (1938): 229–35.
S[tewart], J.R. "Hsinking – Manchuria's Boom Town." *Far Eastern Survey* 6, no. 6 (1937): 68–69. https://doi.org/10.2307/3022573.
Suleski, Ronald. *Civil Government in Warlord China: Tradition, Modernization and Manchuria.* New York: Peter Lang, 2002.
–. "Manchukuo and Beyond: The Life and Times of Zhang Mengshi." *International Journal of Asian Studies* 14, no. 1 (2017): 77–97. https://doi.org/10.1017/S1479591416000206.
–. "Northeast China Under Japanese Control: The Role of the Manchurian Youth Corps, 1934–1945." *Modern China* 7, no. 3 (1981): 351–77. https://doi.org/10.1177/009770048100700304.
Summers, William C. *The Great Manchurian Plague of 1910–11: The Geopolitics of an Epidemic Disease.* New Haven, CT: Yale University Press, 2012.
Sun Jiying. "Tōhoku rinkanki no Chōshun de no shokuminchi doreika kyōiku." In Shokuminchi bunka gakkai, *Kindai Nihon to Manshūkoku,* 92–109.
Sun, Youli. *China and the Origins of the Pacific War, 1931–1941.* New York: St. Martin's Press, 1993.
Sun Bang, ed. *Wei Man wenhua.* Jilin: Renmin chubanshe, 1993.
Tahata Shūichirō. *Boku no Manshū ryokōki.* Tokyo: Jidōtosho shuppansha, 1943.
Tainaka Chizuru. "'Gaichi' no sumō." *Mejiro daigaku jinbungaku kenkyū* 7 (2011): 117–35.
Tajima Daisuke. "'Manshūkoku' ni okeru Kaimin bochi sen'i mondai." *Ritsumeikan bungaku* 619 (2010): 552–29.
Takashima Masaaki. "NichiRo senkōki 'Manshū' (Chūgoku tōhokubu) ni okeru Nikkei jiba ginkō no bunseki." In *Hiroshima keizai daigaku sōritsu yonjūshūnen kinen ronbunshū,* 27–52. Hiroshima: Hiroshima keizai daigaku, 2007.
Takasugi Shingo. *731 butai kinsen no ishi o oe: Ima mo tsutzuku kyōfu no jintai jikken.* Tokyo: Tokuma shoten, 1982.
Takenaka, Akiko. "Architecture for Mass-Mobilization: The Chūreitou Memorial Construction Movement, 1939–1945." In Tansman, *Culture of Japanese Fascism,* 235–53.
Tamaki, Norio. *Japanese Banking: A History, 1859–1959.* New York: Cambridge University Press, 1995.
Tamanoi, Mariko Asano. *Memory Maps: The State and Manchuria in Postwar Japan.* Honolulu: University of Hawai'i Press, 2009.
Tamura Toshio. "Kyōiku kokka ron." In *Ronsō,* vol. 3, edited by Daitō gakuin, 161–297. Shinkyō: Manshū gyōsei gakkai, 1940.
–. *Manshūkoku, rinen to jittai.* Shinkyō: Manshūteikoku kyōikukai, 1941.
Tanaka, Stefan. *Japan's Orient: Rendering Pasts into History.* Berkeley: University of California Press, 1993.
Tanaka Shūsaku. *Shin Manshūkoku chishi.* Tokyo: Kokon shoin, 1932.
Tani Miyuki. *Chōshun Monogatari.* Fukutamachi, Shizuoka: Mittani Yukio, 1989.
Tanner, Harold Miles. *The Battle for Manchuria and the Fate of China: Siping, 1946.* Bloomington: Indiana University Press, 2003.
Tansman, Alan, ed. *The Culture of Japanese Fascism.* Durham, NC: Duke University Press, 2009.

Tashiro Shigenori. *Omoizuru mama.* Tokyo: Tashiro Shigenori, 1935.

Tatsuo Nakami, ed. *Manshū to wa nan datta no ka.* Tokyo: Fujiwara shoten, 2006.

Taylor, Charles. *Modern Social Imaginaries.* Durham, NC: Duke University Press, 2004.

Taylor, Robert R. *The Word in Stone: The Role of Architecture in the National Socialist Ideology.* Berkeley: University of California Press, 1974.

Tian Shicong. "Dajie xiangbi guanshide xiaocao shuichuande qing." *Qilin* 2, no. 6 (1942): 107.

Tōa keizai chosakyoku. *The Manchuria Year Book, 1931.* Tokyo: Tōa keizai chosakyoku, 1931.

"Tokushū: Manshū to wa nan datta no ka." *Kan* 10 (Summer 2002).

Tsuda Yoshiki. "'Manshūkoku' kenkoku chūreibyō to kenkoku shinbyō no kenchiku ni tsuite." *Kanagawa daigaku 21-seiki COE puroguramu kenkyū suishin kaigi,* March 2008, 71–87.

Tsujita Fumio. "Kyū Manshū Toragashira yōsai no chōsa hōkoku." *Gunji shigaku* 43, no. 1 (2007): 51–72.

Tsukase Susumu. *Manshū no Nihonjin.* Tokyo: Yoshikawa, 2004.

–. "NichiRo sensō mae ni okeru zaiMan Nihonjin no katsudō." *Nagano daigaku kiyō* 22, no. 4 (2001): 138–48.

–. "The Penetration of Manzhouguo Rule in Manchuria." In *China at War: Regions of China, 1937–45,* edited by Stephen R. MacKinnon, Diana Lary, and Ezra F. Vogel, 110–47. Stanford, CA: Stanford University Press, 2007.

Tucker, Anne Wilkes, Dana Friis-Hansen, Kaneko Ryūichi, and Takeba Joe. *The History of Japanese Photography.* New Haven, CT: Yale University Press, 2003.

Tucker, David. "Colonial Sovereignty in Manchuria and Manchukuo." In *The State of Sovereignty: Territories, Laws, Populations,* edited by Douglas Howland and Luise White, 75–93. Bloomington: Indiana University Press, 2009.

–. "France, Brossard Mopin, and Manchukuo." In *Harbin to Hanoi: The Colonial Built Environment in Asia, 1840 to 1940,* edited by Laura Victoir and Victor Zatsepine, 59–81. Hong Kong: Hong Kong University Press, 2012.

–. "Labor Policy and the Construction Industry in Manchukuo: Systems of Recruitment, Management, and Control." In *Asian Labor in the Wartime Japanese Empire: Unknown Histories,* edited by Paul H. Kratoska, 25–57. Armonk, NY: M.E. Sharpe, 2005.

Tucker, David Vance. "Building 'Our Manchukuo': Japanese City Planning, Architecture, and Nation-Building in Occupied Northeast China." PhD diss., University of Iowa, 1999.

Uchida, Jun. *Brokers of Empire: Japanese Settler Colonialism in Korea, 1876–1945.* Cambridge, MA: Harvard University Press, 2011.

United States Department of State. *Foreign Relations of the United States, Diplomatic Papers, 1941.* Vol. 5, *The Far East.* Washington, DC: US Government Printing Office, 1956.

–. *Foreign Relations of the United States, Diplomatic Papers, 1945.* Vol. 7, *The Far East: China.* Washington, DC: US Government Printing Office, 1969.

–. *Foreign Relations of the United States, Diplomatic Papers, 1948.* Vol. 7, *The Far East: China.* Washington, DC: US Government Printing Office, 1973.

Valliant, Robert B. "Japanese Involvement in Mongol Independence Movements, 1912–1919." *Mongolia Society Bulletin* 11, no. 2 (1972): 1–32.

VanderVen, Elizabeth R. *A School in Every Village: Educational Reform in a Northeast China County, 1904–31.* Vancouver: UBC Press, 2012.

Waldron, Arthur, ed. *How the Peace Was Lost: The 1935 Memorandum "Developments Affecting American Policy in the Far East."* Stanford, CA: Hoover Institution Press, 1992.

Wang, Di. *Street Culture in Chengdu: Public Space, Urban Commoners, and Local Politics, 1870–1930.* Stanford, CA: Stanford University Press, 2003.

Wang Lin and Gao Shuying, eds. *Wanbaoshan shijian.* Jilin: Renmin chubanshe, 1991.

Wang Wenfeng. "GiManshūkokugun no kaimetsu." In Shokuminchi bunka gakkai, *Kindai Nihon to Manshūkoku,* 265–67.

Ward, Rowena. "Delaying Repatriation: Japanese Technicians in Early Postwar China." *Japan Forum* 23, no. 4 (2011): 471–83. https://doi.org/10.108%9555803.2011.617461.

"Wato Shōkō." *Zaisei keizai* 3, no. 11 (1919): 43–44.

Watt, Lori. *When Empire Comes Home: Repatriation and Reintegration in Postwar Japan.* Cambridge, MA: Harvard University Press, 2009.

Weale, B.L. Putnam. *The Fight for the Republic of China.* London: Hurst and Blackett, 1918.

–. *Manchu and Muscovite: Being Letters from Manchuria Written during the Autumn of 1903.* London: Macmillan, 1904.

–. *The Re-Shaping of the Far East.* Vol. 2. London: Macmillan, 1905.

Westad, Odd Arne. *Decisive Encounters: The Chinese Civil War, 1946–1950.* Stanford, CA: Stanford University Press, 2003.

Westney, D. Eleanor. *Imitation and Innovation: The Transfer of Western Organizational Patterns to Meiji Japan.* Cambridge, MA: Harvard University Press, 1987.

Whigham, Henry James. *Manchuria and Korea.* London: Isbister, 1904.

Williams, E.T. "The Open Ports of China." *Geographical Review* 9, no. 4 (1920): 306–34. https://doi.org/10.2307/207732.

Williams, William Appleman. *The Tragedy of American Diplomacy.* Rev. ed. New York: Dell, 1962.

Williamson, Alexander. *Journeys in North China, Manchuria, and Eastern Mongolia; With Some Account of Corea.* 2 vols. London: Smith, Elder, 1870.

Willoughby, Westel W. *The Sino-Japanese Controversy and the League of Nations.* Baltimore, MD: Johns Hopkins University Press, 1935.

Wilson, Sandra. "The Discourse of National Greatness in Japan, 1890–1919." *Japanese Studies* 25, no. 1 (2005): 35–51. https://doi.org/10.1080/10371390500067652.

–. *The Manchurian Crisis and Japanese Society, 1931–33.* London: Routledge, 2001.

–. "Rethinking the 1930s and the '15-Year War' in Japan." *Japanese Studies* 21, no. 2 (2001): 155–64. https://doi.org/10.1080/10371390120074336.

Wingrove, Paul. "Mao in Moscow, 1949–50: Some New Archival Evidence." *Journal of Communist Studies and Transition Policies* 11, no. 4 (1995): 309–34. https://doi.org/10.1080/13523279508415293.

Wolff, David. "Bean There: Toward a Soy-Based History of Northeast Asia." In *Harbin and Manchuria: Place, Space, and Identity,* edited by Thomas Lahusen, 241–52. Durham, NC: Duke University Press, 2001.

–. "Open Jaw: A Harbin-Centered View of the Siberian-Manchurian Intervention, 1917–1922." *Russian History* (Pittsburgh) 36, no. 3 (2009): 339–59. https://doi.org/10.1163/187633109X412898.

–. *To the Harbin Station: The Liberal Alternative in Russian Manchuria, 1898–1914.* Stanford, CA: Stanford University Press, 1999.

Won, Kim Sang. "The Chinese Civil War and Sino-North Korea Relations, 1945–50." *Seoul Journal of Korean Studies* 27, no. 1 (2014): 91–113.

Woodhead, H.G.W. *A Visit to Manchukuo.* Shanghai: Mercury Press, 1932.

Wright, Gwendolyn. *The Politics of Design in French Colonial Urbanism.* Chicago: University of Chicago Press, 1991.

Wright, Tim. "Growth of the Modern Chinese Coal Industry: An Analysis of Supply and Demand, 1896–1936." *Modern China* 7, no. 3 (1981): 317–50. https://doi.org/10.1177/009770048100700303.

Wynne, Waller, Jr. *The Population of Manchuria.* Washington, DC: US Government Printing Office, 1958.

Xu Xueji, ed. *Rizhishiqi zai Manzhou de Taiwanren.* Taibei: Zhongyang yanjiuyuan jindaishi yanjiusuo, 2004.

–. "Zai Manzhouguo de Taiwanren gaodengguan: yi Datong Xueyuan de biyesheng weili." *Taiwanshi yanjiu* 19, no. 3 (2012): 95–150.

Yamada Hisetarō. *ManMō toyū zenshi.* 2 vols. Tokyo: Nikkan Shina jijōsha, 1926.

Yamaguchi Takeshi. *Maboroshi no kinema Man'ei: Amakasu Masahiko to katsudō gunzō.* Tokyo: Heibonsha, 1989.

Yamamuro Shin'ichi. *Manchuria under Japanese Dominion.* Translated by Joshua A. Fogel. Philadelphia: University of Pennsylvania Press, 2006.

Yanagisawa Asobu. "'Manshū jihen' o meguru shakai keizai shi kenkyū no shodōkō." *Rekishi hyōron* 377 (September 1981): 50–59.

–. "'Manshū' shōkō imin no gutai zō: NichiRo sengo no Manshū tokō jijō." *Rekishi hyōron* 513 (January 1991): 42–53.

–. *Nihonjin no shokuminchi keiken: Dairen Nihonjin shōkōgyōsha no rekishi.* Tokyo: Aoki shoten, 1999.

–. "ZaiMan Nihonjin." In Shokuminchi bunka gakkai, Chūgoku tōhoku rinkan jūyonnenshi sōhenshitsu, *Manshūkoku to wa nandatta no ka,* 219–26.

Yang, Daqing. "Resurrecting the Empire? Japanese Technicians in Postwar China." In *Japanese Empire in East Asia and Its Postwar Legacies,* edited by Harald Fuess, 185–205. Munich: Iudicium, 1998.

–. *Technology of Empire: Telecommunications and Japanese Expansion in Asia, 1883–1945.* Cambridge, MA: Harvard University Press, 2010.

Ye, Yu, and Xiuqi Fang. "Land Use Change in Northeast China in the Twentieth Century: A Note on Source, Methods and Patterns." *Journal of Historical Geography* 35, no. 2 (2009): 311–29. https://doi.org/10.1016/j.jhg.2008.08.007.

–. "Spatial Pattern of Land Cover Changes across Northeast China over the Past 300 Years." *Journal of Historical Geography* 37 (2011): 408–17.

Yokohama shōkin ginkō chōsaka. *Manshū mengyō no gaikan.* N.p.: Yokohama shōkin ginkō, 1941.

Yokote Shinji. "Soviet Repatriation Policy, U.S. Occupation Authorities, and Japan's Entry into the Cold War." *Journal of Cold War Studies* 15, no. 2 (2013): 30–50.

Yoneda Masabumi. "Shinkyō Kitsurin kokudō kōji hōkoku." *Doboku gakkaishi* 21, no. 11 (1935): 1611–26.

Yosano, Akiko. *Travels in Manchuria and Mongolia: A Feminist Poet from Japan.* Translated by Joshua A. Fogel. New York: Columbia University Press, 2001.

Yoshihashi, Takehiko. *Conspiracy at Mukden: The Rise of the Japanese Military.* New Haven, CT: Yale University Press, 1963.

Yoshimi Yoshiaki. *Grassroots Fascism: The War Experience of the Japanese People.* Translated by Ethan Mark. New York: Columbia University Press, 2015.

Yoshioka, Bunroku. "Manchoukuo in Co-Prosperity Sphere." *Contemporary Japan* 11, no. 11 (1942): 1584–91.

Young, C. Walter. *Japan's Special Position in Manchuria.* Baltimore, MD: Johns Hopkins University Press, 1931.

Young, Louise. *Japan's Total Empire: Manchuria and the Culture of Wartime Imperialism.* Berkeley: University of California Press, 1998.

Yūki Seitarō. "Kokuto daiShinkyō kensetsu to nisan no mondai." *Manshū gijutsu kyōkaishi* 10, no. 58 (1934): 548–50.

Zarrow, Peter. *After Empire: The Conceptual Transformation of the Chinese State, 1885–1924.* Stanford, CA: Stanford University Press, 2012.

Zenkoku toshi mondai kaigi, ed. *Dai rokkai zenkoku toshi mondai kaigi: sōkai bunken 4: sōkai yōroku.* Tokyo: Zenkoku toshi mondai kaigi, 1939.

Zhang Shenfa. "Return of the Chinese Changchun Railway to China by the U.S.S.R." In Elleman and Kotkin, *Manchurian Railways*, 171–94.

Zhang Zhenglong. *Xuebai xiehong: guogong Dongbei dazhuezhan lishi zhenxiang.* Hong Kong: Dadi chubanshe, 1991.

Zhang Zhenjia and Yang Jianping. "Watakushitachi kara mita 'Shinkyō to Daitōkō no kensetsu kōsō.'" *Doboku gakkaishi* 79, no. 12 (October 1994): 53–55.

Zhao, Quansheng. "Japan's Aid Diplomacy with China." In *Japan's Foreign Aid: Power and Policy in a New Era,* edited by Bruce M. Koppel and Robert M. Orr, 163–87. Boulder, CO: Westview Press, 1993.

Zhigalov, B.S. "KVZhD v Dal'nyvostochnoy Politikye Rossii, 1906–1914." *Vestnik Tomskovo Gosudarstvennovo Universiteta* 1, no. 2 (2008): 24–44.

Zhu, Zixuan, and Reginald Yin-Wang Kwok. "Beijing: The Expression of National Political Ideology." In *Culture and the City in East Asia,* edited by Won Bae Kim, Clyde Michael Douglass, Sang-Chuel Choe, and Kong Chong Ho, 125–50. Oxford: Clarendon Press, 1997.

Zukowsky, John, ed. *The Many Faces of Modern Architecture: Building in Germany between the World Wars.* Munich: Prestel, 1994.

Index

Note: "(i)" after a page number indicates an illustration; "(m)" indicates a map; "(t)" indicates a table. For abbreviations in subentries, please see the list on page xv.